S0-AYT-084

EDUCATIONAL INNOVATION

An Agenda to Frame the Future

Edited by

Charles E. Greenawalt, II

UNIVERSITY
PRESS OF
AMERICA

Lanham • New York • London

THE
COMMONWEALTH
FOUNDATION
for Public Policy Alternatives

Copyright © 1994 by
**The Commonwealth Foundation
for Public Policy Alternatives**

University Press of America®, Inc.
4720 Boston Way
Lanham, Maryland 20706

3 Henrietta Street
London WC2E 8LU England

All rights reserved
Printed in the United States of America
British Cataloging in Publication Information Available

Copublished by arrangement with
The Commonwalth Foundation
for Public Policy Alternatives

Library of Congress Cataloging-in-Publication Data

Educational innovation : an agenda to frame the future
edited by Charles E. Greenawalt, II.
p.   cm.
Includes bibliographical references.
1. Educational innovations—United States.   2. Educational
innovations—Pennsylvania—Case studies.   3. Educational
change—United States.   4. Educational change—
Pennsylvania—Case studies.   I. Greenawalt, Charles E.
LA217.2.E387   1993   370'.973—dc20   93–35877 CIP

ISBN 0–8191–9193–0 (cloth : alk. paper)
ISBN 0–8191–9194–9 (pbk. : alk. paper)

 The paper used in this publication meets the minimum requirements of
American National Standard for Information Sciences—Permanence
of Paper for Printed Library Materials, ANSI Z39.48–1984.

Dedication

This book is dedicated to the memory of my father,
Charles E. Greenawalt,
a lifelong teacher and educational innovator
who brought energy and excitement into his classroom
and his home.

Contents

Preface

The unparalleled efforts to reform basic and secondary education in the United States over the past ten years have a common root in the National Commission on Excellence in Education's report, *A Nation At Risk*. The social and political forces that gathered to try and ameliorate the problems of public schools in response to the Commission's stark findings are still at work today. There has been no flagging in the energies of those who see the public schools as the one enduring public entity that can assist in solving the ills of society. The myriad of proposals for educational reform from all sides of the political spectrum have highlighted the almost universal agreement that our public schools mirror what is both best and worst in our society.

Educational change and innovations are large-scale attempts to deal with societal problems that seem incurable on other economic, political, and social levels, and are thus destined to fall short of the high expectations they create. Each effort to create new educational paradigms is a specific attempt to deal with an American society that many believe has gone awry. The accelerated deterioration of our values; disruptions in our economy; challenges to our political system; increases of poverty among the young; reductions in community safety; increases in drug usage in some segments of society; the decreases in the presence of the nuclear family; and many more, are then seen as elements driving the school reform movement.

Can our society use the schools as a place to begin a regeneration, or will the schools remain as a mirror image of the dimming quality of life that has come to our communities, our society, and our nation? Do we have the political will to move from didactic discourse, political bandwagonism, and self-centered political ambition to see what we might do in a coordinated manner to improve education and make schools starting points for the transition to a brighter tomorrow?

In Tom Peters' newest book, *Liberation Management*, he describes management in the era of the nanosecond 1990s. He believes that success in this global economy with instantaneous communications and access to information will lie with those whose paradigms are re-created almost daily. His prime example of instantaneous organizational re-creation is the Cable News Network (CNN). He explains that on a daily basis, successful 1990s corporations do not rely on hierarchical structures and time-tested truisms. Their organizations are almost completely horizontal, with supervisors and workers changing roles almost daily. Projects run by these new organizations hire staff based on need and skills. In some of these companies, there are few permanent desks or offices. Personal possessions may be carried or transported about in mock supermarket shopping carts.

In a world of impermanence, of instant gratification, of almost complete mobility, of frequent career and job change, of rapidly evolving technology, how can we operate our schools on either an agrarian or a "Taylorized" factory model? The answer is that we cannot. Irrespective of the debates between those who would raze the entire public system of education and those who believe that the nation simply needs to improve the present system with minor changes and major infusions of new funding, society continues to evolve. It may well be that Tom Peters is correct. The most perfect of paradigms for education may be no paradigm at all.

The 1960s brought with it the accumulation of a century of thought about social engineering on a governmental level unparalleled in American history. The beginning of the 1990s has brought a deep distrust of governmental interference, of social programs aimed at repairing society, and of the ability of political institutions to cope with national problems. While traditional educational reformers attempt to reconstitute the system, others see the current system as the problem preventing effective schooling. The movements towards choice, entrepreneurial and charter schools, home schooling, privatization, parochial education, and equity challenges are symptoms of a general skepticism of central authority and government's ability to provide excellent and affordable education.

The political side of this mistrust is evidenced by term limitation movements for elected officials, one-term presidencies, the development of a new third party movement led by H. Ross Perot, the rise of one issue candidates, and low voter registration and turn-out rates. The malaise of our times is an uncertainty as to the direction of our nation. This is a frightening prospect for many. An examination of our strongest allies, Japan and Western Europe, also reveals a scene with the same problems and the same uncertainties as to how to address them. Which of these nations, however, has the vast heterogeneity of the United States combined with a long history of anti-elitism? Even traditional enemies of our nation have fallen by the wayside to be replaced with problems that are as incomprehensible as the "Evil Empire" was so clearly a threat.

Education reformers all have one thing in common. It is fruitless to dwell on the 1960s concept that schooling has little effect on children. Despite the old argument that children are only in school for six or seven hours and that the home and other parts of society have more time to act on children, many of the new reformers are convinced that school, in any number of forms, has a significant impact. Can a classroom whether public or private, religious training or home schooling, cause positive changes in children? The answer is surely, "Yes." Is there any other *public* institution in our society that can effect such changes? All school reformers would say "unfortunately, no."

The outpouring of literature on school reform over the past ten years has been astonishing. Terrell Bell, the former Secretary of Education under President Ronald Reagan, was concerned that after *A Nation At Risk* was published that the country would once again retreat into indifference so that education issues would be relegated to the second section of the nation's major newspapers. On the contrary, the debate on education reform and innovations has not abated at all. There have been lengthy reports, studies, treatises, and discussions on education at all levels of government since 1983. Indeed, *A Nation At Risk* has stimulated a far-reaching review of the state of education in the United States.

Educational Innovation, An Agenda to Frame the Future is an attempt to capture these discussions within a national and statewide context. The book uses Pennsylvania as a case study. Pennsylvania has a history of serving as a case study since it was founded and built as a social experiment. In fact, the Commonwealth of Pennsylvania has been blessed by its founder, William Penn, with the over-arching obligation to look over all of its inhabitants in a most benevolent manner. Therefore, Pennsylvania has a history of moderate and deliberate change. It is a state that thought long and hard before eliminating its "Blue Laws," establishing a lottery, and reforming its schooling through educational innovations.

Pennsylvania is also a state steeped in custom and tradition. Change is not easily accepted by the state's institutions or its populace. Consequently, it is perennially the number one or two state in rankings of people who are indigenous to the state in which they were born (over 80 percent). Therefore, its history and sociology make discussions on issues of major import very personal across the state. The recent debates about "outcome-based education" (see Judith Witmer's chapter) were played out across every business, community building, and residence in the state.

The nature of this book would have been somewhat different if a different state had been examined. Many of the actual players in the school reform movement in Pennsylvania have contributed to this volume. Bob Coldiron was the creator of a statewide assessment program; Susan Arisman, in her role as the director of the Academy for the Profession of Teaching, did help to change teacher training in the state; Bill Moloney is a leading national reformer as the superintendent of the Easton School District; Dave Kirkpatrick is one of the leaders of the choice movement in Pennsylvania; and Annette Palutis is the President of the Pennsylvania State Education Association (PSEA).

On a national level, the insights and contributions to educational innovations by figures such as Bruce Cooper, Denis Doyle, and E. D. Hirsch have channeled the current of education reform. The reform movements and educational innovations that these figures lead have influenced the nation as well as the Commonwealth of Pennsylvania. But what has the extent of their influence been and what results have their innovations wrought in the school buildings and school yards of America? This volume attempts to answer these questions in order to examine the progress of improving the educational system throughout the nation.

The background of Pennsylvania's educational system makes it a useful case study and a promising location for a genuine school reform effort. This examination will see the extent to which this promise has been realized. Education does frame the future, and to ensure the brightest possible future for the nation's children, the best educational innovations available must be identified and implemented in America's schools.

Acknowledgments

I am extremely grateful to the Commonwealth Foundation for its sponsorship of this project. The Foundation's Board of Directors, President, and staff made this anthology possible. The Foundation's President, Don Eberly, has provided strong support and guidance for this project in all of its phases, and its completion is a testimony to his leadership.

Further, this anthology would not have been possible without the generous financial support of the individuals, corporations, and foundations that enable the Commonwealth Foundation to conduct its work.

I am indebted to each of the knowledgeable authors whose work follows as well as the numerous educators and public policy analysts across the country and the Commonwealth who contributed advice and ideas to this project.

Thanks is extended to all Commonwealth Foundation staff members and interns--Keith Bashore, Clifford Frick, Doug Lehman, Wendy Lentvorsky, and Debra Wolford. Clifford Frick not only typeset this book, but he also assisted with its editing and was a constant source of encouragement.

Finally, I also appreciate the advice and assistance provided by Dr. Arnold Hillman. Dr. Hillman's knowledge of the Commonwealth's educational system, his assistance in drafting the Preface and the Epilogue, and his enthusiasm for this project were key ingredients in completing this project.

Charles E. Greenawalt, II, Ph.D.

Chapter 1

From Active Teaching to Active Learning

Susan Arisman

INTRODUCTION: TWO SCENARIOS

Scenario 1983: The day's teaching objective is written on the blackboard. The desks are set expectantly in rows. The teacher stands at the front of the room: it is time for math. She provides the students with a set of math problems that relates what they are about to learn with what has already been learned either in the classroom or through other experiences. She checks the homework assignment for the day. Then she points to the objective and sets the parameters for the day's lesson. Carefully, she determines whether the students understand the day's lesson. Then she presents new content, checking for understanding as she proceeds. Examples are given on the board. Students receive work to begin at their seats. After a short review to conclude the lesson, the homework assignment for tomorrow is given. Class is over for the day.

Scenario 1993: Computers surround the classroom space, which resembles a large work room. Announcements are written on the remaining blackboard. Some students are working in clusters around the computers. Others are seated in groups around large work tables. Some are off in corners doing small experiments to prove propositions. The teacher can be identified only because she looks older. She argues a proof with a small group, then pauses to exchange a few words with two students who are manipulating string; she passes by the computer group but does not stop; they would not pay any attention anyway. Three students are working together on an exhibition which they will present first to a jury of their peers and then to a jury composed of teachers and other school community members. This exhibition will serve as the basis for assessing their knowledge of this material. Other students enter the room, returning from checking experiments that are located in different areas of the school. About one-half the class is out in the community, some on service projects helping in an elementary school, some in internships with community organizations and businesses.

When *A Nation at Risk* was published in 1983, the ideal educational environment was believed to be teacher-directed and curriculum-centered, much like the first scenario. Lesson plans were designed to be followed, objectives were listed on the board, and all eyes were directed toward the teacher. Whether or not the document advocated a particular kind of education, it was interpreted as supporting essentially more of the same kind of education that was judged to be successful for the upper ten percent of the students around the world--a passive experience in which books were outlined, facts were reduced to flash cards, and tests were geared to the regurgitation of what was learned.

Publications such as *What Works: Research about Teaching and Learning* described "direct instruction" as having the following basic components:

- Setting clear goals for students and making sure that they understand these goals,
- Presenting a sequence of well-organized assignments,
- Giving students clear, concise explanations and illustrations of the subject matter,
- Asking frequent questions to see if the children understand the work, and
- Giving the students frequent opportunities to practice what they have learned.[1]

These components were quickly transformed into checklists and formulas for lessons that became part of the evaluation of teachers. Supervisors looked for some combination of objectives, anticipatory sets, input, modeling, checking for understanding, guided practice, and independent practice. All of these activities reinforced the idea that teachers were the center of the classroom, directing the learning of all the students.

In ten years, the reform movement developed in ways its first advocates never dreamed. In the descriptions of the eleven New Generation of American Schools sponsored by the New American Schools Development Corporation, the emphasis on direct instruction, sequenced lesson plans, objectives, and teacher direction has been muted. Instead, the second scenario prevails. An analysis of the basic ingredients of the different designs reveals that they are all concerned, at least on paper, with the following: learning characterized by the active involvement of students; an integrated curriculum; the cultivation of relationships with the larger society and community; collaboration among students, teachers, parents, administrators, and community members; the use of technology; and alternative assessment systems that test more than facts. The words used to describe the changes planned in the schools do not include such phrases as "direct instruction" or "standardized tests." No school chose to demonstrate that what was advocated in the 1980s, if implemented well, would produce acceptable results.

What caused these changes in the schools? Are they real? Will they last? In this chapter, three threads leading to this change will be explored: 1) the new meaning of learning, which is linked to a new understanding of knowledge; 2) the economic and political forces that sanction and support these changes; and 3) the growing dissatisfaction from within the educational community. These threads provide a basis for reform and are reflected in its basic components. The threads and the components provide a consistent, holistic approach to change. Whether change will succeed is also considered in the final section of this chapter.

THREE THREADS LEADING TO REFORM

THE NEW MEANING OF KNOWLEDGE AND LEARNING

While behaviorism and its mechanistic approach to education were flourishing in the post-World War II era, a quiet revolution was taking place in how knowledge and learning were viewed. The "behaviorists" talked about the mind as a "black box" and captured the imagination of educators with their success in training troops for combat and modifying the behavior of handicapped students. Meanwhile, the work of Piaget and other researchers, in contrast, was leading to an understanding that learning was not just a response to stimuli that were reinforced. Something was happening within the "black box," and that something shaped what and how people learned. Eventually, the latter group of psychologists and educators came to be called "constructionists" because they believed that people contribute to and shape knowledge as they assimilate it.

To understand how different these two groups are, one can look at how they influenced expectations about computer instruction. The behaviorists viewed computers as providing direct instruction to students, who would receive praise and encouragement as reinforcement. Computers were heralded as harbingers of what could be put into that black box for all students. In contrast, the constructionists viewed computers as interactive, capable of being programmed to help students control and shape the knowledge they contained. The computer was seen as one tool in an ongoing quest to make knowledge the learner's own. Although the content might be the same, the whole approach to how it is learned and retained is different.

Whereas behaviorists limited themselves as much as possible to what could be described accurately by language and talked a lot about the scheduling of reinforcement, different types of praise, and the breaking down of knowledge into discrete pieces that could be programmed either through a computer or a text, constructionists talked about conversations and dialogue, about the setting of conditions under which students can learn. Constructionists would applaud this description by Lewis Thomas of the scene at the Woods Hole Marine Biological Laboratory in *Lives of a Cell*. Thomas writes about the "buzz of conjoined intelligence...made by confluent, simultaneously raised human voices, explaining things to each other."[2] Bruffee describes that "buzz" as "the conversations among scientists making sense out of what they observe by negotiating their differences."[3]

In classrooms, constructionists encourage this "buzz" by posing challenges, contradictions, and essential questions that invite inquiry and promote investigation.

This change did not take place in a vacuum but was based on changes in how knowledge in natural and physical sciences was viewed. The proposition that objective truth exists and can be known has been challenged by scholars in all disciplines. What one can know, they suggest, is that there are approximations of truth that can be explored, keeping careful account of the processes of investigation and interpretation so that the level of approximation can be measured and decreased.

The attitude toward knowledge has undergone a revolution since Einstein's theory of relativity first was accepted.

For some three centuries (roughly speaking, from Newton to Einstein) the empirical, "positivist" language, assumptions, and methods of the sciences were revered as the most powerful intellectual processes ever devised. "Unscientific" disciplines--the humanities and, especially, the social sciences--aspired to increase their rigor and influence by making themselves over in the image of what they supposed to be "scientific."

...social scientists these days..."are chattering about actors, scenes, plots, performances, and personae, (while) humanists are mumbling about motives, authority, persuasion, exchange, and hierarchy."[4]

This change in the world's view of knowledge in some ways parallelled the changes proposed in schools, teaching, and learning. In many cases, reformers proposed changes without once mentioning changes in the view of knowledge. But, in retrospect, the changes in fundamental thinking about reality, about what is known and knowable, provided the basis for what emerged. The change from behaviorism to constructionism was well under way before the name "constructionism" entered common educational parlance. It found much of its strength, however, in its ability to converge with similar movements in science, mathematics, and the social sciences.

ECONOMIC AND POLITICAL FORCES ON REFORM

Just as educators did not intentionally set out to develop a constructionist rather than a behavioristic philosophy of education, they also did not prove prescient about the new political and economic realities which emerged simultaneously.

Although the economic workplace had been dominated by manufacturing well into the 1970s, a quiet revolution was in progress. First, the world shrank. In an incredibly short amount of time following World War II, the world that had seemed so vast and unknowable became ever-present through television and other communication marvels. During World War II, citizens saw selected movie "shorts" produced by the government and the news media; during the Vietnam War, they saw the conflict "in prime time" and "live." The movement of knowledge increased tremendously as messages filtered through walls and barb wire.

The world economy was also shrinking. Then, and now, what happens on the Japanese stock exchange affects New York and vice versa. A product designed and marketed in one area is examined and cloned in another. Europe is moving closer toward a common market and a common destiny. The United States is negotiating new trade agreements with Mexico and strengthening its commercial ties with Canada. The Japanese are quietly and cautiously courting Chinese business in anticipation of a free economy in the world's largest country.

The world political sphere was also contracting. The old alliances and cabals gave way to the United Nations and a more limited number of nations keeping peace throughout the world. Ideas of governance were more restricted. Democracy in some form is becoming a standard which most nations are trying to achieve. Even though now many old monarchies are maintained for rituals and dictators still have power over too many people's lives, these arrangements are increasingly seen as undesirable. Thousands of agencies have gone international, carrying their agenda to all parts of the globe. For example, CARE, the Red Cross/Crescent, and the World Bank are now accepted almost as "free agents" by virtually all countries in the world. Furthermore, the concern for the proliferation of nuclear weapons supersedes the normal rights of sovereignty that were once accepted.

These revolutions in economics and politics have had a profound effect on the United States and its schools. While the "westernization" of the world culture has created new markets for Euro/American goods, it has also brought this country and others face to face with the realization that these products can be produced more cheaply abroad where the salaries and benefits of workers are woefully low. The disappearance of political barriers has created new markets and new competitors simultaneously. As this nation moves toward a global market, other countries struggle to maintain their trade positions or gain new ones. This burst of economic activity has placed a great burden on the United States, especially because it once enjoyed such a long period of preeminence in the markets of the world. Virtually the only manufacturing country untouched by World War II, the United States came to expect that its products would continually be sought. The retooling of Japan and West Germany, in tandem with American aid to other emerging countries, was seen as a step toward world peace and understanding, on one level concerned with international morality. On the more pragmatic level of international commerce, these actions were seen as creating new economic markets. The U.S. believed that it was invincible.

After Vietnam, the United States learned that not only was it militarily vulnerable; it was economically vulnerable as well. Productivity stalled. According to the Secretary's Commission on Achievement Necessary Skills (SCANS), which takes the Arab oil embargo as its marking point, "Productivity growth (output per hour) in the United States slowed significantly after 1973. Labor productivity actually declined in 1989 and 1990. Some estimate that if current international productivity trends continue, nine countries may exceed the U.S. in output per worker-hour by the year 2020." This stagnation of productivity affects earnings and income. "Median family income increased nearly three percent a year between 1947 and 1973. Since 1973, it has scarcely increased at all. Families with heads of households under the age of 34 have watched their real income decline since 1979."[5]

In addition, nationwide job opportunities are changing as the United States begins to compete globally.

Twenty years ago, manufacturing accounted for 27 percent of all nonagricultural employment in the U.S.; services and retail trade for 32 percent. By 1990, manufacturing accounted for only 17 percent of these jobs, while services and retail trade made up 44 percent. In 1990, manufacturing jobs paid an average of $10.84 per hour; while service jobs paid $9.86 and jobs in retail trade paid only $6.78.[6]

When the number of people who are actually producing something for sale is compared to all those who furnish them with insurance, transportation, and other services, it does not take long to comprehend the vast change that has occurred in the postwar era. Tomorrow, jobs that are now performed by workers in foreign countries or illegal aliens in the United States--underpaid, subsisting in working conditions that mirror those of the sweatshops of the early century--will be done by robots. The natural outcome of the quest for increased productivity is the search for doing more with fewer human resources. The only way to keep ahead of the curve is to constantly improve products to improve the productivity of others.

The computer industry is an excellent illustration of this trend. As the computer industry develops new ideas to make human beings more productive, it also makes workers in other areas obsolete. For example, now that insurance claims can be scanned by computers, there is no more need to hire thousands of data processors in the health services industry. One economic sector's productivity means another sector's unemployment.

In order to stay ahead of other nations in a global economy, the American workforce will have to be more highly trained, more motivated, and more skilled. The SCANS report cites the differences in today's and tomorrow's workplaces that were identified in 1990 by the Office of Technology Assessment, a staff agency of Congress. The fundamental changes that will occur in the workplace can perhaps best be illustrated by the chart below that portrays today's and tomorrow's workplaces in the form of two models: the "traditional model" (today's workplace) and the "high performance model" (tomorrow's workplace).

TRADITIONAL MODEL	HIGH PERFORMANCE MODEL
Mass production	Flexible production
Long production runs	Customized production
Centralized control	Decentralized control
End-of-line quality control	On-line quality control
Fragmentation of tasks	Work teams, multi-skilled workers
Authority vested in supervisor	Authority delegated to worker [7]

This change means that initially workers will have to possess broader basic skills and then continue to develop complex and diversified skills through more comprehensive training sessions. The worker will be seen as "an investment" rather than "a cost."[8]

Whether or not schools want to change, the power of the changes taking place in political and economic worlds will affect them. Employers will need workers who possess more than basic skills, although basic skills will become increasingly important. They will need people who can think and solve problems, who are self-directed and responsible, who can work with others and function as members of a team, and who are capable of being leaders as well as followers. When business wanted assembly line workers, the schools provided them. Now business needs different kinds of people in order to survive; schools will provide them again.

An example of the work an entry-level person does provides a graphic illustration of what the world of work holds for graduating seniors.

John is a warehouse operator--an entry-level position in any company. He is a member of a two-person team that is charged with receiving, storing, inventorying, and distributing chemicals used in car washes. Each chemical must be stored in a proper container and handled carefully.   The consequences of mishandling are toxic fumes and materials released upon the community. He must deal with drivers from all ethnic groups; many of these drivers do not speak English fluently. He must log in what he receives accurately, store it promptly and correctly. If he does not get along with the people he interacts with, he will have difficulty assuring that all chemicals are correctly received. Shortages are frequent and must be dealt with in a sensitive way so that relationships are maintained. Once stored, chemicals must be retrieved for orders so that proper handling reduces spills. Proper equipment must be maintained and used. He is responsible for the welfare of everyone in the near vicinity; he must know what chemicals do if accidents happen; he must care about himself and about others. He must be alert, responsible, accurate. In this entry-level position, there is less margin for error than most university faculty members enjoy. And he does this on a high school diploma.

Just as the fate of a whole community rests in the hands of one 18-year-old warehouse worker, the fate of the nation rests on making our workforce the best in the world. Schools will be different because the workplace will demand these differences.

INTERNAL DISSATISFACTION WITH SCHOOLS

Although educators were less aware of the changes in knowledge development, politics, and economics, they were more aware than the general public of the growing dissatisfaction with schooling itself. In the 1980s, many studies of schools were conducted, but none was as large in scope as those undertaken by Goodlad and Sizer.[9] Both of these national studies examined what schools were like in the 1980s and what they are like today. Both researchers actually visited hundreds of schools and classrooms; talked with administrators, parents, students, and teachers; and emerged with pictures of education that were remarkably similar, even though Sizer's work concentrated only on high schools. Neither study discussed the change in knowledge or the change in the economic workplace, yet their conclusions dovetail with these changes.

What they saw in schools was boredom. They saw students unengaged in their own learning, passively putting in time in order to "get on with real life." They saw schools that had changed little in the past 100 years, operating as assembly lines in which students were homogenized for ease of handling: handicapped students on one line, general education students on another, and the academically gifted on another. Goodlad summarizes the following patterns that he found:

- The dominant pattern of classroom organization is a group to which the teacher most frequently relates as a whole.
- Each student essentially works and achieves alone within a group setting.
- The teacher is the central figure in determining the activities, as well as the tone, of the classroom.
- The domination of the teacher is obvious in the conduct of instruction.
- There is a paucity of praise and correction of students' performance, as well as of teacher guidance in how to do

better next time.
- Students generally engage in a rather narrow range of classroom activities--listening to teachers, writing answers to questions, and taking tests and quizzes.
- The patterns summarized above describe early elementary classes less well than they do classes in higher grades.
- Large percentages of the students...appeared to be passively content with classroom life.
- Even in the early elementary years there was strong evidence of students not having time to finish their lessons or not understanding what the teacher wanted them to do.[10]

The work of Sizer and others filled three volumes: *Horace's Compromise*, *The Shopping Mall High School*, and *The Last Little Citadel*.[11] Each focused on a different aspect of high school life, looking at the insidious dilemmas and trade-offs that underlie the social contract between teachers and students, the proliferation of expectations for students that drain the secondary school system of focus and viability, and the dishonesty that pervades the system. As Sizer writes,

> a common theme of *compromise* throughout [the] three books--of the treaties, however genial or confrontational, that teachers and students and parents and administrators make to keep a school functioning--emerged late in our collective inquiry. All social institutions require tradeoffs, but those in the modern high school seemed to us--each looking at the secondary schools from a somewhat different vantage point--to be ill considered, harmful, and corrupting, however well intentioned.[12]

These two studies of education provide the data base upon which many of the restructuring efforts have been built. They are continually used as justification for doing things differently, for innovating, and for rethinking the fundamental premises underlying how schools are organized and experienced by all constituencies. Sizer and Goodlad made it clear that all schools need to rethink what they are doing. When these studies are used in connection with data on the rise of drug use, dysfunctional families, and violence in all segments of society--urban, rural, and suburban--they provide incontrovertible evidence that something is fundamentally wrong with schooling as we know it.

A new understanding of knowledge, political and economic changes, and growing dissatisfaction with schools provided the basis for a call for reform in the 1990s that grew from the limited recommendations of *A Nation at Risk* to the sweeping rethinking that characterizes many of the reform projects today. For the first time in decades, data are available to serve the reform efforts. What is likely to emerge is considered in the next section of this chapter.

Moving From Reform To Restructuring

The language on education reform has shifted. Reform is seen as the more generic term--implying a whole host of change efforts. Restructuring, on the other hand, means "fundamental changes in rules, roles, and responsibilities that result in more powerful learning for all students."[13] Restructuring affects systems because it cannot survive without changes in the policies of those systems. Restructuring is results- oriented; it focuses on how the lives of students change, not on improvements that make the system better for adults.

Because restructuring is such a fundamental change in the way people think about schools, it is exceedingly difficult to implement. Citizens rarely complain when a teacher changes the way in which he presents a lesson on the verb *to be* to a class of eighth graders. Although he has reformed his own teaching, he has not made a fundamental change in the system. However, when a teacher changes the organization of a class from didactic to cooperative learning, he changes more than just his classroom--affecting the resources and culture of the school. When two or more teachers begin to question what they are teaching and how they are teaching it, and begin to work together to change the way in which students learn, the whole system faces changes. Many reforms have gotten to the classroom door in education but have been squelched when they step beyond into the larger school community. Such changes attack the essence of the schools. Those changes are at the heart of restructuring.

In a recent article in *Education Week*, Lauren B. Resnick comments on what is seen as an "emerging oral consensus" on what schools of the future should be.

> In the schools that these futurists envision, understanding and intellect would be as valued as athletics are today. Students would become active learners who assume an increased responsibility for their own education. And learning would occur in context, in environments that are laden with stimulating and resource-rich materials and that enable students to learn through a variety of avenues.
>
> The emphasis would be on applying and using knowledge to solve real-world problems, not just on regurgitating facts. And the traditional walls

between education and the broader community would come tumbling down.

In such schools, every student would be expected to meet high standards for what he or she knows and can do. And the vision of what a successful high school graduate should look like would drive both the curriculum and the assessments.

Most of all, these schools would be communities of learners--in which as much attention is paid to the intellectual and developmental needs of adults as of children. Decisions would be made as close to the classroom as possible. And teachers and principals would have a far greater say over curriculum, budgets, and hiring.[14]

At the heart of these new schools are four components that must be addressed: student learning, high expectations, the involvement of a wider community of players, and alternative measures of achievement. A description of these four components follows.

STUDENT LEARNING

At the heart of the restructuring movement is student learning. If restructuring succeeds or fails, it will do so on the basis of how it affects student learning. In the same way, individual efforts must be judged in relation to how closely they affect this component. For example, site-based management might facilitate student learning, but it can occur without any change in student learning whatsoever. Decentralization and choice are other examples of changes that can occur without any change in student behavior. The emerging consensus on what must change about student learning is based in large part on how the view of knowledge has changed and on how economic life has changed. Both of these were described above and form the basis for what is written below.

In order for restructuring to succeed, there must be a new image of what teaching and learning mean. This image includes an acceptance of the following beliefs: 1) knowledge is created and developed collegially; 2) knowledge begins with an accumulation of facts and principles but is achieved only when those facts and principles can be used to solve problems, answer important questions, and serve as guides to new learning; and 3) students are responsible for their own development as learners. Each of these three components must be examined.

First, students now work in an atmosphere of individual competition that stifles teamwork. The only place within the schools where students learn about working together is the athletic field, and until recently, a full slate of team sports was not available for women. Such individual competition is no longer functional in the workplace where the players and the plays are constantly shifting, nor is it compatible with the way in which knowledge is created in most fields. The images of the lone scientist working against criticism and ridicule, of the architect hunched over the drafting board, of the businessperson operating as the "self-made person," have been replaced by images of teams, quality circles, and networking. Student learning that proceeds on an interactive basis is encouraged by such reform movements as Paideia, the Coalition of Essential Schools, and the Accelerated Schools.

But collegiality extends beyond the students. One of the first things that principal Mark DiRicco did upon taking charge of Sullivan County High School in Pennsylvania was to take down the sign for principal and hang one that said "Chief Learner."[15] In most schools that are making significant changes, the principal is characterized as almost a compulsive learner, constantly seeking the best for his teachers and students. Saranson, in his book entitled *The Predictable Failure of School Reform*, states that schools will not change until they become places in which the learning of teachers is appreciated.[16] If teachers are not treated as learners and their learning is not valued, then little change in student learning will occur.

In schools, enormous barriers stand in the way of becoming what would seem to be an easy thing--a community of learners. Colleagues belittle and scorn anyone who tries to be different. Teachers are intimidated by the reactions of colleagues and will not report on or share their accomplishments in their own schools. Often they look to university and other consultants to tell them what they already know: it is safer that way. Teachers do not take responsibility for their own development. They rely on the in-service offerings of the school district and master's degrees from the colleges, but not on themselves. Study councils and classroom research are frequently conducted in the face of great opposition. Although many teachers give of themselves constantly, all are aware that there is a fine line that they cannot cross.

Second, although it is axiomatic that facts and principles must be learned, it is also true that they must be used in order to be remembered. Most of the New American Schools incorporated some type of project approach to learning that focused on essential questions, challenges, and dilemmas to be solved. In order to be successful, students must not only know facts and principles, but they must be able to apply these facts and principles to new situations. Knowing geometric shapes is one thing; using them to design a developmentally appropriate playground for three-year-olds is another.

Third, all of these forms of restructuring focus on the student as worker, engaged with others in addressing and creating knowledge. The bored, passive students portrayed in the books listed above give way to energized, engaged, purposeful students who are responsible for their own learning and for demonstrating this learning through exhibitions and other methods of assessment.

In restructured schools, the curriculum needs to be redesigned to enable students to assume this new role of collegial worker. Consider this example. At McCaskey High School in Lancaster, Pennsylvania, ninth-grade students were confronted by a group of teachers dressed as aliens and challenged to develop evidence to justify the continuing existence of life on earth. Within nine weeks, students created exhibitions that demonstrated why they believed that human beings should be allowed to continue to exist. Students who would normally not be expected to know or care about Beethoven and Bach, Matisse and Gauguin, Newton and Einstein were using them to defend life on earth. They needed to know what made them great and what they had contributed that would uplift life everywhere. These are the kinds of problems that students can address when the curriculum changes from a dull presentation of "Great Artists and Musicians" to a challenging exercise in addressing one of life's more interesting questions.

HIGH EXPECTATIONS FOR ALL STUDENTS

Perhaps one of the major shocks for anyone studying educational policy in the 1990s is how few people really want *all* children to succeed. This is seldom publicly voiced. But when confronted with the implications of what success means both personally and fiscally for all students, dramatic shifts of power begin to occur. Consider the following scenario.

In reforming education, one of the major battles has been waged with those who fear the success of children who have not yet been successful. These students will ultimately compete with those students who are expected to succeed. When at-risk students from restructured schools declare an interest in higher education, "warm fuzzies" are raised in the hearts of student advocates across the nation. But to a parent whose own child is applying to college, these students represent more competition for placement and financial aid.

The achievement scores of the upper ten percent of American students are comparable to those of all other nations. This upper ten percent knows the rules and plays by them. When the rules change or when new types of learning are introduced into the schools, the current members of this ten percent of the student population frequently feel threatened.

Slavin states that all children can succeed in meeting the expectations of primary education if certain conditions exist. These conditions include: 1) strong preschool programs that include parent education; 2) early identification and intervention in potentially handicapping conditions; and 3) continuous advancement or progress programs in the early grades that allow students to move at their own pace through an articulated program. He summarizes what it would take

> to ensure the success of *all* at-risk students.... There is a large category of students who would fail to learn to read without intervention but would succeed with good preschool and kindergarten experiences; improved reading curriculum and instruction; and perhaps brief tutoring at a critical junction, eyeglasses, family support, or other relatively inexpensive assistance.

The cost and intensity of the assistance needed grow as the complexity of the student's problem increases. But Slavin optimistically states that

> one could imagine that any child who is not seriously retarded could succeed in school if he or she had some combination of the intensive birth-to-3 services used in the Milwaukee project; the high quality preschool programs used in the High/Scope model; the tutoring provided by Reading Recovery or other models; and the improvements in curriculum, instruction, family support, and other services (along with tutoring) provided throughout the elementary grades by Success for All.[17]

The programs he refers to are all highly tested and successful programs with young children. What it means is that the nation can achieve its goal to provide a good start for all children, but it cannot do so without providing the necessary resources and programs. While these programs are expensive, they are less expensive than prisons, drug assistance, and job training, which are the natural consequences of children failing in the early grades. In fact, the greatest predictor of who will drop out of high school is failure in the first three grades. Early intervention is the key to success.

In the middle years, expectations are being raised through programs that address the needs of the early adolescent while challenging his intellect and channeling his energy as his physical characteristics change rapidly. Making school more important to these students strikes a balance in their lives that all the tender loving care cannot provide. High expectations, instead of causing problems, can help solve the problems of this age group if these expectations are embodied within a caring and supportive learning environment.

In its recent study on the education of young adolescents, the Carnegie Council on Adolescent Development recommended that middle schools take the following steps to improve their efficacy:

Create small communities for learning where stable, close and mutually respectful relationships with adults and peers are considered fundamental for intellectual development and personal growth.

Teach a core curriculum that results in students who are literate, including in the sciences, and who know how to think critically, lead a healthy life, behave ethically, and assume the responsibilities of citizenship in a pluralistic society.

Ensure success for all students through elimination of tracking by achievement level and promotion of cooperative learning, flexibility in arranging instructional time, and adequate resources (time, space, equipment, and materials) for teachers.

Empower teachers and administrators to make decisions about the experiences of middle grade students....

Staff middle grade schools with teachers who are expert at teaching young adolescents and who have been specially prepared for assignment to the middle grades.

Improve academic performance through fostering the health and fitness of young adolescents....

Reengage families in the education of young adolescents....

Connect schools with communities, which together share responsibility for each middle grade student's success....[18]

Students who are engaged in these kinds of schools look forward to the school day, appreciate the fact that people respect their potential to care about their success, and give more of themselves to the whole enterprise.

In the Middle-School-of-the-Future project designed by California University of Pennsylvania at Woodlawn Middle School in Munhall, Pennsylvania, students are actively involved in their own learning, whether it is in the biomes of the science lab, the computer writing room, the on-line broadcasting facilities, or the ecologically balanced pond. As one student succinctly stated, "we don't sleep here any more."

Given the high expectations for all students to learn to read in the early years, and to become responsible for their own learning of meaningful and rich content in their middle years, the results will be senior high schools where students need to be continually challenged to achieve outcomes that exceed the minimal. The first reaction to educational reform was to institute tests of basic skills that assured the public that all students were at least performing at a minimal level. Although these tests were helpful, particularly to students in the general studies component, because they assured that students would at least learn something, they quickly became trivialized. Students in the general track in high schools across the country are currently in a holding pattern. They work hard for cars and other consumer goods, but they do not expect to study, to do homework, or to be challenged. Their high school diplomas have little qualitative meaning. As many educators have continually pointed out, transcripts of students and recommendations from high schools are generally not used by business as a means of hiring new employees. The message quickly becomes: put in your time and get your "C"; other efforts devoted to education are a waste of time.

Standing outside a typical urban high school at dismissal time, one is shocked by the lack of books and other academic gear with which the students emerge. They leave the high school as they leave any other activity--free to spend their time as they choose. This scene stands in sharp contrast to students emerging from a local, private college preparatory school. These young adults leave with backpacks bulging with books and paraphernalia. They know that they are going home to another four to five hours worth of homework and study. In fact, the greatest difference might be that they realize that studying is expected. Without developing good and consistent study habits, these students will not achieve their goals, which usually include entry into the best higher education institution that their intellect and resources can procure.

When a recent Coalition of Essential Schools project site in Pennsylvania tried to institute a rigorous new course for seniors, school officials were told that no one wanted to work that hard during his senior year. This phenomenon of the "senior year entitlement" is one of the dismal little secrets of American education. With college applications due in January, the last year frequently becomes a wasteland. Even though students are cautioned by colleges to maintain their achievement levels, many feel more inclined to take easy courses, party, and glide into the world of work or higher education.

The recent trend toward outcomes-based education tries to address this issue. By setting high standards for achievement for all students but by also eliminating the time factor for meeting those standards, school districts hope to move some students into work or higher education sooner, provide more time for those who need it to achieve the outcomes, and revitalize the senior year experience. Whether these standards will be high enough to develop the kind of student that is envisioned remains to be seen. Whether schools will be able to develop appropriate assessments for those outcomes is another problem that is looming on the horizon. If the experiences of states like Vermont are any indicator, the assessment will be the crucible upon which higher expectations will be tested.

NEW PLAYERS IN EDUCATION

If student learning is the center of reforming education, then its first line of support is made up of a host of different people who assist in making that learning possible.

First, parents are being reinvited into the schools and into the lives of their children. Head Start and other early childhood programs demonstrate the power of involved parents who are trained and committed.

Joyce Epstein has done extensive research on parent involvement programs and has developed a topology program, which links the type of involvement with the outcomes it will produce. For those who doubt the efficacy of these programs, Epstein maintains that the type of parent involvement most clearly linked to achievement "provide[s] ideas to parents on how to help [a] child at home." She states that she "would like to see more attention to the type of involvement parents want most: how to work with their own child at home in ways that help the student succeed and that keep the parents as partners in their children's education across the grades."[19] These types of activities have a clear link to achievement and can be undertaken by all parents, not just those with the time and resources to volunteer, attend meetings, and serve on school committees.

Epstein found the following situation:

> A small number of children and families need special attention from health
> and social service professionals. But in some schools educators have used
> these few as excuses for not developing partnerships with all parents. From
> research on parent involvement in urban, rural, and suburban schools, we
> believe that about 2 to 5 percent of parents may have severe problems that
> interfere, at least for a time, with developing partnerships; ...and that about
> 20 percent of all parents are already successfully involved.
>
> But the other 75 percent would like to become more effective partners with
> their children's schools. ... All schools have the opportunity to build strong
> partnerships with parents.[20]

Comer's work on the School Development Program (SDP) presents a
carefully researched and documented approach to education that has
achieved success with students. In this model, teachers, parents, and other
professionals and community members work collaboratively through a
model consisting of the following:

> 1) *a governance and management team* representative of the parents,
> teachers, administrators, and support staff; 2) *a mental health* or *support
> staff team;* and 3) *a parents program.* The governance and management
> team carried out three critical operations--the development of 4) *a
> Comprehensive School Plan* with specific goals in the social climate and
> academic areas; 5) *staff/development* activities based on building level goals
> in these area; and 6) periodic *assessment* which allows the staff to *adjust*
> the program to meet identified needs and opportunities.[21]

This model is typical of those that advance the proposition that the
teacher is not enough, particularly for at-risk students. The teacher brings
certain skills and understandings to the group but cannot address all
problems that students have--with parents, with living conditions, and with
mental and physical health. Not enough time nor expertise exists for
teachers to be everything to every student. Although many adults
reminisce about teachers who cared for children above and beyond the
demands of learning, such care is more difficult and complex today. What
today's children must overcome in order to be students is far greater than
years ago. Despite the nostalgia that colors these reminiscences about
teachers who were more caring, the truth is that these teachers reached
only a limited number of students. When many people honestly examine
their school experiences, they admit that although they were the

beneficiary of these teachers, many students, including their own siblings and friends, were not so fortunate.

What Comer and others have done is expand the team responsible for assisting the student, without expanding the responsibilities of team members. In many schools, teachers complain bitterly about taking on new roles and responsibilities when they cannot fulfill their main one: providing the conditions for student learning. Getting parents reinvolved in schools to promote student learning has its problems, of course. In the Chicago School District, Councils have been formed at each school with a balance of community/parent/professional participation. These Councils have sweeping powers, ranging from firing principals to developing the school vision to hiring new teachers. The participation of parents and other community leaders in the education program of the schools on the broad scale of the Chicago Councils has largely been untested. But the limited and structured participation that Comer advocates has been honed and tested over a 15-year period of study and development.

NEW METHODS OF ASSESSMENT

One of the consequences of the behaviorist view of knowledge that has dominated this century has been the proliferation of standardized and other tests that measure only that which can broken down into discrete pieces. Standardized achievement tests were attempts to assure that the progress of all students was measured against one standard so that equity could be gauged. Without a standardized form, the nation would be unaware of the disparity between different racial groups, socioeconomic levels, and regions. Unfortunately, the unintended consequence of such tests was the same as the unintended consequence of the view of knowledge described above: a reduction in expectations. When teachers and other educators claimed that the tests would eventually govern the curriculum, they were correct. It was not long before people realized that if fractions were not taught at a certain grade level, then their students would not be able to pass that part of a nationally standardized test. Whether students were ready for fractions or not, they had to meet that standard at a particular time. This led to curriculum alignment with the tests--which certainly appeared to be a sensible response. Those who did not suffered the consequences.

This point is important because the tests themselves were not at fault--it was the view of knowledge and of the aims of education that undergirded these tests that became outmoded and dysfunctional. Although most people decry the disparity in achievement on these tests by minority group members and women, the nation would have no way of assessing the differences between the educations that these groups receive if these tests were not available. The differences that writers have uncovered is remarkably the same for all minority/majority groups throughout the world, supporting the conclusion that the causes of that difference are the issue, and not the test itself.

Given that standardized tests perform a specific function of keeping all players honest, how can they be improved without losing the needed information the tests yield? Several test makers have risen to the challenge and are in the process of developing new types of tests that will address this need. For example, the traditional National Teachers Examination that was a crucible for minorities is being replaced by PRAXIS, which is a more complex measure of readiness to teach. Alternatives to the Scholastic Achievement Test (SAT) are also being developed.

In the meantime, schools and colleges are increasingly faced with the pressure to become more accountable. Forces outside the schools and colleges realize that the cost of education continues to soar and claim that the educational results of that cost are minimal. Legislators continue to respond to this pressure but are unsure about what the public wants. The tests of basic skills, the standardized tests, and the national assessment are examples of what the public wants, yet even with the implementation of these measures, the public remains dissatisfied.

In the meantime, a new kind of assessment called "authentic assessment" is emerging. This method of assessment more closely mirrors what students are expected to do in real life; thus, it is authentic to what needs to be learned. Filling in circles on a standardized test is not what people do in life. They do not display facts or principles in a vacuum. What they do is use these facts and principles to solve problems, to marshal arguments, to think about new and creative solutions. In an effort to assure that what students are accountable for in school matches what they are accountable for in life, educators such as Sizer advocate starting with the end--which he calls the exhibition--and working backwards. Exhibitions are public displays of what has been learned in much the same way in which an artist displays his portfolio of work; a musician, his virtuosity; a chef, his meal. There is nothing new here, only an adaptation from the more visual to the more hidden intellectual products of learning.

Sizer gives this example of an assessment that demonstrates what all students should have learned in a specific instance:

In the eye of the Constitution, in the eye of the law, there is in this country
no superior, dominant, ruling class of citizens. There is no caste here. Our
Constitution is color-blind, and neither knows nor tolerates classes among
citizens.... If evils will result from the commingling of the two races upon
public highways established for the benefit of all, they will be infinitely
less than those that will surely come from state legislation regulating the
enjoyment of civil rights upon the basis of race. We boast of the freedom
enjoyed by our people above all other peoples. But it is difficult to
reconcile that boast with a state of the law which, practically, puts the
brand of servitude and degradation upon a large class of our fellow-citizens,
our equals before the law. The thin disguise of "equal" accommodations
for passengers in railroad coaches will not mislead any one, nor atone for
the wrong this day done.

Please explain what this segment from a decision of the United States
Supreme Court says.

Speculate on the subject of the case represented here and on the period of
American history during which it was rendered. Give reasons for your
opinions.

Extract from this segment its enduring constitutional principles, cast it in
the form of a hypothetical case that might reach the Supreme Court today--
a case arising from today's particular social realities--and express how you
personally would act on such a case if you were an associate justice of the
Court.[22]

Although this exhibition seems complex, Sizer goes on to say that
without such skills it is difficult for any student to be a citizen, to
understand the fundamental agreements under which this nation operates,
and to make intelligent choices about leadership. Without understanding
these fundamental principles of the development of law in this land, it is
difficult to appreciate much of what is on the front page of our papers:
abortion rights, civil rights issues, and special prosecutors. In much the
same way, and looking at the same newspaper, it is difficult to make
choices without knowing a great deal about how the physical world
operates. Citizens and policymakers have been increasingly confronted
with difficult public policy questions as modern society and its technology
have the potential to affect various biological lifesystems; but this debate
was never heard. Again, the complexity of the issues that people face
today to be informed citizens falls back on the schools: how are all

students to be the kind of citizens that only a small elite was once expected to be?

Authentic assessments are characterized by their appropriateness to what must be mastered; by their expectations that all students will achieve; by their public nature; and by the involvement of the students themselves. Time will have to be adjusted in the school schedule to provide for these assessments and for their evaluation. In art schools today, portfolio assessments are an accepted part of the year's schedule; time is set aside at the end of the semester to allow students and teachers the opportunities to ˈ᷄ a good job on them. Many art schools stagger the assessments, using a lottery or another system, so that students can leave or stay depending on their placement on the list. This timetable is not viewed as cutting into instructional time, but as part of instructional time.

The assessments described above are critical to the success of the restructuring movement. When the public becomes aware of what students from all tracks know and can do, the benefits of reform will become more apparent.

These four components: new images of student learning, high expectations for all students, new players, and alternative and authentic assessment undergird many of the different models in the reform movement. In fact, most of the school designs submitted to the New Schools Development competition included different configurations of these components. And the emerging consensus on reform refers to these as constants.

Although there are other components to educational reform, such as governance, interdisciplinary courses, class size, choice, and scheduling, to mention a few, the components described in this section are at the heart of the change effort. Without changing ideas about learning, without creating communities in which learning is respected, without setting high expectations for all students, without opening education to others who have a stake, especially in the lives of their own children, and without changing the assessment systems, little will be accomplished. Those involved in these change efforts agree that what emerges is often a different sort of governance which allows much more input and flexibility; flexibility in scheduling that provides more time to think and learn coherently; and differences in the ways in which students are assigned to teachers and others in the learning community. These are the situational conditions that support the changes described above. In some cases, such as scheduling and assignment, it is difficult to implement the components of restructuring without recasting these conditions.

The changes described above cannot be achieved easily. Although many have already been incorporated into parts of our educational system, no system today can demonstrate that it has implemented all of these components. Although there is a growing consensus on how education can improve, there is little evidence that such improvements have been adopted systematically.

GETTING TO REFORM

Everywhere barriers are rising against the new and more comprehensive reform movements. It is one thing for *A Nation at Risk* to advocate more subjects and more time in schools, the setting of higher expectations for entrance into colleges and universities, and the allocation of the resources necessary to make these reforms happen; it is another thing to re-examine the basic assumptions of schooling itself and to advocate changes in its goals, structure, curriculum, and instruction.

Perhaps the first barrier to reform is its growing complexity. When it was a question of advocating a few additional required courses for graduation, it was understandable. Now some reformers are calling for the abolition of courses as the basis for a high school diploma. Outcomes-based education (OBE) by its many names is urged instead. Furthermore, when it was a question of changing someone else, it was easy; now all segments of the system, including the parents and the community, are being asked to change. Achieving this wholesale change is a much more difficult task.

Leadership from business people and politicians is needed to support the changes described above. Setting national educational goals was the first major step. But within every state, politicians and business people must come forward to support these changes, defend the need for all students to achieve at higher levels, and help schools do things differently.

A second problem with reform is the demand placed upon teachers. Even though schools will change, some form of teaching will still be required. Questions about what form that teaching will take and uncertainties about the qualifications of the present teaching force concerning not only how they teach, but how they think about teaching, are also before the nation. The image of the teacher in front of the classroom, in control of what goes on in that classroom, has changed. Whether or not teachers will have the will and the resources to respond to the reform efforts is still a question.

"Please send money" might be the plea of most people trying to implement reform. They know better than anyone that money can buy time to think and to plan, provide support for travel to educational reform models and visits from experts, and fund curriculum development efforts. Teachers are expected to change while doing just that--teaching. Few people are expected to learn a new piano concerto while playing the old one or master a new tennis stroke while playing in tournaments every day. Whether the time will be available is problematic. With decreasing school budgets, it is difficult to meet present demands, much less address new ones.

Third, an infrastructure is lacking that can support reform. The education system is divided by history, mission, language, and strategies. For example, higher education, where knowledge is created and developed, is separated from the classroom where it is taught. No resources have historically been earmarked for working with schools. Funds to cover honoraria of cooperating teachers and other agreements for the support of teacher education are the most commonly accepted ways of interacting with schools. There is no way in which to gain access to the liberal arts and science faculty without confronting the promotion and tenure system of higher education. Involvement by faculty is frequently on an individual basis, for which faculty members expect a fee.

Neither is there an infrastructure built with business. Although the number of business-school partnerships and collaborations has grown, there is no systematic way in which to make these partnerships accessible throughout the system. In many cases, business works in opposition to education by reducing its tax base or by hiring its newly trained experts. In Baltimore City, it was a legend that every time the school district trained a teacher in an advanced computer language, he was hired away by business. No newly trained teacher ever went back into the classroom. Yet businesses complained about the lack of computer training of students.

Attempts by states to create an infrastructure either inside or outside their departments of education are extremely fragile. When budget cuts are made, these types of operations are often eliminated. Although some states like South Carolina have created high-level positions charged with enhancing school-university collaboration, in most cases no one owns the means to bring all parties together to implement reform.

Fourth, changes in professional development are part of the necessary conditions for change and are part of the reform itself. Professional development that works becomes more like the kind of learning that is described above: active; teacher-designed and implemented; public and accessible; meeting high expectations; and enriched by partnerships with community, business, and social service participants.

At this time, professional development for experienced teachers follows the pattern of states and/or districts requiring the completion of certain amounts of hours in return for a certain amount of credits. Teachers largely become passive recipients of in-service days, advanced degree courses, or workshops. They are not required to be responsible for their own learning or to meet high standards of achievement. In fact, as Hawley pointed out recently in his study of teacher education in Pennsylvania, teachers are free to shop around for degrees and courses that make the least demands on them.[23] When these courses are linked with what normally happens with school district training, little excitement or challenge is present. In these experiences, sometimes teacher behavior mirrors that of their most disengaged student, with teachers reading books, correcting homework, developing activities, working on outside activities, and/or disrupting speakers with challenges and angry ripostes.

When teachers become a learning community as described above, these types of dysfunctional behaviors disappear. People start taking responsibility for their own learning, linking their individual goals with those of the students they serve. They start learning new skills of consensus building, communicating, and leading. Sizer's Re: Learning Project has done much to provide these new skills in the TREKs that it runs for teams of teachers and other educators. In these team experiences, educators learn the skills that are needed to work with other adults. As classroom walls come tumbling down, teachers will increasingly be called upon to take on an expanded role in a learning community which they help to create and operate.

In order to do this, colleges and universities must change their teacher preparation programs to allow students to work with other professionals who will be important in the lives of their students, to develop team and community building skills, and to experience assessments that model for them the assessments that are required from all students.

Staff development programs and graduate degree programs will be required to change to allow for more flexibility and to provide the challenging curriculum that teachers must create for their own students. Interdisciplinary learning advocated by many of the national learning associations also will need to be incorporated into the total higher education curriculum.

A fifth concern is the lack of caring for children that is rampant in some parts of this nation. As the Children's Defense Fund has so poignantly documented, the needs of children have grown in the past decade while the resources to meet those needs have decreased.[24] Economically, it does not make sense to care about or for children. Some individuals consider children to be a burden, and the presence of children in a family makes it more likely to be on welfare. Television is the great caregiver of the decade, with children logging more hours in front of the "tube" each day. Parents care for their own children but often feel overwhelmed by the sheer physical and emotional demands associated with raising them. Children are pacified with consumer goods, television, and junk food.

Finally, reform takes simple courage--the courage to say that things must change for all children and to take the criticism that will follow. Educators in many of our reportedly finest schools see the desolation of drugs, lack of caring, and low standards that face the majority of the students. Politicians understand that school funding is frequently inadequate or inequitable. State officials know that the easy changes are those that probably do not matter. If large-scale, authentic educational reform is to be conducted somewhere along the line, jobs will be lost; careers dimmed; electoral defeats suffered. There is no escape from this truth. Therefore, the policymakers who implement genuine educational innovations and reform will probably "pay a price" in the political realm for their actions. It is to be hoped that the convictions of educational innovators will carry them forward. Today's schools await innovation and reform.

CONCLUSION

The reform movement is fragile, capable of being deterred and derailed; nonetheless, it is a movement that will grow because the conditions for it are right. The nation must recognize that knowledge has changed, that the economic and political worlds have become increasingly intertwined and global, and that our schools and colleges are not meeting the needs of the majority of the students. The emerging consensus on what must be changed will continue to grow, to become more articulate and reasoned, and to be integrated into all levels of learning. All that remains is for the nation to find the leadership, the courage, and the conviction to make the changes necessary. Not an easy task, but the work has started.

ENDNOTES

1. Department of Education, *What Works: Research About Teaching and Learning* (Washington, D.C.: Government Printing Office, 1986), 35.

2. Kenneth A. Bruffee, "Science in a Postmodern World," *Change* 24 (September/October 1992): 25.

3. Ibid., 25.

4. Ibid., 22-23.

5. The Secretary's Commission on Achieving Necessary Skills (SCANS), *What Work Requires of Schools: A SCANS Report for America 2000* (Washington, D.C.: Government Printing Office, 1991).

6. Ibid., 2.

7. Ibid., 3.

8. Ibid., 3.

9. John I. Goodlad, *A Place Called School: Prospects for the Future* (New York, NY: McGraw-Hill Book Company, 1984); and Theodore R. Sizer, *Horace's Compromise: The Dilemma of the American High School* (Boston, MA: Houghton Mifflin Company, 1992).

10. Goodlad, *A Place Called School*, 123-124.

11. Theodore R. Sizer, *Horace's School: Redesigning the American High School* (Boston, MA: Houghton Mifflin Company, 1992); Arthur G. Power, Eleanor Farrar, and David K. Cohen, *The Shopping Mall High School: Winners and Losers in the Educational Marketplace* (Boston, MA: Houghton Mifflin Company, 1985); and Robert L. Hampel, *The Last Little Citadel: American High Schools Since 1940* (Boston, MA: Houghton Mifflin Company, 1986).

12. Hampel, *The Last Citadel*, xii.

13. Phillip C. Schlechty, *Schools for the 21st Century: Leadership Imperatives for Educational Reform* (San Francisco, CA: Jossey-Bass Publishers, 1990), xvi.

14. Lynn Olson, "The Future of School," *Education Week*, 10 February 1993, 15-16.

15. Jack Shaw, Sullivan County School District, interview by author, n.d..

16. Seymour Sarason, *The Predictable Failure of School Reform: Can We Change Course Before It Is Too Late?* (San Francisco, CA: Jossey-Bass Publishers, 1990).

17. Robert Slavin, Nancy L. Karweit, and Barbara A. Wasik, "Preventing Early School Failure," *Educational Leadership* 50 (December 1992/January 1993): 17.

18. Carnegie Council on Adolescent Development, *Turning Points: Preparing American Youth for the 21st Century* (New York, NY: Carnegie Corporation of New York, 1989), 9-10.

19. Ron Brandt, "On Parents and Schools: A Conversation with Joyce Epstein," *Educational Leadership* 46 (October 1989): 156.

20. Ibid., 157.

21. James B. Comer, "A Brief History and Summary of the School Development Program," New Haven, CT: privately printed, n.d..

22. Sizer, *Horace's School*, 98-99.

23. Willis D. Hawley and Carolyn M. Evertson, "Revisioning Teacher Education in Pennsylvania," Nashville, TN: privately printed, 1993.

24. Clifford M. Johnson and others, eds., *Child Poverty in America* (Washington, D.C.: Children's Defense Fund, 1991).

Chapter 2

Educational Reform Movements Among the States in the Last Ten Years

Thomas V. O'Brien

> If an foreign power had attempted to impose on America the mediocre educational performance that exists today we might well have viewed it as an act of war.[1]

It has been just over ten years since the National Commission on Excellence in Education published *A Nation At Risk* and declared a state of educational emergency. That federal report, which billed itself "an open letter to the American people," used "provocative and scathing language"[2] to fuel a period of educational reform that continues into the mid-1990s. The report began with a discussion of the dismal condition of America's system of public education. It then recommended intensifying the existing curriculum, raising students' academic performance standards, increasing the length of the school day and school year, increasing teacher pay, rewarding good teachers, and firing bad ones.

In the wake of *A Nation At Risk* over 300 commissions and task forces were created to develop educational reform proposals. In the first year alone, over 250 were formed and asked to develop reform programs.[3] Between 1983 and 1987 task forces, composed primarily of nonspecialists, developed concrete, "simple and in some cases simplistic solutions" for school reform.[4] By 1988 state leaders, aware that their programs were yielding mixed results, called on "university thinkers"[5] for help. This chapter briefly examines the major educational reform movements among the states that came about in response to *A Nation At Risk*. It concentrates on some of the key efforts that were made to improve secondary public education in the fifty states during the first and second "waves" of reform. It is organized around several, but not all of the reforms that took place in the last ten years.

A CHALLENGE TO THE STATES

Unlike other federal educational initiatives in public education since World War II, *A Nation At Risk* did not initiate reforms, but instead challenged state governments to "gather in their authority from local authorities" to launch reforms at the state level.[6] The document reflected the Reagan Administration's decision to provide advice but no additional money to carry out the reforms. Indeed, Reagan's 1980 campaign pledge to abolish the Department of Education served notice that the new Republican administration wanted the national government to get out of the business of education altogether, and would not provide large chunks of new funding. While the Reagan Administration was ultimately persuaded to leave the Department of Education intact, for the next twelve years the primary responsibility of educating America's children would remain with the state and local authorities. As *A Nation At Risk* put it, "state and local officials, including board members, governors, and legislators have the primary responsibility for financing and governing schools, and should incorporate the reforms we propose in their educational policies and fiscal planning."[7]

The challenge to the states did not fall on deaf ears. Perhaps anticipating the letter and spirit of *A Nation At Risk* and not wanting to get caught behind the political "eight-ball," several governors across the country were already taking the lead in what some would call the "first wave" of educational reform. The first wave of educational reforms encompassed great breath, scope, variety, and intensity,[8] but were generally "top-down" reforms. They were designed, framed, and evaluated by those at the top of state government--governors, state legislators, state boards of education, and state related organizations as well as those that influenced state officials (business leaders, corporate heads, etc.). The changes the first wave reforms initiated were targeted at those at the local level, the district superintendents, building principals, and ultimately, classroom teachers and students.

By 1988 a second generation of school reform was underway. Unlike the first swell, the second wave of reform was and continues to be characterized by decentralized reform programs that rely on the ideas and theories of "university thinkers."[9] During this wave, top level officials, with notable exceptions,[10] have been less inclined to take a hands-on approach to school reform. Consequently, they have left many of the complex tasks involving the teaching and learning process to some of America's best educational minds. Top level state officials, nevertheless, have continued to set broad educational goals for America's children, as they did with President Bush at the Education Summit in the fall of 1989, and later when they endorsed the President's education strategy in "America 2000."

THE EVOLVING STATE ROLE IN EDUCATIONAL FINANCE

While thousands of state reforms were undertaken during the 1980s,[11] perhaps the most significant development at the state level was in the area of finance. Historically, the financial responsibility of providing educational services has been left to the states by the federal government. Although there is arguably a vague constitutional provision for a federal role in education because education relates to the nation's "general welfare" and "national defense," most scholars agree that states, under the Tenth Amendment, have the primary constitutional responsibility for the provision of education.[12] Yet, during the early national period and well into the 20th century, states left the bulk of the task of funding and administrating public schools to local school districts.

Shortly after World War II, however, states dramatically increased their involvement in the education enterprise. On the eve of the post-War period of prosperity, and in a climate of idealism and a renewed faith in democracy, Americans looked inward. What they saw, however, was not comforting. Scores of studies reported that the quality of public education across the country was uneven, and in many districts inadequate. One study in 1944, for example, found "shocking variations" in school expenditures, ranging from $400 dollars per classroom in Mississippi to $4,100 dollar per classroom in New York.[13] Most reports agreed that the disparities and inadequacies would result in damage to the children and the infrastructure,[14] and would ultimately compromise America's newly acquired status as a superpower.

In the decade that followed World War II, state governments rethought and acted upon their hands-off educational policies. In moves that aimed to secure "'reasonably adequate and well rounded opportunities for all children,' . . . states began enacting bills that reflected the fresh principle that public education was not only a local enterprise, but also a state affair. The new partnership between the state and local districts placed major legal and financial responsibilities on the states."[15]   A survey in 1953 found that most states had stepped up their contribution significantly, kicking in an average of 39 percent of the total expenditure.[16]

By mid-century, state level "Foundations Programs," which assured "a basic level of expenditure . . . for every child," were in operation in over three-quarters of the states. The "Foundations Programs" movement in the late 1940s and 1950s was perhaps the most powerful idea in educational finance in its day.   The movement set the stage for the "Equity Movement" that would follow in the 1960s and early 1970s. In state after state, leaders developed and approved school-aid formulas that provided more general state aid for poorer localities.[17] That period of educational reform, which also contained the seed of greater state accountability for what happens in schools, set the stage for what became known as the "Excellence" Movement, which emerged in the 1980s.

THREE TRENDS

As one surveys the literature on school reform in the last ten years, three important trends are evident.   First, beginning in the late 1970s and continuing into the 1990s, state governments have emerged as the primary suppliers of revenue to support and maintain the schools.[18] Moreover, as state governments have become increasingly active in financing elementary and secondary public education, they have also used these increases "as a vehicle to develop, in many cases, state reform of education programs."[19] Thus, the shift in who contributed most for funding public schooling was accompanied by a shift in who controlled the reform agenda.

A second trend that emerges from the literature is that the theme of "equity" that had anchored educational reform in the 1960s was replaced by the theme of "excellence" in the late 1970s. Consequently, the decade of school reform following the publication of *A Nation At Risk* has come to be known as the "excellence movement." Although prompted in large part by the publication of the now-famous report, the excellence movement in American public education finds its roots in the back-to-basics movement of the 1970s. In the mid-1970s growing numbers of policy makers, business leaders, the media, and U.S. citizens perceived that the public schools had declined in quality. Consequently, the back-to-basics movement, which promised Americans a return to an emphasis on "the three R's," and a reinstatement of respect for teachers and elders, good manners, politeness, and a return to the old ways of teaching, received tremendous approval from all corners of American society. A Gallup Poll in 1977, for example, found that 83 percent of those polled favored a return to the basics.[20] Anchored firmly in the educational theory of *essentialism,* the movement has dominated American educational reform up to the present day.[21]

A third development in the 1970s was a growing perception that America's system of schooling was in decline. By the mid-1970s Americans were concerned that public education was in deep trouble.[22] The media was also aware of the public loss of confidence in the schools. Reporters began comparing scores on the Scholastic Aptitude Test (SAT), a standardized test that was designed to predict a high school senior's potential for college success, and discovered that since 1963 there had been a steady decline in scores. Although the SAT was not designed to identify the quality of public secondary schools, the decline in SAT scores in the late 1970s came to be seen as synonymous with a decline in the quality of schooling.[23]

American public policy makers, corporate leaders, and the media began to use SAT scores as evidence that the schools were coming apart at the seams. Although a study by the College Entrance Examination Board (CEEB) in 1977 pointed out that the major cause for the decline in scores was a large increase in the number and types of students who took the SAT, many of whom in the past who were discouraged from taking the SAT because higher education was not open to them, the public and policymakers "paid little attention to this conclusion."[24] The public also ignored warnings from the CEEB that the SAT measured student *aptitude* (potential for further academic work), but not student *achievement* (how much students had learned). What stuck in the minds of most Americans was that something had gone wrong in the schools.[25]

All three trends--the emergence of the state as the primary revenue provider, the new emphasis on excellence, and the general perception of decline--gave governors, state legislators, business groups, and others who controlled the purse strings--potent political issues upon which to launch American education into a new direction of reform and to increase state financing for public education. As historian David Tyack remarked recently, the doctrine of decline, in particular, served an important political agenda.[26] "Reform periods in education are typically times when concerns about the state of society or economy spill over into demands that the schools set things straight."[27] In this instance, *A Nation At Risk* cited the threat of losing our economic edge to Germany, Japan, and South Korea that provided the impetus for reform. State politicians seized on public fears of declining American competitiveness and on the general widespread support for American public education to garner support for centralized, state-mandated reforms.

OMNIBUS REFORMS, 1982-1987

It was against this backdrop that the "excellence movement" of the 1980s emerged. Even before the publication of *A Nation At Risk*, state politicians had been working toward passage of extensive "omnibus" reform packages with impressive price tags. In December of 1982, the Mississippi Legislature passed a $106 million reform package that included mandatory kindergarten and a big pay raise for teachers. In January of 1983, Governor Lamar Alexander of Tennessee proposed a $210 million reform plan that included mandatory kindergarten, a basic skills elementary curriculum, tougher math and science requirements, and a controversial merit pay for teachers plan.[28] Working with key lawmakers, Alexander funded "A Penny for Their Thoughts" package with a one cent increase in the state sales tax.

Governor Bill Clinton of Arkansas, followed Tennessee's lead in September 1983, when a task force headed by Clinton's wife, Hillary Rodham Clinton, proposed mandatory kindergarten, increases in teacher pay, decreases in the student-teacher ratio, teacher competency testing, higher graduation standards, and a longer school year. Clinton, who campaigned and won the governorship on a "better schools, more economic growth" platform, was also encouraged by a 1982 Arkansas Supreme Court ruling that held the school finance system unconstitutional. In a special session in late 1983, the legislature passed Clinton's Quality Education Act and allocated $527 million state dollars toward that program.[29]

A 50 state survey published by *Education Week* in November of 1983 found that after the release of *A Nation At Risk* in April of 1983, 54 state-level reform commissions had been formed. The article reported that two states had approved differentiated pay for teachers and 33 others were considering the issue. It also reported that seven states had lengthened the school day, one state lengthened the school year, and 16 other states were considering lengthening the school year. Also 26 states stiffened high school requirements, and seven states approved teacher competency tests.[30] In July 1983, three months after *A Nation At Risk* was published, Illinois and California lawmakers passed major school finance reform bills.[31] In 1984 New York, which had evaluated its system prior to *A Nation At Risk*, added a $634 million increase to fund its reform package.

Other states, notably Texas, Wisconsin, Florida, and South Carolina enacted similar state level reforms. The 1984-85 Texas initiative, led by businessman Ross Perot, raised the minimum starting salary for teachers from $11,000 a year to $15,200 and the average teacher salary from $17,910 to $20,080.[32] Wisconsin increased teacher salaries and per pupil expenditures by almost nine percent, as did Florida. Florida's omnibus reform was similar to the Tennessee initiative in that it too was funded by a one cent sales tax increase and a unitary tax on corporations.[33] In Florida, by 1986, the sales and corporate taxes had generated $256 million, with an estimated $203 million that went to basic school aid.[34]

Perhaps "the most comprehensive and well funded educational reform programs" during the first wave belonged to South Carolina.[35] Concerned about their students' relative rank in average SAT scores (50th) and their below average scores on other standardized tests, South Carolinians were anxious to do something to improve the quality of their schools. South Carolina began making state level educational reforms during the late 1970s.[36] South Carolina passed legislation for a basic skills assessment program, a minimum competency testing program for students, and a literacy exam for incoming teachers in the 1980s. With leadership from Governor Richard Riley and State Superintendent Charlie Williams, the state introduced the Educational Improvement Act (EIA) of 1984,[37] a program that surpassed all other state efforts. The EIA carried a price tag of $210 million in the first year and was set up to receive future funding through a one percent increase in the sales tax.[38] Revised in 1985, 1986, 1987, and 1989, the EIA increased the state appropriation to public education by twenty percent.[39] The South Carolina program came closest to the 20-28 percent increase in revenue that experts estimated would be necessary to implement the recommendations called for in *A Nation At Risk.*[40]

By 1987 virtually every state had taken steps to reform their public schools.[41] *A Nation At Risk* had been quite successful in challenging governors and lawmakers to take steps to finance educational reforms in the 1980s. Because of the recession in the early 1980s, however, the increases in actual state revenue increases for education ranged from six percent to 17 percent and were significantly below what experts in 1985 were estimating would be needed to carry out the reforms.   When the recession subsided, many state leaders, who were enthusiastic about educational reform, adopted a "quick fix" approach to set public education back on course. By the mid-1980s, overall expenditures on education had increased 25 percent after inflation,[42] with the state maintaining its proportion of the contribution. In the early 1990s there is some evidence that states and local districts are continuing to maintain their commitments to finance reform. One recent study, for example, found that state, local, and federal expenditures on K-12 education rose 30 percent per pupil in constant dollars during the excellence movement.[43]

As we move into the mid-1990s, however, there is some concern over whether states will continue to endorse increases in school funding. The continued national "economic downturn" and a turnover in political leadership[44] have placed many state school finance reforms in jeopardy. Incumbent state politicians are also aware of the unpopularity of a recent shift in attention in some states to a "new round of finance-equalization measures."[45]   These politically controversial finance reforms, that redistribute tax dollars more evenly to the local districts, which are underway in Kentucky, New Jersey, and Texas have been criticized sharply throughout the states. All of these factors may cause state reformers to shy away from finance reform in the near future.

THE STATE AND THE CURRICULUM

Unlike the Sputnik inspired reforms of the late 1950s, which attempted to rethink the content of the curriculum, the state reports following *A Nation At Risk* took no issue with the kinds of subjects being taught.[46] What seemed to be putting our nation at risk, according to the Commission on Excellence, was the low amount of time spent on these subjects. The Commission recommended raising high school graduation requirements to four years of English, three years of math, three years of science, three years of social studies, one-half year of computer science, and up to six years of foreign language.   The Commission also recommended more homework, longer school days, a longer school year, and more "time on task" for students and teachers.

By May of 1983, the message that our nation was at risk was driven home again, this time by the Education Commission of the States' (ECS) National Task Force on Education for Economic Growth, a group primarily composed of governors and corporate leaders. Even more so than *A Nation At Risk*, the ECS report *Action for Excellence* linked improving our schools to economic development, and argued that schools had failed to educate for today's workplace. Four months later the National Science Board's Commission on Precollege Education in Mathematics, Science, and Technology added to the reform agenda, warning that American school children were in danger of becoming "stragglers in a world of technology."[47]

HIGH SCHOOL GRADUATION REQUIREMENTS

It was not long before several states took steps to adjust the curriculum and thus put the excellence movement "into orbit."[48] By September 1983 California, Colorado, Florida, and Iowa had taken steps to "ratchet up" high school graduation requirements in the subjects identified in *A Nation At Risk.* Iowa had even taken the unusual step of putting in place per-pupil incentive grants of up to $50 for students in advanced math and science courses.[49] By April 1984, one year after the release of *A Nation At Risk,* six more states (Alaska, Arkansas, Missouri, New York, Texas, and Wisconsin) had raised graduation standards.[50] One month later the National Center for Educational Statistics reported that more that half the districts in the United States had increased graduation requirements in "core subjects" and another 38 percent of districts were planning to do so.[51] By the summer of 1986, 34 states had increased their graduation requirements over 1980 levels.[52] A study conducted by the Educational Testing Service in 1990 found that 42 states had raised graduation requirements during the first six years of the excellence movement, although the requirements in many states still fell short of the recommendations made in *A Nation At Risk.*[53] The study found that 37 states required four or more years of English, 28 states required three or more years of social studies, but only ten states required three years of mathematics and only four required three years of science.[54]

In general, nearly all of state curriculum reforms undertaken in years following *A Nation At Risk* assumed that education did not have to be fundamentally changed in order to make schools "excellent." What needed to be done, according to state reformers, was to intensify the existing curriculum. It was thought that this could be accomplished by placing a greater emphasis on math, science, computer literacy, and other "core" subjects, while at the same time discouraging the study of vocational subjects such as photography, auto mechanics, or home economics. In the words of a first wave state legislator, the key to educational reform was to "make the little buggers work harder."[55] Although these curricular assumptions in the first wave of reform were authoritarian and somewhat simplistic, they were shared by large numbers of Americans who accepted the doctrine of school decline, and were genuinely concerned about improving academic performance. In this sense the theory of intensifying the curriculum kept Americans in touch with state level actions. Making familiar courses more rigorous, the states sustained public interest in the education enterprise and provided momentum for "a second wave" of reform in the late 1980s and early 1990s.

By the late 1980s the successes and limitations of intensification were evident. First, the state initiatives had affected the proportion of students taking core subjects such as math and science. A state-by-state analysis of pupil enrollment patterns conducted by the Council of Chief State School Officers, for example, found that the percentage of high school students taking math and science had "increased dramatically during the 1980s."[56] These increases, however, had not had a significant impact on student achievement in these core subjects. Another state-by-state analysis, for instance, revealed that only 5 percent of high school seniors had the necessary math skills needed for high technology or college level work.[57]

Such findings pointed out that the state level initiatives could revise official curriculum, but had little or no impact on the way those changes were played out in the classrooms across the country. State reformers, driven by the assumption that international and interstate competition was linked to education,[58] could determine what subjects students studied, but could only cross their fingers when it came to the actual learning process. The state reformers would need to enlist the help of educational experts and the teachers in order to make possible the kinds of changes they had envisioned a decade earlier.

STATE MANDATED STUDENT TESTING

While state reform initiatives such as increasing graduation requirements and lengthening the school day and school year caught the media's attention in the 1980s, the practice of assessing students with standardized tests was discovered to be the most powerful policy for influencing student learning and teacher behavior.[59] Like other strands of the excellence movement, the move to use standardized tests to evaluate student achievement emerged during the back-to-basics movement of the 1970s. By the time *A Nation At Risk* appeared, student testing was "already extensive."[60] While the SAT continued to be used to measure school decline, other standardized tests, some of which sought to measure student achievement, became quite popular. Perhaps the most popular standardized tests that the states began to use were "minimum competency tests." The idea behind minimum competency was to ensure that no student escaped public school without basic competencies to function in our complex society.[61]

A brief survey of minimum competency testing reveals that in 1983, New Jersey, Tennessee, and Florida, modified their minimum competency testing programs. State reformers in New Jersey, led by Governor Thomas Kean, raised the difficulty level of their test, while in Florida lawmakers passed a law that withheld a student's high school diploma if he did not pass the test. Tennessee's state board of education approved granting students who failed the minimum competency test a "certificate of attendance" instead of a diploma.[62]

In the mid-1980s other states played "follow the leader" with regard to modifying minimum competency testing. Encouraged by state-by-state "wall chart" comparisons, state reformers endorsed minimum competency testing programs and concentrated on raising test scores. Although tests differed among the states, most states chose to reward students who passed minimum tests with promotion or graduation, while forgetting, overlooking, or in some cases, dismissing students who failed. Although the efficacy of minimum competency testing in promoting achievement has not been established,[63] two independent studies found that by 1990 over 40 states required state mandated testing of students.[64] By 1990 state mandated testing of students was in effect in every region in the country.

Two problems with minimum competency testing programs became evident. First, as mentioned above, many states developed policies that only rewarded students who passed the tests. For those students who failed to reach the minimum, the options were quite limited as most states neglected to set up systematic remediation programs.[65] Students below "grade level" were often overlooked or in some cases discouraged from continuing in school. Another unanticipated result of minimum competency testing was that some teachers, whose performance was being evaluated based on their students' test scores, began to over-emphasize the test material, thereby encouraging rote learning and ignoring critical thinking skills. In the mid-1980s, educators and policy-makers began to respond to this problem by modifying the tests to encourage and evaluate higher order thinking skills. Such misapplications of test scores led, in the late 1980s, to a series of conferences that focused exclusively on educating policymakers about the proper use of tests scores, such as curricular alignment and student remediation. As we head into the 1990s, however, the misuse of test scores continues to be problematic.

Recently, perhaps due to criticisms by action groups and educational researchers that testing basic skills was not adequately preparing students to be "economically competitive and socially competent," there has been a move in several states, particularly in Florida, Georgia, and Pennsylvania, to reduce minimum competency testing.[66] Vermont took an innovative step in late 1988 when school reformers and educators announced that in addition to test scores, students would be assessed on the basis of portfolios.[67] A second trend has been a move in some states, such as Arizona, California, and Michigan, to modify testing programs to address higher-order thinking skills.[68]

A recent variation of state mandated testing is the development of Outcomes Based Education (OBE) at the state level. A few states, notably Kentucky, Maine, Minnesota, Pennsylvania, and Virginia, are pioneering efforts to develop state outcomes, which all students must meet, before earning a high school diploma. An "outcome" is a broad statement describing what students are expected to know and be able to do upon graduation.[69]   Most outcomes require some type of culminating demonstration, usually in the form of a multifaceted student performance.[70] State outcomes programs generally leave local communities with the tasks of interpreting the outcomes, developing a strategic plan and curriculum for reaching the outcomes, defining the standard for reaching those outcomes, and evaluating whether or not that standard has been reached. In this regard, OBE represents a significant break from the top-down reforms of the 1980s. It also can be distinguished from other first wave reforms in that it is driven, in part, by school reform research and tested educational theory.[71]

TEACHER STANDARDS

Perhaps the most controversial and most intense state level reforms undertaken in the 1980s were those that addressed teachers. Between 1980 and 1986, for example, over 1,000 pieces of legislation dealing with teacher compensation and certification were introduced at the state level.[72] Teachers, who were excluded from setting the reform agenda during the first wave, became central targets of many state leaders. Although *A Nation At Risk* was careful not to scapegoat teachers, many of the state reform packages that followed the report insisted that teachers be held accountable for low student performance. Underneath the rhetoric of accountability and accentuated by the doctrine that the schools were regressing, was a not-so-subtle disrespect and disregard for public school educators. Most teachers did not take kindly to suggestions that they as a group, were lackluster educators that needed to be held more accountable for their performances. Nevertheless, state leaders during the excellence movement persisted with several plans that sought to improve the quality of the teaching force and hold teachers accountable for their work. Some of the more popular plans among the states involved increasing teacher pay; raising teacher certification standards for both in-service and pre-service teachers through testing; assessing teacher performance; and linking that performance to promotion or demotion.

TEACHER SALARIES

Initially, in the period immediately following *A Nation At Risk,* state reformers showed lots of interest in improving teacher salaries. By November of 1983, six months after the report's release, for example, Arkansas, California, Florida, and New Jersey had called for some kind of increase in teacher salaries, with some of these states pushing for lower student teacher ratios. By January of 1985, nearly one third of all states had raised teacher salaries.[73] These early initiatives led to continued increases in average salaries during the 1980s. A 50 state survey in *Education Week* in January of 1985 found that approximately one third of the states had raised teacher salaries in response to *A Nation At Risk.*[74] California in little more than a decade, for instance, had increased minimum starting salaries from $15,000 to $22,000 by 1987.

TEACHER LITERACY

By the mid-1980s, however, the call for higher salaries had been drowned out by leading reformers' schemes to link salary increases to good teaching and to rid the profession of "deadbeat" teachers. Realizing perhaps that the tax-paying public was at best lukewarm to policies that rewarded teachers monetarily, governors, lawmakers, and other policymakers moved ahead with more punitive policies. With new evidence from the Educational Testing Service that concluded the decline in test scores was caused by "decreased rigor in the high schools and by a drop in the amount of time spent on homework,"[75] some 30 states approved "literacy or competency" testing for teachers. In January of 1984, 12 others were considering the idea.[76] Also adding fuel to the literacy/competency testing movement in August of that year was a RAND Corporation study that predicted a shortage of qualified teachers would soon undermine the excellence movement.   That same month Albert Shanker, the President of the American Federation of Teachers, put his prestige behind a national professional exam for teachers. By July of 1985, even the National Education Association, the largest teachers' union in the country endorsed the testing of new teachers and the dismissal of teachers deemed incompetent. During the summer of 1985, it seemed as if literacy/competency testing had been accepted by all quarters, except, perhaps, by classroom teachers who felt burdened and insulted by the requirement.

The literacy testing movement, aimed primary at identifying incompetent in-service teachers, began to run into difficulty by 1986.   First, the programs remained costly. Most state-initiated omnibus reform packages had ebbed early in the year,[77] and continued support for this type of testing was waning. In Texas, for instance, the state legislature had allocated $4.8 million for the development, administration, and scoring of the Texas Examination of Current Administrators and Teachers (TECAT), only to find that it would actually cost nearly $36 million.[78] When nearly all of the Texas teachers and administrators passed the TECAT literacy test in the spring of 1986, many lawmakers questioned the value of the test. Second, an unintended side effect became apparent. Literacy testing of teachers was screening out relatively high percentages of African-American and other minority teachers, many of whom were considered very good teachers. This effect was particularly strong in the deep South. Thus, while competency testing initially appeared to be a fool-proof idea, the reality of developing and administering a valid test that would reliably screen out ineffective teachers was an expensive, if not unattainable, goal.

Triggered, in part, by a federal civil rights lawsuit filed in Alabama in the spring of 1986, state support for literacy testing abated for in-service teachers. In the mid-1980s a handful of states, as an alternative to literacy testing of in-service teachers, developed and mandated performance instruments. Within a four year period Georgia, for example, developed and required and then abandoned the Teacher Performance Assessment Instrument (TPAI). The TPAI sought to require a performance assessment before certifying new teachers. The assessment program was abandoned in 1990 for a variety of reasons. These reasons included the test's costs and its negative effect on the state's efforts to attract out-of-state teachers to Georgia.

PRE-SERVICE SCREENING

Soon most states began endorsing more vigorously the idea of testing teachers *before* they received certification or in some states before they gained admission to a college teacher preparation program. Several states, Pennsylvania and South Carolina for example, required prospective teachers to pass the National Teacher Examination (NTE) before they would be granted a teaching certificate. The concept of centralizing certification received support from the National Governors Association, which in 1986 issued *A Time For Results*, a report, that among other things, recommended a national certification board to oversee teacher licensing. In January 1985 *Education Week* reported that more than half the states had toughened teacher-licensing requirements. By 1990, 46 states used the NTE or some other standardized basic skills test for pre-service teachers.[79] Thus, screening pre-service teachers rather than in-service for competency emerged as a major development during the 1980s.

While this new trend of state required pre-service testing remains popular into the 1990s and is likely to stay, policymakers should realize that pre-service competency tests have the same shortcomings as the literacy tests for in-service teachers. The tests are subject to criticism for their cultural bias and speculative validity. Indeed, it is difficult, if not impossible, to write a single instrument that could reliably predict effective teaching in the variety of educational situations among the myriad of public school systems in the 50 states. Notably, the tests have had a negative impact on recruiting minority teachers because a disproportionate number of minorities in teacher education programs have failed to reach the state-mandated cut-off scores.[80] Meanwhile, recent educational research suggests that by the year 2010 one out of three school children will be non-white and that "cultural synchronization" will be critical in educating these children.[81] In other words, although prospective teachers who are non-white may score lower as a group on the existing pre-service tests, they may have a distinct advantage in reaching and teaching non-white students. For these reasons, state policies on pre-service testing may require an in-depth rethinking.

TEACHER ASESSMENT AND THE CAREER LADDER

Among the most publicized reforms undertaken by state government during the excellence movements was assessing the performance of teachers and linking the results of that assessment to pay bonuses, career ladder promotions, or increased school or district responsibilities. Lamar Alexander, the Governor of Tennessee, and Robert Graham, the Governor of Florida, took the lead in 1983 in moving their states toward master teacher plans for teachers and administrators and merit pay for quality instructors. In the meantime California moved ahead with its "Mentor Teacher Program." This program aimed to reward exemplary teachers with a $3,000 stipend above their regular salary and a quasi-sabbatical that allowed them to spend up to 40 percent of their time in professional growth activities.[82] By the summer of 1986, after battles between state reformers and educators in several states, various career ladder plans emerged as the preferred performance-reward arrangement. The National Governors Association's *A Time For Results*, for example, recommended the "development of new career patterns for teachers, including the opportunity to earn more money . . . new methods of training in which outstanding practicing teachers and administrators would have much more important roles."[83] In 1986 Chris Pipho, a columnist for *Phi Delta Kappan* and a proponent of merit pay, reported that approximately 25 states had taken some type of action on career ladders structures,[84] and in 1988 at least 30 states had implemented some variety of career ladders.[85]

THE SECOND WAVE

The National Governors Association's *Time For Results* contained some of the ideas that would make up what some called the "second wave" of education reform. Although the report could not completely break away from the top-down, centralized policies that characterized the first generation of reforms, there was a sense that most governors were more willing to cooperate with educators than they had been in the three years following *A Nation At Risk*.[86] In summing up the report, Lamar Alexander, Chair of the Association, remarked that "the Governors are ready for some old-fashioned horse trading. We'll regulate less, if the schools and the districts produce better results."[87] Thus, while Alexander's remark anticipated and perhaps even precipitated a move toward more decentralized decision making at the district or site level, it still held onto the excellence movement's principal themes of accountability and quality.

The reforms that made up the second wave were in many ways a response to what had not been accomplished in the first wave. Second wave initiatives sought to penetrate the thick skin of American education by radically rethinking and reworking the schools. Thus, the reforms from 1988 to the present called on and relied upon the efforts of educational experts, not state politicians. What follows is a brief examination of two of the many decentralized reform efforts taking place in the second wave of the excellence movement--parental choice and school restructuring.

PARENTAL CHOICE

A Time For Results, the National Governors Association report of 1986, also resurrected the politically charged issue of parental school choice. The basic idea of parental choice is that public and private schools would compete freely for students in an educational marketplace where parents could decide which schools their children would attend. Parental choice would theoretically give parents more motivation and responsibility in their children's education and would improve schools through competition.

Specific plans to implement parental choice, however, have not been widely developed or supported. According to the annual Gallup polls on education, the American public has been increasingly supportive of the concept of the "right" of parents to choose which school their children would attend. Encouraged by President Ronald Reagan and William Bennett, the U.S. Secretary of Education from 1985 to 1988, seven out of ten Americans favored parental choice with regard to the local school that their children attended.[88] Yet, when asked specifically whether they would support adopting a voucher system which would enable parents to choose public, parochial, or private schools, Americans were much more divided on the question. Gallup and Clark, the pollsters, concluded that the "lukewarm" support for vouchers stemmed from the belief that educational coupons would ultimately hurt the public schools.[89]

The results of the annual Gallup Poll did not go unnoticed by state reformers. Indeed, given all the political capital in the concept of choice-- freedom, quality through competition, empowering voters--state reformers scrambled to endorse a variety of choice schemes that fit nicely with their economic theme of better preparing the future work force through excellence in education. Reformers argued that choice would maximize accountability by rewarding "good" schools, both public and private, while encouraging "bad" schools to either "shape up or ship out." For many it was simply a matter of allowing the realities of the free market to work on the education enterprise. In effect, the concept of choice was driven by a sort of social Darwinism mentality that the healthy ("fit") schools would survive, while the unfit schools would fade way.

What many reformers had overlooked was the fact that many actual choice policies, which resembled a rebate plan, threatened to decrease the amount of total revenue allocated for public schools--precisely where many of the most thorny learning problems were occurring. By allowing families to make "any choice," parents that already could afford private school tuition, would receive a bonus in the form of a $700-$1,000 rebate[90] for their choice, while poorer families would be granted that same stipend with one option--returning their children to a public school that now had a reduced staff and fewer resources and equipment. At the risk of oversimplification, non-qualified choice proposals in education represent an inverse "Robin Hood" plan. Many choice plans would steal from the poor and give to the rich. Such plans not only go against America's claim that it is a land of opportunity, but also give an unfair advantage to those already who have secured a piece of the American dream.

Nevertheless, the reformers during the first wave of reform made much ado about choice in their reform proposals. Again, it was Tennessee's Lamar Alexander who took the bully pulpit to call for choice in the early 1980s and mid-1980s. *Education Week* reported in January of 1985 the issue had reached a "critical mass," when Minnesota's Governor Rudy Perpich proposed an "open enrollment" for 11th and 12th graders. In the same month Colorado's Governor proposed a modified voucher plan aimed at high school dropouts. The plan involved giving dropouts a "second chance" voucher to attend the public school of their choice and by the spring of that year the Colorado Legislature approved that plan.[91]

As conservative educators and bureaucrats tinkered with ways to make choice plans more egalitarian, liberals, many of whom were vehemently opposed to choice, revisited the concept. Albert Shanker, President of the American Federation of Teachers, for example, came out in favor of limited choice plans within the system of public education.[92] Shanker's move set the stage for the Clinton Administration's position on school choice in the 1992 presidential campaign.

Choice also received added boosts from two groups of scholars in 1987 and 1990. First, Thomas Hoffer and James S. Coleman, the controversial sociologist from the University of Chicago, added fuel to the small, but vocal choice movement when they published *Public and Private High Schools: The Impact of the Communities* which reasserted Coleman's 1981 claim that Catholic schools provide a superior education to all kinds of children than do public schools. Then in June of 1990, John E. Chubb and Terry M. Moe published *Politics, Markets and America's Schools* and called for an open market system of school governance with school choice as a central feature.

In April of 1988, Minnesota became the first state to enact a parental choice plan since the "white flight" freedom-of-choice plans that were enacted in response to school desegregation in the 1960s. Advocates of school choice received an additional boost in the early 1990s when President George Bush, following the lead of Ronald Reagan, introduced a $200 million federal initiative to encourage local districts to implement choice plans. By late 1990, five other states had enacted school-choice plans.[93] Only one of these states, Wisconsin, had succeeded in allowing low-income parents the option of sending their children to private school at the state's expense.[94] Wisconsin succeeded in implementing this program in Milwaukee. Other choice plans in the early 1990s were unsuccessful. Colorado voters, for example, rejected a more comprehensive voucher plan, while the New Hampshire Supreme Court ruled against a voucher plan that would have allowed local taxes to pay for parochial school tuition.[95]

It seems that many Americans are suspicious of large-scale choice plans. While most Americans are philosophically liberal on the concept of parental choice in education, many are also operationally conservative when asked if they want to implement a choice plan. Such apparent contradictions suggest that Americans are deeply concerned about improving their schools, but at the same time are reluctant to abandon the notion that public schools rather than private schools are the primary vehicles that promote equal opportunity.

RESTRUCTURING SCHOOLS

By 1987, soon after the first wave of educational reform had "crashed upon the beach," many observers were aware that other waves were "forming at sea."[96] The second wave that rolled in during 1988 was in many ways a reaction to the top-down state mandates discussed above.[97] It brought in with it the word "restructuring," which was *vague* enough to accommodate a variety of conceptions of what was wrong with American schooling, but was also *vogue* enough to rekindle many people's interest in education.[98] By 1988 the American public, which had supported the excellence movement, had become disillusioned with its failure to produce the kind of dramatic results that state reformers had envisioned would come through state level mandates.[99] For many in the educational community, "restructuring" was an opportunity to resume control over the educational enterprise and to develop new strategies of school reform at the local level.

One study, for example, aware that a swing of the pendulum to a more decentralized mode of decision making was on the way, noted that although local school boards had lost a great deal of power and influence during the first wave of reform, "they [we]re far from obsolete."[100] Those disappointed with the first wave viewed the second wave of reform "as an effort to balance out the wrongs of state mandates," while the sympathetic observers remarked that "it was a logical extension of the first wave."[101] People from both views agreed, however, that in spite of the billions of dollars spent on public schooling in the 1980s, there were "weak links" at the classroom level between reform policy and practice that called out for attention. As one group of researchers summarized, "state and district activity were not quickly reflected in classroom practice and student learning."[102]

It was during this time that several educational foundations and university-based educational researchers were called upon to help provide the expertise to restructure America's schools. Influenced by several of the major reports and observational studies of the mid-1980s, such as Ernest Boyer's *High School,* Theodore Sizer's *Horace's Compromise,* and John Goodlad's *A Place Called School,*[103] state reformers slowly warmed up to an idea that they really didn't understand--restructuring. At a conference sponsored by the Education Commission of the States in February of 1990, for example, 150 participants endorsed the principle of restructuring while also agreeing that there was no single definition of the term.[104] Nevertheless, there was a consensus that the new phase of reform would have to go "right to the heart of the teaching and learning process."[105]

The recommendations of John Goodlad's study were among the first to be piloted on the eve of the restructuring, when ten states, including Goodlad's home state of Washington, began working toward making classrooms more exciting places to learn as well as to teach. The application of Goodlad's reform agenda which happened primarily in the West, was soon matched by an East coast effort that relied on the reform agenda of Theodore Sizer. In 1988 Sizer's reform initiative, known as the Coalition of Essential Schools, formed a partnership with the Education Commission of the States. The partnership project that emerged, called "Re: Learning," sought to connect second wave school-based restructuring efforts with state policies. Although more than 20 states had districts or individual schools that were involved in the restructuring initiatives by 1989, the reforms are still being piloted unevenly and sporadically within the states. Such limited penetrations led many devoted, but discouraged teachers to lose their optimism about restructuring.[106]

In spite of these problems, restructuring efforts persist. In 1988, for example, Washington's State Board of Education chose 21 schools to "take part in a pioneering statewide effort to experiment with reforms of their own design."[107] Three years later lawmakers in Minnesota approved experimental "charter schools," that would be run by experienced teachers and would be free from the state's rules and regulations. By late 1991 school-site, state-supported reforms were taking place in hundreds of districts throughout the country, a development that led reform leader Ted Sizer to remark that while schools had a long way to go, "there was a 'growing army' of reform minded teachers ready to reinvent schools, if given the opportunity."[108] But, as two educators involved in a restructuring effort in a Colorado high school explain, "Restructuring takes time, particularly teacher time; and time costs money."[109] Thus, there are at least three critical variables that will determine the fate of restructuring-- time, money, and opportunities for classroom teachers.

CONCLUSION

One recent study[110] found that the excellence movement of the 1980s was characterized by "a massive and sustained public interest" in schooling. The study also found that, in spite of this interest, student achievement held steady during the movement.[111] A cursory review of literature also reveals that the excellence movement was also characterized by a new, larger, and more authoritarian state role over the educational enterprise. This new state role, where states assumed more power and control, forcefully influenced certain types of reforms--such as increasing funding for schools, increasing graduation requirements, and testing student and teacher competence--but was far less conspicuous and had much more limited impact on deeper changes in the ways schools were structured. Thus, while many of the state initiatives during the 1980s were effective in raising standards throughout the country, few fundamentally changed the ways in which teachers and students behaved in the classroom. Reform at the school and classroom levels was uneven and isolated.

State level reforms, charged many critics, could not alter or influence the most critical relationship in education, the relationship between the student and the teacher. Most of the critics of the state level, top-down reforms appeared to be as interested in change as were the governors, legislators, and business owners. In 1984 most of these critics accepted the statistics that suggested that the quality of a public school education had declined since 1963, and they were supportive of the idea of school reform. Many applauded the attention to education wrought by the reform reports. Some found value in the essentialist qualities of the reports in recommending that Americans put the established disciplines above life-adjustment courses like driver education and home economics. Others celebrated the call that all citizens, not just teachers, should be held accountable for improving schools. Most critics, however, took issue with the failure of the state reformers to rethink the curriculum or to assess ways in which that curriculum was delivered. As one observer put it, "the reports are telling us that what we have been doing in the basic subjects is just fine, but we need to do much more of it."[112]   Others pointed out that the reformers were operating on the false assumption that schools were like factories and could be fixed quickly by better management. Pointing to more academic and less politicized studies, conducted by Theodore Sizer, John Goodlad, and Ernest Boyer,[113] critics suggested that the state reforms did not go far enough. Many called for more radical changes in the ways schools should be organized, with the harshest critics predicting that the reforms would ultimately fall short due to a lack of vision and the failure of leaders to include teachers in the reform discussions.

Only one of the 18 members of the National Commission on Excellence in Education who wrote *A Nation At Risk* was a public school teacher. With most states closely following that report as a blueprint for change, teachers were never directly recruited or enlisted by the states in the war against "mediocre educational performance"[114] during the decade of reform. Such an oversight was perhaps the most costly mistake of the excellence movement. As David Tyack points out in his historical analysis of educational reform movements, teachers can make or break changes in the educational structure. "Teachers have become experts in accommodating to, deflecting, or sabotaging changes they do not desire."[115]   Real improvement of classroom instruction requires that teachers buy into the reforms. When they make reforms their own business and become energized by changes in the classroom, they can energize their students.[116]

During the mid to late 1980s, state politicians became aware of this oversight, and enlisted leading educators in the reform crusade, some of whom were more in tune with the capabilities and needs of classroom teachers than were the policymakers. While some of the more conservative scholars suggested that greater parental choice would be the best path toward "excellence," other scholars called for a "reinvention" of the teaching-learning process at the school level.

Ultimately, the excellence movement can be seen as one of many reforms that make up the ebb and flow in education. Given the unyielding faith that Americans place in their schools, it is no wonder that many people are dissatisfied with the marginal results of the excellence moment. Still, it is important for Americans to begin to realize that there are no quick and easy answers to "fixing" our schools. Reforms in education, Tyack reminds us, should not and cannot be thought of as permanent. American educational reforms have historically swung back and forth between a more centralized structural decision making system and a more pedagogically influenced decentralized arrangement. Both trends bring with them positive and negative results. Americans would be wise to accept the notion that there is "no magic wand" in the hands of state leaders, teachers, business leaders, or educational researchers. Given the faith we place in the institution of public education, we are ultimately left with the task of "tinkering toward utopia" with our system of schools.[117] In the end, schools will never become places with which we will all be happy.[118] But that prediction should not keep us from trying to attain such an educational utopia.

ENDNOTES

1. National Commission on Excellence in Education, *A Nation At Risk: The Imperative For Educational Reform* (Washington, D.C.: Government Printing Office, April 1983).

2. *Newsweek*, 9 May 1983, 53.

3. Allan Odden, *Educational Finance in the States*, Report F84-1 (Denver, CO: Education Commission of the States, June 1984), vi.

4. Thomas J. Sergiovanni and others, eds., *Educational Governance and Administration*, 2d. ed. (Englewood Cliffs, NJ: Prentice Hall, 1987), 241.

5. Chris Pipho, "Stateline," *Phi Delta Kappan*, June 1988, 710.

6. Sergiovanni and others, eds., *Educational Governance and Administration*, 241.

7. National Commission on Excellence in Education, *A Nation At Risk*, 28.

8. Pipho, "Stateline," October 1988, 102-103.

9. Pipho, "Stateline," June 1988, 710.

10. Pipho, "Stateline," June 1990, 750-751.

11. William A. Firestone and others, eds., *Education Reform from 1983 to 1990, State Action and District Response*, Report RR-021 (Rutgers, NJ: Consortium for Policy Research in Education, 1990).

12. Sergiovanni and others, eds., *Educational Governance and Administration*, 240.

13. John K. Norton, "The Myth of Educational Equality," *American Mercury* 265, no. 62, (1946): 16-23.

14. Thomas V. O'Brien, *Georgia's Response to Brown v. Board of Education: The Rise and Fall of Massive Resistance, 1949-1961* (Ph.D. diss., Emory University, 1992), 40.

15. Ibid..

16. Ibid..

17. Sergiovanni and others, eds., *Educational Governance and Administration*, 240.

18. Jack Flanigan, Rosalyn Flanigan, and Michael Richardson, *State Reform, Separating Perception from Reality*, Paper presented as part of the meeting of the American Education Finance Association, Las Vegas, NV, 15-17 March 1990, 1-3.

19. Ibid., 1.

20. Stanley M. Gallup and others, eds., *A Decade of Gallup Polls of Attitudes Toward Education, 1969-1978* (Bloomington, IN: Phi Delta Kappa, 1978), 299.

21. Joseph W. Newman, *America's Teachers, An Introduction to Education* (White Plains, NY: Longman, 1990), 253.

22. Ibid., 254.

23. Ibid., 255.

24. Ibid., 256.

25. Ibid., 256.

26. David Tyack, *Progress or Regress*, Paper presented as part of the meeting of the American Educational Research Association, Atlanta, GA, 15 April 1993.

27. David Tyack, "'Restructuring' in Historical Perspective, Tinkering Toward Utopia," *Teachers College Record*, Winter 1990, 171-191.

28. "Charting a Course for Reform: A Chronology," *Education Week*, February 1993, 1-20(S).

29. Odden, *Educational Finance in the States*, 6.

30. "Charting a Course for Reform," 5(S).

31. Pipho, "Stateline," October 1993, 83; and "Charting a Course for Reform," 4(S).

32. Flanigan, Flanigan, and Richardson, "State Reform," 11.

33. Ibid., 16.

34. Ibid., 16.

35. Ibid., 17.

36. Odden, *Educational Finance in the States*, 9.

37. Robert Green, "School Reform South Carolina Style," in *The Origins of Public Education in the South*, ed. Walker, Richardson, and Parks, Dubuque, IA: privately printed, 1993, 49-51.

38. Ibid., 50.

39. Flanigan, Flanigan, and Richardson, "State Reform," 17.

40. Odden, *Educational Finance in the States*, 19.

41. Michael W. Kirst, "Recent State Education Reform in the United States, Looking Backward and Forward," *Educational Administration Quarterly*, August 1988, 319.

42. Ibid., 321.

43. Robert M. Huelskamp, "Perspectives on Education," *Phi Delta Kappan*, May 1993, 720.

44. Pipho, "Stateline," January 1992, 350 and February 1992, 431.

45. William A. Firestone and others, eds., "Recent Trends in State Educational Reform: Assessment and Prospects," *Teachers College Record*, Winter 1992, 254-255.

46. Charles E. Strickland, "Sputnik Reform Revisited," *Educational Studies*, Winter 1985, 15-21.

47. "Charting a Course for Reform," 4(S).

48. Pipho, "Stateline," September 1983, 5.

49. Ibid., 5-6.

50. "Charting a Course for Reform," 5(S).

51. Ibid., 4(S).

52. Pipho, "Stateline," June 1986, 702.

53. Educational Testing Service, *The Educational Reform Decade, Policy Information Report,* (Princeton, NJ: Educational Testing Service, 1990).

54. Ibid..

55. Kirst, "Recent State Education Reform," 320.

56. "Charting a Course for Reform," 17(S).

57. Ibid..

58. Kirst, "Recent State Education Reform," 319.

59. Firestone and others, eds., "Recent Trends in State Educational Reform," 17 and 19.

60. Educational Testing Service, *The Educational Reform Decade,* 29.

61. Sergiovanni and others, eds., *Educational Governance and Administration,* 240.

62. "Charting a Course for Reform," 1-20(S).

63. Firestone and others, eds., "Recent Trends in State Educational Reform."

64. Van E. Cooley and Jay C. Thompson Jr., "A Study of the 50 States to Determine the Effect of Educational Reform on Seven Educational Improvement Areas," Paper presented as part of the meeting of the Mid-Western Educational Research Association, Chicago, IL, October 1990; and Firestone and others, eds., "Recent Trends in State Educational Reform."

65. "Charting a Course for Reform," 6(S).

66. Firestone and others, eds., "Recent Trends in State Educational Reform," 17-18.

67. "Charting a Course for Reform," 12(S).

68. Firestone and others, eds., "Recent Trends in State Educational Reform," 18; and "Charting a Course for Reform," 6(S).

69. David Silvernail, "Definitions from the Common Core of Learning Project," *Educational Leadership,* May 1993, 33.

70. William Spady and Ron Brandt, "On Outcome-Based Education, a Conversation with Bill Spady," *Educational Leadership,* December 1992/January 1993, 66.

71. Ibid., 66-70; Benjamin S. Bloom, "The 2 Sigma Problem, the Search for Methods of Group Instruction as Effective as One-to-One Tutoring," *Educational Researcher,* June/July 1984; and Theodore Sizer, *Horace's School: Redesigning the American High School* (Boston, MA: Houghton Mifflin, 1992).

72. Firestone and others, eds., "Recent Trends in State Educational Reform," 11.

73. "Charting a Course for Reform," 6(S).

74. Ibid..

75. Ibid., 5(S).

76. Ibid..

77. Ibid., 7(S).

78. Firestone and others, eds., "Recent Trends in State Educational Reform," 22.

79. Ibid., 21.

80. Ibid., 22.

81. Jacqueline J. Irvine, *Black Students and School Failure: Policies, Practice, Proscriptions* (Westport, CT: Greenwood Press, 1991), Chapter 2.

82. Pipho, "Stateline," November 1983, 165.

83. Pipho, "Stateline," October 1986, 101.

84. Pipho, "Stateline," June 1986, 701.

85. Pipho, "Stateline," April 1988, 550.

86. Pipho, "Stateline," October 1986, 101.

87. Ibid., 101.

88. Gallup and others, eds., *A Decade of Gallup Polls*, 17-30.

89. Ibid., 17-30.

90. "School Choice Bills Reintroduced," *Intelligencer Journal* (Lancaster, PA), 12 May 1993, 3(A).

91. "Charting a Course for Reform," 6(S).

92. Ibid..

93. Ibid..

94. Pipho,"Stateline," September 1992, 7.

95. "Charting a Course for Reform."

96. Kirst, "Recent State Education Reform," 319.

97. Pipho, "Stateline," June 1988, 710.

98. Tyack, "Tinkering Toward Utorpia," 171.

99. Ibid..

100. "Charting a Course for Reform," 9(S).

101. Pipho, "Stateline," June 1988, 710.

102. Firestone and others, eds., "Recent Trends in State Educational Reform," v and 4.

103. Pipho, "Stateline," June 1988, 710; and Sergiovanni and others, eds., *Eduactional Governance and Administration*, 233.

104. "Charting a Course for Reform," 14(S).

105. John O'Neil, "Piecing Together the Restructuring Puzzle," *Educational Leadership*, April 1990, 6.

106. "Charting a Corse for Reform," 9(S).

107. Ibid., 12(S).

108. Ibid., 18(S).

109. Tim S. Westerberg and Dan Brickley, "Restructuring a Comprehensive High School," *Educational Leadership*, May 1991, 24.

110. Firestone and others, eds., "Recent Trends in State Educational Reform," 3.

111. Ibid., 4.

112. Strickland, "Sputnick Reform Revisited," 17.

113. Sergiovanni and others, eds., *Educational Governance and Administration*, 233.

114. National Commission on Excellence in Education, *A Nation At Risk*, 5.

115. Tyack, "Tinkering Toward Utopia," 171-191.

116. Ibid..

117. Ibid..

118. Lawrence A. Cremin, *Popular Education and Its Discontents* (New York, NY: Harper & Row, 1990).

Chapter 3

One State's Effort to Redeem
A Nation At Risk: School Reform
in Pennsylvania 1983-1993

William J. Moloney

A SUPERINTENDENT'S SAGA

Mike Farrell was beginning to perspire as the television lights steadily raised the temperature in the Capitol's ornate Executive Conference Room. Hemmed in by a throng of reporters, state workers and invited educators, he strained to hear the voice of Governor Robert Casey: ". . . Exactly what we expect our students to know and do will be crystal clear for the first time."

As soon as the Governor concluded his remarks, a reporter quickly turned to Mike saying, "Dr. Farrell, you've been a Superintendent ever since the *Nation At Risk* report came out. Do you think things have gotten any better for Pennsylvania school children? Will the Governor's outcomes-based education make a difference?"

"Young lady," he replied, "I'll be retiring in a few months, so I'd like to believe that what we've been doing these last ten years has meant something. As for the outcomes, it'll be a good while before we know if they've put our kids on the road to success, or whether they're just another dead-end street. Believe me, these answers will be clearer to tomorrow's historians than to today's reporters or educators."

INTRODUCTION

Pennsylvania school reform in the decade following *A Nation At Risk* can be divided into three distinct phases. As these phases correspond very closely to nationwide trends, Pennsylvania is thus a very representative state in which to explore America's crusade to repair its ailing education system.

Large and highly diverse in its composition, the Keystone State as a reform entity would be neither at the top or the bottom of the class. On the one hand, it witnessed nothing so dramatic as the Texas reform effort led by Ross Perot--or the root and branch structural change occurring in Kentucky under Tom Boysen, but neither was it one of those quieter precincts where change and conflict were muted and routinized.

The Pennsylvania story is a rich mixture of politics and personalities, principle and expedience, and all those other social variables that form the backdrop to education reform at every level.

Economic factors would be profoundly important. The decade in question began and ended in a recession, while the middle period was one of the sunniest economic eras our nation has known. While finance was not the starting point for thinking on school reform, nonetheless by decade's end, it had become the dominant issue that was driving all else before it.

Second only to economics as an issue was governance. At decade's end, the fatigue, frustration, and sense of stalemate felt by education reformers were closely connected to the failure of the state's tangled educational jurisdictions to initiate or sustain coherent reform policy. This institutional gridlock was nowhere better illustrated than by the outcomes morass. Here, Executive Branch, Legislature, State Board, Education Department, Independent Regulatory Commission, and various education and business organizations all became stuck in a glue pot of overlapping jurisdictions and interests in a process that few understood and none could control.

PHASE I (1983-1987): "INPUTS OR MORE IS BETTER"

In the Spring of 1983, Richard Thornburgh was widely held to be one of the most successful politicians in Pennsylvania history. The previous November he had won a second term as Governor despite a recession that many chose to blame on his Republican Party.

Like President Ronald Reagan who had off-handedly commissioned it and every other governor, Thornburgh was greatly surprised when the *A Nation At Risk* report seemed to loose a tornado of interest in education reform.

The hyperbolic language of the report ("rising tide of mediocrity," "act of war," etc.) and its timing seemed to strike a raw nerve in the American public. Continued economic sluggishness, the drumbeat of foreign competition, media focus on ineffective but costly schools, and a long-simmering public unease over schools all contributed to bringing the education issue to the highly combustible stage that the landmark report ignited.

Retrospectively, one of the most striking things about this reform era is that from beginning to end it was in the hands of politicians, not educators.

In the past, reform had generally been run by educators. There were limited exceptions such as those reforms in the aftermath of Sputnik and at the height of the Great Society, but usually education was not viewed as a sufficiently high priority to command high-level political address.

Why was it different after 1983?

The main reason seemed to be that people worried about their country came to see its future as dependent on the economy and the economy as dependent on education. Therefore, effective schools went right to the top of the national agenda.

Three successive Presidents during this era endorsed with growing urgency the notion that the schools were in deep trouble and that their rescue was indispensable to the restoration of America's competitive dominance.

In our federal system, however, it would not be Presidents who would be chief craftsmen of reform but rather Governors and legislators.

Educators would not be wholly left out of the reform process. Those who wrote books--Adler, Boyer, Finn, Goodlad, Ravitch, and Sizer, among others--would serve as major idea banks though most of them were much better at describing the problem than prescribing the solution.

In the states, the education organizations representing school boards, administrators, and particularly teacher unions would be major players in the reform process but nowhere would they find themselves in the driver's seat. That role was always held by the political leaders and their minions on State Boards, and in Departments of Education.

It should also be noted that, after a slow start, the business community, through its various organs, would be a major reform participant in states like Pennsylvania.

In the wake of *A Nation At Risk*, there followed a torrent of books, task force reports, commission studies and the like. Across the land the cry was to do something about our schools--now.

As Dick Thornburgh pondered the question of what to do, he was pleasantly surprised to find the Democrats more than willing to help. This bipartisan tendency was not unique to Pennsylvania. Across the nation, school improvement had an almost patriotic halo, and it was widely viewed to be of such compelling importance that it should not be a partisan issue. As the years went by, this bipartisan euphoria waned but, in the first blush of reform, it was an important factor in the speed with which events moved.

As the political leaders looked for useful things to do, it was significant that they thought in terms of legislation and by extension regulation.

This impulse could hardly be viewed as surprising because after all passing laws is what elected officials do. The situation is worth dwelling upon because it would have much to do with the failure of reform in the first phase or "wave" as some called it.

The political impulse is to do something quickly, pass a law, start a program, and complete it in time to claim some credit during the next campaign season which seemed never more than a year away.

The difficulty was that this approach does not work well with problems that are broad based, deeply rooted, and systemic in nature as is the case with education or, to name another, health care.

These kinds of problems require an understanding, a patience, and a complexity of address that is generally foreign to the normal legislative process.

In looking back on this first phase of reform, it is remarkable how quickly a consensus developed in regard to fixing the schools. The consensus derived directly from *A Nation At Risk*. In a phrase, it said, "More is Better."

Students needed to take more courses--particularly math and science, do more homework, be more disciplined, study more foreign languages, and take more tests to prove that all of the above was happening.

Schools needed more technology, more teachers making more money (particularly the better ones), more clarity of mission, and above all, more accountability for getting the job done right.

Educational regeneration based on the theme of "More" had broad appeal. Republicans liked the martial tones of national revival; Democrats warmed to the summons to government activism; business resonated with the stress on math, science, technology, and response to foreign competition; and the education establishment grasped immediately that the whole thing added up to major money coming their way.

Legislative action on education hummed into high gear. The 1983-84 sessions were the prelude to national and state elections and politicians were determined to show the public concrete action on this suddenly popular national imperative.

A critical element was the fact that the recession was now over and a surging economy was producing the kind of revenues that would be needed to fund major education initiatives.

Playing off the rhetoric of *A Nation At Risk,* the Thornburgh administration dubbed its education crusade as "Turning the Tide."

The centerpiece of this effort would be major changes in the state curriculum regulations aimed at increased graduation requirements in general and at more math and science in particular.

Because opinion in Pennsylvania reflected the national consensus on what needed to be done, the required action by legislative and executive branches and their regulatory adjuncts moved with relative speed.

These new curriculum standards represented the final triumph of inputs, a "Last Hurrah" of the more-regulation-is-better approach to school reform. Not surprisingly, the crowning piece of this new improved learning machine was a test that would validate the inputs and show who was following the new regulations best. Called TELLS (Test of Essential Learning and Literacy Skills), this item would check up on all 3rd, 5th, and 8th graders to be sure they were on their way to world class educational attainment.

As in the other 49 states, this rush to educational judgment was unstoppable. Those who posed questions or suggested difficulties were dismissed as carping critics or somehow not team players. It just seemed certain that by raising the bar of this scholastic high jump we were about to see an educational "Great Leap Forward."

With the legislative/regulatory framework in place by 1984, the next three years would witness a gradual process of implementation during which all of the state's 501 school districts would have to integrate the new standards into their own policies and practices.

This as always they dutifully did ("Theirs was not to reason why..."). New math and science courses had to be invented to accommodate the extra year to be taken by all students; pupil schedules had to be tightened up to reflect increased credit requirements; and of course, more staff had to be hired.

All across the Commonwealth, committees of teachers and administrators labored through a million meeting hours working diligently to make the new standards fit with the old realities.

In this task, they in fact succeeded so well that the old realities were hardly inconvenienced at all. This, in fact, was the main problem. As the famous French adage put it, "All was changed, yet all remained the same."

How did this happen? What went wrong?

What went wrong was that the reforms were essentially bureaucratic and not educational in nature. Therefore, other than an alteration of the paper trail, nothing happened. No human behaviors were changed.

Responding to political direction, the State Board of Education altered its regulations. Accordingly, the Department of Education altered its procedures and directives.

Responding to said direction, altered regulations, procedures and directives, 501 school districts altered their policies, procedures, and directives. In sum, the local paper trail was adjusted to fit the state paper trial, and then business as usual resumed.

In effect, existing variables of time, space and work were rearranged but not expanded in any significant way. The school day remained six and one-half hours, the school year 180 days, and all that occurred therein remained the same, too.

The new regulations did not cause increased homework for students, or greater exertion for teachers; they did nothing about grade inflation, or social promotion; and they introduced nothing that would make anyone--students, teachers, administrators, board members, or parents--more productive or more accountable.

Severe critics might liken this exercise to the proverbial rearrangement of deck chairs on the *Titanic*, but it would be wrong to think that nothing changed. The internal shifting of variables did have certain consequences. There were some winners and losers.

Vocational education was a loser because students were compelled to spend a greater portion of their fixed amount of school time pursuing academic subjects in their home schools. Therefore, the under-enrollment of area vocational schools (AVTS) which had been merely bad, now became disastrous.

The increased student time in academic courses might have been useful except that the quality of such courses declined in proportion to their increase in quantity. Instead of academic content and rigor going up, it went down as schools adjusted to the changes simply by stretching out the seat time and credit hours of existing content areas.

More courses, for instance, had the words "math and science" attached to them so that the lower-ability students could get the newly mandated additional credits simply by sitting still for more time on the same tasks.

Needless to say, no one was going to admit publicly that this was happening because to do so would be upsetting to all those parties who wanted to believe that the changes were useful. Also, such admission might well invite negative responses from politicians and bureaucrats who would be quick to blame you rather than themselves if anything were seen to be amiss.

All of this reality avoidance was greatly facilitated by the fact that neither before or after the changes was there any kind of testing system that measured student achievement with any reliability at all. The scandalous state of American standardized testing as exposed by Thomas Toch (*In the Name of Excellence*, 1991) and others provided the perfect vehicle to accommodate this flight from reality. No matter what the schools were doing, there was a test publisher who could guarantee that they would remain eternally "above the national average."

As the Thornburgh administration drew to a close in the winter of 1986-87, it was increasingly evident to thoughtful school people that the campaign for "Turning the Tide" had not done so.

For the above-noted reasons, however, it was in nobody's interest to make an announcement to this effect. Only years later with the advent of Outcomes-Based Education (OBE) would the state tacitly admit the complete failure of its earlier effort.

Instead, the education world followed its usual instinct to nimbly dance away from its failures while loudly proclaiming the virtues of the latest astonishing "breakthrough" (i.e., fad).

PHASE II (1987-1991): RESTRUCTURING OR THE TRIUMPH OF PROCESS

The inauguration of Democrat Robert P. Casey in January of 1987 meant not just a new governor but a new party inhabiting the executive branch of government.

Opinion sampling done for Casey by pollster Patrick Caddell revealed that education as an issue retained a powerful hold on the minds of Pennsylvanians. As the new governor put together his administration, he talked with experts across the country and searched for ideas in education that could be translated into initiatives that would bear his distinctive stamp.

Just as Dick Thornburgh had embraced *A Nation At Risk* as the policy underpinning of his education endeavors, so too would Bob Casey find inspiration in a powerful landmark education report released right around the time of his election.

The Carnegie Report on Teaching--*A Nation Prepared: Teachers for the Twenty-First Century*--would have in this decade of reform an impact second only to *A Nation At Risk.*

This study was endorsed by the nation's major teachers' unions--The National Education Association and the American Federation of Teachers--and adopted by the National Governors Conference as its "centerpiece of educational reform." Further, the report had the added impetus of the Carnegie Foundation and its commitment to spend up to $50 million over a decade to promote acceptance of its recommendations.

From the beginning, it was clear that the educational ideas of the Casey administration had their principal origin in the Carnegie Report. Thus, like Thornburgh before him, Casey would tie his educational fortunes to the hoped-for success of a national report's basic idea.

Carnegie marked a basic and lateral shift away from the "input" orientation of *A Nation At Risk.* Simply stated, Carnegie asserted that whatever was wrong with American education could be fixed only by fixing whatever was wrong with the teaching profession. The report further asserted that what was wrong with the teaching profession--aside from inadequate financial rewards, of course--was that it lacked real decision-making power within the schools.

The remedy for this problem was teacher "empowerment" or as it referred to schools, "site-based management." The way to accomplish this remedy became known under the all encompassing generic term, "Restructuring."

What American schools needed according to Carnegie was to be completely restructured so that empowered teachers could engage in site-based management. If this was done, then all those things constraining student achievement and school productivity would somehow disappear.

Beyond question, the Carnegie analysis was a powerful one and there was great truth in its insights about schools and teaching. Its flaw, like most of the major reports, was not in its astute description of problems, but rather in the shakiness of its prescribed solutions.

To begin with, Carnegie's implied motto of "All Power to Teachers" was very off-putting to other education stakeholders such as school boards, central administration, principals, and parents.

These flaws, however, would not become "perfectly clear" until much later. In the spring of 1987, the "Carnegie impulse" was at its zenith and it would be the educational lodestar by which Bob Casey would set his compass throughout his first term.

To lead his Education Department, Casey chose Thomas Gilhool, an attorney best known in school circles as the special education advocate who filed the landmark *PARC* case in 1972. As had been the case when Democratic Governor Milton Shapp chose Attorney John Pittenger as Chief State School Officer, the selection of Gilhool was a non-traditional move which would be the spark to no small amount of controversy.

Usually, the top education post went to a superintendent or other stalwart of the education establishment, thus insulating the Governor from serious conflict with said groups. Imbued with the restructuring zeal of the Carnegie Report, Casey at the outset, however, was not averse to some jousting with the established order.

It is valuable to pause a moment to look at the Education Department (PDE) that Gilhool inherited from Thornburgh's departing Secretary, Margaret Smith.

In terms of its structure and statutory authority, the Department had to be ranked as one of the most powerful in the nation. At its peak, it had more than 1,600 employees. Though not large by New York standards (more than 4,000 employees), PDE had great leverage in local school districts.

Under Thornburgh, however, the Department had become a prime target for the budgetary axe. By 1987, a long-running hiring freeze had reduced the staff to just a little over 600 employees.

Those who operated the Department never could accept this decline as permanent, and so rather than reorganize in light of new realities, they constantly redistributed the responsibilities of departed employees to those who remained. As one wag put it, "We've got more people acting here than a dramatic academy."

The institutional disinclination of the Department to change itself was greatly symbolic of the general unwillingness of the entire education establishment to adapt to change. As one educator put it to Secretary Gilhool, "You've little chance to restructure Pennsylvania education if you can't even restructure 333 Market Street (PDE)."

As state bureaucracies go, PDE through most of its recent history had a good reputation for responsiveness and integrity. As the attrition-induced decline set in, however, competence levels began to suffer. The best staffers became overworked and under-recognized. A steady exodus began. Low salaries made finding capable replacements very difficult, if not impossible.

Only redesign of the sweeping Kentucky or Virginia type could re-establish effectiveness and good morale. Sadly, for the many fine people who worked in the Department--and the districts dependent upon them--this never happened.

It did not take the new Secretary long to clash with the educational establishment. The subject was testing and the ensuing crossfire illuminated one of the great dilemmas of American school reform.

Thornburgh was gone but his TELLS test lived on and, in 1987, Gilhool released the district-by-district results in rank order from highest to lowest along with a press statement that clearly implied that the scores were somehow indicative of the relative quality or effectiveness of individual school districts.

Gilhool's major error was in basing his rankings on an instrument of measurement that was clearly inadequate for such a purpose. Obscured by this error, however, was the fact that he also violated one of the great unwritten commandments of public education: "Thou Shalt Not Compare."

Compounding the indignation of education officials over this "unfair" comparison was the fact that the media and much of the public thought that ranking was a dandy idea. Like William Bennett's much reviled (among educators) "Wall Chart," Gilhool's rankings played well with a press and public that liked to see an educational equivalent of "League Standings" and didn't care much about finer points like "psychometric validity."

Improperly or not, Gilhool had held the education establishment's feet to the fire, and for this they would never forgive him.

Aside from its strong support by unions--always a plus in a Democratic administration--a major appeal of Carnegie's teacher "empowerment" doctrine was that it might prove an antidote to Pennsylvania education's perennial status as the most strike-ridden state in the nation.

Ironically, the most renowned educator in the Casey Administration was not in the Education Department, but rather the head of the Department of Labor and Industry, Harris Wofford.

Wofford joined Gilhool in a cross-departmental effort to create what was called the Schools Cooperation Program. This program was essentially an effort to promote harmony among labor and management elements in school districts. The state recognized key districts that were models in this regard and sought to encourage others to follow this path through a series of conferences and extensive literature.

A premier example of this program was the Easton Area School District* where on May 9, 1988, Gilhool, joined by the heads of the four major education organizations--School Boards, Superintendents, Principals and Teachers--went to recognize a remarkable series of Carnegie-based agreements ratified that day.

The teacher and principal units ratified labor pacts and the Board adopted policies with significant features of "empowerment" including a Master Teacher Panel, Peer Assistance Program, and a degree of Site-Based Management.

While a prime exemplar of Carnegie's central idea adapted to include Board and Principals, Easton was also a prime example of the limitations of that idea. While "Shared Governance" did transform a district of frequent strikes and cascading grievances into an enduring model of "labor peace" (three successive teacher contracts and not a single teacher grievance in nine years), the price of that peace was a tacit agreement not to promote any change that was unacceptable to any of the parties. This meant that while modest improvements could be advanced, essentially the status quo remained unchanged--hardly a recipe for educational transformation.

The lesson of Schools Cooperation and Casey's other Carnegie-type initiatives--the establishment of nine Lead Teacher Centers and the Re-Learn Program (a borrowing from Ted Sizer's Coalition of Essential Schools)--was that you could do some useful things to improve the working atmosphere of schools and you could do some marginal tinkering with program but that none of the above was going to significantly alter the basic reality of schools. In a phrase, the structures of public education proved impervious to "restructuring."

In the end, restructuring proved to be form without content, a "process" reform that left substance essentially untouched. In the end, like Thornburgh's "reform" of curriculum regulations, Casey's restructuring touched only the surfaces of education while leaving the core variables of time, work, and accountability unchanged. Yet another attempt to raise student achievement and school productivity had failed.

---

*The author served as Superintendent in Easton after 1984.

This failure should not obscure the fact that an energetic and sincere effort had been made or that the frustration experienced in Pennsylvania was part of a national pattern of state-based efforts that consistently fell short of the mark.

In fact, the energy of Gilhool's promotion of Carnegie's ideas was not without political cost to Governor Casey. Across the state, both Gilhool and the Carnegie Report were widely viewed as excessively pro-teacher.

The friendship of the politically powerful state teachers union (PSEA) proved a mixed blessing for Secretary Gilhool. In the end, it was not enough to offset the steady drumbeat of criticism from other education organizations.

Rather than hurt the re-election campaign of his long-time friend and mentor, Bob Casey, Tom Gilhool tendered his resignation as Secretary in the summer of 1989.

The new Secretary of Education, Donald Carroll--most recently Superintendent in Harrisburg--was a genial ex-Marine, politically adroit, and a long-time education insider. Warmly received by the education establishment, Carroll with skill and loyalty would provide continuity to Casey's program and also mend his political fences during the run up to the election campaign.

Part one of Bob Casey's effort at education reform was over. Part two would begin only after his triumphant re-election and would occur in a very different environment.

PHASE III (1991- PRESENT):   OUTCOMES-BASED EDUCATION

The first two phases of this Pennsylvania school reform era--"inputs" and "restructuring"--had corresponded closely to the national reform style. Inputs was now thoroughly discredited and restructuring was moving into eclipse as well; both had failed to meet expectations and the seminal reports that launched them were now little spoken of. The doctrine of "empowerment" lingered on but its main national exemplars--Rochester and Chicago--had slipped into disarray and bickering over finance. Schools and the children in them remained essentially unchanged.

The reform impulse both nationally and in Pennsylvania became fragmented. There were no more landmark reports and no discernible major trend that could be acclaimed as reform's "Third Wave." Many people who had enthusiastically endorsed earlier failed nostrums were now skeptical and more inclined to quietly go their own way.

This change, however, did not mean that education had dropped out of the news or ceased to be an object of widespread concern. When George Bush and the nation's governors had gathered for an "education summit," there was no lack of fanfare.

The six national goals that emerged as the cornerstone of the President's "America 2000" program were widely discussed but curiously seemed to have little cumulative impact. They were widely thought to be either too vague ("all children ready to learn") or too unrealistic ("first in the world in math and science").

Nonetheless, emulating most other states, the Commonwealth dutifully launched "Pennsylvania 2000" to correspond with the national effort. Many communities and school districts within the state followed suit at their level as well.

The major reason for this general distraction and lack of direction in school reform was money--or more pointedly the lack thereof. The continuing recession of the early nineties had pushed state governments into a horrendous financial mire that was distorting every priority, but none more than education.

Compounding the state's recession woes was the fact that a deficit-obsessed Federal government was off-loading its own financial responsibilities onto the states almost every time Congress passed a law. None of these unfunded mandates was more devastating than Medicaid which, with spiralling health costs and court-expanded eligibility, became a battering ram aimed at every other account in the state budget.

Not surprisingly, a major consequence of this Federal irresponsibility was that the states themselves began off-loading whatever financial burdens they could onto local authorities including school districts.

All of these lamentable trend lines came together in the budget of 1991.

Until this time, education had enjoyed a relatively favored status among the major budget categories. Educators who had come to take this status for granted were now in for a rude awakening.

Between 1983 and 1991, Pennsylvania had paralleled a national trend which saw real education expenditure (adjusted for inflation) rise 31 percent. In the eyes of legislators seeking to distribute pieces of a shrinking economic pie among a myriad of expanding entitlements and priorities, these ever-rising education costs seemed increasingly hard to justify. In their view, the schools didn't seem to be getting any better despite all this new money, and the demands for even more money seemed never to end.

Attitudes towards education and educators began to change. Seen through the eyes of legislators (and the executive) educators seemed ungrateful for the increases they had received and unrealistic about what they could hope for in the future. They seemed oblivious to such things as the juggernaut of Medicaid or the fact that building prisons was more popular with a populace increasingly worried about crime.

The budget of 1991 marked a decisive turning point in Pennsylvania education finance. Having deferred many hard decisions until after the election, Casey in 1991 called for the largest tax increase in state history. Given prevailing economic conditions, this was necessary just for the state to keep its head financially above water. At the same time, it was also necessary to unload discretionary spending wherever possible. Regarding education, the chosen vehicle for this divestiture was special education. 1991 began a three-year process of inexorably moving this high cost center off the state's expenditure page and onto that of local districts.

The budget of 1991 would also be a turning point in local school districts as many chickens came home to roost.

Economic pressures rippled across the state and affected all levels of government. State share of total educational expenditure had been steadily dropping (from 44 percent in 1983 to a projected 34 percent for 1993), but this decline had been offset by strong local revenues in a pre-recession economy. Now those local revenues were waning at the same time the state was escalating its own cost-dumping campaign.

Rising pressures on local property taxpayers were exacerbated in many places by long-deferred county-wide reassessments. These politically explosive exercises only fanned taxpayer anger at a time when increasing proportions of the population were hurting economically.

A final piece in this mosaic of unrest was provided by growing resentment over what were widely viewed as exorbitant teacher contracts. Benefitting in this reform era from the general desire for better schools, teachers had done well economically. When times were good, this trend drew little ire, but when the economy began "downsizing" most other industries, more and more distressed citizens began to wonder why education should be the exception.

The financial vise would also lead, as it had in many other states, to a lawsuit challenging the wide disparity in per pupil expenditure in districts across the state. Brought by the Pennsylvania Association of Rural and Small Schools (PARSS) and eventually having 176 districts as plaintiffs, this suit would build a steady pressure on the Governor and the Legislature to address extreme funding inequities. At the outset, many in the education establishment saw the courts as a useful device for leveraging total dollars upward despite taxpayer resistance. As suits in other states demonstrated (notably Texas), the more likely effect was a highly divisive "Robin Hood" effect that threatened to weaken allegiance to public schools.

The financial crisis was also putting a brutal squeeze upon the private schools which educated nearly one-sixth of Pennsylvania's children. The Catholic parochial school system, in particular, suffered because their cost margins were so thin to begin with. These pressures became a major motivation for the Catholic Conference to go all out in support of a voucher plan.

Vouchers and other variations of educational choice had been percolating all across the nation for some years. In addition to finance, this movement was being driven by appalling educational conditions in many big city systems. Most polling showed growing support for choice, particularly among minority parents.

Choice bills of one kind or another were to be found in most states and in Pennsylvania the issue burst into public prominence when the State Senate in December 1991 passed a bill to grant vouchers worth $900 per pupil to parents who wished to choose an educational alternative other than their own public school.

The Senate vote galvanized the education establishment to mount a massive campaign to defeat the bill (HB 1133) in the House and pro-voucher forces responded in kind. There followed a distortion-filled media campaign that did credit to neither side.

By successfully painting the voucher bill as requiring a huge tax increase, the anti-choice forces narrowly succeeded in preventing its passage. The issue did not go away, however, and Pennsylvania remained among the states providing the most fertile ground for voucher initiatives.

Ever since the decline of the restructuring impulse, the Casey Administration had been casting about for a new vehicle to promote education reform. Ultimately, it selected Outcomes Based Education, a theoretical descendant of the old mastery learning idea that had gained new currency in recent educational literature.

OBE rested upon the highly laudable concept that results (outcomes) were a better measure of educational progress than inputs.

In embracing OBE, state authorities had now come full circle from the positions they had taken immediately following *A Nation At Risk*. Then inputs--the more the better--had been triumphant. Now the state was returning to those very same curriculum regulations and with great passion declaring them a complete failure. All of the traditional input measures--clock hours, seat time, credit, certification, prescribed courses, etc.--were now held up to public scorn as meaningless. A new rubric swept across education land: "Inputs are out, and outcomes are in."

Launching the OBE campaign in his 1992 State of the State Address, the Governor somewhat oversimplified the concept in words that would came back to haunt him: "Exactly what we expect our students to know and do will be crystal clear for the first time."

Alas, for the Governor and the state, things would not be quite that simple. While everyone could applaud the notion of concentrating on results, nobody knew what OBE would look like in practice.

Essentially, there were two ways the state could go in implementing the outcomes concept.

The first way would very much resemble the approach adopted by other industrial nations who also focused on results. That path led directly to a "high stakes" test, usually by way of a national curriculum. Since both high stakes testing and national (and even state) curriculums were traditionally abhorrent to the education establishment, this route was never seriously considered.

The second option was to list and partially define the desired outcomes and then tell 501 school districts to go figure how they wanted to achieve them--sort of a study guide with no test attached. This vague and "non-coercive" approach very much resembled the current status quo and hopefully would not offend too many people.

Option two carried the day with apparently little debate, and the Department of Education was handed the task of carrying it out.

The work product of this effort, however, turned out disastrously in a set of no fewer than 575 specific but hopelessly vague outcomes, each one more fatuous than the one before. Examples: "All students develop an understanding of their personal characteristics (e.g., interests, needs, attitudes, and temperament)," or "All students understand and appreciate their worth as unique and capable individuals, and exhibit self-esteem."

Even the State Board of Education's assessment acknowledged that these "outcomes" as written into regulations, included "too much jargon," were "not clear enough, not subject to assessment, too redundant," and involved "too much process and too little content knowledge."

Even though the outcomes were withdrawn, rewritten, and boiled down from 575 to 57 separate--but still vague--items, the damage to their credibility seemed irreversible. To many thoughtful people, the idea of outcomes without tests made about as much sense as playing tennis without a net.

The final doom of the outcomes was probably sealed by an unanticipated but furious controversy over references in the outcomes to "values."

At last, the outcomes gained the attention of the public, but not at all in the manner that their authors might wish. Across the state a firestorm of grassroots criticism enveloped the outcomes. Though frequently based on misinterpretation of the outcomes, the wave of criticism proved immune to all efforts at damage control and soon overwhelmed the legislature and even the governor himself.

By early 1993, Governor Casey had found himself in the unusual position of asking the State Board of Education to delay, delete, or rewrite key portions of the outcomes that his own administration had submitted. More unusual was the fact that they refused and passed the outcomes over his objections.

Passage of the outcomes by the State Board was already quixotic in nature since it was evident that the legislature was primed to at least rewrite if not completely overturn them.

The outcomes--once heralded as a "nationwide precedent"--had now become a "statewide disaster."

Though the Governor in the spring would make yet another effort to retrieve the situation through cosmetic changes he described as a "compromise," it was clear that the outcomes were a spent force with the unmistakable label, "damaged goods." Even if they survived in some truncated form, the likelihood of overcoming widespread skepticism and imposing them on a wary public seemed a remote possibility for a badly bruised lame duck administration.

A SAGA CONCLUDED

As Mike Farrell sat at the head table barely touching his food, he reflected on how many retirement dinners he had attended both as a teacher and administrator. Now it was his turn to be an "honoree." With affection, he recalled his father who long ago told him that retirement was like adolescence--you only do it once in life and nothing that goes before prepares you for it.

It was nearly time for him to speak. Still in his reverie, he half heard the emcee giving an overly long introduction. "Dr. Michael Farrell, our honoree as the county's Penn State Alumni of the Year...43 years in education...former President of the State Superintendents Association. Tonight Dr. Farrell will speak to us on "*A Nation At Risk*--Ten Years After: Where We Go From Here."

Mike looked out at the relaxed and expectant gathering, adjusted his notes on the dais and began:

"My friends, if I really knew where we go from here, why would I be retiring?" As the laughter subsided, he continued, "Most of you are not educators so I'll try to tell you what I think without a lot of that gobbledygook we educators are notorious for. My friends always told me I was a much better communicator as a football coach than I ever was as a Superintendent. I'm going to tell you where I think we are but I'm going to do it in kind of a different way. I'm going to tell you what I remember of the way we were, and then what I think has happened since.

"Just before I began that wonderful 43 years, I served a couple of years as a young soldier in what was then called, 'Occupied Germany.' The Berlin Blockade was still going on when I arrived and, let me tell you that that country and those people--even three years after the war's end--were in mighty rough shape. It wasn't just the Germans, though. I had a chance to do a little travelling and that whole continent was filled with uncleared rubble. Unless you were there, you can't imagine what it was like to be an American soldier in those days. We were like some kind of new Roman centurions sent from afar by a great empire then enjoying an Augustan Age. If a thing had a motor in it, it must have been built in Detroit. More steel came out of Bethlehem, Pennsylvania, than from Germany, France, and Britain combined. Made in USA was the standard for the world. We GIs used to naively joke that there were only two kinds of people in the world, Americans and those who wanted to become Americans.

"When you looked at the Europeans, you felt sorry for them. Our school books told us how they had a glorious past, but it seemed now like they had no future. Well, let me tell you we were sure wrong on that score. Those people picked themselves up out of the dust, worked hard, and built themselves a future.

"In the early Eighties, my son Tom was over there as a young Army officer, and let me tell you, his experience was different from mine. My wife and I have also gone over on vacation though not in recent years because the prices are too high.

"Now, you're wondering what this has to do with education. Well, let me tell you what I think.

"For at least 25 years after 1945, we went through a very abnormal historical period, a time when America had no real competition. World War II was bad for everyone else's economy, but good for ours. In 1945, all our competitors--allied and enemies alike--were down and out.

"It took them a long time to get to a point where they could compete. Still, if you looked, you could see it coming. First, they copied everything we had to offer, particularly our democracy and our education system.

"Everybody's hearing about Edward Deming and Total Quality Management today, but how many of us noticed him when he was teaching it to the Japanese 45 years ago?

"One writer called this the 'Age of American Exceptionalism' meaning that we were the exception to every rule. Well, now we're not. We're in the pack with everyone else--still the big guy in volume, but now having to fight for market share with everyone else.

"We used to know how to compete, but then we forgot, because for a generation and more we didn't have to.

"During this period of exceptionalism, we developed some bad habits. We began to think that every progression was a permanent trendline pointing upward. Every year meant bigger salaries, more sales, longer vacations, and shorter work weeks.

"Education wasn't the first American industry to be touched by this American Exceptionalism, but it looks like we'll be last to recover. We still haven't got the message that the party is over. We still basically think that people should keep giving us money whether we produce or not.

"We're a monopoly industry, yet we don't think of ourselves that way. Our plans for reform resemble the 'Five-Year Plans' of Soviet bureaucrats, but we don't see that.

"O.K., now here's the good news.

"The alarm bell has gone off at last. Most of us are waking up. Anyone who's attended school budget hearings in recent years, watched the turnover of school boards, seen the 'Mellow' exodus of superintendents like me, or paid attention to state budget trendlines knows that a new day is dawning.

"The structures of school finance are crumbling at the state and local level. Either we redesign them or watch them collapse. Already it is clear that redesign is the choice.

"So, what's the new dawn going to look like? What are the schools of tomorrow going to be like?

"In the ten years since *A Nation At Risk*, we've been on a long march from inputs through process to outcomes and somehow we didn't get where we wanted to be. Teachers didn't teach differently, managers didn't manage any better, and kids didn't work any harder despite everyone saying that all these things needed to happen.

"The outcomes had potential. It rested on a great idea. Everyone in the world knows that results are the bottom line. But we walked through the wrong door when it came to implementing it. Our thinking was still back in American Exceptionalism. We thought that, unlike all other countries, we could have results without tests or agreed-upon curriculum.

"However, I think we learned a lesson. I think we're getting on the right track. I think you're going to see those high stakes tests--and they'll be more fair than the ones we have now. You're going to see a national curriculum--though maybe with state and regional variations like the Germans use.

"And here's the best part. When we start giving those tests, our kids and our teachers are going to astound the world.

"We do badly on these international comparisons because over here those tests don't mean anything. Our tests don't get you promoted, don't get you a diploma, don't get you into college, and don't get you a job. In the rest of the world, tests do all of those things and, believe me, people pay attention when something is on the line.

"In my rather ordinary school district, I've never seen a test that teachers couldn't prepare kids for it if they knew it was important. I never saw a test that kids wouldn't work hard for if they knew it was important.

"Flexibility really hasn't helped us. Being able to do anything has just meant that we get blamed for everything.

"People resist accountability when they don't understand what is wanted. If expectations--a curriculum, a test--are defined clearly, then people can accept accountability.

"We'll have to deregulate our schools just as much as we can because the price of regulation has become exorbitant and wholly counterproductive. Deregulation per se or through devices like Charter Schools is the best way to defeat vouchers if that's what we're afraid of. Really though, we shouldn't fear choice. All those other countries have it. If it hasn't hurt public education there, why should it hurt us here?

"Let me sum up by saying that there is enough money, if we only use it differently. The scandal of financial inequity can and must be ended. The even greater scandal of inner city education can and must be ended.

"Give us the tools and give us the strategy and our people will do the job. If we have the courage and the will to change ourselves, then the Dream shall live on.

"Good night, Good-bye, and Godspeed in this great American journey."

Chapter 4

Education and Values: Study, Practice, and Example

Denis P. Doyle

Culture is activity of thought, and receptiveness to beauty and humane feeling. Scraps of information have nothing to do with it. A merely well-informed man is the most useless bore on God's earth. What we should aim at producing is men who possess both culture and expert knowledge in some special direction. Their expert knowledge will give them the ground to start from, and their culture will lead them as deep as philosophy and as high as art.

> Alfred North Whitehead
> *The Aims of Education*

Education does not mean teaching people what they do not know .... It is a painful, continual and difficult work to be done by kindness, by watching, by warning, by precept, and by praise, but above all--by example.

> John Ruskin
> *The Stones of Venice*

The views in this chapter do not necessarily reflect the views of the trustees, officers, or staff of the Hudson Institute.

INTRODUCTION

When this writer began to write this essay, he took the occasion to return to his own work to find a quote that would illustrate the theme *Education and Values*, and, as Pat Moynihan says, "backwards reels the mind ...." More than a decade ago I wrote an article for *The College Board Review*, titled "Education and Values: A Consideration." If anything it is more apt today:

> Since ancient times, philosophers and scholars have known that values and education are indissolubly bound together. Their connection was so obvious and important that it was virtually impossible to imagine value-free education. Even if education did not transmit values explicitly and self-consciously, it did so implicitly and by example. Can anyone remember a distinguished teacher or philosopher, ancient or modern, who was morally neutral?

As a people we have come to understand that no nation that ignores values in education can hope to endure. No democracy that neglects values and education can expect to remain free. The reasons, though they should be obvious, bear repeating.

The American experiment in self-government is now two centuries old. Indeed, we are not only the oldest democracy in the world; we have an unbroken tradition of self-government marked by a long history of enlarging the franchise. When our experiment began, only white men of property could vote; today all citizens over 18 may do so. They may do so because we are convinced that all adults can responsibly exercise the franchise. They may do so if they are educated.

Philosophically, the reason for including values in education is clear enough: a democracy committed to the twin principles of equality and liberty must have an educated citizenry if it is to function effectively. By "educated" one means not just a knowledge of basic skills, but people who are liberally educated. In this connection it is worth remembering the purpose of a liberal education: it is to suit men and women to lead lives of ordered liberty. It is the embodiment of the Jeffersonian vision of a free and equal people.

CIVIC VIRTUE

Such observations, of course, would hardly surprise the Founders. To them civic virtue was the *sina qua non* of a democratic republic, and it was in some large measure imparted by the formal institutions of society, among them schools. Indeed, without such norms, civilization itself is unimaginable. Born naked, ignorant and full of appetites, each child must learn the facts and values of the culture anew. It is no surprise that formal schooling plays a major role in that process. Schooling and civic virtue cannot be separated.

In place of the hereditary aristocracy of the Old World, the New World, according to Thomas Jefferson, would witness the emergence of a natural aristocracy of talent. In a great democracy, as all men are equal before God and the law, so too are all men free to develop their talents to the fullest. This elegant and radical idea survives to this day and for its full development, the people of a democracy must be educated.

As Lord Brougham said, "Education makes a people easy to lead, but difficult to drive; easy to govern, but impossible to enslave."

The ancient Greeks, from whom we inherit our intellectual and educational traditions, knew that there was one purpose for education and one only: to fit man to live in the polis. And the key to life in the polis is values, "civic virtue"; without it the polis, the state itself, would founder. They had the insight to know how one acquires civic virtue. Their threefold lesson is as true today as it was then. It is study, example, and practice.

STUDY

First, values are acquired by study, knowledge acquired didactically. Teachers teach and students learn. Study requires submission to the discipline of learning. Second, values are acquired by example. Virtuous men and women by example communicate values to the young and to their fellows. Third, and perhaps most important, values are acquired by practice. Virtue is acquired by behaving virtuously.

Long before the "excellence movement" there were two broad schools of thought in such matters. One is the vision of school as agent of the state, familiar enough to anyone who cares to peer beyond the totalitarian state. John Stuart Mill, who was spared the excesses of modern totalitarian and authoritarian regimes, thought that no other objective could characterize government schooling. Government education, whether the dominant power be a priesthood, monarchy, or majority of the exiting generation is

> a mere contrivance for moulding people to be exactly like one another: and as the mould in which it cast them is that which pleases the predominant power in the government ... it establishes a despotism over the mind ...

By way of contrast there is the perspective of a supporter of government as the instrument of civic virtue, Simon Bolivar. Addressing the Congress of Angostura, he solemnly observed:

> Let us give to our republic a fourth power with authority over the youth, the hearts of men.... Let us establish this Areopagus to watch over the education of the children ... to purify whatever may be corrupt in the republic...

There is, however, a less extreme way to think about education and civic virtue in a democracy. How should a free people inculcate those values and attitudes essential to public welfare, domestic tranquility, and the pursuit of happiness? How can order and freedom be reconciled? The task, while not easy, is not impossible. And the American experience of the past century and one half with public education--or the education of the public--is instructive.

What are the values of civic virtue? First, explicit knowledge, mastered to the point of habit, about the rights and responsibilities of citizenship, and the opportunities and obligations imposed by a constitutional republic. It is knowing, as sociologist Morris Janowitz observed, that the corollary of the right to trial by jury is the obligation to serve on a jury when called. It is knowing that one man's freedom ends where another's begins. It is knowing that rights are earned and must be protected if they are to survive. It is knowing that Supreme Court Justice Oliver Wendell Holmes was right when he observed that "taxes are what we pay for civilized society."

What is it our public schools should do to teach values? What knowledge and habits must children acquire to make them virtuous citizens? Let one look first at example, then study, then practice.

The most striking example of citizenship in all of history was offered by Socrates. He accepted the hemlock cup, not because he believed himself guilty of corrupting the youth of Athens, but to demonstrate the supremacy of law. His wisdom and his courage are captured by John Ruskin in words which contain the essence of my point:

> Education does not mean teaching people what they do not know .... It is a painful, continual, and difficult work to be done by kindness, by watching, by warning, by precept, and by praise, but above all-by example.

As a practical matter, this means that schools must be staffed by moral men and women who care about their calling and their craft. By the pure force of personality they must communicate their sense of commitment to their students. There is no mystery as to who these people are. They are the teachers we each remember, the teachers who made a difference in our own lives. The problem is not identifying them after the fact, but before the fact. They are the teachers who are connected to their disciplinary traditions, who are broadly and deeply educated, and who believe in the life of the mind.

These are not empty homilies. There is an internal dynamic to study and scholarship, and there are canons of the profession that themselves embody the values of a democratic society. They include honesty, fidelity, accuracy, fairness, tolerance for diversity, flexibility, and a willingness to change when new evidence is presented. Indeed, what one expects of better teachers, is precisely the set of traits that one associates with civic virtue.

THE INVISIBLE CURRICULUM

Another name this writer uses to describe this cluster of attributes and the outcomes they help foster is "the invisible curriculum." It is the message sent by teachers to students about what is right and what is wrong, what is acceptable and what is not. A school, for example, that sets low standards sends a powerful message: nothing much matters, get by. That is a dangerous message to give a young person because it programs him for failure. The invisible curriculum undergirds and reinforces the student's visible curriculum.

It has become fashionable in certain circles to think that education is a process, a set of skills divorced from their substantive context. That is not true. Education is contextual. It is a substantive experience which requires, among other things, learning about the great documents of citizenship. At a minimum these include an acquaintance with Aristotle's *Politics and Ethics*, Plato's *Republic*, The Magna Carta, *The Prince* by Machiavelli, *An Essay Concerning Human Understanding* by John Locke, The Declaration of Independence, the 10th *Federalist Paper*, The United States Constitution, John Stuart Mill's *On Liberty*, The Gettysburg Address, Lincoln's Second Inaugural Address and Martin Luther King's Letter from Birmingham Jail. Education is an empty concept if it is stripped of the values these documents embody. As King reminds us, "Freedom is never voluntarily given by the oppressor; it must be demanded by the oppressed."

This is first and foremost a normative statement, a statement of values. To be fully educated the student must master a body of knowledge, fact, myth, history, anecdote, not as an exercise in memory, but as an exercise in understanding and critical thought. History and context are important to education both for themselves and as the instrumentality by which people learn to think and to reason. It is simple but true: people learn to think by thinking and thinking hard. That is the essence of the Socratic dialogue, the most enduring and important teaching technique ever devised.

Think of the centerpiece of the Fifth Amendment as simply a phrase to be recapitulated without an understanding of its underlying meaning: *"nor shall be compelled in any criminal case to be a witness against himself."*

Without understanding its purpose and its historical context it is truly nonsense. Why should a suspected criminal not have to testify against himself? Protecting all of us from testifying against ourselves emerged from a long and bitter history of the rack and thumbscrew -- if a man may be compelled to testify against himself who is to say no to the torturer? Certainly not the victim. Freedom from self incrimination is no more and no less than freedom from the Inquisitor and the tools of his trade. It is a strange thing in a century so convulsed by violence of every kind that this simple truth is frequently overlooked when people "take the fifth." It may be the single most important protection a free people enjoy.

As George Santayana observed, "something not chosen must chose." In exploring the idea of values and education we must remember that values are a part of our world that is not scientifically derived. They include such human but unscientific attributes as love, loyalty, courage, devotion, piety, and compassion. These attributes give dimension, scope, and meaning to being human. It is precisely with these attributes that great literature concerns itself.

HUCK FINN

Let me draw upon a particularly telling and appropriate example, Mark Twain's *Huckleberry Finn*, published more than a century ago. It is arguably the greatest American novel, a book of such importance that no American who has not read it can be considered educated. What makes this book important? Its scope and sweep, certainly, but above all, its values. In shape it is a book for the masses. Like the Bible or *The Iliad* it tells a universal story, accessible to all. Just as it contains much with which to agree, it contains much that shocks, provokes, and even offends. As a consequence, reading the book and discussing it in a classroom requires sensitivity and discretion. It is not a book to be taken lightly.

It is interesting that the book is attacked today just as it was when first released. The far right believes Huck is venal at best, and hostile to religion at worst. They say his language is abominable, his behavior unacceptable. In sum, he is a poor example. The left is even more outspoken in its hostility to Huck. They level against him the worst of modern epithets: racist.

I will stipulate to this: Twain's purpose was to subvert the state, undermine the morals of the young, and challenge the smugness and complacency of the American *haute bourgeoise*. To this accusation I plead Twain guilty. And this is precisely the power of the book: to confront the conventional wisdom. Twain railed against the organized religion of the day and its sanctimonious piety and hypocrisy. Indeed, he found organized society, particularly the state, the cause rather than the cure for social ills. Huck and Jim, children of nature, could escape the corrupting forces of contemporary life only by physical escape.

So far as one can tell, Twain really believed that society was a sentence and the only hope was escape. The development of this idea in *Huckleberry Finn* is the best known of Twain's repeated efforts to deal with it. If this interpretation of Twain is correct, as this writer believes it to be, he is far more dangerous than either the left or right wings know. He is an enemy of the state.

Whether or not he should be read by callow youths, then, becomes a question with meaning. The direction assumed by other great works across the ages is the same. While the first purpose is to entertain, the more important purpose is to instruct. Such literature is almost never the servant of the state nor the advocate of the *status quo*.

Jean DuBuffet, champion of "*l'art brut*," raw or unschooled art, in a splendid twist on Plato asserted that art was subversive, that the state should attempt to suppress it, and that the artist worked best and most effectively when he was disdained by the prevailing culture. That is, in fact, a rather exaggerated version of the hypothesis offered here. Suffice it to say that the artist should question, at a minimum, the conventional wisdom and make the *bourgeoisie* uncomfortable.

Without dwelling on Twain, it is useful to consider great literature in general to see if the example is idiosyncratic. Are there common threads? The direction assumed by great literature across the ages is the same. While its first purpose it to entertain, its more important purpose is to instruct. It provides examples of courage, strength, and love. It shows the effects of hubris, greed, and the will to power. It reveals transcendent accomplishment and abject failure. Such literature is almost never the servant of the state or the advocate of the *status quo*. Great literature challenges assumptions, it breaks with the conventional wisdom.

Not all great books are offensive, or irreverent, or hostile to the state, but they challenge the conventional wisdom, they provoke the reader, they insist upon engagement with the subject. This is even true of science, particularly in its early stages when it is concerned with breakthroughs in basic knowledge. Galileo, Kepler, and Darwin are only the best known examples.

The controversial nature of a work, then, is a product of its power and authenticity, and it is for this reason that the inexperienced reader will frequently find the great book difficult--it is often very tough sledding. It is tough sledding because it raises fundamental questions about right and wrong. For the inquiring mind, it induces an interior Socratic dialogue.

VALUE FREE EDUCATION: AN OXYMORON

At issue in the teaching of values is an error of judgment that continues to plague our schools. An assumption was made, in all good faith, that our schools could be value-free, neutral, and objective; this would defuse the potentially explosive question of which values to teach and how to teach them. This vision of American education is an old one.

In the nineteenth century, what was described as value-free education was really non-sectarian Protestantism. It was not quite ecumenism, but a robust Unitarianism. Indeed, it is no accident that the early public school reformers were visionary and romantic Unitarians, builders who would use the public schools to uplift and transform each generation. As Horace Mann, with a striking sense of modernity, said in his *Annual Report to the Board of Education* in 1848:

> If all the children in the community from the age of four to that of seventeen could be brought within the reformatory and elevating influence of good schools, the dark host of private vices and public crimes...might...be banished from the world.

When it came to values education, Mann, as well as his supporters and colleagues, had little problem identifying what schools should do. They knew that most teachers were poorly trained and they were the inheritors of a classical tradition that brooked little interference. In essence, the curriculum chose itself. So it was in the late nineteenth century that the *McGuffey Reader* enjoyed unparalleled success. It was full of pious homilies and entreaties to civic and religious virtues, the values widely shared by the community that patronized the public schools. In the 19th century, the patrons were almost exclusively white Protestants.

The emergence of a highly diverse, democratic, and pluralistic modern society means that we can no longer rely on either the classical curriculum or the Protestant consensus of the 19th century.

THE DISCIPLINARY TRADITION

In an attenuated way this disciplinary tradition does exist in the best public and private college preparatory schools. In these institutions, for example, teachers are free to choose Dryden or Donne, Spencer or Marlowe, Shakespeare or Cervantes, Twain or Hawthorne--but the freedom to choose is nearly ephemeral, because the educated person, the student, must eventually read all of them.

What has happened in American education, of course, is the virtual abandonment of the disciplinary tradition. Instead of vertical integration, elementary and secondary schools are organized horizontally.

They are not only characterized by self contained classrooms, they are self contained organizations with few links to the outside world. Great bands of children are grouped by age and they are given "problem areas" to study. Communications skills replace English, social studies replaces history and geography; is it any surprise that bachelor living and power volleyball enter the curriculum?

Is it any wonder that there are periodic attempts to purge Huck Finn from the classroom? With no intellectual and disciplinary anchor, the school is subject to the fads and vicissitudes of the moment. When the watchwords of the school become "value neutrality," "relevance," and "relativity," anything goes.

Nothing is imposed on anyone, except the notion that there are two sides to every question. The philosophy of the ancient Greeks and the great revealed religions, both based on moral absolutes, no longer provide answers. Not even the existential answer that teachers know more than students can be offered with conviction. It is for these reasons that the disciplinary tradition is essential.

PRACTICE MAKES PERFECT

Let this writer turn briefly to his final point: practice. "Happiness," Aristotle tells us, "is activity of the soul in accord with perfect virtue." We achieve this state by practice. Ironically, it is not so much in the exercise of our rights that we learn this, but in meeting our obligations. It is through submission to a higher principle that we learn to appreciate the importance of our hard-won rights.

At the level of friend and family, practice means satisfying the reciprocal demands that loyalty and filial responsibility place upon us. At the level of the community, it means meeting minimum standards of civility and good conduct.

More than just obeying the law, it means accommodation to unspoken standards of behavior. At the level of the state, it means honoring the full and explicit demands of citizenship from honesty in paying taxes, to citizen participation, to the ultimate sacrifice for a higher good in time of mortal danger.

At the level of the school, practice means doing what is expected and doing it well. But it could and should mean much more. It could and should mean service, both to the school and to the community. Although an old idea in private education, service is just now being taken seriously in the public sector.

The North Carolina School of Science and Mathematics, one of the nation's few public boarding schools, enrolls some of the best and brightest youngsters in North Carolina. There is a special graduation requirement that says no student may graduate without performing three hours a week of school service and four hours a week of community service.

Students from NCSSM spend time in nursing homes, orphanages, day care centers, and hospitals. And they do so week in and week out.

Every high school student in America should be expected to perform community service as a condition of graduation. No one is so poor or so elevated as to not profit from it, for that is surely its purpose. The help these young people provide, while important, is the least of what they do.

What is really important is that they are learning through practice the habits of service. That is the very foundation of civic virtue and the personal satisfaction it can provide.

What this means, of course, is that we cannot avoid the question of curriculum. What we teach we value and what we value we teach. The curriculum, both visible and invisible, is value laden. What is it we need to know as Americans, both to have a shared sense of community and a shared destiny?

COMMUNITY

At the same time, we need the support, solace, and integrity of the smaller, organic communities of which we are naturally a part. No one can be a member of a "family" of 240 million people. We can be citizens, and owe obligations and expect rights to flow from this larger body politic, but the kinds of association that most of us find deeply satisfying flow from smaller units of organizations. Any curriculum--particularly a "core" curriculum--must reconcile the demands of a continental democracy and the need to belong to a more intimate community. It must reflect the values of the whole and the part, respecting both while supporting the individual.

The need is acute because in the final analysis "excellence" in any endeavor is a solitary pursuit, requiring self discipline and commitment. Excellence also assumes many forms--music, art, the quantitative disciplines, languages and the Humanities. And over the life of a student the pursuit of excellence calls for progressively greater specialization and more complete immersion in the peculiarities of a given discipline.

This is not to say that a "core" curriculum cannot coexist with specialization: it can. It is just more difficult to pull it off successfully. And this raises the most important question of all. If curriculum is central, and values are central to the curriculum, who will choose and of what will the curriculum consist? If it is chosen by the wise and judicious, the penetrating and the discerning, the discriminating and the disciplined -- in short, by the reader and this writer--the curriculum will be a wonder to behold.

But if is chosen by the ideologues of the left or right, the Babbits and Buffoons of American intellectual life, it will be a disaster. The fear of the latter is a real one as anyone who has read Francis FitzGerald's study of American history texts must admit. Anti-intellectualism in America is an old, powerful, and even honored tradition and it is not at all clear that the excellence movement will, even over the long haul, change that.

Lurking beneath the surface of any discussion about the quality of American education is the nagging suspicion that we already have the schools that we both want and deserve. We do have citizen control; we do have a voice in what our schools do and how they do it, however attenuated it may be. Perhaps, after all is said and done, Americans prefer football to the life of the mind. That, after all, is what values are all about.

CONCLUSION

The life of the school, then, is defined by what is taught, and the life of the student is defined by what is learned.

What has this to do with education and values? A good deal, this writer thinks, because we are what we value, and schools cannot escape this simple truth. And at the heart of the excellence movement--if indeed it has a heart--lies the conviction that it makes a difference what children are taught and what they learn.

This quintessential and timeless expression of values and education is carved in stone on the B'nai B'rith headquarters in Washington, D.C.: "The world stands on three foundations: study, work and benevolence." And so it does.

Chapter 5

Service-Learning

Phyllis V. Walsh

SERVICE--PAST AND PRESENT

Much has been written on the subject of service to one's community. Many of us can vividly remember the late John F. Kennedy's words: "Ask not what your country can do for you--ask what you can do for your country." Or perhaps it is Martin Luther King's message that still rings loud and clear: "Every person must decide whether to walk in the light of creative altruism or the darkness of destructive selfishness. This is the judgment. Life's most persistent and urgent question is, What are you doing for others?" The great humanitarian Albert Schweitzer said, "I don't know what your destiny will be, but the one thing I know; the only ones among you who will really be happy are those who will have sought and found how to serve." Few of those who spoke so eloquently about service had the opportunity of President Kennedy, who, just a few weeks after his inauguration in 1961, created the Peace Corps. Since its inception, corps members have traveled to every corner of their country and the world to assist others in their quest for a better life. The Peace Corps continues to be an exemplary program. Approximately 125,000 Americans have served in its ranks, and they have assisted large numbers of the world's peoples.

Throughout our country, many individuals who are not as famous as Kennedy or King have taken these thoughts and adopted a philosophy of life reflecting those ideas. Some of these people are involved in the educational community and have chosen to spread the "good news" to others. Two of the most notable and most often quoted are Dan Conrad and Dr. Ernest Boyer.

Mr. Conrad has had extensive experience with service-learning in both the public schools of Minnesota and the realm of higher education at the University of Minnesota. His philosophy, research, and statistics are often cited when the pedagogy of service-learning is examined. Ernest Boyer's thoughts were reported as early as 1986 in *High School*, in which he recommends that high schools require 120 hours of community service for graduation.

In addition to these and other individuals who have published numerous papers and studies related to service-learning, a number of support organizations operate on varying levels to assist educators with their reform and restructuring efforts. Primary among these are the Association for Experiential Education and the National Society for Internships and Experiential Education, both operating for more than 20 years.

DEFINING THE EXPERIENCE

The term "service-learning" is used to describe a wide range of voluntary, mandated action, or experiential education programs. Since there are so many variations on the theme of "service-learning," it is difficult to establish a firm definition of the term. Perhaps it is more relevant to establish a philosophy of the principles of service-learning, rather than a "Webster's definition" of the concept. It would seem logical that in education, the idea would mean something like this: "providing public service to reinforce classroom teachings," or "combining hands-on activities to supplement curriculum," or perhaps "integrating classroom theory with community involvement." Essentially, what is happening in the student's culture and his community environment can and should be connected to the information expected to be mastered in the classroom. Therefore, service-learning, also known as "experience-based learning," combines the pursuit of a significant social purpose with the goal of fostering the personal and intellectual growth of the participants.

Dr. Gary Phillips, President of the National School Improvement Project, has conducted research that shows that people retain learned material at different levels that correspond directly to the amount of personal involvement the individuals invested in each effort. Simply hearing and seeing material is not enough of a process to ensure effective education, since the learner retains only about 20 percent of this material. The percentages for retention of material increase dramatically when the material is actively experienced, jumping dramatically to a rate of 80 percent. When learners teach material to other students, it increases retention levels of the learner for that material to an optimal level of 90 percent.

These statistical findings indicate that our classrooms and curricula should be changed drastically so as to give students more time and opportunity to have "hands-on" experiences which aim to enhance and augment more traditional learning techniques. Current pedagogy recognizes undeniably, that all students' most efficient and effective knowledge-gathering mechanisms are not limited to left-brain auditory learning modes. These learning modes are the techniques upon which traditional American schools are predicated.

Service-learning provides flexible options for the recognition of alternative learning styles and strategies. Service-learning provides educational activities; concurrently, it supplies needed services to the community. This experience helps students become aware of the world around them through reality-based experiences and assessment measures that can provide an "authentic" view of what the students learn during this experience. When students are asked to help design these activities or projects, they develop a sense of ownership in the activity and a sense of commitment toward the people to whom these projects are directed. When later asked to reflect on and evaluate these projects, the students are able to add other dimensions to their knowledge. It is likely that during the course of a project, they will develop new attitudes toward themselves, their community, and learning in general.

By linking subject matter to the implementation of that information, academic learning and curricular content can be improved and retained longer and in greater depth. When schools integrate social action and service into their traditional academic programs, students learn much more than the planned behavioral and content objectives. They learn to communicate, solve problems, think critically, and practice higher-level thinking skills.

The highest levels of Bloom's "Cognitive Development Taxonomy"-- analysis and synthesis--are admirably served by experiential education. Students become immersed in a "real" activity with results and consequences, not a simulation of life devoid of problems or possibilities. They experience working collaboratively, they assume responsibility, they accept the logical consequences of their actions, they become reliable and dependable, and they recognize the ramifications of rendering service, both positive (when the service is well conceived and well executed), and negative (when the service is merely "window dressing"). In conclusion, this type of service-learning experience will also give students a sense of worth and pride; will enhance their self-esteem; and will allow students to explore new identities, interests, and roles.

Of critical importance to any service-learning program is a strong component of reflection and evaluation. This aspect was actually the process part of a definition of learning by John Dewey, who said: "Learning is reflection on experience." More than twenty years of research on how people learn has shown that the effectiveness of our learning increases as the number of senses that are involved with the learning project increase. Reflection provides us with the opportunity to engage our senses through memory.

In an article entitled "Documenting Learning Through Service" published in *The Generator*, Spring 1992, Gerry Ouellette wrote the following passage:

> If one finding from my study stands out above all others, it is that reflection is the key to learning from the service experience. Students who wrote in journals or who responded appropriately to essay questions at the end of each quarter all posted significant gains in self-concept and problem solving. Those who did not participate in structured reflection showed no such statistically significant results. Through reflection, students deal with the problems they learn to solve. They evaluate their progress and their personal development, and they revisit the people, knowledge, and feelings that have made up their experience.

Reflection allows students to relive and evaluate the way they feel about an experience, to organize their thoughts, and to share thoughts with and get feedback from others. If the reflection is written, those thoughts and feelings can be reviewed at a later time. Reflection should not be thought of as unimportant simply because it usually occurs at the end of a particular experience. It should be the culminating activity that ties the experience together; it ensures that learning is not left up to happenstance.

Once the philosophy of service-learning is understood, the possible applications of the concept seem almost endless. Most practitioners would agree that several general principles should be followed. An effective service-learning program has the following components:

1) Clear service and learning goals for everyone involved, and it is an option made available to all students.

2) A clear statement of the responsibilities of each person and organization involved in terms of procedure, expectations, and evaluation.

3) Planning and monitoring by the servers and servees, and flexible evaluative instruments to allow for growth and change.

4) Training, supervision, recognition, and reflection for the students.

Implementation of a service-learning program may occur in many ways. Careful thought should be given to the options so that the maximum benefit is achieved. One way of distinguishing among these options is to view a continuum developed for comparison of curriculum offerings.

Volunteer Information Center	Club or Co-curricular Activity	Community Service Credit	"Lab" for Existing Courses	Community Service Class	School-wide Focus or Theme
1	**2**	**3**	**4**	**5**	**6**

Less a part of regular school program	More a part of regular school program

Some of these categories are discussed briefly in the following text. Each one is unique and has its own advantages and limitations.

Beginning at the left of the continuum, some schools offer a type of "match-maker" service to the students, in which they help students to identify organizations that could benefit from a contribution of a particular talent or block of time from students. This "match" provides an interested student with information about various organizations in the community and their particular needs, but its implementation depends on student initiative, and its results may, therefore, be limited in scope.

Clubs and co-curricular programs are most often used as service opportunities, as they require a minimal commitment of time from school staff. Students generally do not miss any class time and do not receive academic credit for their service. This type of program is strictly voluntary and traditionally attracts those students who already possess an altruistic ethic. A common example of this type of program is the traditional Key Club activities. While many worthwhile activities occur through the efforts of this type of school group, sometimes it can become a major obstacle to real service-learning infusion because the mindset that "we already do that" becomes a built-in impediment to change. Change is important in our schools, particularly as we look toward outcome based education, school restructuring, school re:learning, and other school innovations and reforms.

In-school activities involving peers may be categorized as service within the school environment. Peer helpers, peer tutors, students trained as conflict managers, big-brother/big-sister relationships, and aides for students with special needs are all examples of student involvement in service-learning as part of their school experience. These activities traditionally are limited to the school day and immediate school environment. Student participation may be limited to those self-assured students who are personally motivated to help others and to become involved in their school activities.

Individual classroom teachers may choose to integrate service projects as part of expected activities, for "extra-credit," as an optional activity, or as a planned "for-credit" assignment. This integration allows the student to connect the topics in the classroom with the world around him. Often several teachers will collaborate on projects affecting common students across several disciplines. Students benefit from the connections between subject areas, the experience of working with other students and teachers, and the chance to be involved with their community.

Further along the continuum, offering community service for elective credit is another way for schools to become involved in service-learning. By initiating a process in which students perform service in approved organizations or projects, document required hours, and earn graduation credits, schools are exploring yet another variation on the theme. Most of these programs utilize out-of-school hours for the service activities, as the students initiate the effort largely independent of other classroom requirements. Typically, this type of offering attracts few students, most of whom already are interested and involved in the volunteer sector.

A response to this lack of initiative on the part of other students might be to mandate after-school service involvement. Credit is given for the experience when it meets minimal standards established by the school district. This type of service-learning should be flexible enough to adjust to students needs, schedules, and other commitments, while remaining structured enough to be a meaningful learning experience. Students, however, are left to their own resources to connect their service experiences with classroom expectations, unless a structured reflection component is also mandated. Structured reflection opportunities are significant in helping the students to make those connections. A program of this type is explored in more depth later in this chapter.

Some school programs offer or require students to complete a course on community service. These courses are often presented as part of the social studies curriculum, with flexible scheduling to facilitate community involvement without infringing on other class time. In this option, students have the benefit of regular class participation, scheduled service times in the community, and a structured reflection component. A direct connection between classwork and service-related activities, the ultimate goal of service-learning is also inherent in this option.

At the furthest end of the continuum, developing a school-wide focus for service-learning may be appropriate for some areas of education. Large cities often sometimes use this approach to offer specialty high school programs which are often referred to as "charter schools." By defining a theme of service, the entire school community is involved in the spirit of combining daily lessons with activities benefiting the out-of-school environment. This idea is one of the most infusive, as the primary goal of the school and its programs is defined with service-learning as its base. As an added dimension to this type of program, direct links and cooperation between the school and community agencies foster intensely satisfying relationships and positive results. Local businesses are also ideal partners in this collaborative effort.

The general methods for combining service with learning, briefly described above, can be refined to become as unique as the individuals involved in the creation of the specific program. Understanding that our schools and the communities that surround them are culturally, financially, and philosophically discrete bodies demands that service-learning programs have the flexibility to meet the needs of the people they serve.

Program materials to aid in the implementation of service-learning programs are available from numerous sources. One of the most renowned organizations producing service-learning materials is The National Youth Leadership Council. Located in Minnesota, this group has developed a wide range of resource documents covering all aspects of service-learning. Another source for materials is The Pennsylvania Institute for Environmental and Community Service Learning. This institute has also prepared a handbook of suggested projects for secondary school students, which combine service and classroom topics. In Pennsylvania, both the Governor's Office of Citizen Service (PennSERVE) and The National Center for Service Learning and School

Change are available to act as resources and disseminators of information related to service-learning theory and programs.

SERVICE-LEARNING ACROSS THE NATION

In the 1980s, public school systems throughout the United States began instituting service-learning programs. By 1986, a total of ten states had developed policies or guidelines on school-based community service programs and seven others were in the developmental stages. Approximately 900,000 students and 5,400 high schools were involved, representing 27 percent of all high schools nationally.[1]

Eight states were recognized as "leader states" in 1992 by the Commission on National and Community Service. The leader states named were Colorado, Maryland, Minnesota, Pennsylvania, South Carolina, Vermont, West Virginia, and the District of Columbia.[2] Federal grants were allocated to these states for proposals that "hold especially significant promise" for service-learning projects from kindergarten through high school.

Of the "leader states," Maryland was the first state in the nation to require community service as a condition of high school graduation. In July 1992, a mandatory service-learning plan was approved despite qualms voiced by many educators. For example, the service rule was vociferously opposed by the Maryland State Teachers Association, whose president asserted that the new requirement was unconstitutional. With the backing of Maryland Governor Donald Schaefer, the community service plan was passed by a 7-to-3 vote of the State Board of Education.[3]

The service-learning requirement calls for students to perform either 75 hours of community service during the middle and high school years, or to comply with a locally designed program approved by the state superintendent. The option of a locally designed requirement was added to the original student-service proposal late in the process to provide greater flexibility. Under either community service option, the service must be developmentally appropriate and the school district must set up a way to monitor the service activities.

Another state trailblazer in implementing school-based service learning is Minnesota. The Minnesota Youth Service Plan is a combination of state policy and financial incentives that both compel and encourage school districts to develop community service programs.[4] The State Board of Education requires all K-12 schools to provide opportunities for students to participate in youth service activities.

Additionally, schools in Minnesota must integrate service-learning into their curriculum. For those high school students participating in youth service, credit toward graduation must be awarded. The Minnesota program provides opportunities for students to engage in peer tutoring, drug use prevention, work with infants and children, care for seniors, hunger relief efforts, environmental projects, and many other forms of service. Minnesota has made financial assistance available to districts by allowing a local levy of 50-cents per capita to implement a "youth development program." If service is a part of the plan, the local school district will gain an additional 25-cents per capita in state funds for the district.

At the national level, the National and Community Service Act of 1990 created the Commission on National and Community Service to provide program funds, technical assistance, and training to states and communities to develop and expand service opportunities. Total funding of $73 million was available to the Commission in fiscal year 1992.

President Clinton recently created a White House Office of National Service. This office is overseeing the implementation of a tuition-for-service plan, which enables pre-college students to do community service in exchange for government funding of university education or training. A demonstration program in the summer of 1993 will employ 1,500 students in a variety of projects.[5] Those who take part will receive the minimum wage for their eight weeks of service, plus a $1,000 stipend towards college costs.

SERVICE-LEARNING PROGRAMS IN PENNSYLVANIA

Pennsylvania is becoming well-established as a leader in the field of service-learning. Leaders of this state, notably Governor Robert Casey and U.S. Senator Harris Wofford, have deep roots in such distinguished service activities as the Peace Corps and have been instrumental in enacting legislation supporting service-learning programs at all levels of public education. In October 1988, the Governor's Office of Citizen Service, "PennSERVE," was created to advance the Commonwealth's policy of promoting public service and to foster the Governor Casey's belief that service should be the common expectation and experience of all Pennsylvanians.

PennSERVE acts as a clearinghouse for advice, expertise, ideas, and information related to service-learning. Conferences, seminars, and workshops are developed here to be presented across the state for interested agencies, groups, and school districts. PennSERVE also serves as the vehicle for dispensing money committed by the state and by the federal government to service-learning programs across the Commonwealth. Finally, PennSERVE has spawned the Pennsylvania Conservation Corps for youth under age 18 and at-risk of not graduating from high school. Additionally, it was instrumental in establishing the Pennsylvania Service Corps for people ages 17 and older that requires service in exchange for college loan forgiveness.

In early January 1989, the Pennsylvania State Board of Education adopted a resolution which stated:

> Resolved: That the State Board of Education believes that programs of community service should be an integral part of education at all levels and strongly urges schools, colleges and universities to institute or strengthen community service programs so that every student is encouraged to serve and participate in volunteer services.

As community service programs expanded in number and strength over the past few years, additional personnel were designated to assist PennSERVE's management and their staff. The state was "divided" into service areas and Fellows were selected in each area to provide some of PennSERVE's services at the local level. These Fellows serve as process consultants and regional facilitators. They have been recognized as key service-learning professionals in the field and were selected competitively. Their territories were multi-county segments of the state. In 1991-1992, six Regional Fellowships were established across the state. The Fellows held bi-monthly meetings for participants in their areas for the purposes of information dissemination, networking, and training. As interest and participation in service-learning programs increased in early 1993 in many school districts, the state was further divided into 12 regions. By creating smaller geographical areas, more participants are now able to attend the meetings for sharing information, and the Fellows are better able to meet the needs of those they represent and serve. Fellows also bring sound ideas and approaches from one region to another through the Fellows Council.

The Fellows work closely with the newly created National Center for Service Learning and School Change, established in Pennsylvania in late 1992. The Center states that its mission is to:

> Support school communities to redesign school structures, curriculum, assessment, and instructional practice through Service-Learning, Re:Learning

and a system of performance-based education. The Center implements a state model of regional networks designed to bring together educators and community stakeholders to create opportunities to establish the community as the extended classroom and to jointly support further systemic change in schools. Each of the twelve regions in the Commonwealth has both a Service-Learning Fellow who understands the concepts and processes of service-learning as a pedagogical strategy and a Re:Learning Fellow who understands school change as a systemic process.

One of the functions of PennSERVE and The National Center for Service Learning and School Change is to disseminate available funds to school districts and community organizations, in concert with school programs, which are interested in developing or enhancing programs of service learning. Since 1988, PennSERVE has distributed funds to 129 programs, each representing at least one school district in the Commonwealth. Some of these programs received small planning grants, while others were awarded more substantial funds to develop more intricate programs. The funds are awarded on a competitive basis after proposals are submitted to the PennSERVE Office for review. The proposals must meet specific criteria outlined by PennSERVE at least once a year. In 1988, grants were awarded to program proposals in 22 counties. By 1993, PennSERVE funds had reached programs in 35 counties.

The 1992-93 school year marked the largest dollar amount ever dedicated to school-supported programs of service-learning, enhanced by PennSERVE funds. Thirty-two proposals for mini-grants were approved by PennSERVE for programs in 28 communities. Mini-grants are $7,500 per year for three years, or a total of $22,500.

In addition to the mini-grant programs which were awarded in 1992-93, PennSERVE also funded 12 programs as disseminators. The designation of "disseminator" indicates that these personnel and programs were approved to be available as resources for other districts while also receiving funds to enhance their own proposed service-learning agendas. These grants were extended over a three-year period with specific expectations in each of these years. Regular interaction with PennSERVE occurs throughout the grant period so that districts and organizations can "keep on track" and exchange ideas with other program participants. The total amount of $75,000 per grant was spread equally over the three years with specific budget allocations for different portions of the proposed project.

Presently, 129 school-supported service-learning programs are aided financially by PennSERVE. This figure is not, however, truly reflective of the number or the strength of educational programs in Pennsylvania which embrace service and learning as partners. Many districts have incorporated the service-learning idea into their curricula, their philosophies, and their procedures, without funding from the Commonwealth. They have created partnerships with community organizations, have been innovative where organizations did not exist, and have met the needs of their communities by creating programs for their school students that focus on "real-life experiences" to learn traditional subject matter. While many of these programs are part of classroom activities or club functions, a growing number of schools offer graduation credit for service activities. In 1989, approximately five percent of Pennsylvania school districts offered credit for service; that percentage increased to 20 percent by 1992. According to a survey completed by PennSERVE in April 1992, 53 high school programs in the Commonwealth offer academic credits for community service, with eight of those high schools mandating service as a condition for graduation. These schools are in the following districts: Bethlehem, Fox Chapel, Keystone Oaks, Lycoming, Mill Creek Valley, Montrose, State College, and Steel Valley.

BETHLEHEM AREA SCHOOL DISTRICT: A CASE STUDY

Probably the most publicized Pennsylvania service learning program is the one in Bethlehem Area School District. Bethlehem is a medium-sized city located in eastern Pennsylvania. The school district currently has 12,685 students, almost 3,600 of them in the two high schools, grades 9 - 12. Faced with the typical problems of schools during the 1980s, curriculum specialists in the district began to explore alternative styles of curriculum, the grouping of students, and programs for students who were judged to be at-risk of failure or drop-out. While many programs were available in the elementary grades to enhance reading and writing skills and to improve or establish proficiency in English for the non-English-speaking student, additional program revisions were needed to address the needs of middle and high school students.

PLANNING

One of the programs explored was a service-oriented one. To facilitate the program's implementation, research literature was solicited from as many sources as possible and reviewed by the school district's administration. A task force was assembled in the fall of 1989 to further review the idea of service-learning in the district. The backgrounds of the task force members were diverse, consisting of school board members, school district administrators, parents of high school-aged students, teachers and guidance counselors of the school district, and service agency representatives. These agency representatives included the Director of the Spanish Speaking Organizations of the Lehigh Valley and the Director of the Volunteer Center of the United Way. (The latter agency is a clearing-house for volunteer activities, playing "matchmaker" for the prospective volunteer and more than 500 not-for-profit agencies in the Greater Lehigh Valley.) Also providing input and advice were representatives from the Pennsylvania Department of Education and the Intermediate Unit 20. After several months of regular meetings with intense discussion and debate on many aspects of the ideas and issues of service learning, two high school administrators visited Atlanta, Georgia, where a program of community service had been mandated in the public school system for several years. This visit provided the group with first-hand exposure to complement the written materials previously studied.

Public hearings were held in late winter at several locations in the district to address issues and concerns related to the new program of studies. In April 1990, the Board of School Directors adopted a revised Program of Studies for the high school, increasing the number of "credits" or Carnegie Units needed for graduation to 23.7, strengthening academic requirements, and requiring community service. Some fierce resistance to the service aspect of the changed curriculum surfaced, escalating into a federal lawsuit by the fall of 1990. This aspect of the issue will be addressed later in this chapter.

IMPLEMENTATION

Since the curricular changes were to be implemented in the fall of 1990 with the incoming freshman class, the process began to accelerate. A Community Service Coordinator was hired to oversee the program and to prepare policies, procedures, and paperwork. The coordinator's position was created with a full-time teacher contract, flexible hours, and an additional stipend for summer work. Special thought was given to the background of the person selected for the coordinator's position, since the job description would involve a wide range of responsibilities. These job requirements included a working knowledge of the school system--its policies, programs, staff, and students--as well as a comfortable relationship with the public agencies and organizations that would be involved with the program. A degree of comfort with job visibility turned out to be a desirable asset as well, as the program has generated much interest. The coordinator's position acts as the liaison between the school district and other parties involved in the service experience. The coordinator also maintains the records of students' selected placements and their hours.

Many local groups requested presentations on the Community Service Program and its impact on the students, their families, and the community at large. These presentations are given by the program coordinator. Since the Associated Press carried the news story about the legal questions related to the program, requests for information have poured in from all parts of the country. Two major television networks, NBC and ABC, have covered the Bethlehem program. Peter Jennings' staff completed a five-minute "spot" highlighting different types of service-learning for the "American Agenda" portion of *World News Tonight* in May 1991. NBC's coverage in the fall of 1992 focused on Maryland's statewide mandated program, with highlights from Bethlehem included in that broadcast. Students and staff from Bethlehem have also been interviewed by several magazines, including *Family Circle* and *Seventeen*, and by students completing college-or graduate-level papers. Numerous newspapers from across the country have published articles related to service-learning, using Bethlehem as a focus as well.

ORGANIZATIONAL INVOLVEMENT

The process of selecting agencies and organizations to serve as service-learning sites began with a letter of introduction to all non-profit groups in the Greater Lehigh Valley. A description of the school district's program was included, as well as a definition of each agency's expected involvement. Those organizations interested in receiving students into their program and providing the expected educational supervision responded with an application to the Bethlehem Area School District (BASD) Community Service Coordinator. Upon receipt and review of each application, the coordinator visited the proposed site to meet the volunteer supervisor, to gain first-hand knowledge of the activities offered by that site, and to answer questions posed by the organization. Recommended agencies were then submitted to the Board of School Directors for approval. After notification of approval, the agencies were asked to send representation to an orientation meeting conducted by the Community Service Coordinator. This meeting provided an opportunity for the agencies to fully understand the paperwork and procedures required by the school district for the tracking of its students as they complete their service experience. Follow-up meetings occurred yearly, with phone communications and site visitations frequently throughout the year.

Agency selection focuses on several criteria. Agencies should have tax-exempt, not-for-profit status (501 C3). They must be free from any illegal discriminatory practices related to sex, age, race, or religion. They are required to provide appropriate adult supervision and direction for the students at all times. Agencies must also comply with BASD's policies and procedures, as required by the Community Service Program guidelines. The activities should be ones designed to actively engage students in tasks that meet the following goals:

1) Are developmentally appropriate and supervised by a responsible adult,
2) Provide needed services to the community or to the service agency's clientele,
3) Provide tangible benefits rather than being limited to housekeeping duties or chores,
4) Promote healthy psychological, intellectual, and social development including self-esteem and self-actualization,
5) Promote career exploration and work force skills,
6) Emphasize benefits to both youth and society, and
7) Emphasize assumption of the responsibilities and obligations of life as well as the enjoyment of its privileges.

The service activities should not do the following:

1) Pose unusual safety risks,
2) Involve operation of motor vehicles or use of machinery that requires technical training,
3) Displace paid employees,
4) Provide private or personal financial gain,
5) Promote doctrinal or religious issues, or
6) Be illegally discriminatory in regard to age, sex, religion, or race.

NUTS AND BOLTS--A PROGRAM OVERVIEW

Although not required for participation in the BASD program, nearly all of the participating agencies maintain liability insurance covering all volunteers on site, including students. If the agency did not provide such insurance coverage, that information was clearly noted on the agency's description page in the student handbook.

A for-profit agency can be considered as a placement site for service, if the service being provided benefits agency clients in ways that are not addressed by paid employees and does not contribute to the profit of the organization. An example of this would be a nursing home, where the student might be a companion or "friendly visitor" for the client. Nevertheless, these situations are screened very carefully, to prevent any controversy.

After these steps were taken to lay the groundwork for the program, it was officially launched in the fall of 1990. Bethlehem's current service-learning program requires students to compile 60 hours of approved, documented service during the four years of high school, grades 9 -12. This unpaid service is to be completed between September of the freshman year and May of the senior year, and may not be performed during regular school hours. The student receives one-half credit upon the satisfactory completion of the approved service hours and the submission of a double-entry reflective journal. Students make the selection of their service sites and activities with the help of their parents, guidance counselor, and, on occasion, the Community Service Coordinator. To aid in the selection process and for a more complete understanding of the program, each student, at the beginning of the freshman year, receives a complete booklet containing step-by-step instructions, and descriptions of each organization approved by the district as a service site. The descriptions include site locations, the name of on-site supervisors, activities available for student involvement, and hours that are appropriate. The procedural portion of the booklet is printed in Spanish, as well as English, to assist those students and parents who are more comfortable in their native language. At the present time, the 1992-93 edition of the Community Service booklet contains descriptions of 121 local agencies and organizations.

Students and parents receive two brief orientation sessions prior to the beginning of the ninth-grade year. These programs are optional and address numerous issues related to the high school curriculum and experience. One of these sessions occurs during the eighth-grade year, and the second, in August, just prior to the start of the freshman year. Early in the ninth-grade year, the coordinator meets with all students, usually as part of an English or social studies class, to fully explore the idea of service-learning and to thoroughly explain the procedures required by the district. Since the guidance counselors are the vital link for the students in the selection and reflection aspects of the program, they discuss service-learning and specific projects with the students individually and in small groups several times during each school year, in accordance with the overall counseling plan. The program coordinator is also available to meet with students and parents upon request. The counselor/student ratio is kept at a level conducive to facilitating such regular meetings, not only for the community service aspect of the curriculum, but also to address the many other concerns of the 1990s student. Currently, the counselor/student ratio in BASD is approximately one to 250.

Students are encouraged to peruse the information booklet and to select their service opportunities carefully. Service sites are located throughout the greater Lehigh Valley in the hope that there will be a convenient location for each student. Transportation to and from the service site is the responsibility of the student and his family. Organizational focuses and learning opportunities are varied to meet all ranges of students' abilities and interests. Students are encouraged to use their service experience to explore a possible career choice, to pursue a personal interest, or to provide a response to an immediate need in the community. Often a news article, television show, conversation with a friend, or a chance encounter will spur enough interest in a topic for a teen to become involved. The student is able to select more than one agency or activity and may be involved in several simultaneously if he so chooses. Students are also urged to select opportunities that complement their other activities. On occasion, an agency or organization will have a specific need that is advertised in the high school announcements for the students to consider, particularly to highlight opportunities that are seasonal or unexpected.

Another option available to Bethlehem students is the pursuit of independent projects. These projects may be of the students' design or may consist of service to an organization not previously approved by the school district but which nonetheless meets the established criteria. Many of the local churches and their outreach activities fall into this category. Another example of this would be a student living outside the area during the summer months and choosing to perform service at that time for an agency located in another community. The independent projects are screened and approved by the Community Service Coordinator on an individual basis.

As part of the selection process, the student must complete an application for each service organization or independent project. This contract must be completed and signed by the participating agency, the student and his parents, the guidance counselor, and the Community

Service Coordinator prior to beginning service time. Once the student has selected an agency, he must abide by the training requirements and other rules of that agency. The organization is responsible for conducting its own orientation and training sessions, for providing appropriate supervision for the students, for keeping accurate time records and submitting them to the school district on a timely basis, and for generally helping the student feel comfortable as part of the organization. Regular communication is necessary between the agencies and the school district coordinator. Agencies are reminded that they not only have the right, but also the responsibility, to interview and accept only those students who will complement the existing staff, and who will further the mission of the organization. The agency must be willing to serve as an extension of learning for that student and to provide corrective guidance when necessary.

During the course of the service experience, each student is expected to maintain a double-entry journal related to his service activities. As part of the English curriculum for ninth and tenth grades, journal writing is explored as a writing technique. Since several purposes are served by journal writing, several styles of journals are taught. When the double - entry journal is presented, the community service experience is used as the teaching example. This lesson will give the students background that will be helpful whenever the service experience is carried out. Journal directions, questions for thought, and a double-entry example are included on an instruction sheet that is attached to each community service application. Throughout the high school years, the student meets with his guidance counselor several times each year for discussion related to many topics, including service-learning. The journals may be discussed at these times. Finally, this journal must be presented to a guidance counselor or a district teacher of the student's choice for perusal at the conclusion of the 60 hours of required service. A signed journal and the verification of service hours is then presented to the guidance counselor for input into the computer grading program. One-half credit is issued with a Pass/Fail grading system.

MOVING FORWARD AND BACKWARD-- EXPANSION AND LEGAL CHALLENGES

As with any educational program, evaluation and revision help make lessons and experiences more meaningful and relevant to the students' lives. The adoption of the journal was a direct result of students' input.

Previously, each student completed an end-of-experience summary sheet after performing the required 60 hours of service. This summary focused on the student's reflection of the total experience after the fact. Many students felt that an on-going commentary would help them see personal growth and the effect of the experience more clearly. The journal provides that opportunity. A second advantage of using a journal is that each student is given another opportunity to enhance his writing skills.

Presently, Bethlehem's program is a self-contained service experience, with discussion and reflection taking place with the guidance counselor. Although some teachers are making regular connections between classwork and service opportunities, much remains to be done to truly integrate service-learning into the high school curriculum. During the next several years, extensive curriculum revision will take place to embed service opportunities into most traditional classroom curricula.

As mentioned earlier, Bethlehem's Community Service requirement was not embraced by all in the community. During the research and public meeting phases of the proposal, a group of approximately 30 persons actively lobbied for the rejection of the program on several grounds. Liability, transportation, time, supervision, and appropriateness of the activities were the most common objections raised during the planning and discussion stages. Although district personnel attempted to satisfactorily address those concerns, two families proceeded with a threatened lawsuit in the fall of 1990, as the program began. The suit, filed in Federal Court, charged that the district was in violation of the children's First, Thirteenth, and Fourteenth Amendment rights. A common cry was that "involuntary servitude" or "slavery" was being forced on the teens of the BASD. The suit further stated that the program would force certain beliefs and standards on those students, and that they might come in contact with people whose criminal backgrounds were not investigated.

In April 1992, the Federal Judge assigned to the case dismissed the charges, ruling the program constitutional. Attorney Michael Levin, representing the school district, said in response to the decision that the judge made three main points: mandatory community service does not violate the students' 13th Amendment rights and does not make them involuntary servants; it does not violate students' First Amendment rights; and it does not violate the parents' rights to raise their children. In addition, the Judge considered community service an educational activity, much like other educational activities in schools. Within days of this ruling, the parents filed an appeal of the decision with the Third Circuit Court of Appeals. Testimony on the appeal was presented in early

November 1992, and a unanimous decision by the Appeals Court in March 1993, upheld the lower court decision. The plaintiffs had indicated that they would pursue this issue to "the Supreme Court if necessary." True to their word, in June 1993, a petition was filed with the United States Supreme Court to review this case against the school district.

CONCLUSION

As the first group to be affected by this requirement is the 1994 graduation class, it is expected that the final legal decision will be reached prior to their graduation in the spring of 1994.

There is no doubt that service-learning is not part of a passing fancy, but is here to stay. How school systems and communities use this idea will vary. Experiential learning techniques and outcomes based educational processes may be the educational innovations that change the entire focus of our educational system. Certainly, service-learning theories and pedagogy have tremendous potential to exert a dramatic impact on the students of the 1990s and beyond. We have reached the crisis point in preparing our youth for the adult roles they will play into the 21st Century. "We must do what America does best: offer more opportunity to all and demand responsibility from all. I challenge a new generation of young Americans to a season of service--to act on your idealism by helping troubled children, keeping company with those in need....In serving, we recognize a simple but powerful truth: We need each other and we must care for each other."[6]

ENDNOTES

1. F. M. Newmann and R. A. Rutter, "A Profile of High School Community Service Programs," *Educational Leadership*, 1986, 64.

2. Millicent Lawton, "Programs to Share $63 Million Through GI Bill for Service," *Education Week*, 17 June 1992, 5.

3. Millicent Lawton, "Maryland Becomes First State to Mandate Student Service," *Education Week*, 5 August 1992, 32.

4. John Backes, "Youth Service: A Profile of Those Who Give More Than They Take," *The High School Journal* (April/May 1992): 234.

5. Lucy Hodges, "Clinton Plays for High Stakes on Service," *Times Magazine*, 12 March 1993, Education Supplement, 12.

6. President Clinton, *Inaugural Address* (Washington, D.C.: January 1993).

Chapter 6

Fairness and Core Knowledge

E. D. Hirsch, Jr.

Overcoming educational injustice is the new frontier in the struggle for civil rights. But it is a more subtle and confusing struggle than the one involving sit-ins and freedom rides. It is a battle of experts and slogans in which ignorant armies clash by night, where it is hard to tell good from evil, true from false. Both the left and the right genuinely desire a good education for every child, and believe that our national well-being hinges on educating all children to their potentials. Yet as American children move from first grade to second, and onward, the academic gap between privileged and disadvantaged children grows wider.[1] In several other countries, the opposite occurs; the learning gap between haves and have-nots grows smaller and in some cases disappears as children move through school.[2] Is America really so different--so "diverse" as compared with other countries--that we cannot learn from them how to give all children an equal chance?

In France, disadvantaged children enter a school system that has explicit requirements for each grade. Each child's progress in meeting those requirements can be monitored in detail, so that extra help can be quickly provided when needed. Under these circumstances, disadvantaged children in France soon catch up. Why are our results so completely different?

© 1991, 1993 E. D. Hirsch, Jr. & Core Knowledge Foundation, 2012-B Morton Drive, Charlottesville, VA 22901

One plausible explanation is that our children enter a public school system which is so fragmented that, in effect, every school or even classroom follows its own sequence of study. Teachers and remedial specialists lack guidelines to the specific knowledge and skills that each child should acquire in each grade. The contrast with French specificity could hardly be more dramatic. The American vagueness about what a child needs to learn in a grade seems more than any other circumstance to cause the learning gap to widen.

Apart from some thoughtful scholars like James Comer and Henry Louis Gates, experts concerned with helping disadvantaged and minority children have badly misunderstood my argument in *Cultural Literacy* (1987) that, in order to overcome unfairness in schooling, it is necessary to impart a universally shared core of knowledge.[3] Only by doing so, I argued, could we surmount the fundamental injustice of educating some children to their potentials while allowing others to stay mired in ignorance and semi-literacy. Many experts jumped to the conclusion that my advocacy of a shared core of knowledge was really a plan to impose WASP culture on people who are entitled to their own. They proposed that *multicultural* education would be a more effective way to avoid educational unfairness. But their response did not really touch upon the fundamental issues that I raised concerning educational justice.

After all, it would be a simple matter to include multicultural school content as part of the specific knowledge that all children should share. The question of multiculturalism is a significant one, and I have written about it elsewhere in an accommodating spirit.[4] But I shall put aside entirely the question of multiculturalism for the space of this essay in order to explain in detail why fairness demands that elementary schools impart a core of shared knowledge--however defined. In the years since 1987, the issue of fairness has become ever more pressing, and new evidence has appeared that strengthens the connection between core knowledge and educational justice.

Educational justice means equality of educational opportunity. It does not mean (since some children are apter and harder-working pupils than others) that all students should get high test scores. Nonetheless, you can tell whether a school offers its students an adequate educational opportunity by looking at its *average* level of achievement. This overall outcome is an accurate index to educational fairness, because the human potential of a schoolful of elementary-school children, whether in the inner city or in the suburbs, does not vary enormously from one school to another. A national school system that is fair will not exhibit huge variations in the average outcomes of its schools. (This observation suggests that fairness is strongly correlated with the overall quality of schools--a point I shall touch on later.)

Adopting this reasoning about the significance of variations in school outcomes, the International Association for the Evaluation of Educational Achievement (IEA) has begun to report on the proportion of schools in a nation that fail to offer students adequate educational opportunity. The fairness of a nation's educational system can be correlated with the IEA's rating of the percentage of a nation's schools whose average outcomes fall below a minimal international standard. On this criterion, the United States, with some 30 percent of its elementary schools below the minimal standard, has, after Italy, the least fair educational system in the developed world.[5]

SOURCES OF UNFAIRNESS IN PUBLIC SCHOOLING

On average, all children will learn relatively well in an effective school. Research data about how to make individual schools effective are inconsistent and complex, but the large-scale evidence about school effectiveness, covering entire school systems across many cultures, is quite unambiguous.[6] Systems that achieve across-the-board effectiveness in early schooling are systems that specify a core of knowledge which children should acquire in each grade of elementary school. All the national systems that are fair by the IEA standard do in fact use this core-knowledge approach. By contrast, *no* national system that fails to use a core knowledge approach has managed to achieve fairness. The cross-correlations between fairness and core knowledge are 100 percent.

Most Americans know that our various school districts have diverse standards for the skills and knowledge that children should acquire in each grade. But few know that the districts rarely mandate specific knowledge for *any* grade. Here is a typical set of district guidelines for history in first grade:

> The child shall be able to identify and explain the significance of national symbols, major holidays, historical figures and events. Identify beliefs and value systems of specific groups. Recognize the effects of science and technology on yesterday's and today's societies.[7]

Let us focus on just one phrase in those guidelines: *Identify beliefs and value systems of specific groups.*

Compare that highly general admonition with the following excerpt from a more specific guide to first-grade history:

> Introduce ancient civilizations and the variety of religions in the world, using maps of the ancient world. Specifics: *Egypt*: King Tutankhamen; Nile; Pyramids; Mummies; Animal Gods; Hieroglyphics. *Babylonia:* Tigris and Euphrates; Hammurabi. *Judaism:* Moses; Passover; Chanukah. *Christianity:* Jesus. *Arabia*: Mohammed; Allah; Islam. *India:* Indus River; Brahma, Hinduism; Buddha. *China:* Yellow River; Confucius; Chinese New Year.[8]

Detailed guidelines provide clarity where there is now confusion. They help by distinguishing between knowledge that is required and knowledge that is merely desirable. By privileging specific concepts and information, explicit guides reduce the total amount of concepts and information that a teacher needs to consider essential. They thereby encourage greater depth and coherence in teaching. On the debit side, detailed guides also tend to generate disagreement--a fact that partly explains why school districts continue to issue vague guidelines. Why be specific when vagueness will avoid controversy?

But against this bureaucratic convenience stands the great value of highly detailed standards to disadvantaged students and those who try to remedy their educational deficiencies. Explicit guides enable tutors to focus on the specific knowledge that students need in order to attain grade level. Absent such specific guides, disadvantaged students and their tutors in this country play a game whose rules are never clearly defined. Soon the unlucky are consigned to slow tracks from which they can never enter the mainstream of learning or of society.

By contrast, tutors in West Germany, having the benefit of detailed guidelines, are able to bring the highly disadvantaged offspring of Turkish "guest workers" up to grade level, despite the enormous educational handicaps of Turkish children in Germany.[9] In all of the core-knowledge systems of the world, the standard method of remediation is to diagnose the knowledge and skills that each child lacks, according to detailed grade-by-grade standards, and then focus on those specifics. This process of remediation begins in first grade and continues at need in subsequent years, enabling every normal child to be kept at grade level.

THE WIDENING GAP AND THE 4TH-GRADE SLUMP

While the IEA report discloses that the American system is unfair to the thirty percent of students who attend ineffective schools, additional evidence of another kind shows that our system is universally unfair to disadvantaged students. In the United States, the gap between academic haves and have-nots grows wider in each successive early grade, until, by fourth grade, it is often unbridgeable.

This tragic process currently seems inexorable. The longitudinal researches of Loban in the 1960s (replicated by Chall in the 1980s) tracked the acquired learning abilities of cohorts of disadvantaged and advantaged students as they moved from grade one to grade four and beyond.[10] To grasp the results of this research, imagine a graph with the vertical representing learning ability and the horizontal representing time. The lines on the graph that represent the median abilities of the two groups over time will then look like a V that is turned about 45 degrees to the right, with the narrow end at kindergarten. Loban and Chall show that a small educational disadvantage in kindergarten normally becomes a huge learning gap by grade four, a result that unfortunately applies even to graduates of Head Start.[11]

But this disheartening characteristic of American schools seems less than inevitable when we look at the successes of Swedish, German and French schools in teaching third-world and other disadvantaged students.[12] As children progress through those systems, the gap between haves and have-nots grows narrower rather than expands! The main reason these other systems are fairer to disadvantaged students is that they are able to compensate for the snowball effect of background knowledge upon early learning--a snowball effect that allows a small knowledge difference in kindergarten to become a huge gap in learning ability within a few years.

For most young children, new knowledge expands exponentially, as anyone can testify who has watched a three-year-old acquire new words and build new knowledge upon old. The words that children hear in school are like so many snowflakes falling on the school ground. (To continue the snowball metaphor, we would need to picture the children rolling among these flakes like so many snowballs!) Disadvantaged children may hear the words, but they do not pick up the meanings, whereas children who have already accumulated a covering of knowledge and vocabulary will be picking up knowledge rapidly. As their academic snowball grows, so does their ability to accumulate still more knowledge --in strong contrast to disadvantaged students whose initially meager learning abilities get smaller and smaller by comparison, humiliating them still further and destroying their motivation. *This continual widening of the learning gap cannot be halted unless schools make a systematic effort to build up the specific background knowledge that disadvantaged children need.*

BEING UNFAIR TO NEWCOMERS

What makes our schools unfair, then, is that some students are learning less than others because of systematic shortcomings in their schooling rather than because of their own innate lack of academic ability. This injustice arises from the systematic failure of our schools to teach all children the knowledge they need in order to understand what the next grade has to offer. How can any teacher be sure that a child is ready to learn the lessons of third grade, if we don't define explicitly what second-graders ought to know? How can a third-grade teacher reach all children in a class when some of them lack the necessary building blocks? Probably one of the most important tasks of early education is to insure that all children have the background knowledge they need at each stage of schooling. Yet our system currently leaves that supremely important job to the vagaries of individual districts, schools, and, very often, individual classrooms.

It is a fundamental injustice that what American children learn in school should be determined by whether their homes have given them the background knowledge they need for academic work. A nation's public schools have a duty to educate all students to their potentials. A disadvantaged child's initial lack of preparation is not a mere given that the school is powerless to change; it is a challenge that some schools in the world are meeting and which all our schools could rise to if we launched a serious effort to overcome the incoherence of our system regarding the content of elementary education.

As an illustration of that incoherence, consider the plight of Jane in Calhoun County. In school A, first-grade teachers have deferred all world history until grade four, but in school B, in the same district, first graders are learning about ancient Egypt. Leaving school A after first grade, Jane goes to school B where the other children had studied Egypt in the previous year. The new teacher's references to the Nile, the Pyramids, and hieroglyphics simply mystify her, and fail to convey the *new* information that the allusions to ancient Egypt were meant to impart. Multiply that day's failure of comprehension by many others in Jane's new environment, and then multiply those by further comprehension failures that will accrue because of the initial failures of uptake, and we begin to see why Jane is not flourishing in her new school.

Still greater handicaps are inflicted on a newcomer who must go to a new school in a totally different part of the country. Some of the schools around metropolitan Washington and in parts of Florida, California, and elsewhere now report that forty percent of their students are newcomers.[13] When one of these new children happens to be a disadvantaged child (as is disproportionately the case in our society, because low wage earners are the most frequent movers), the inherent handicaps of being a newcomer in an American school are greatly exacerbated. It is again the disadvantaged who suffer most from the structural incoherences of the American educational system.

RESISTING A UNIVERSAL CORE SEQUENCE

It will not surprise the reader to be told that the only and obvious antidote to incoherence in school content is to reach agreement on a grade-by-grade core of content for elementary school. The core need not take up more than 50 percent of total classroom time, leaving plenty of room for local variation and imaginative approaches. But it is exceedingly difficult to reach agreement about school content in the United States. The practical hurdles are no doubt great, but the top priority in surmounting them must be to spread awareness of the problem itself and to resist attempts to deny its existence. The direct solution to the educational problem--defining a specific and universally-accepted core of knowledge--goes so much against the American grain that experts have developed astonishingly resourceful techniques of avoidance to resist the idea of core-knowledge standards. But the public needs to recognize these denials for the evasions they are.

Here, by way of example, are a few characteristic arguments or slogans that experts use to deny the need for a core of universal content standards.

We already have an informal core-knowledge system in the United States, determined by the widespread use of just a few textbooks.

We do not need to emphasize *particular* content at all. Knowledge is changing and increasing so rapidly that the best approach is to teach children *how* to learn.

There is a danger that standardization of content would be imposed by the Federal government and would open the way to Federal control of education.

We have educated children reasonably well in the past without using a core of universal content standards.

It is illegitimate to compare the United States with other countries, which are in every case far less diverse than we are.

A common core of knowledge would obliterate the distinctive characteristics of American localities, and make schools in to cookie cutters that turn out the same product everywhere.

Elsewhere, I have responded to each of these highly dubious expressions of resistance to change, none of which can stand up to detailed examination.[14] I haven't the space to repeat that exercise here, and in any case, there are straws in the wind that indicate a growing recognition of the need to define core knowledge. Various professional groups such as the National Councils of Teachers of Mathematics, of Science, and of Social Studies have passed resolutions committing their organizations to develop guidelines for their particular subject matters. A few states have created or resolved to create grade-by-grade core curricula for their schools.

These recent moves by a few states are promising insofar as they begin to define, however vaguely, a definite sequence for elementary-school content. With luck, all fifty states will someday agree with each other about a common core sequence. Until such time, however, which may be far-off, it is essential that *at least at the school level,* a core of shared knowledge be defined in a specific, sequenced way, if a school is to achieve excellence and fairness.

My co-workers and I at the Core Knowledge Foundation, while advocating the teaching of a sequence of specific knowledge, also realize that it is not feasible, nor necessarily desirable, to wait for a top-down consensus on what this knowledge should be. Accordingly, the Foundation has undertaken an effort that combines scholarly research with grassroots experience to develop a working consensus upon a specific sequence for grades one through six. This working consensus, known as the *Core Knowledge Sequence for Grades 1-6,* is a planned progression of specific knowledge in history, geography, mathematics, science, language arts, and fine arts. The *Core Knowledge Sequence* does not presume to stipulate *everything* American schoolchildren should know. Rather, it represents a working agreement regarding the *minimum* knowledge that children should acquire in grades one through six. The *Sequence* is meant to comprise about 50 percent of a school's curriculum, thus leaving ample room for local requirements and emphases.

The content of the *Core Knowledge Sequence* is the result of four years of research, debate, and consultation with parents, teachers, scientists, professional curriculum organizations, experts on America's multicultural traditions, and the curricula of other countries with proven success in elementary education. The *Sequence* represents a consensus of many diverse groups and interests: a provisional version was debated, modified, and finally ratified by a group of about 100 persons representing diverse areas and constituencies at a conference in March 1990. The *Sequence* is part of an ongoing process that we keep democratic and grounded in experience by involving many teachers in schools around the nation. As these teachers use the *Sequence,* they are asked to draw upon their classroom experience to help determine revisions of the *Sequence.*[15] Other revisions of the Sequence are based upon suggestions from the Foundation's technical and multicultural advisors.

We do not claim that the specific grade-by-grade guidelines in the *Core Knowledge Sequence* are better than some other well-thought-out core: no specific guidelines could possibly constitute the Platonic ideal. But, in order to offer something useful, and to get beyond talk to practice, we created the best specific guidelines we could.

The *Core Knowledge Sequence,* and publication of a series of resource books based on the *Sequence,*[16] are two of the initial moves of a campaign to start a discussion of core knowledge for the early grades. Our hope is that even if the Foundation's model core sequence is not the one that will be finally accepted nationwide, its mere existence will dramatize the need for a specific core in grade school. We also hope it will help insure that if ever there is any officially accepted core, it will be as effective as the *Core Knowledge Sequence* has already shown itself to be.

At this time, the curricular recommendations of the *Core Knowledge Sequence* have been accepted, wholly or in part, at more than fifty elementary schools around the nation. (In the state of Pennsylvania, one school in Philadelphia has started out by integrating Core Knowledge content into grades K-2, while the Wilkes-Barre Area School District has made long and careful investigations of the *Core Knowledge Sequence,* and is in the process of considering implementation in the fall of 1993.) A few schools that are well along in implementing Core Knowledge-- schools in Texas (San Antonio), New York (South Bronx), Indiana (Richmond), and Florida (Ft. Myers)--are reporting improved test scores, higher attendance rates, tremendous student enthusiasm, and greatly increased professional collaboration among teachers who, for once, share some solid, sequenced, clearly defined content guidelines.

CONCLUSION: FAIRNESS AND EXCELLENCE

In this brief essay I have tried to show concisely how a lack of agreement on a specific core of content in early grades is an insuperable barrier to fairness in American schools. My arguments (generally accepted by educational experts outside the United States) have not depended on any particular conception of what that content should be. Any sensible version of core content would be about as effective as any other sensible one for developing a fair system. I want to conclude by observing that there is a strong connection between the use of core knowledge and the achievement of excellence in early education. It is highly significant that core-knowledge countries have the best fairness scores and the best achievement scores in early grades.

Some of the underlying reasons for these favorable results are similar to those I have already traced. An educational arrangement that enables all children to learn at grade level will cause classrooms to be more lively and conducive to learning. When all children have the background knowledge they need for understanding new material, the teacher need spend far less time in boring review and special treatment of those who are behind. Moreover, when teachers share specific, well-defined curricular goals, they can address those goals cooperatively as a community, and cooperate to make sure that each child learns certain things in each grade as part of the gradual, multi-year process of education. In such classrooms, in such schools, everybody learns more.

And, just as specific guidelines help a tutor diagnose what a disadvantaged child needs, so do they help teachers diagnose an *advantaged* child's academic progress. A teacher who knows exactly what the essentials are is in a position to demand those essentials from all students. Students, in turn, are able to understand what is expected of them, knowing that the teacher will be able to find out whether they have met those expectations. In short, the guidelines that permit accurate diagnosis also permit genuine accountability for everyone--the child, the teacher, the school, the district, the state. Definite expectations and clear accountability focus everyone's performance. They help concentrate the mind.

In the last IEA report on science achievement (1988), two nations of Western Europe were still using the local-choice system for determining school content. These were England and Holland. The other developed nations of Europe and Asia that were analyzed in the report were all core-knowledge countries. The percentage of schools that fell below the minimal standard in the best core-knowledge countries ranged between one and five percent. By contrast, the fairness ratings for Holland and England were respectively 16 percent and 19 percent.[17] (Remember, the fairness score for the United States was 30 percent of schools below standard.) Because of findings like these, England recently decided to switch to a core-knowledge system. That left Holland. Recently I learned that the Dutch have now decided to switch to a core-knowledge system.

To my mind, the only half-way persuasive argument left to American opponents of core knowledge is the idea that America is a much more diverse nation than all those other countries. But if the analyses of this essay are right, a diverse country has greater need of a core-knowledge system than does a homogeneous one--for some of the same reasons that a disadvantaged child has greater need of it than an advantaged child. The tired idea of American exceptionalism seems increasingly outmoded in the modern world, where the educational needs of young children are everywhere very much the same. As I have learned from studying the curricula of Bavaria, France, Japan, and Sweden, there are far more similarities than differences in the most effective educational systems of the developed world.

Our persistence in following a purely local-choice arrangement for early education has created a conflict between traditional American attitudes and modern educational realities. Our sentimental attachment to American exceptionalism, our resistance to change when confronted with rising educational standards, are not different in principle from the resistance to change exhibited by Soviet and Chinese bureaucrats. Stubborn traditions may succeed in perpetuating themselves through powerful bureaucracies, but a persistence in old ways in the face of new circumstances cannot succeed in creating a better life for the people of a nation. In a conflict between outmoded theories and new historical realities, the reality principle may be tragically evaded, but it cannot be defeated.

ENDNOTES

1. W. Loban, *Language Ability: Grades Seven, Eight, and Nine*, Project 1131, ed. T.G. Stricht and others, eds. (Berkely, California: University of California, March 1964); Human Resources Research Organization, *Adding and Reading: A Developmental Model* (Alexandria, VA: Human Resources Research Organization, 1974); J.S. Chall, *Families and Literacy, Final Report to the National Institute of Education*, privately printed, 1982; and J.S. Chall and others, eds., *The Reading Crisis: Why Poor Children Fall Behind* (Cambridge, MA: Harvard University Press, 1990).

2. S. Boulot and D. Boyzon-Fradet, *Les Immigres Et L'ecole: Une Course D'obstacles*, Paris: privately printed, 1988, 54-58; and Centre for Educational Research and Innovation, *Immigrants' Children At School* (Paris: Organization for Economic Cooperation and Development, 1987), 178-259.

3. James Comer, "Ignorance Is Not Bliss," *Parents Magazine*, March 1991, 193.

4. E. D. Hirsch, Jr., "Towards a Centrist Curriculum: Two Kinds of Multiculturalism in Elementary School" (Charlottesville, VA: Core Knowledge Foundation, n.d.).

5. International Association for the Evaluation of Educational Achievement, *Science Achievement in Seventeen Countries: A Preliminary Report* (Elmsford, NY: Pergamon Press, 1988), 5 and 42.

6. R. Kyle and others, eds., *Reaching for Excellence: An Effective Schools Sourcebook* (Washington, D.C.: Government Printing Office, May 1985); and S.C. Purkey and M.S. Smith, "Effective Schools: A Review," *The Elementary School Journal* 83 (n.d.): 427-542.

7. Florida Department of Education, "Lee County District Guidelines" (Tallahasse, FL: Florida Department of Education, 1991).

8. Core Knowledge Foundation, *Core Knowledge Sequence* (Charlottesville, VA: Core Knowledge Foundation, n.d.).

9. *Amtsblatt des Bayerischen Staatministeriums fur Untericht und Kultur, Sondernummer 20, Einfuhrung des Lehrplans fur die Bayerische Grundschulen*, Munich,: privately printed, 1981.

10. W. Loban, *Language Ability*, ed. Sticht and others, eds.; Human Resources Research Organization, *Adding and Reading: A Developmental Model*; Chall, *Families and Literacy, Final Report to the National Institute of Education*; and Chall and others, eds., *The Reading Crisis: Why Poor Children Fall Behind*.

11. Constance Holden, "Head Start Enters Adulthood," *Science* 247 (23 March 1990).

12. Centre for Educational Research and Innovation, *Immigrants' Children At School*.

13. Marylou Tousignant, "Area Schools Struggle with Increasing Student Turnover," *Washington Post*, 20 May 1991, 1.

14. Core Knowledge Foundation, "Common Misconceptions About Core Knowledge" (Charlottesville, VA: Core Knowledge Foundation, n.d.).

15. "Three Oaks School," *Education Week*, 20 November 1991; *Wall Street Journal*, 6 September 1991; and *Life Magazine*, September 1991.

16. E.D. Hirsch, Jr., *What Your First [Through Sixth] Grader Needs to Know* (New York, NY: Doubleday, n.d.).

17. International Association for the Evaluation of Educational Achievement, *Science Achievement in Seventeen Countries*, 42.

Chapter 7

Heroes and Heroines and Children Belong Together

Dennis Denenberg

THE DILEMMA

Ask almost any six or seven year old child to describe a stegosaurus, and you will most likely hear a complete and accurate description, including the correct spelling of the creature's name. By the way, you'll also have to listen to details about tyrannosaurus rex, because kids love that ferocious beast.

Ask that same child who "Old Joe Camel" is, and after some giggles, you will hear a fairly precise accounting of not only his appearance, but also the product he represents. In fact, according to research published in the December 1991, *Journal of the American Medical Association* and reported in major news magazines,[1] kids can identify that commercial symbol as readily as they recognize Mickey Mouse! Remember, cigarette commercials are even banned from television. Interesting too is another portion of that study about teenage smokers, a third of whom select that brand compared with less than ten percent of the over 21 year old smokers making the same choice.

Now ask that child a third question: Who is Thomas Jefferson? You will probably receive a blank stare and an "I don't know" response. You might hear an amusing guess, such as "I think he's the man who brings our mail," or maybe a defensive reply: "We didn't learn about him." But the chance that you'll hear any accurate information about the author of our Declaration of Independence is quite remote.

Why? Because neither in our schools nor in our homes do children learn about the great men and women who have made positive contributions to our nation and our world. We teach dinosaurs "ad nauseam" in the elementary grades because they arouse kids' imaginations. Meanwhile, the all-pervasive advertising industry uses cartoons to capture kids' hearts and minds. But we ignore the many wonderful real people-- HEROES--from whom children could learn so much.

HEROES

A hero is an individual who can serve as an example. He has the ability to persevere, to overcome the hurdles which impede others' lives. While this intangible quality of greatness appears almost magical, it is indeed most human. And it is precisely because of that humanness that some individuals attain heroic statue. They are of us, but are clearly different.

We look to heroes and heroines for inspiration. Through their achievements we see humankind more positively. They make us feel good. They make us feel proud. For some of us they become definite role models, and our lives follow a different direction because of their influence. For others, while the effect may be less dramatic, it is of no less import, for these heroes make us think in new ways. Their successes and failures lead us to ponder our own actions and inactions. By learning about their lives, our lives become enriched.

Molly Pitcher saw what had to be done and did it. Women had a defined role in the war; they were a vital support to the fighting colonials. But when her husband was wounded, and the cannon needed to be fired, she knew what she had to do. Molly Pitcher was, and is, a heroine, and her story deserves to be told and retold. Neither a great statesman or soldier, she was an ordinary person who performed an extraordinary deed.

Michelangelo spent a lifetime at his craft, leaving the world a legacy of magnificent paintings and sculptures. His hard work was a daily reaffirmation in his belief of a human's creative potential. Through toil, he produced artistic monuments which have continued to inspire generations.

This world has had (and still has) many Molly Pitchers and Michelangeloes, people who set examples which inspire others. Some had only a fleeting moment of glory in a rather normal life, but oh, what a moment. Others led a life of longer-lasting glory and had a more sustained impact on humankind. All were individuals who through their achievements made positive contributions.

Where are the heroines and heroes for children today? They are everywhere! They are the figures from our past, some in the historical limelight, others still in the shadows. They are the men and women of the present, struggling to overcome personal and societal problems to build a better world.

Indeed they are everywhere, but most children know so very few of them. Quite simply, in our schools and in our homes we have removed these great people from our focus. They have become "persona non grata" instead of persons of importance. Where at one time nearly every American classroom had portraits of Washington and Lincoln gazing down upon the children, now Mickey Mouse and Snoopy hold court. The greats are still around; they have merely been removed from everyone's view.

YESTERDAY

"Once upon a time..." kids had heroes, and lots of them. Some of these great individuals were real (Lincoln, et.al.); others were legendary (such as Paul Bunyan and Casey Jones); still others like Hercules were of a different realm altogether. Most of them were male and white, as if heroics somehow knew gender and racial lines of distinction. Frequently, kids pretended to be these heroes or at the very least their followers. Since not every boy could be King Arthur, the others could be knights of the Round Table. Yes, it was clearly better to be the King, but even as a knight, one got to slay a dragon now and then. All--kings and knights-- were capable of great deeds!

These heroes seemed to be everywhere. They were part of the curriculum, so textbooks and other reading materials (even the classic comic books) provided details of their adventures. The movies portrayed them in action, adding an exciting visual dimension not found in the books or classroom. Heroes truly came alive for kids, who not only learned about them but, often, learned values from them.

Whether or not "the Father of Our Country" ever did chop down a cherry tree is not a question of significant historical importance. What is telling is that for generations the story helped children understand the meaning of honesty. Even heroes had faults, but they were moral enough to admit their errors.

The inclusion of heroes in schools served dual purposes. In addition to learning about specific great individuals, students also were exposed to the ethical nature of those persons. The presence of heroes provided a focus for children's dreams and wishes, and those heroes were cloaked in mantles of virtuous behavior.

In some instances, those deeds were even accomplished by children. Who has not marveled at the brilliant accomplishments of that most famous of child prodigies, Wolfgang Amadeus Mozart? George Westinghouse began his successful career as an inventor and entrepreneur at the age of 12. For the next 56 years until his death at age 68, he continued building a legacy based on hard work, creativity, and a desire to improve people's lives. Indeed, heroes for children were real children of achievement.

TODAY

As the advertising industry grew, however, heroes became displaced persons and virtually disappeared from children's views. Through the wonders of the mass media, a whole new array of characters became a daily part of American culture. Cartoon creatures and company advertising mascots existed for many decades, but not until the advent of megacommunications did they intrude into everyone's lives in a seemingly unending manner. Billboards, print ads, television and radio programs, commercials, videotapes, and many other avenues provide ads "ad infinitum." Even while relaxing on the beach, one's attention is pulled skyward to read the fly-by advertisements. Mickey Mouse and his companions, Charlie Brown and his associates (especially his dog), and countless other purveyors of the popular culture are everywhere today.

The issue is not so much that they have joined the ranks of known figures, it is rather that they have totally replaced real heroes for children. Today the role models are often whatever the latest commercial fad creatures happen to be. Once the new character catches the public's attention, the merchandising machine marches on. The tee shirts, buttons, books, book bags, greeting cards, games and toys, trading cards, movies, and of course, television series all follow in rapid succession. The presence of the latest sensation dominates the child's world. Consciousness leads to conversation demanding the newest marketable item bearing the creature's image. And everywhere--in the child's mind, in the home, and in the classroom--the character assumes a new status of heroic proportions. It's out with Ben Franklin entirely; here comes the Mouse!

En masse the animated beings invade--everywhere into the classroom and the school. Out go the pictures of Washington and Lincoln (except in February for a two-week period) to make room for cutouts of Donald and Goofy. This transformation occurs not because teachers think the latter are more significant than the two presidents; rather, it is most frequently done under the guise of "good teaching." Many elementary teachers genuinely believe the furry fad figures motivate and inspire kids. Because the child already recognizes Mickey from his numerous media appearances, those special ears make the child feel comfortable. An instantly friendly, known climate for learning is established, as familiar faces and figures abound to evoke feelings of security in the child. So teachers use the Mouse and his many compatriots on bulletin boards and every conceivable type of instructional resource. In the name of motivation, cartoon characters take over many classrooms.

Instead of seeing displays of real people or even time-tested legendary heroes, kids primarily see and experience the latest kid-culture fad hero. In the 1980s and 1990s one could guess the correct year simply by entering a typical elementary school, visiting the classrooms, and identifying the creatures that dominated the display areas. Had the students been present, many of their personal belongings--tee shirts, notebooks, book bags, pencils, and occasional lunchbox--would most certainly have matched the bulletin boards. So, not only was the Mouse already there to welcome the kids to school, he often came along with them. There simply was no escaping the influence and impact of commercialism.

Do you remember the movie about Roger Rabbit? In it, there was an entire city populated by cartoon characters--they co-existed with humans, and each was able to enter and leave the other's realm whenever and wherever they chose. Farfetched, wasn't it?

But it really isn't that far off the mark, is it? Children today are so surrounded by cartoon fad figures that indeed they enter and leave cartoonland every day. It is possible they awake to see Garfield emblazoned on their pillowcases, drink their morning juice from a Little Mermaid glass, grab their Snoopy lunch pail, and leave for school, wearing, of course, their Batman shirt. Once in their fourth grade classroom, they will be surrounded by these same images, staring at them from bulletin boards, ceiling mobiles, and fellow classmates' clothing. Assorted worksheets and stickers will carry the familiar fad faces too.

Following school, they'll return home, where most likely bedroom posters will carry the same theme. With any luck (their opinion), tonight's rented video might be the latest Turtle adventure! It's their world, and welcome to it!

STRIVING FOR BALANCE

Should the fad figures be expelled from school and the home? No, such a drastic step is neither realistic nor desirable. Undoubtedly, the furry creatures do at times motivate students to perform well. For instance, Barney's footprint stamped on a child's perfect (or near perfect) math study sheet may be the reward sought eagerly by the youngster. But the comic characters must be moved to the backseat, and the real heroes and heroines should move to the front and start driving. Let Jonas Salk, the discoverer of the polio vaccine, be given attention and space in the classroom instead of being relegated to a token five minute portion in a health lesson. He, not some purple dinosaur, should be prominently displayed.

Envision this issue of cartoon versus real figures as a continuum. In most classrooms, all of the displays and instructional techniques fall at the cartoon end; the emphasis is clearly skewed in favor of fads. What is needed at the very least is a balance; what is desirable is a skewing toward the great people's end of the continuum.

The balance between commercially-derived figures and real people of significance is easy to achieve in some cases. For example, when Mickey Mouse is used in the classroom, give credit to the genius who created him. Walt Disney's picture should be alongside his famous drawing. His life story can be just as inspirational, or even more so, than any of the exploits in his cartoons. Mr. Disney's triumphs and failures, and most of all his perseverance, are worthy of attention and emulation.

The over-presence of fantasy characters in our schools and homes contributes to a confusion for our children and adolescents about the value of real-life human accomplishments. It is not surprising that when in 1991, a Pennsylvania school district in the Harrisburg area asked its fifth to twelfth graders to name people they most admired, the teenagers chose rock stars, athletes, and television personalities, people who often seem to be larger than life. Other than Nelson Mandela, no famous people from any other field of endeavor were mentioned. No great artists, inventors, humanitarians, political leaders, composers, scientists, doctors--none were mentioned by the 1,150 students.

It is readily apparent that as elementary-aged children grow up, their attention is turned from fad creatures to fad people. Bedroom posters of the latest animation figure suddenly become life-size posters of sports, music, or movie stars. These human idols are in many instances even less desirable than the cartoon icons were!

There are real people to whom kids can turn for role models. Hard work is what makes productive people succeed. Let children learn about the creative spark humans possess, so they begin to understand that it is individuals who make a difference. If Mickey is used as the motivator, surely Mr. Disney is the real hero who ought to be given recognition too. Balancing the message requires at least equal time, space, and effort between the cartoon and the cartoonist. It is the human, not the animation, which ought to be the focus in classrooms and in homes.

A New Approach

Important individuals will be quite different from those prominently referred to before the 1960s. The heroic people we recognize today as great are of every race and ethnic origin and of either gender. No longer are heroes only white and male. The women and men who shaped this nation and the world, but who were not given a fair shake because of earlier historical shortsightedness, should now be given their day in the sun--and in the schools. Their presence is needed in classrooms to teach and to inspire. They, not the mice, cats, and dogs, should be the role models for tomorrow's leaders. Remember the child with the near-perfect math paper? Build a situation so that the student wants a Sally Ride sticker (or the letters "SR" stamped on the paper) instead of a dinosaur print. Good mathematicians can become good scientists and even astronauts; they cannot become extinct animals! Sally Ride, not Barney, can show children what hard work and dedication can achieve for real people, so it is most fitting to reward achievement in her name. She is only one of the many new heroes and heroines waiting in the wings.

Enlivening classrooms and curriculum materials with great people does not mean overwhelming children with them. Very little, if anything, is achieved by the good intentioned teacher who displays pictures of all the presidents. The outstanding men and women who never reached that high office or who earned distinction in other fields are overlooked. "Less is more" is clearly a guideline to follow in moving toward the continuum's hero/heroine end. Key individuals representing all types of heroic deeds should be employed judiciously throughout the year. By focusing on a limited number and by planning carefully their appearance and reappearances, a teacher can guarantee that these individuals will have an impact.

Think of the impression on young minds if teachers and principals begin using real heroes regularly in the school's curriculum. Currently, it takes a special day (usually a day off from school) to honor the few key people still receiving recognition. Martin Luther King, Jr.'s photos appear in mid-January; at the end of the month, they are removed and replaced by the old dynamic duo of Washington and Lincoln just in time for Presidents' Day. Sometimes, a teacher will make a sincere attempt during "Women in History" week to spotlight famous females. But these efforts are too transitory and too limited to achieve any lasting effect--especially when they are compared to the continuing and permanent presence of fad figures. The effort to inspire and motivate through great people must be ongoing and lasting if indeed it is going to influence children's thinking.

NATIONAL SUPPORT

Encouraging signs of the re-emergence of heroes and heroines are already appearing, as some historians present strong arguments favoring the inclusion of more history in the school curriculum. For example, the Bradley Commission on History in Schools has asserted:

> ...Well-taught, history and biography are naturally engaging to students by speaking to their individuality, to their possibilities for choice, and to their desire to control their lives...[2]

> Young children are fascinated by heroes, amazing deeds, fantastic tales, and stories of extraordinary feats and locales. History offers a wide range of materials to delight and engage the young learner.[3]

The *History-Social Science Framework for California Public Schools, Kindergarten Through Grade Twelve* strongly endorses the inclusion of heroes/heroines in children's studies:

> To understand the common memories that create a sense of community and continuity among people, children should learn about the classic legends, folktales, tall tales, and hero stories of their community and nation....Children should listen to biographies of the nation's heroes and of those who took the risk of new and

controversial ideas and opened new opportunities for many. Such stories convey to the children valuable insights in the history of their nation and its people;....[4]

Aimed at reshaping social studies education in our largest state, that important curriculum document sprang from ideas espoused by such individuals as E. D. Hirsch, Jr., and Diane Ravitch. Their thinking and writings have created a needed dialogue over the issue of more meaningful content in elementary schools.

In his 1987 best-seller, *Cultural Literacy: What Every American Needs to Know*, Hirsch develops his major premise that all citizens should share a common core of cultural information to enable communication and progress to occur.[5] To be "culturally literate" means to be familiar with a body of knowledge seen as important to the development of America and for its continuation. Hirsch argues that the disadvantaged children are particularly hurt by lacking fundamental background knowledge. "The American vagueness about what a child needs to learn in a grade seems more than any other circumstance to cause the learning gap [between privileged and disadvantaged children] to widen."[6] Today, the newly established Core Knowledge Foundation promotes the establishment of a "core knowledge" curriculum in elementary schools. A defined sequence for grades one through six has been developed, and a series of resource guidebooks (*What Your First [Second, Third, etc.] Grader Needs to Know*, has been written. "Model" core knowledge schools have been started in several states, with Florida and Texas in the forefront. While critics have sometimes labeled the effort as a form of "Trivial Pursuit," Hirsch clearly does not advocate memorizing endless lists of facts. "Teachers in Core Knowledge schools bring the knowledge to life in active creative ways."[7]

Hirsch's work and emphasis on engaging the young learner with meaningful content is closely related to Diane Ravitch's philosophy. In extensive writings, she has severely criticized the emptiness of the elementary school curriculum, especially in the so-called expanding environment framework of kindergarten through grade three social studies teaching.

This curriculum of "me, my family, my school, my community" now dominates the early grades in American public education....It contains no mythology, legends, biographies, hero tales, or great events in the life of this nation or any other. It is *tot sociology*. (emphasis added)[8]

Ravitch, along with Charlotte Crabtree, were the principal writers of the California Framework, which clearly promotes the inclusion of heroes into the curriculum at all grade levels.

One textbook company, Houghton-Mifflin, has taken the ideas found in the California Framework and based a new elementary social studies textbook series on them.[9] This comprehensive work incorporates great men and women into every grade level, beginning with kindergarten.

A more revolutionary approach aimed solely at the upper elementary grade (4, 5, and 6) is *A History of Us*, a ten volume set by Joy Hakim.[10] It restores the story to hi*story* without sacrificing the need for well researched facts. Real people are brought to life as America's story is told, and heroes again reappear in social studies instruction.

In addition, to help teachers and parents in promoting real heroes, more children's books are being published about the lives of famous people. *Hooray for Heroes! Books and Activities Kids Will Want to Share with Parents and Teachers*[11] provides over one hundred clever, hands-on activities and comprehensive age-appropriate lists of biographies for children. Thousands of titles are organized so kids and adults can easily find books about inventors, humanitarians, artists, and so on, and then can use the activities to become actively involved with their heroes and heroines. Likewise, *Toward A Human Curriculum: A Guide to Returning Great People to Classrooms and Homes* is a brief practical guide to help make heroes come alive.[12]

PENNSYLVANIA SUPPORT

Are any of the national efforts taking hold in Pennsylvania? With the current drift in curriculum reform caused by the Outcomes Based Education debate, it is difficult to answer that question; however, some observations can be offered.

Very few schools in the Commonwealth are involved in the Core Knowledge program. The Richmond School in Philadelphia has some primary grade teachers incorporating its ideas into daily lessons. One very positive step is the increased use of authentic literature instead of basals at the school.

Clearly, more elementary schools are moving toward some variation of a "whole language" program, and one of the assets of that approach is the use of quality reading materials, including biographies and historical fiction. Increased interaction with good books, especially the growing number of well-written stories of famous men and women, will help focus children's attention on positive role models.

There is also growing state-wide membership in the National Council of History Education, Inc. (the successor to the Bradley Commission). Its monthly newsletter regularly addresses the need for more content dealing with real heroes, so ideas are being disseminated.

Some districts engaged in social studies curriculum revision have been reviewing the Hakim series, and other districts planning on the more standard textbook approach have expressed interest in the Houghton-Mifflin texts. All or part of the K through 8 social studies series have been adopted by these districts: Ambridge Area, Bristol-Borough, Coatesville Area, East Penn, Hatboro-Horsham, Millcreek Township, Neshaminy, Palisades, Pennridge, and Pennsbury, and some individual schools in the Philadelphia School District. Nevertheless, the recent curriculum regulation revision outcome-based-education (OBE) plans, as well as difficult financial problems, have slowed many districts in committing resources to new materials.

CAN IT BE DONE?

Can children--young children, "older" children, teenagers--learn all this "stuff," this "core knowledge," all these heroes and heroines? The answer is an unqualified *YES*--if we who teach them in schools and in homes spend as much time making learning about heroes as interesting and exciting as we make learning about dinosaurs.

Commitment is needed first if changes are to be made, and that commitment is quite simply the recognition that most children are far more capable of learning enriching content than what we give them credit for! Someone puzzled by that statement need only count the number of questions kids ask in one day! They are eager to learn, and every good teacher and parent knows it. If students are actively and creatively engaged in their learning, any content can be taught. Brachisaurous and its companions can give way to Albert Schweitzer, Harriet Tubman, Beethoven, and on and on.

And, more importantly, Thomas Edison, Elizabeth Blackwell, Peary and Henson, and so many others can take the places of Mickey, Snoopy, Barney, et. al. The *real* Leonardo, not his turtle namesake, should be our focus.

Why focus on great women and men as part of our necessary knowledge base? Kids need role models, that's why. The presence of people of achievement is needed once again in today's helter-skelter world and, especially, in the lives of children and young people. Parents and teachers working together through creative teaching can make a difference by exposing children to these role models. The strategy to move away from cartoon fads and toward real heroes is obviously not a quick fix for society's ills, nor is it one the results from which can be easily measured. But it is a common sense, "feels good" notion that can help change the focus in schools and homes.

Heroines and heroes and children belong together.

ENDNOTES

1. Geoffrey Cowley, "I'd Toddle a Mile for a Camel," *Newsweek*, 23 December 1991, 70; *Time Magazine*, 23 December 1991; *Business Week*, 23 December 1991; and *Science News*, 14 December 1991.

2. Bradely Commission on History in Schools, *Building a History Curriculum: Guidelines for Teaching History in Schools* (Indianapolis, IN: Educational Excellence Network, 1988), 5.

3. Ibid., 16.

4. History-Social Science Curriculum Framework Criteria Committee, *History-Social Science Framework for California Public Schools, Kindergarten Through Grade Twelve* (Sacramento, CA: State Department of Education, 1988), 43.

5. E. D. Hirsch, Jr., *Cultural Literacy: What Every American Needs to Know* (Boston, MA: Houghton-Mifflin, 1987).

6. E. D. Hirsch, Jr., "Fairness and Core Knowledge," *Common Knowledge: A Core Knowledge Newsletter* 4, no. 2, (Fall 1991): 6.

7. E. D. Hirsch, Jr., "Esprit de Core," *Common Knowledge: A Core Knowledge Newsletter* 5, no. 1, (Winter 1992): 2.

8. Diane Ravitch, "Tot Sociology, or What Happened to History in Grade Schools," *The American Scholar*, Summer 1987, 343-354.

9. Houghton-Mifflin, Social Studies (Boston, MA: Houghton-Mifflin, 1991).

10. Joy Hakim, *A History of Us* (New York, NY: Oxford University Press, 1993).

11. Dennis Denenberg and Lorraine Roscoe, *Hooray for Heroes! Books and Activities Kids Will Want to Share with Parents and Teachers* (Metuchen, NJ: Scarecrow Press, 1993).

12. Dennis Denenberg, *Toward a Human Curriculum: A Guide to Returning Great People to Classrooms and Homes* (Unionville, NY: Trillium Press, 1991).

Chapter 8

Educational Assessment

J. Robert Coldiron

INTRODUCTION

The role of educational assessment has changed considerably over the past 40 years. In the late 1950s, assessments were confined to producing descriptive data about the inputs to the educational system, such as indices of class size, expenditures per pupil, number of teachers with masters degrees, and so forth. The presumption was that schools or districts with averages not too discrepant from the overall average were good schools.

Assessment, as used here, is a more encompassing term than testing or evaluation in that it refers to any number of methods that may be used to gather information about the achievement of students and the conditions that may affect that achievement. A test is considered to be narrower in implication than either assessment or evaluation. For our use, the term test will denote a presentation of a specific set of questions to be answered, a task to be performed, or a problem to be solved. The test is tangible and structured and can be administered within a specified period of time. Evaluation refers to what one does with the information gathered by the assessment program. One gathers the assessment data, using tests and other means, compiles the data into a useful form for decision makers in anticipation that their decisions will be based, at least to a considerable degree, on the assessment results. Such is the desideratum.

The major shift in the role assessment plays in judging student achievement and school quality began with the report of "Equality of Educational Opportunity" by James Coleman and others.[1]   Known popularly as the Coleman Report, this study related the inputs of education to the outputs or achievement of students and so began the use of assessments that focused on the outcomes of schooling rather than the demographics of schooling.

Each decade since the 1950s has also witnessed the increased reliance on commercial, standardized tests as measures of school quality. In their formative years, these tests were viewed as supplements to the judgment of the classroom teacher, but their impact on educational programs grew steadily as they were increasingly used as the summative measures for federal initiatives, then as the arbitrators of school and district quality, and now for state and national educational quality as well.

But the overuse, and often misuse of the commercial, standardized tests has caused a considerable backlash among educators. Many see these tests as the dominating influence of classroom instruction and claim that all too often the focus of instruction is simple recall of isolated facts because that is all that is needed for high scores on the achievement tests. The criticism has grown from calls to ban standardized testing in the decade of the 1970s to the current movement to develop assessments that provide data about what students can do, create, demonstrate, and produce as a result of their educational experiences.

In some ways, the current assessment scene portrays the evolution of assessment and the beginnings of a changing culture of how we think about the determination of levels of achievement, that is, what assessment should do *for* students and other stakeholders in the educational enterprise rather than what assessments do *to* them. The evolution of assessment is seen in the call for educational indicator systems which represents an expansion from considering just inputs as measures of school quality.[2] The proponents of indicator systems point to their usefulness in providing valuable information about the status of various educational entities, the interaction of various indicators, and how they change over time. Such systems call for not only indicators of inputs but also measures of process and output as well. This evolution reflects not only the inclusion of process and output variables, but the more precise measurement of all variables used in such systems.

The changing culture of assessment is still in the formative stages, but it is clear that the methods that will be used to assess achievement in the future will more closely align with the understanding of how students learn than how proficient they are in recalling bits of information. Performance assessments in writing have been used in many states for several years[3] and other states such as Connecticut and New York have employed performance assessments in other curricular areas as well. Maryland and Vermont have begun to develop statewide assessments that require students to produce and demonstrate an array of skills and understandings, in Maryland across the curriculum, in Vermont via portfolios in reading and mathematics. The move by states to a greater reliance on performance assessments will likely set the trend for district and school assessments in the future.

Specific examples of the move away from the multiple-choice format to performance assessment are the revised California Assessment Program (CAP)[4] and the New Standards Project (NSP)[5].

After years of administering a sophisticated, technically elegant assessment system that employed multiple-choice items to obtain data from students, the California Assessment Program is moving to assessments which will tap students' abilities to solve problems, work collaboratively, and carry out investigations. The program envisions eventually using portfolios as an additional source for ascertaining student achievement. This major departure in methodology will be carefully watched by other states.

The New Standards Project (NSP) is but one of many plans for setting national standards and developing a new kind of assessment system to examine student progress toward those standards. The promise of the NSP is the development of performance assessments that will be relevant to the classroom teacher but will be benchmarked to a common national standard. The system intends to build in the flexibility needed to accommodate the needs of schools, districts, and states. The NSP assessments will emphasize the ability to think well, to demonstrate a real understanding of subjects studied, and to apply what one knows to the kind of complex problems encountered in life. Data will be gathered through performance assessments, portfolios, projects, and timed performance examinations based on real-life tasks that students are asked to do alone and in groups. Directors of this project feel the results can be the cornerstone of a strategy to greatly improve the performance of all students, particularly those who perform least well now.

These movements away from the substantial reliance on multiple-choice tests portend future changes in instructional programs. It is widely believed that testing programs greatly influence what gets taught and how it is taught.[6] If other programs follow the lead of California and the New Standards Project, then changes in American classrooms should be forthcoming before the end of this decade. But will it really happen?

Assessments have been employed by government officials before to rank and rate schools in attempts to bring about changes in the ways schools operate. The "Wall Chart" used by the Reagan Administration is a prime example of using indicator data to promote change in school programs. The minimum competency testing programs are other examples of state government officials employing assessment to leverage change.

An expanded National Assessment of Educational Progress program, moving from the matrix sampling program testing a few select areas, which has existed for 25 years, to an expanded state by state assessment for all major content areas, has now completed the first round of field testing. This is another federal attempt to bring about change via assessment.

It is very clear--educational assessment has moved from a bit-player role to star billing as a means to change the educational experiences offered to American students. What do past experiences tell us about the potential of assessment programs to move school systems from the status quo to realizing the vision of world class standards? What have we learned that can help us avoid the potential pitfalls of such an enormous challenge?

SOME LESSONS

Even though there have been many advances in the educational assessment field since the late 1960s, it may be useful to examine the development and demise of a large-scale assessment program and compare the relative components of then and now in order to anticipate possible problems. We propose to examine the standards/goals; interpretation of the standards for assessment purposes; the level of assessment, e.g., student, school, district, or state; the assessment procedures; the analysis; and the communication of results. To do this we will use the Pennsylvania assessment program, referred to as EQA (Educational Quality Assessment) which was created in 1965 and discontinued in 1989.

In 1963, the Commonwealth of Pennsylvania passed legislation that led to the consolidation of over 2,000 school districts to just over 500 districts. In order to make this consolidation legislation acceptable to some legislators, a compromise was reached which included the establishment of a statewide assessment program to produce information about the relative effectiveness of large and small districts. From this inauspicious beginning came one of the most comprehensive state assessment programs of the last 25 years.

The legislation required the State Board of Education to proceed with assessment reform in the manner outlined below. The Board was mandated to:

caused to be developed an evaluation procedure designed to measure objectively the adequacy and efficiency of the educational programs offered by the public schools of the Commonwealth. The evaluation procedure to be developed shall include tests measuring the achievements and performance of students pursuing all of the various subjects and courses comprising the curricula. The evaluation procedure shall be so constructed and developed as to provide each school district with relevant comparative data to enable directors and administrators to more readily appraise the educational performance and to effectuate without delay the strengthening of the district's educational programs.[7]

GOALS/STANDARDS

The type of statewide assessment desired by the State Board was specified: one that would provide administrators and school directors with relevant, comparative data. The State Board's directive was inclusive about the data to be collected: data from students pursuing all of the various subjects and courses comprising the curricula. Note that the data were to be from all the curricula areas, not just the cognitive or even more restrictive, reading and mathematics areas.

In 1965, the Pennsylvania State Board of Education adopted the Ten Goals of Quality Education. In addition, the Board directed the Department of Education (PDE) to base the assessment program on those ten goals and to find or develop measures that would address each goal. The assessment was not to be based on only the easy to measure goals.

The program that evolved, called the Educational Quality Assessment (EQA), incorporated both inputs and outcomes. The ten goals were broadly stated and called for mastery of the basic skills; positive attitudes toward self, others, and learning; responsible citizenship; good health habits; opportunities to be creative; preparation for a productive life; appreciation of human achievements; and preparation for a changing world.[8] These goals were, in effect, the high standards for Pennsylvania schools, standards that the State Board would employ to provide direction for Pennsylvania schools.

As can be readily noted, this broad set of goals included more than the usual academics as represented by the traditional reading, writing, and arithmetic goals for schools. Furthermore, the State Board pointedly directed the Pennsylvania Department of Education to provide measures for every goal, recognizing that some goals would be much more difficult to assess than others.

Since the goals were so broadly stated, definitions or descriptions of them could vary considerably. In order to develop assessment devices for the goals, the Bureau of Education Quality Assessment first had to develop rationales for their measurement with the understanding that other possible interpretations could be possible and that the rationales may be modified over time.

For example, the rationale for measuring the goal ". . . help every child acquire the greatest possible understanding of himself and an appreciation of his worthiness as a member of society" was broadly interpreted to include factors that influenced self-esteem both at school and outside of the school environment. Over time, this interpretation was modified to include only the more direct effects of school factors on self-esteem. This was done because school staffs felt they were being held accountable for factors over which they had no control.

ASSESSING THE OUTCOMES

For the EQA program, outputs or student achievements, now often referred to as outcomes, were difficult to measure. First, there was the problem of determining what outcomes to measure. This problem was delineated somewhat for the Educational Quality Assessment staff, the group charged with developing the assessment program, in that the State Board directed that measures be developed for all goals. Measures could not be devised for the broadly stated ten goals until some interpretation and delineation of their meaning was conducted. This process, described in a division publication[9] (*EQA, Phase II Findings, The Ten Goals of Quality Education, Rationale and Measurement*) points out there are many ways to interpret the goals and that the rationales contain only a sample of possible definitions. Likewise, there could be several measurement approaches taken and the assessment design must specify what approach is being taken and the process used to arrive at that decision.

The problem of defining a goal or outcome statement in terms from which a measurement instrument can be selected or designed is one of the most difficult for any complex assessment program. Large-scale assessments must usually confine their tests to items and forms that can be optically scanned for economy and time considerations, thus limiting their choices of assessment approaches. Today, with the advent of holistic scoring and the emphasis on performance assessment, the opportunity to include an array of assessment approaches is substantially increased. Still not settled, however, are the considerable cost and time factors needed to conduct large-scale performance assessments. Will legislators appropriate funds over the long-run, and will the performance designs be such that they supplement the student's instructional program?

Those persons charged with the formulation of standards for the National Standards Project or other large-scale assessments will face the similar interpretation problems. A prime example of this problem comes from Pennsylvania when the Commonwealth moved to adopt new curriculum regulations in 1993 which included the goal of understanding and appreciating persons belonging to social, cultural, and ethnic groups different from his own. Even though this goal had been part of the State Board set of goals for 25 years, it was challenged by a contingent of persons who felt it subversively meant students would have to develop "politically correct" attitudes toward persons with whom they may not want to be associated. The goal was eventually removed from the final set in order to obtain the votes necessary to approve the new regulations. If the influence of similar groups grows, it could mean that any new standards would represent only the fundamental goals associated with schools--reading, writing, and arithmetic. It remains to be seen if the new standards will encompass goals promoting thinking, problem-solving, citizenship, and collaboration.

After the establishment of the goals and rationales for measuring them, comes the task of developing methods to collect data that reveal how well the goals are being addressed by schools. In the late 1960s when the EQA was being developed, this task was accomplished by developing multiple-choice questions (items) and following the standard procedures of pilot testing, revision, tryout, and so forth until reliable and valid measures were ready to be used for the state assessment. The development of indicators followed a similar set of procedures. This process required two years before a preliminary set of instruments was ready for pilot testing in schools.[10]

The initial field testing provided the empirical data needed to make adjustments in both the instruments used to gather data from the students and the indicator data. What was clear from this initial assessment was that inputs often did not account for substantial amount of variation in outputs. It was assumed that process indicators would add to the predictability of the outputs but the model had no way to include them. The data from the field testing of the EQA instruments and procedures demonstrated that such a large-scale assessment could be done for a reasonable expenditure of resources and that, in fact, most districts welcome such an assessment.

INTERPRETATION

Even though the program was voluntary until 1974, the Assessment Bureau of the Department of Education drew representative samples of districts, based on district tax effort and enrollment from the districts participating, in order to develop normative data for comparisons. The Bureau developed normative tables for both the student achievement results and the indicator data. Schools could locate their standing on all the variables included in the total assessment package.

A feature of the EQA program not found in most other large-scale assessment of the early 1970s, was the use of regression equations to predict the students' outcomes based on the input condition variables (indicators). The Bureau developed equations for each goal area, predicted the school's score, based on the indicator data for that school, and then added and subtracted a standard error of estimate to obtain a "band" around the predicted score.

The "band" proved to have both positive and negative qualities when it came time to interpret the results. For schools with limited resources that drew the majority of their students from low socioeconomic areas, the bands were welcomed because in addition to the percentile score which indicated their absolute standing in the normative group, the band provided a relative position based on the conditions under which the school operated. For example, a 15th percentile score in reading might have been within the predicted band. This would indicate that even though the school scores were low compared to the normative sample, the school was scoring about the same as other schools with similar resources. At the other end of the continuum, a school could score at the 82nd percentile and be below their predicted band. This would indicate that the school operated under very favorable conditions but did not produce results commensurate with those conditions.

Unfortunately, school district administrators began to interpret scores within the band as "where the department expected them to score" and any score in the predicted band was acceptable. The intent of the predicted score was not to indicate that a low score was acceptable but rather to present a way to show results relative to resources. Many analysts found this format to be a self-fulfilling prophecy; moreover, it provided the decision-makers of low scoring schools with convenient excuses for not improving their programs.

A second problem, relative to the interpretation of scores, was the use of multiple-matrix sampling by the EQA program. This means that for a given grade level, say fifth grade, three forms of the assessment were distributed randomly to the fifth graders in a given school. Each form contained a different set of items, the forms were balanced based on the difficulty of the items. The problem is not with the technical aspects of using this sampling procedure or similar procedures but rather the problem is in convincing the recipients of the results that those results reflect an accurate measure of achievement. This is especially a problem when the scores are low.

School leaders and teachers are not well-versed in sampling processes and tend to be skeptical if all students are not assessed on the same material. This will be a significant problem for large-scale performance assessment programs that may, for cost reasons, need to employ sampling designs to obtain data. The National Standards Project will also face this problem as it converts its various measures to estimates of aggregate achievement. Legislators are also skeptical of sampling results, particularly if those results are at variance with their perceptions of school quality. This issue will be discussed in more detail in the "Communication of Results" section of this chapter.

UNIT OF MEASUREMENT

One of the problems with some past assessments was that data gathered for one level of decision making was applied to another level without consideration of the validity of the application. One of the best examples of this is the use made of the Scholastic Aptitude Test (SAT) results. The SAT is designed to gather data from students to help decide their readiness to cope with higher education courses. The SATs are designed for individual level interpretation. But widespread misuse of these data occur each year as legislators and school board members use the data to rate schools, a clear misuse of the data.

It is possible to aggregate data across levels, but the aggregations and conclusions from them must be drawn carefully. All too often, that is not done by the user of the assessments.

The focus of the assessment is crucial. Assessments at the classroom level can assist teachers in making instructional decisions; at the school level, assist principals with decisions about instruction and programs; at the district level, assist the superintendent and school board members with decisions about the adequacy of programs; at the state level, assist legislators with allocation decisions. In designing an assessment program, one must always keep in the forefront the decisions that might be made based on the data and who will be making those decisions.

FOCUSING THE ASSESSMENT

The assessment design is driven by the need for data to support a decision that needs to be made. Who, then, are the decision makers? Classroom teachers? Principals? Superintendents? School Boards? Legislators? And what are the decisions for which they need data? Assessment designs need to reflect the needs of the decision maker; thus, the immediate problem is to determine the level at which to focus the assessment. There are many levels at which an assessment might be focused.

In response to the Commonwealth's legislation and with a knowledge of the organizational arrangements of most Pennsylvania school districts, the EQA program selected 5th, 8th, and 11th graders from which to collect data and to call those levels representative of schools. The unit of measure was the average school score at those grade levels; the normative data were then relative to mean school scores. This design provided administrators and directors with data about their elementary, middle/junior high, and high school programs. Since schools do differ within districts, information was available to compare individual schools as well. This was a mixed blessing as some district leaders did not want to recognize that their schools were achieving at different levels, usually as a result of the differing inputs, particularly the socioeconomic difference found in the populations of the neighborhood schools.

With respect to sampling, another problem that appeared when scores were low was that the 5th or 8th or 11th grade class that responded to the assessment was the "worst" class that had come through that school in years and was not really representative of the school. While this may have been true in some isolated cases, EQA found, by assessing consecutively over a period of years in the same school, that scores, across all measures tended to be quite stable.

This, again, is a problem that may be more pronounced in performance assessment where it may not be possible to include enough students in the assessment to convince the local staff that the results reflect class achievement let alone school or district achievement.

For the EQA program, the data were to be comparative and were to also address the adequacy and efficiency of the educational programs. Thus, more than just outcome data would need to be collected. Consequently, the model developed measurements for inputs, called "condition variables" by the Assessment Bureau.

INDICATORS

In current approaches to assessment, what Pennsylvania referred to as "condition variables" are now referred to as "indicators." Over time, Pennsylvania used as many as 50 different condition variables, not at the same time, to assist in the interpretation of outcomes. Variables were considered by the possible impact they might have on a given outcome. The model was based on a series of concentric circles with the student at the center point. Circles were delineated as classroom, school, and community. Included in the classroom variables were class size, homework, teacher expectations, and several variables relating to teachers. Some of the school variables were percent low income, accessibility of library, grade enrollment, and tuition rate. Finally, some variables for the community were parental education level, type of community, teacher/ parent relationships, and parental educational expectations.

Scales were developed for the variables using guidance from the research literature and data from pilot studies. Today, assessment designers can call on a wealth of research on indicators[11] to aid them in the design of indicator systems.

Problems with indicators. There are critics who say the use of indicators in the interpretation of outcomes is a self-fulfilling prophecy. They maintain that all schools should be held to the same standards and that those standards should be achieved by students by a designated time.

One might agree with such critics if all schools were created equal or if students were randomly assigned to schools. Since neither is true, nor likely to be true in the foreseeable future, indicators are essential if fair comparisons are to be drawn about the adequacy and efficiency of school programs.

All students do not come to school ready to learn as recognized by former President Bush and the governors of the 50 states. Two to three years are required for some schools to ready their students for learning. Consequently, their achievement as measured by most tests will likely be far below schools that have students who come from environments that prepare them for school. The best measure of school effectiveness would be a value-added measure that would show how much the school has contributed to the achievement growth of each student since the student enrolled in that school. As yet, no such measure exists.

Another problem with indicators is the sensitivity in collecting some indicator data. Some of the best indicator data may be personally sensitive, thus not collectible. For example, socioeconomic status (SES) is strongly related to achievement when the unit of measure is a school or a larger unit. Parents' educational levels or occupational levels are good proxies for SES, but there is an understandable reluctance to provide such information for assessment purposes. The assessment designer is then faced with either finding another proxy or dropping that variable from the system. Sometimes one can find a good proxy that will suffice for statistical purposes, but it may be difficult to "sell" to the consumers of the assessment results.

An example comes from the assessment of outcomes. In order to save three hours of test administration time, the Pennsylvania assessment program dropped the standardized test requirement from its array of tests and substituted short vocabulary and mathematics tests that correlated highly ($p = 0.90$) with the standardized achievement tests and thus could serve as proxies for reading and mathematics achievement. In schools, where scores on reading and math were reported to be low, these measures were often challenged. Rarely were they challenged if the scores were comparatively high. In other words, it is very important that the decision maker can see the direct relationship between the indicator and the decision to be made.

COMMUNICATION OF ASSESSMENT RESULTS

There is an enormous gap in the ability of assessment designers to develop and analyze assessments and the communication of those results to their intended audiences. While assessment procedures have steadily grown in technical sophistication, no corresponding growth has been witnessed in the interpretation of those results, especially for school staff and school board members.

As mentioned earlier, EQA employed percentiles as the main interpretive statistic and used the predicted score as a supplementary interpretation. Over time, the reports began including item data as well so that more precise interpretations could be made of the results.

Another feature of the EQA program was that the reports were interpreted at the school district site by an EQA staffer for any local district staff invited by the local superintendent. These sessions, usually lasting about two hours, provided an excellent forum for the exchange of viewpoints about the assessment results and their interpretation.

All too often assessment results are packaged and sent to the respective decision makers who may open them, glance at the summary results, and place them on the nearest shelf, intending sometime to review them more carefully. That review seldom occurs.

Initially, one of the underlying perceptions of the EQA staff was that if the results indicated problems in one or more of the student achievement areas, school administrators and board members would take action to change that condition. The EQA staff believed that this corrective action would occur by first perusing the condition variables and then by taking action to change conditions. Such perceptions were seldom born out.

When a school district received reports that indicated low achievement in one or more areas, the first response of the district would often be to challenge the test, followed by a challenge of the sampling technique. If the problem area was other than reading or mathematics, the school district would then frequently argue that the achievement area was lacking in relevance. Districts were not required to publish the reports; thus, they could ignore the results if they chose to do so.

Exceptions to this observation, were those districts where a problem was suspected but not confirmed. When the EQA results indicated the suspicions were probably well-founded, action would be taken. In essence, the results of an assessment need to be perceived by the decision maker to be directly relevant to his concerns. Unless the results are so viewed, one can expect little to come from the assessment.

The role of publicity is important in the use of assessment results by local decision makers. In 1984, Pennsylvania instituted a minimum competency testing program, Testing for the Essential Learning and Literacy Skills (TELLS). Since remediation funds were directly related to test results, TELLS data had to be released to the local media. School districts that had ignored low reading and mathematics scores provided by EQA, took quick action once TELLS scores were published in local newspapers. The TELLS scores were no more reliable or valid than the EQA scores, but the publicity resulted in action.

Large-scale assessments are faced with the problem of how to convey their findings to various audiences. Seldom do results of large-scale assessments reach the classroom teacher in any usable form; and even if they did, one would find that the teacher has received virtually no training about how to interpret the results or using them in any meaningful way.

Much the same can be said for school administrators.

Obviously, if assessments are to have much impact on what happens in schools, considerable staff development must take place to prepare the local staff to use the data. Most of the efforts in assessment, however, goes into developing assessment tasks or more elegant analyses, and the local school-based user continues to be ignored. Until this condition changes, assessments will have no more impact in the future for changing the course of American schooling than they have had in the past. From the initial descriptions of the New Standards Project and new state assessment programs, it is not clear how the problem of communicating results to the classroom will occur.

POLITICAL INFLUENCES

The educational landscape is dotted with the remains of many innovations and reform efforts, but these past efforts have not discouraged the development of new efforts. Some of the new efforts would include re-structuring, re-learning, and re-inventing. Reformers are also examining the organizational features of schooling, making learning the central goal of schools, or using current understandings of learning, organizations, and technology to create different ways of orchestrating learning experiences. Some educational analysts view the structure of the school organization as the major target for change; others see a need to focus on learning; and still others want to start over by recognizing and using societal influences, research on learning and organizations, and technology to maximize the effectiveness and efficiency of education. These efforts often include just a small percentage of the 15,000 school districts that educate American children.

Political authorities do support the "RE:" movements, but political agendas often call for wider and faster changes than can be achieved through the deliberate, focused efforts of targeted change. Thus, politicians turn to large-scale assessments, state or national, in their attempts to change school systems.[12]

In Pennsylvania, the birth of the EQA program came about as a legislative compromise. The program was to provide some guidance about the relative effectiveness of large districts versus small districts in terms of student achievement. However, in the time interval between the passage of the legislation and the implementation of the assessment program, that question was apparently forgotten. There was never any request from the legislature for an analysis of achievement based on the enrollment of students in school districts.

The EQA was relatively free from political influence for most of its existence with the exception of controversy created over the inclusion of non-cognitive measures in the assessment instruments. Several of the goals--self-esteem, attitude toward learning, appreciation of human achievement, understanding and appreciating differing others--required that non-cognitive instruments be developed. For other goals, such as citizenship, the rationale for measurement called for more than just knowledge of historical facts and knowledge of government functions. Some legislators and some citizen groups felt the Commonwealth should not collect any type of noncognitive data from students. They claimed that by doing so the state was invading parental rights and violating the national Constitution. PDE responded to this criticism by noting that EQA was a program assessment and students responded anonymously to all questions. Thus, no privacy was invaded and parental rights were not usurped. The majority of legislators and citizens accepted the PDE position, and noncognitive items were included in the battery of test questions until the program was discontinued in 1989.

The decision to discontinue EQA was a political decision. In October 1984, a decision was made by Governor Richard Thornburgh to create a minimum competency testing program for Pennsylvania. The need for such a program was not clear, since the PDE had done a survey of Pennsylvania districts the previous year and found that most districts conducted extensive standardized testing programs which produced data very similar to that to be generated by the minimum competency testing program. Nevertheless, the Governor's Office recommended that the minimum competency testing program, Testing for Essential Learning and Literacy Skills (TELLS), be administered at grade levels 3, 5, and 8. Since two of these levels, 5 and 8, overlapped with the EQA program, EQA was adjusted to include grades 4, 6, and 9 omitting 5 and 8.

The Division of Educational Testing and Evaluation (formerly the Bureau of EQA) was assigned the responsibility of administering both testing programs and did so until 1989. TELLS was designed to identify students who needed extra help with reading and/or math and to provide state remediation funds to assist districts in developing programs for their identified students. The tests were designed to focus on individual achievement, as opposed to the EQA program assessment. Because the focus was on minimums, there were few questions that would challenge above-average students. Clearly, the scores should not have been averaged to reflect a school score, nor should they have been averaged to produce a district score.

School and district averages were not produced in the initial years of the program. However, after the election of a new governor in 1986 and the subsequent appointment of a new secretary of education, the testing and assessment programs were considered, by the new secretary, to be the most promising levers for motivating districts to change their modes of operation.

The Secretary concluded that the EQA was not bringing about the desired changes because most scores fell into the predicted band (as they should have, based on the prediction model); therefore, districts were content with their results. He decided to discontinue the EQA program in favor of TELLS.

He proceeded to direct that average school scores be produced for TELLS as well as average scores for districts and that the district scores be ranked from 1 to 505, the number of districts in the state. He was repeatedly given advice about why such scores should not be generated, the invalidity of the probable interpretations of such scores, and the probable adverse reaction that would follow. The advice was discounted as bureaucratic nonsense.

Scores and reports were generated as ordered by the Secretary, and these reports were sent to all districts and public libraries in the Commonwealth. The reports were sent to libraries so that citizens could have unrestricted access to them. Newspapers printed the scores and rated districts and schools as "A," "B," "C," and so forth. Numerous parents called PDE asking how they could transfer their children to schools that had a 95 percent passing rate because their school only had a 91 percent passing rate.

The uproar that followed the dissemination of TELLS results led to the Secretary requesting that the reports be returned to the Department or destroyed. School administrators felt they had been betrayed by the Department. They believed that promises had been broken regarding how test data would be reported, and they were naturally skeptical of plans for future assessments.

In this case, the change of administrations brought about a significant change in assessment policies. The second administration, led by Governor Robert P. Casey, was, in effect, not committed to the original assessment plan. Any assessment data can be misused. If safeguards are not put into place and honored by those in charge of the assessment, then school officials are correct in their apprehension about having their staff and students participate in large-scale assessment programs. When the law requires mandatory participation, school officials are well advised to insist that all conditions, from administration of the assessment instruments to the reporting of the results, be agreed to prior to any student reponding to any item. Technical correctness cannot overcome political incompetence. Before concluding, an overview of educational assessment innovations across the nation would be useful.

STUDENT ASSESSMENT MEASURES USED BY STATES

Forty-eight states, excluding New Hampshire and Wyoming, assess student achievement in some manner. Some states utilize criterion-referenced (measure student achievement relative to an established standard) and/or norm-referenced tests (measure student achievement relative to a national average or sample group), while others use informal surveys or student achievement portfolios. Generally, most states use performance-based assessments (measure student achievement relative to established performance tasks) to test student achievement in the subject areas of language arts, math, reading, science, social studies, and writing.

The following excerpts summarize innovative assessment measures used by selected states to test student achievement.

CALIFORNIA

The California Learning Assessment System (CLAS) has three major assessment components: 1) performance-based assessments, administered to students in grades 4, 8, and 10, evaluate student knowledge in language arts, reading, mathematics, and writing; science and social studies will be added in 1994; 2) Golden State Examinations (GSE), end-of-course exams that are voluntarily taken by students, evaluate student knowledge in algebra, biology, chemistry, economics, geometry, and U.S. history; and 3) career-technical assessments, which are presently being developed through California's Career-Technical Assessment Project (C-TAP), will indicate if students possess the knowledge and skills to be successful beyond high school. After CLAS is fully established, it will be augmented by student achievement portfolios.

FLORIDA

Four measures of assessment are used by the Florida Department of Education to evaluate student achievement: 1) Grade 4 and 8 norm-referenced tests evaluate student knowledge of reading and mathematics; 2) the Florida Writing Assessment Program provides information about the writing performance of students in grades 4, 8, and 10; 3) the Grade Ten Assessment Test (GTAT) is a standardized, norm-referenced achievement test that measures student performance in the subject areas of reading comprehension and mathematics; and 4) the High School Competency Test (HSCT), which must be passed to obtain a high school diploma, measures student ability to apply basic skills in mathematics, reading, and writing to everyday life situations. HSCT is first administered in 11th grade and may be taken no more than five times before the end of grade 12.

NORTH CAROLINA

Students enrolled in grades 1 through 12 are tested through the use of informal surveys that are developed by North Carolina's Department of Education. Students enrolled in elementary and middle school grades are informally surveyed to assess performance in language arts, mathematics, reading, science, and social studies. Students enrolled in high school are informally surveyed to assess performance in "11 priority courses," which include algebra, chemistry, composition, geometry, history, and science. North Carolina is the only state to use informal surveys as a form of student assessment.

VERMONT

Vermont has developed statewide assessments that require students to produce and demonstrate an array of skills and understandings. Student skills and understandings, along with one piece of work the student considers his best, are "showcased" in a portfolio. All portfolios are augmented by standardized assessment data which indicate student knowledge in the subject areas of mathematics, reading, and writing. New Mexico and Rhode Island also use student portfolios; New Mexico in the area of writing and Rhode Island in language arts and mathematics. In addition, California and Wisconsin plan to implement a student portfolio assessment system before the year 2000.

CONCLUSION

For the most part, large-scale assessments have had little impact on the way schools operate or the curriculum they offer, with the possible exception of students' writing. There are many possible explanations for the lack of impact. Foremost among these explanations is the lack of any real incentive to use the results combined with little training on how to interpret assessment results.

There is little indication that performance assessment programs will change the usage situation at all. Again most of the emphasis is being placed on the development, administration, and scoring of the assessments, and, as yet, little emphasis is being placed on the interpretation of results for use at the school level. Staff development is the key to changing this situation, but most school boards place little value on staff development and typically do not budget for significant programs. Since in-service and staff development programs have typically lacked relevant substance, teaching staffs have not made increased staff development opportunities a priority. Without the needed training in performance assessment for administrators and teachers, this movement is not likely to have any more impact on changing schools than its predecessors.

Large-scale performance assessment may change classroom instruction not via the results they generate but rather in offering classroom teachers models on which to base their own assessment. Performance assessments may renew the credibility of teacher judgments of students' achievement. Today the external tests, the state or a national assessment, receive the media coverage and, for the minimum competency tests like TELLS, supersede the teacher's judgment of student achievement. Performance assessment approaches should reduce the heavy reliance on multiple-choice tests as the primary means of ascertaining student achievement. Teachers should be offered a wide array of methods to assess student achievement that will be viewed as credible outside the classroom. If assessment would drive instruction, the trip to implement educational innovations and reform could be much more adventurous in the future.

ENDNOTES

1. Department of Health, Education, and Welfare, *Equality of Educational Opportunity* (Washington, D.C.: Government Printing Office, 1966).

2. William W. Cooley and Carole A. George, *Educational Indicators for Pennsylvania* 14 (Pittsburgh, PA: University of Pittsburgh, 1992); and Jeannie Oakes, *Educational Indiciators: A Guide for Policymakers* (New Brunswick, NJ: Center for Policy Research in Education, Rutgers University, 1986).

3. U.S. Congress, Office of Technology Assessment, *Testing in American Schools: Asking the Right Questions,* OTA-SET-519 (Washington, D.C.: Government Printing Office, February 1992).

4. California Department of Education, *A Sampler of Mathematics Assessment* (Sacremento, CA: Office of State Printing, 1991).

5. University of Pittsburgh Learning Research and Development Center, *New Standards Project* (Pittsburgh, PA: University of Pittsburgh, n.d.).

6. Pennsylvania Department of Education, *Educational Quality Assessment, Phase II Findings: The Ten Goals of Quality Eduction, Rationale, and Measurement* (Harrisburg, PA: Pennsylvania Department of Education, 1970).

7. Pennsylvania Department of Public Instruction, *Progress Report: Educational Quality Assessment* (Harrisburg, PA: Pennsylvania Department of Public Instruction, 1968).

8. Pennsylvania Department of Education, *Phase II Findings.*

9. Pennsylvania Department of Public Instruction, *Educational Quality Assessment.*

10. James Welsh, *Pennsylvania Looks at Its Schools* (Harrisburg, PA: Pennsylvania Department of Education, 1971).

11. Cooley and George, *Educational Indicators for Pennsylvania*; and Oakes, *Educational Indicators: A Guide for Policymakers.*

12. Pennsylvania Department of Public Instruction, Bureau of Educational Quality Assessment, *Phase I Findings* (Harrisburg, PA: Pennsylvania Department of Public Instruction, 1969).

Chapter 9

School Report Cards

D. Michael Fisher

Introduction

When moving into a new neighborhood, people have the option of asking neighbors or their real estate agent about the school district's reputation. In Pennsylvania, no reporting mechanism is in place to help parents determine whether or not a school provides a good or bad education.

It is unfortunate that Pennsylvania does not generate comprehensive, relevant information to help its residents answer even basic questions such as: How good are the schools? How good are the teachers? And how useful is the information being taught to students?

With such uncertainty, how can we expect individuals to make rational choices for their children? Also, without such reporting mechanisms, the incentives for our school districts to improve are much less.

School Report Cards Across The Nation

According to the Education Commission of the States, 23 states had adopted new laws, amended old laws, or passed regulations to report data on the educational system and its performance by 1987. The number of states utilizing this educational innovation rose to 29 by 1990. These state school report cards collected data from different sources and reported a number of varying statistics in the attempt to depict the state of education within their jurisdiction.

ILLINOIS

In 1985, the Illinois General Assembly began requiring its public school districts to report to the taxpayers on the performance of schools and students. The legislation referred to this requirement as a report card that would be disseminated to all parents whose children are enrolled in the school district and kept on file by the district, thus making it accessible to taxpayers.

Specifically, the report card includes the following information:
1) Student Characteristics--Student demographics, such as percent that are low-income and attendance rates.
2) Student Performance--Percent of K-8 students not promoted, graduation rates, state assessment data, ACT composite score, and national percentile rank.
3) Instructional Resources--Average class size; percent of high school enrollment in math, science, English, and social science; average minutes per day devoted to math, science, English, and social science in elementary school.
4) District Information--Teacher ethnic characteristics, average years' teaching experience, average teacher and administrator salaries, pupil-teacher ratio, operating expenditure per pupil, per capita tuition charge, expenditure by fund, administrator-student ratio, and counselor-student ratio.

MARYLAND

Maryland's state Department of Education requires each of its 24 school systems to publish a free, magazine-size guide called the school performance report. These reports describe their students' performance countywide which is measured against expected state standards. These reports allow Maryland residents to review the successes and failures of the state's public schools.

Maryland's reports include minimum, satisfactory standards, as well as standards for excellence that include the following:
1) Attendance rates;
2) Drop-out rates;

3) Percentage of ninth-or 10th-graders who passed basic skills tests in citizenship, math, reading, and writing on their first try;

4) Percentages of 11th-graders who passed the basic tests they were first given in the ninth or 10th grade;

5) Percentages and counts of students who earned 20 high school credits and completed the basic requirements to obtain entry into the University of Maryland system; and

6) Percentages and counts of students who completed an occupational training program.

NEW JERSEY

In New Jersey, the Department of Education has cooperated with the Business Roundtable Education Initiative of New Jersey to issue an annual school district report card. This report card is intended to give the public some insights into how school districts spend taxpayer dollars and how each district's students perform.

SCHOOL REPORT CARDS FOR PENNSYLVANIA

As other states move toward the goal of better educating their students through increased accountability in their educational system, Pennsylvania has remained on the sidelines.

Therefore, on March 18, 1991, I introduced Senate Bill 720 in an effort to focus on the issue of greater accountability for the state's school system. Senate Bill 720 would have helped to measure the performance of schools and school districts through the establishment of school report cards. School report cards would not only help parents to determine the level of education that the local schools are providing but would also serve as an incentive for improved performance.

Under my proposal, schools would have been graded in various areas, including student performance, instructional resources, and student characteristics. In addition, schools and school districts would have been compared to other schools and districts. The report card would have also assessed a school's performance and a district's performance compared to others of similar demographic characteristics. Comparisons of this type provide incentives for school improvements.

Specifically, my legislation called upon the state Department of Education to prepare and provide a report card form which would be completed by every school district each year and forwarded to the

Department no later than June 30 of each year. The content of the school report card would have included these items:

1) *Student Characteristic Indicators*

- Attendance rate per district and attendance rate per type of school.
- Economic characteristics, including the percentage of low income students.
- Student mobility, as determined by percentage of transfers in and out of each district.
- Chronic truancy.
- Percentage of limited-English proficient students.
- Percentage of students for each racial-ethnic group.

2) *District Indicators*

- Percentage of teachers for each racial-ethnic group.
- Percentage of teachers by gender.
- Average years of teaching experience.
- Percentage of teachers with masters degrees and above.
- Student-teacher ratio.
- Student-administrator ratio.
- Counselor-student ratio.
- Average teacher salary.
- District expenditure per student.

3) *Student Performance Indicators*

- Graduation rate.
- Percentage of students not promoted to the next grade.
- Percentage of students placed in the top and bottom quarterlies of nationally normed achievement tests.
- State assessment data.
- Composite means for college-bound students.

4) *Instructional Resources Indicators*

- Average class size.
- Percentage of high school enrollment in English, mathematics,

science, and social studies.

- Percentage of time per day devoted to English, mathematics, science, and social studies at the elementary, junior high, and senior high grade levels.
- Percentage of enrollment in college preparatory, general education, business, and vocational-technical education programs.

Upon receipt of all the districts' report cards, the state Department of Education would provide a statewide comparison and performance targets in accordance with the following guidelines:

- A comparison of statewide averages to the individual school and school district data.
- A comparison of averages of demographically similar schools and school districts to the individual schools and school districts.
- Performance targets for each school and school district in the following year.
- A statement that the school district is or is not educationally deficient as determined by the indicators included in the report card.

In regard to the dissemination of this school report card data to the public, each school district, no later than September 30, would have been required to publish the final report cards for each school and school district in a newspaper of general circulation serving the district. Each school district would also have provided a copy of the report card to parents of children enrolled in the school and school district and keep the report cards on file for inspection by the taxpayers.

A failure to file a report card when required would have subjected the school district to the withholding of all money due the school district out of any appropriation made by the Commonwealth for any purpose until such time as the appropriate documents were filed.

The type of school report card described above will assess a school's performance and a district's performance compared to others of similar demographic characteristics. These comparisons will help to create an incentive for improvement. Unless a vehicle is provided that identifies potential problem areas, the state cannot proceed to establish priorities for resource allocation and the improvement of school and student performance.

EVALUATION OF SCHOOL REPORT CARDS

The practical benefits realized by the implementation of school report cards in other states have already been plentiful. The Illinois program has been successful in disseminating a wealth of information regarding the performance of public schools and districts. In the 1988-89 school year, Illinois issued report cards for 3,927 regular public schools within 967 districts, enrolling 1,766,324 students. The program appears to have fostered teacher and administrator accountability and resulted in a slight decrease in both pupil-teacher and pupil-administrator ratios since the first school report cards were issued in 1986.

In Maryland, the reports brought to the public's attention a problem that one county's schools already knew existed--attendance was a problem in some of its schools. When the report was released, that county's residents immediately asked themselves why attendance was a problem and joined with business leaders to seek a solution. This parent, school, and business partnership produced a solution thanks to a special incentive by McDonalds. McDonalds offered a coupon for a free hamburger and fries to all sixth, seventh, and eighth-graders with perfect attendance records.

Moreover, New Jersey's Education Commissioner John Ellis has indicated that, "The report cards show encouraging signs that some schools are improving their performance."[1] Ellis also noted that New Jersey's schools, "simply are not as good as they need to be to make New Jersey internationally competitive."[2] The Business Roundtable, which paid for New Jersey's report cards, expressed concern that the student performance data raised questions as to whether or not New Jersey's state school systems are capable of producing enough workers to compete in high-tech industries.

IMPLEMENTING SCHOOL REPORT CARDS IN PENNSYLVANIA

Questions about educational quality and cost need to be raised by parents, taxpayers, and the business community in Pennsylvania. Why do the citizens of the Commonwealth lack consistent measures of the quality of curriculum, schools, and teachers? The reasons vary, but the following reasons are most frequently mentioned:

1) Complacency by parents.
2) Resistance by educators and school board members who do not like this type of comparison.
3) Fear of federal intervention into local affairs by state and local

politicians.
4) Resistance of test-makers to providing the funding for the creation of tests that better measure what students need to know.[3]

Upon consideration of Senate Bill 720 last year, the Pennsylvania State Education Association (PSEA) opposed my legislation. According to PSEA's policy statement on Senate Bill 720, it was opposed because, "Senate Bill 720 is directed at identifying problems in schools and publicizing them, but proposes no remedies for those problems once they are identified. Assistance to districts which receive poor report cards is essential. Without it, a bill such as this is punitive, not constructive."

Furthermore, PSEA's policy statement also explained that, "The goal of this type of program must be to identify weaknesses and then to strengthen them, much the same way that teachers work with students. Necessary assistance would include programs to assist parents in their role, to assist staff through professional development, and to assist the schools with curriculum and planning."

Finally, PSEA stated that the language included in the bill attempting to protect districts which might have been labeled "deficient" from lawsuits was inadequate. PSEA stated:

It ought to reaffirm that the Political Subdivision Tort Claims Act fully applies, and that school districts and their employees are immune from actions based on any theory of negligence. Otherwise, a question could arise whether the provision in SB 720 overrides the Tort Claims Act in a limiting fashion. As a result, school districts could be required to spend resources on legal fees instead of education.[4]

The point that PSEA made regarding lawsuits was in reference to language that had been added to SB 720 while it was being considered by the Senate Education Committee. This language is not included in the new version of school report card legislation that I introduced as SB 400 in the current session of the General Assembly.

In addition, the remaining points that PSEA made in regards to financial assistance and proposed remedies by the state are not the focus of the school report cards. Of course, school districts would like additional funding for education, but the question of school funding is deliberated annually during the formulation of the state budget. The enactment of a school report card could accurately assess the performance of state schools and provide needed information to legislators during the appropriations process.

The Pennsylvania School Boards Association (PSBA) also opposed Senate Bill 720 last year. PSBA's position statement focused on the amendment that was added in the Senate Education Committee concerning the determination of whether a school district is "academically distressed." PSBA stated that, "The inclusion of the amendment confuses the issue. The original purpose of SB 720 should be to give the Department and school districts an idea of how each district compares with others on the criteria outlined in the report card, not as a comparison of academic standing."[5]

Without the provision for "academic distress" in SB 400, I am hopeful that both PSEA and PSBA will reassess the school report card bill and offer their support.

It is interesting to note that New Jersey's largest teachers union was also opposed to its state report card program because it believed, "The report cards did nothing to advance a more positive attitude toward schools."[6] The New Jersey School Boards Association was also strongly critical of school report cards because these reports were not reviewed by education organizations.[7] However, the Association supported a later version of the report cards because it believed the data was presented in an unbiased manner and the later version used current-year data on school spending.

CONCLUSION

With all the debate surrounding education reform and innovations, Pennsylvanians deserve school report cards so that schools and communities can accurately assess their school's progress over time. This information will also enable communities to establish goals more effectively for school improvement in the future.

When U.S. Secretary of Education, William J. Bennett proclaimed in a 1987 speech that, "accountability is the linchpin, the keystone, the *sine qua non* of the reform movement," he was reflecting national sentiment. State lawmakers will continue to respond to this sentiment and to seek greater accountability in public education in the years to come.

As state legislators adopt and implement school report cards, it will be useful to them to envision these accountability systems as a tripod. In order to work effectively, school report cards need clearly stated goals, prompt and accurate information about progress toward them, and positive and negative consequences that follow from the information.[8]

While Pennsylvania remains on the sidelines, other states, such as Alabama, California, Connecticut, Illinois, Kentucky, Louisiana, New

Jersey, and South Carolina, lead the experimentation with school report cards. Certainly, if citizens have the right to know the nutritional content of their foods, they are entitled to receive information on the performance of their school system.

ENDNOTES

1. Clyde Leib, "Report Cards Tell Which Schools Make the Grade," *New York Times*, 22 March 1992, 13(A).

2. Ibid..

3. Jeanne Mooney, "State Lacks Yardstick for Comparing Schools," *Beaver County Times* (Beaver, PA), 1 June 1992, 7(A).

4. Pennsylvania State Education Association, *Government Policy Statement* (Harrisburg, PA: Pennsylvania State Education Association, 23 September 1991).

5. Timothy M. Allwein, *Memorandum* (Harrisburg, PA: Pennsylvania School Boards Association, 30 March 1992).

6. Leib, "Report Cards Tell," 13(A).

7. Ibid., 13(A).

8. Chester E. Finn, Jr., *We Must Take Charge: Our Schools an Our Future* (New York, NY: Free Press, 1991), 147.

Chapter 10

Privatization, Policy, and Private Schools: The Irony of Recent School Reform

Bruce S. Cooper

INTRODUCTION

The 1980s and early 1990s have been difficult times for many private schools. Tuition costs have risen, competition with public and other private schools for students has stiffened, and the role of private schools in public life has become more ambivalent. While there has been an incredible flurry of "reform" and "restructuring" activity in the public school sector,[1] private schools have not known quite how to become involved. To confuse matters more, school reformers in the 1980s held private schools up as paradigms (even paragons) of school productivity, innovation, effective organization, and decentralized control,[2] even though they were cut off from valuable federal and state resources. In some cases, private schools were destroyed by the intense competition that many "re-formed," choice-driven "public" schools were now using.

The picture that emerges, then, is complex, even ironic at times, as nonpublic schools are both central and peripheral to the school reform movements of the 1980s and beyond. This essay depicts the role of private education in the most recent reform effort, from about 1983 to 1991, as yet another expression of America's ambivalence toward nonpublic elementary and secondary schools.

In particular, this chapter analyzes private schools from three perspectives: First, *we look at the ways in which private education became a critical, if not central, image of school "restructuring" in the 1980s*-- presenting schools which were competitive, choice/market driven, often with strong missions and clear visions, and which were governed autonomously by those closest to the children and their families. In a sense, private schools provided the living "models" of school change embraced by various national commissions, the Reagan-Bush Administrations, a number of states and their governors, and even innovative school districts (e.g., Dade County-Miami, Milwaukee, New York City, and Rochester, NY).

Second, this essay analyzes *how urban private schools lost ground during the 1980s*, finding it ever more difficult to compete with some of the newly active, more innovative and public relations-conscious public schools. It appears that even though many school reformers were lauding nonpublic schools as the ideal kinds of institution, these same political leaders seemed to weaken (by action or inaction) the condition of many parochial schools. Meanwhile, private school groups themselves were usually unable to muster the political muscle and unity to get much public financial help for their ailing schools, with a few exciting exceptions.

And third, we assess the *"costs" of weakened private sector schools*, as escape valves for local parents, as places to get a religious education, as living laboratories of different kinds of school organization and practice, and as sources of real competition and choice, with several *concrete suggestions* for what government might do to support nonpublic education alternatives.

PRIVATE SCHOOLS AND PUBLIC SCHOOL REFORM

Private schools were hardly critical to the initial efforts to identify and remedy the problems with America's public schools. In fact, *A Nation at Risk*,[3] *A Nation Prepared*,[4] *Tomorrow's Teachers*,[5] and *Time for Results*,[6] and a host of other reports all came and went, with hardly a mention of private education. While educators in the public sector were engaged in a colorful spectacle of studies, attacks, and suggested reforms, private schools--enrolling over one-tenth of the nation's students--were nearly an invisible side-show to the public schools' main attraction.

A LIVING METAPHOR

Yet, making things even more bitter than sweet, many public education reformers were using the private schools as handy exemplars--living metaphors--of institutions dedicated to "competition," "choice," and "character," to use the terms of then Secretary of Education, William J. Bennett. In effect, these reformers were arguing that truly to "restructure" public schools--to use the hottest new term--meant to make them more like private schools. In order to resemble private schools, each public school should possess its own unique mission, be responsive to local needs and demands, which would give it a special niche in the local market-place, and possess autonomy with the ability to make its own decisions tailored to the locality.

This symbolic "privatization" provided *terms* (e.g., "restructuring," education "markets," and "client choice"), *qualities* (responsive schools, inter-school competition, and improvement), and *organizational characteristics* ("bottom-up," decentralized, and school-site) that fueled the reform movement during the second half of the 1980s. The large and growing research literature on school reform and "restructuring" now includes a number of private school qualities which were often but not always recognized during this decade.

EDUCATION MARKETS

Many education reformers during the mid-1980s concentrated on the problems of public education as an unresponsive monopoly and looked to private schools as a means to break this control. For example, the Carnegie Task Force on Teaching, which included a wide array of mainstream education groups (both Albert Shanker of the AFT and Mary H. Futrell of the NEA were members), stated that "Markets have proven to be very efficient instruments to allocate resources and motivate people in many sectors of American life. They can also make it possible for all public school students to gain access to equal school resources."[7]

A few analysts went the whole distance, advocating extensive "privatization" of education provision, situations where all schools compete for students and the government "provides" for education but ceases to own and monopolize it. Perhaps the most comprehensive suggestion to make "public" schools behave like "private" ones (see Lieberman, 1989; Cooper, 1991) is to grant parents the resources (through vouchers or tax breaks) and let them "buy" and control the education of their children. Lieberman argues that "the only ways to improve American education are to 1) foster private schools that compete with public schools and among themselves and/or 2) foster for-profit competition among service providers within the public school system."

SCHOOL ORGANIZATION

Once the ownership, sponsorship, and control issues were raised, reformers during the 1980s had a hard time ignoring the private school. Critics of public education looked to the private sector for models of simple, lean, efficient, and direct forms of management. Even schools under the hierarchy of the Roman Catholic Church were run with a tiny diocesan staff and few non-teaching personnel at the schools.

Chubb and Moe found that the very local, decentralized organization of private schools gave them distinct advantages over top-down, externally controlled, and bureaucratic systems of public schools. They concluded:

> When all else is equal--when schools are serving the same kinds of students and dealing with the same kinds of families, when schools are situated in the same locations, including urban locations where large education institutions are conducive to bureaucratization--schools in the private sector are likely to experience far less administrative and personnel constraint than schools in the public sector . . . . Indeed, the only way a public school enjoys the kind of autonomy routinely enjoyed by private schools is if the public school is lucky enough to be located outside an urban area and serving able students and parents.[8]

A DYNAMIC CONTEXT

The 1980s also saw renewed interest in the "context" in which education occurs. While large public school systems are purported to ignore the "community" and its clients, nonpublic schools must necessarily concern themselves with the parents and the immediate environment in order to survive. Parents, in turn, support nonpublic schools because they selected them and because they pay tuition. This "embeddedness" was critical to the reforms of the 1980s and became a concern of public schools as well--especially as the parent involvement or parent "empowerment" movement, always a factor in private schools, took hold.[9]

Coleman and colleagues concluded that Catholic schools exhibit a particularly distinct sense of community, because of three essential qualities. First, parochial schools often have strong internal "social integration" based on a common purpose;[10] second, such schools are part of an external "functional community" which supports their mission; and third, the "special importance of the *religious community* is that it is one of the few remaining strong bases of a functional community in society which includes *both* adults and children."[11] Parochial schools, then, become unique institutions where community, parents, schools, *and* children all come together in a productive relationship.

Hence, Coleman and colleagues drew upon and reintroduced the complementary concepts of "social capital" (the sum of interrelationships among and between families and their communities, including schools) and "human capital" (the intra-familial resources such as the parents' education and commitment to education). Together, "human" and "social capital" reinforce effective school programs and improved student attainment. As Coleman and Hoffer explain:

> . . . outcomes for children are strongly affected by the human capital possessed by their parents. But this human capital can be irrelevant to outcomes for children if parents are not an important part of their children's lives, if their human capital is employed exclusively at work or elsewhere outside the home. The social capital of the family is the relation between children and parents (and when families include other members, relationships with them as well). That is, if the human capital possessed by parents is not complemented by social capital embodied in family relations, it is irrelevant to the child's educational growth that the parent has a great deal, or a small amount, of human capital.[12]

PRIVATE SCHOOL PRODUCTIVITY

Finally, the 1980s seemed obsessed with education results and school outcomes: the so-called "bottom line." What worked and what failed to work[13] gained high visibility from education reformers, as concerns grew about the apparent failure of America's schools.[14] It appeared to many that we were losing ground in national productivity and international competition and that our schools were not up to the task.

So, when several key researchers reported that private schools were effective--perhaps even *more* effective than public schools, the nation noticed. Several major studies appeared to support the superiority of private schools, especially for the poor, minorities, and children of color. Using a federal government longitudinal data base, the "High School and Beyond," Coleman and Hoffer[15] determined that private school students do better than public ones in finishing high school, completing college, and finding jobs.

In part, these differences are explained by the rigorous academic programs which demanded more of Catholic school students than public ones, accounting for nearly double the achievement results. Coleman and Hoffer concluded:

> Comparing the total estimated effects of these demands with the growth differences [between sectors]. . . suggests that if public schools were as likely to place minorities in academic programs as were Catholic schools, assign as much homework as Catholic schools, and require students to take as many semesters of academic course work as Catholic schools, then public school minorities would do as well as Catholic minorities in mathematics and would reduce the Catholic advantage in verbal skills by almost one-half.[16]

In effect, the greater academic demands in Catholic schools plus the strong "social capital" they possess to support these demands, account for the significant differences in achievement test scores between types of schools. Notably, the stronger discipline of Catholic schools does not explain this difference between the Catholic and public school systems.

Coleman and Hoffer[17] also make the point that "the achievement growth benefits of Catholic school attendance are especially strong for students who are in one way or another disadvantaged: lower socioeconomic status, black, or Hispanic. A corollary of this is that the benefits are least strong for those who are from an advantaged family background."[18] While these findings in the 1980 and 1987 studies of Coleman and colleagues were hotly contested by other researchers,[19] the impact of this "Coleman Report" on private and public school achievement was important in shaping the 1980s reform efforts, directing attention to the benefits of "private" education, and the initiating of an attempt to "privatize" public schools.

MUCH PRAISE, FEW BENEFITS

Despite these accolades, private schools have been receiving little or no benefit from all the publicity and from all the concerns about American education. In fact, private schools--particularly the largest group, those operated by the Roman Catholic Church--suffered the loss of federal resources at the hands of the U.S. Supreme Court, defeats of major federal parochial-aid legislation, and the near abandonment by both political parties. Even leading conservatives like President Ronald Reagan and then Secretary of Education William Bennett realized that to push private school aid through real "privatization" of funding (e.g., vouchers, tax breaks, and direct funding) would so rile the opposition that legislation to "semi-privatize" within the public school sector would founder and die. Hence, private school support was jettisoned while the process of making public schools more private was pursued.

The result has been a general loss of support, schools, and pupils for the private school system, though a few exceptions in this rather bleak picture do exist. Hence, the excitement of school reforms in the 1980s, and the centrality of market-related, "private" approaches to change (decentralization, choice, and competition), have not been of much benefit to parochial and private schools.

FEDERAL AID AND PRIVATE SCHOOLS

In the mid-1980s, the U.S. Supreme Court ruled in *Aguilar* v. *Felton*,[20] and *Grand Rapids* v. *Ball*[21] that providing federally-financed services for poor, under-achieving children *on-site* in the parochial school under Chapter 1 was unconstitutional under the First Amendment's separation of church and state. The court found by a 5-4 vote that the federal requirement to supervise public school Chapter 1 teachers on the premises of religious schools led to the "excessive entanglement" of church and state.

In one shot, the judiciary had undone a twenty-year (1965-1985) relationship whereby poor students in parochial schools received remedial help financed by the federal government but provided by teachers from the public schools. From 1985 on, the quantity and quality of such services, now moved "to neutral sites" or delivered electronically, have declined, just at a time when many inner-city Catholic schools were striving to help the poor and minorities.[22]

Legislative attempts to fix the *Aguilar* problem (i.e., how to provide federal services to children in nonpublic schools) also failed,[23] as the Democratic Party (often thought of as the party of the urban centers and religious-ethnic groups) refused to accept several direct means of aiding nonpublic school children. When the Chapter 1 law was up for re-authorization before Congress in 1986-87,[24] three bills were presented in Congress, all of which would have helped poor children attending private and parochial schools. All three were killed in subcommittee:

TEACH. In 1985, legislation, dubbed the *TEACH* (*The Equity And CHoice*) bill was introduced in Congress. This bill called for the total "voucherization" of Chapter 1 services. Eligible children would command a TEACH voucher worth whatever the local district spent on Chapter 1 children (for example, $400 to $1,300 each). Students would be able to select the location of remedial help they preferred and attend: 1) their public school, 2) another public school outside their district, or 3) a private school.

TEACH was probably constitutional under the First Amendment since it did not intend to teach or further religion (the "establishment" clause), did not restrict or deny religious freedom, and did not "entangle" the church and state. After all, the *Mueller* v. *Allen*[25] decision by the U.S. Supreme Court had earlier held a similar Minnesota law constitutional -- that is, parents could claim a state tax deduction for costs associated with either public or private education. Nonetheless, the TEACH bill died quietly in Congress.

CHOICE. In 1987, a group of Republican Congressmen called the Wednesday Group proposed legislation, titled the *CHOICE* (*CH*ildren's *O*pportunity for *I*ntensive *C*ompensatory *E*ducation) bill, to give poor children, even in private schools, a compensatory voucher and an Individual Education Plan (IEP) much like that which "special" education students receive. The bill detailed how private schools might participate: "Representatives of private schools shall be consulted with respect to the development of such a plan if the child is primarily enrolled in a private elementary or secondary school, or if the child is currently receiving special instructional services from a private school through the issuance of an educational voucher" [Sec. 336,f(s)]. Like TEACH, CHOICE was not sent to committee and died.

AEA. Finally, the Reagan administration introduced the American Excellence Act of 1987 (*AEA*) as part of the Chapter 1 re-authorization. The proposed law authorized school districts "to provide these Chapter 1 certificates [a Chapter 1 voucher] if doing so would be more effective in meeting the needs of eligible children than direct services provided by the Local Education Authority (LEA)."

The advantage of AEA over both TEACH and CHOICE was that it left implementation of the planned "Comprehensive Education Certificates" (CECs) to local public school districts, should they find it cheaper and easier than busing parochial school children to off-the-premises locations for Chapter 1 programs. But the Democratic Congress discarded the American Excellence Act, with its Chapter 1 limited, voluntary, optional voucher, in favor of a Democratic bill (HR 950), which added a small amount ($30 million) to the re-authorization to help public schools transport parochial school children off-site. Again, there would be no "privatization" for private schools. And the door had slammed on any kind of grants to help poor, needy, underachieving children receive the remedial help that the Chapter 1 law supposedly guaranteed.

Hence, by early 1988 the Republican administration and Congress had learned their school lessons: aid to parochial schools was the kiss of death to school reform initiatives in the Democratic Congress. Any attempt to present a "voucher" plan or other direct means to help families was inevitably and inexorably tied up in Congressional committees, preventing otherwise exciting programs from reaching the floor for debate. Even Chapter 1, the nation's most important school aid program, was delayed until the voucher provision for helping families of poor children was eliminated.

In the horse-trading that accompanied the re-authorization of the nation's largest federal aid to poor children in school, lawmakers learned that real "choice" would not fly; instead, resources under Chapter 1 would remain within the public school sector only. "Limited" or "controlled" choice was becoming more acceptable, as long as no funds left the public schools.[26] Chester E. Finn, Jr., Assistant Secretary of Education under the Reagan Administration and an advocate of privatization of education, reached the same hard conclusion that "privateness" was good, though he wisely wished to concentrate on "choice" within the public sector:

> . . . the very "privateness" of private schools confers on them many of the organizational benefits that provide better education for their students. I have been struck by the extent to which today's excellence movement has sought to adopt many private school features to the circumstances of public education. Obviously, choice is one such feature. Nevertheless, here I want to confine myself to the pros and cons of choice *within public education,* while noting that some historic distinctions between public and private schools are already blurring and that this tendency is apt to continue.[27]

Thus, it seemed that nonpublic schools embodied the very constellation of qualities that conservative school reformers preferred: innovation, parental choice, hard work, frugality, moral values, smaller size, personal concerns, closeness and responsiveness to parents as clients (free markets), and decentralized management, among other qualities.[28] But the inclusion of nonpublic schools in a school reform plan seemed to cloud the issues, clog the process, and convince reformers to jettison private school programs (aid, support, inclusion) in the interest of greater unity, acceptability, and "reform."

Albert Shanker expressed the attitude best, indicating general popular support for the concept of "choice" in education but not for private school assistance in particular:

> In principle, choice is a fine thing. Americans cherish their freedom to choose where they will live, what church they will worship in, what stores they will patronize. And public school choice, which allows students to choose the public school they want to attend, has worked well in some places. But schemes that allow public funds to pay for education in private schools are a different beast altogether; they give the real choice to schools, not to the parents or kids.[29]

COMPETITION FROM MORE "PRIVATIZED" PUBLIC SCHOOLS

As reformers moved to make public schools behave more like private ones, with greater intra- and inter-district transfers, competition, specialness of mission, and local school management, private schools found themselves losing students. In New York City, for example, according to the Director of High School Placement, some 20 percent of students applying to many of the high-powered urban Magnet Schools (Brooklyn Technical High, Bronx High School of Science, and Stuyvesant High) were former private school students moving from the nonpublic to the public sectors. Even some "elite" parochial schools, often run by holy orders (Franciscans, Jesuits, and the Sisters of Charity), were struggling to keep the best students. Families seemed to prefer public schools and were turning to the private sector only if students were unable to gain admissions to the exclusive "magnet schools." Many of the private schools' best students were being siphoned off into competitive, high-flying public schools.

Hence, the parochial schools for poor, low achieving children were closing or merging, for lack of fiscal help; meanwhile, the up-scale Catholic schools found some of their best clients fleeing to the tuition-free public schools of choice. The "market" was working, but it was working against the very schools that had upheld market principles. For example, while parents had to pay twice for Catholic education (public school taxes and private school tuition), parents in public schools were getting more "privatized" services (schools with special themes, aggressive recruitment, more Advanced Placement courses for university credit, local school control and decision-making, and responsive staff) *free of charge.*

How, one wonders, could the market work? Giving away good services is a hard bargain to ignore, even for parents who care deeply about their faith, their Church, their schools, and their children. Yet, some scholars, such as Chubb and Moe, found that even "public schools of choice" suffer the effects of bureaucratic control, meaning that the nation will always need some nonpublic alternatives to show the benefits of self-governance, decentralization, and responsive education.

On the private school side, a few commentators[30] welcomed the competition from more market-oriented public schools, to keep nonpublic school leaders on their toes. One might even make an argument that when private schools cease to be useful as real prods to public ones (thus becoming less of an alternative to privatized "public" schools), private schools will wither away. Their function as models of competition and excellence may no longer be essential--though obviously we are a long way from having a highly entrepreneurial, open market public school system in the United States.

CATHOLIC SCHOOL DECLINE

The 1980s saw the continued slow death by attrition of many inner-city parochial schools, despite their importance to the poor. While James S. Coleman and colleagues discovered parochial schools high in "social capital" and more effective in helping the impoverished in comparison to many urban public high schools,[31] Catholic schools were themselves low in *financial* capital--and mergers and/or closings were the rule.

As Table 1 shows, Catholic schools increased in number and size steadily, sometimes dramatically, between 1880 and the mid-1960s. They have declined ever since. The peak year was 1964, with some 5.66 million students enrolled in over 13,000 Roman Catholic schools nationwide. The 1980s saw a 20 percent drop in enrollments and a 8.8 percent dip in the number of schools. Research shows that a large number of the school closings were in cities, often at schools serving low-income, minority pupils.[32] Even middle-income schools, however, were hit hard in the last few decades, as costs of Catholic education rose and competition from public schools increased.

TABLE 1

GROWTH AND DECLINE OF U.S. CATHOLIC SCHOOLS & ENROLLMENTS
1880-1990

YEAR	Pupils + (% Change)	Schools + (% Change)
By Decade:		
1880	405,234 --	2,246 --
1890	633,238 (+56%)	3,931 (+75%)
1900	854,523 (+35%)	5,012 (+27%)
1910	1,237,250 (+45%)	7,405 (+48%)
1920	1,925,616 (+56%)	8,103 (+9%)
1930	2,464,522 (+28%)	10,046 (+24%)
1940	2,396,329 (-3%)	10,049 (+0%)
1950	3,066,419 (+28%)	10,778 (+7%)
1960	5,288,705 (+72)	10,892 (+1%)
1964*	*5,622,328*	*13,296*
1970	4,363,633 (-18%)	11,262 (-3.4%)
1980	3,106,378 (-29%)	9,560 (-15%)
1990	2,498,870 (-20%)	8,719 (-8.8%)
By Year:		
1985	2,902,787 --	9,340 --
1986	2,816,787 (-3%)	9,219 (-1.3%)
1987	2,726,004 (-3.2%)	9,102 (-1.3%)
1988	2,623,031 (-3.8%)	8,992 (-1.2%)
1989	2,551,119 (-2.7%)	8,867 (-1.4%)
1990	2,498,870 (-2%)	8,719 (-1.7%)

* Peak Enrollment Year

Source: *A Statistical Report on U.S. Catholic Schools*, 1985-1990, Washington, D.C.: National
Catholic Education Association, pp. 8-12. (Fisher Publishing Ganley's)

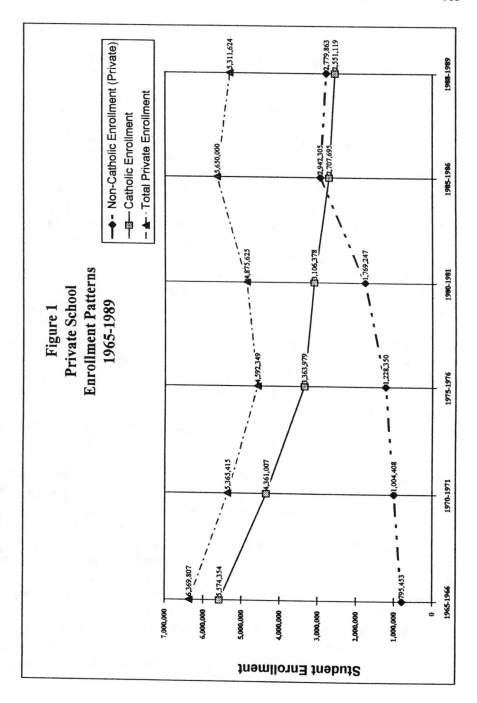

Figure 1
Private School
Enrollment Patterns
1965-1989

Figure 1 shows the overall condition of private education in the United States. Included are Catholic schools (the double line) in comparison to other nonpublic schools (dotted line), with a total (top line) between 1965 and 1989 in all kinds of private schools, allowing some interesting analysis of trends by time periods.

Between 1965 and 1980, for example, the total private school enrollment went from 6.369 million to 4.876 million students, a dip of 23 percent. Meanwhile, the Catholic school enrollment declined by 43 percent during this period (1965-80), while other private school enrollment grew from .795 million to 1.769 million students, or a jump of 123 percent. Data show a somewhat different pattern between 1980 and 1989. During this time Catholic school enrollment declined by 18 percent (from about 3.1 million to 2.5 million), while non-Catholic private school pupil populations *grew* by 57 percent (from 1.770 to 2.780 million in 9 years), increasing the total national enrollments in private schools from 4.875 million in 1980 to 5.34 million in 1989 or plus 9 percent in 9 years.

Finally, Figure 1 shows a total drop in private school pupils between 1965 and 1989. The major loss leader again were schools run by the Roman Catholics, which declined by 54 percent, from 5.574 million to 2.551 million pupils in 24 years. Meanwhile, schools sponsored by other religious groups (e.g., Lutheran, Jewish, Quaker, Seventh-day Adventists, Greek Orthodox, and "independents") have increased during this same period from .795 million to over 2.55 million for a jump of 221 percent since 1965. Because of Catholic school enrollment declines, the overall number of children in the United States attending all kinds of nonpublic schools dipped from 6.369 million in 1965 to around 5.312 million in 1989, or a decrease of 17 percent.

One may draw several conclusions from these data. First, one can assume that the growth in non-Catholic schools (+57 percent), typically more expensive and more middle-class, indicates continued concern about the public system. Parents with resources were availing themselves of the "choice" which the affluent have long had: to select a private school in communities where public schools are in trouble because of strikes, racial problems, declining quality and test scores, violence, or other factors).

Second, as the courts enforced bans on school prayer and religious practice in public schools, a growing number of families abandoned public education. Some of these families helped to establish a vital, fast-growing "Christian" school sector, while other families among this group kept their children home for Christian "homeschooling," rather than risk, in their terms, endangering the souls of their youngsters in "Godless" ("value-free") and "secular humanist" public schools.[33]

Third, private, usually Catholic, schools that attend mainly to poor students found the 1980s a difficult period, with steady declines every year of around two to three percent. Such small, consistent drops probably reflected an attempt on the part of bishops, pastors, and other Catholic leaders to minimize the damage of school closings by careful planning and, where possible, the merger of two (or even three) costly schools into one that was more viable.

It seems quite clear, then, that America's Catholic schools did not benefit from the interest in "privatization" of education in the 1980s. In fact, direct attempts to help poor children in Catholic schools were foiled by the public school lobby (e.g., the NEA and AFT) and the Democratic Party, both of which resisted attempts to "privatize" public funding for private education in the U.S. Though many reformers at the federal level seemed to worship the special qualities of private schools in theory, they were unable to help these schools in practice.

Several states, such as Minnesota and Wisconsin, however, made some modest efforts to aid nonpublic schools. For example, Minnesota passed the most extensive school choice plan in the nation: parents could transfer their children out of their home school district, select regional magnet schools for their children, or apply for a state tax break if they chose a private school for their children. In Wisconsin some 400 children in Milwaukee were funded in order to attend private, non-sectarian schools under a state law championed by state representative Polly Williams, a Black Democrat. Even this modest effort, however, has encountered a few snags.

First, the enabling law for this Wisconsin experiment was attached inappropriately to a general state appropriations law, an illegal act in the state. Second, one of the participating private schools in Milwaukee has already asked to be released from the plan, since it wishes to affiliate with a religious group. Imagine being penalized for wishing to pursue religious convictions in a nation dedicated to "freedom of worship." Despite these minor glitches in Milwaukee, these experiments hold promise, as seen below.

Most interesting, perhaps, has been the suggestion by John Coons and his colleagues that black students be permitted to attend parochial schools under a federal, court-ordered desegregation order (a response to the *Jenkins* v. *State of Missouri* decision declaring the schools segregated) that created a massive "magnet school" choice plan in Kansas City,

Missouri. Since real racial balance is difficult or impossible to attain within this city (given that the public school population is 80 percent African-American and Latin), Coons and others have filed a brief in federal court to permit Black parents and their children to choose among *local, integrated parochial schools*, a position not well received by the federal judiciary.

Most Black parents in Kansas City, Missouri, had found it difficult to exercise choice, since so few whites were available to desegregate the city's schools; hence, whites could go to any public school of choice while Blacks had to wait for the right racial balance (i.e., more whites to apply). Hence, Coons and colleagues questioned this situation and the following conditions: 1) making Black children wait; 2) denying them their first choice; 3) busing them into white suburbs; 4) or moving them across town to find white pupils for an "integrated education." They asked, "Why not take advantage of the high-quality, private schools that are located in the community, are willing to take poor black children, and can educate them at *half* the cost of the public system?" Their plan has been rejected thus far, however, since public systems--afraid of losing their students--have exerted considerable influence to block it. Nevertheless, the debate about this plan suggests that parochial schools may have promise as a way of helping inner-city private schools, furthering racial and social integration (de-segregation), and expanding choice for the nation's poorest, most deprived children.

SUMMARY, COSTS, AND POSSIBILITIES

It seems that the more society looks to private schools as "models" of change, as centers of "excellence," and exemplars of hope for the poor, the less willing it is to assist them in substantive ways. Several attempts in Congress to aid nonpublic schools in the 1980s through Chapter 1 vouchers, tax breaks, and parochial-aid were killed in subcommittee. Private schools, instead, received mobile vans, computers, and off-site services under Chapter 1. Nevertheless, public assistance to private schools, adjusted for inflation, has declined by 40 percent since the *Aguilar* decision.

Hence, society has "used" private schools as paragons of virtue and reform, without tending to their real survival needs and without letting them share in the best aspects of the school reform movement, which they helped to stimulate. By the end of the Reagan and Bush Administrations, private schools had almost vanished from the national reform agenda.

Many conservative reformers, trying to make radical changes in public schools, eschewed helping private schools, for fear that upon introducing religious issues into the equation, the controversial issues of "church-state" and "vouchers" would kill wider legislative support for public school reforms. By the end of the 1980s, private schools were banished to a quiet corner, to be cited and intoned when convenient but not to be substantively helped.

Religious school leaders watched the Democrats--the party of the poor, the urban areas, the many ethnic groups of America, the Catholics, the Jews, and the Blacks--turn against restructuring parochial school aid. U.S. Representative Augustus "Gus" Hawkins, Democrat of California, had chaired the House Subcommittee on Education with an iron hand: no aid to private schools would ever come from that source. Not only had the Democratic Party lost the white South, but it was also now ignoring some of its constituents in the Northern cities, where parochial schools were critical. When Chapter 1 was re-authorized in 1988, parochial schools received little direct help from the Democratic Congress, and remedial assistance for the poor in parochial schools has waned ever since.

Even Chubb and Moe,[34] in their important 1990 book on the advantages of private, autonomous, market-driven schools, would require that nonpublic schools become state-chartered ("public") institutions in order to receive public help. The difference between "public" and "private" would practically disappear, though not all private schools would be eligible or would want to join the state sector. "Existing private schools will be among those eligible to participate," the authors write:

> Their participation should be encouraged, since they constitute a ready supply of often-effective schools. (Our own preference would be to include religious schools as well, as long as their sectarian functions can be kept clearly separate from their educational functions.) Any private schools that do participate *will thereby become public schools*, as such schools are defined under the new system.[35]

Irony of ironies. Note that private schools are included in Chubb and Moe's privatization scheme, not because of their needs and commitment to poor children, but because they are functionally a "ready supply of often-effective schools." But most telling, to participate, a private school becomes a *public* school--absorption into the public sector? And if a nonpublic school has a religious mission, as most do in the U.S., they are excluded from help unless they can isolate their religiousness from the rest of the school. School leaders that believe that religious convictions should permeate the entire school program--and many do--would have their schools excluded from this program.

Although the Chubb and Moe approach welcomes choice, variety, and local autonomy within a nonsectarian domain, most American private schools would find it difficult to adopt since they exist to promote their religious goals. Many committed Christians, Jews, and Muslims, would find it difficult to take public funds for their schools, if this aid was dependent upon the condition that the school's religious message be kept in an air-tight compartment, safely away from the non-religious curriculum.

The "chartering" of private schools as state-aided institutions has several obvious advantages, including the government assuming some or most of the costs of educating children in the private sector. Already, private schools receive tax benefits on property and income; some take special needs children in placements paid for by the public; and for the first time, chartering would put public and private schools on equal footing, playing the competitive game on a "level playing field," to use the current term for economic equity.

> The important institutional innovation here is the New *Public* School which is a novel legal creature; each such school would take the form of a separate public corporation organized and designed by a local school board (or public university) and financed by the scholarships of its patrons. Its counterpart in the private sector would be the New *Private* School operating according to the same rules except for its entitlement to teach religion.[36]

Furthermore, as national data show, not all private schools are in financial distress or in the process of closing, though the recent recession (1991) has made its mark on many of even the most elite preparatory schools. With a sagging economy and lay-offs in many sectors, parents have been finding it more difficult to raise the tuition for private schools. Schools which serve a strong faith community, which reach more affluent parents, and which are aggressive in recruiting students and accumulating an endowment were likely hurt less than those serving low-income and non-Catholic students.

In summary, then, private schools have made a significant contribution to America's school reform effort, supplying ideas, concepts, dedication, and productivity. But friends and foes alike have faced the naked realization that these schools confuse policymakers with sticky issues such as the separation of church and state, privatization, voucherization, selectivity and elitism, and real hard-nosed competition--most of which most public school monopolies cannot accept.

Most analysts realize that monopolies cannot long exist without laws and policies to suppress choice and competition. Education markets are as "natural" in the U.S., it seems, as are economic markets in Eastern Europe. Witness the vitality and productivity of American *higher* education, where families and students have enormous diversity and choice. Still the 1980s has seen the public school lobby working overtime to maintain its hegemony over public funds, policies, and programs.

The Future

In the future, private schools will continue to lead in the development of the intellectual and organizational innovations necessary for public school reform. What can be done to facilitate this process given the complex history of private schools in America[37] and the nation's schizophrenia about religion and education?

A Steady Decline

Without dramatic action, many cities and towns will lose their effective parochial schools for the poor, especially as costs go up, competition builds, and available resources are expended. Private and parochial schools seem trapped; they need desperately to raise funds. Perhaps this can be done through more effective marketing. Those parochial schools that help the least affluent families are the schools on the verge of closing and have the least access to financial resources (rich endowments, industrial contributions, private help) with a few exceptions.

If things continue on course, then, we shall probably see a widening gap between those families that can afford real choice (either by moving their residence to a "better" public school district or zone or by paying increased private school tuition and fees) and those poor families that have fewer life-chances and much less choice. While "controlled choice" programs (e.g., magnet schools, open enrollment schemes, and metro-transfer plans) within the public schools have promise for all students, affluent and poor, some critics have argued convincingly that public school choice is limited and a passing trend. These critics have observed the difficulties of expanding and continuing programs of public school choice due to mounting public school costs and rigid bureaucratic controls and regulations.

Myron Lieberman,[38] a noted educational theorist, has predicted the failure of choice and "privatization" within the public systems. As he explains, "At bottom, choice within public schools is an effort to incorporate the features of a market system in government provision of services. Unfortunately, such efforts usually fail, no matter what service or country is involved."[39] Real choice cannot easily flourish in a state-run monopoly, for several reasons:

Limited Variety. Public schools, no matter what their "theme" or concept, tend to look more alike (than the vast range of private, parochial, and alternative schools), are staffed by teachers drawn from the same "certified," state-licensed pool, under the same strictures. Some school types would be totally unacceptable to government-run schools, including religious and doctrinal schools.

Diffusion of Mission. Public schools that attempt to be all things to all people, offering a shopping list of choices, may lose their sense of mission. Hence, while a private school, for example, a Missouri Synod Lutheran school, focuses on the goals of this sect and this community, a "public" school must offer programs for all groups, and thus loses a focus. Lieberman explains,

> To make matters worse, by catering to a wide range of choice, public schools end up trying to be all things to all parents. Inevitably, they cannot provide choices as attractive as those available in schools which focus on particular choices. Anyone who doubts this should consider what choice of automobile would be available if limited to those made by a single monopolistic automobile manufacterer.[40]

Perservering Bureaucracy. Many "choice" plans are implanted in school systems which are highly regulated and bureaucratic. The New York City school system, which boasts one of the nation's most diverse public school options programs with 364 different "magnet," or "educational option," programs in its 116 secondary schools, also possesses the most elaborate system of centralized control in the U.S.. Principals find it difficult to "be different" in a system which is rule-bound and centrally controlled. Funding, testing, staffing, programming, and allocating of resources come from the top; janitorial, security, and food services are also "run from downtown," even though school-site leaders are held accountable for these functions.

Thus, private schools are not different simply because they have a variety of missions and programs; they are structurally, managerially, and economically different as well.[41] Thus, to rely solely on educational choice programs conducted within the public sector is to cede control not only of school curriculum but also of models of school governance and control to the public sector. This would inevitably have a negative effect on the nation's educational system since private schools have much to contribute.

Are private, particularly parochial schools, being hurt by mounting competition from more "choice-oriented" public schools? The answer is likely, yes, though exact data and research are yet to be available on this important topic. Probably, the schools most affected are those dedicated to the children from the least affluent families, these private city schools may be engaging in efforts that will constitute their "last chance" for survival. Private schools for the poor are being hurt most by increased public-private competition, or at least that is what private school leaders proclaim.

Perhaps we should have expected as much. Private education, being closer to the local economic realities of societal change, may be reflecting America's widening differences between rich and poor, older and younger people. Why should inner-city Catholic schools be doing better in a society that has turned its back on the cities, the poor, and the non-white? Given an opportunity, we know that nonpublic schools can work for children; they're doing it now, according to "High School and Beyond" data[42] with very limited help. But these nonpublic schools cannot do it alone for much longer.

In part, the future of private education depends, sadly, on the (perceived) failure of public education. This zero-sum game (one must lose if the other is to win) is the result of how the United States has constructed its educational services. The more choices that are offered within the public system, the greater the negative impact on private schools will be. The more public schools act like private ones, the worse are the consequences for the private schools which must charge fees to survive. Conversely, where public schools are in disarray, private schools are in demand.

Arthur Powell[43] urges that we avoid this contentious relationship between public and private schools--and have the two school systems work together. He explains:

> The point is that when the stakes are perceived as wholly competitive, a zero-sum game where there are only winners and losers, the polemical pressure increases both anger and generalities . . . . Much of the debate so far suggests two monolithic armies poised to engage in bitter and decisive conflict on the field of battle. The two central images are of inevitable competition between the sectors, on the one hand, and of fundamental

differences between them, on the other. The either/or quality of political debate . . . helps reinforce these two images.[44]

Somehow, the two sectors should be working toward the same ends: better education for all children, regardless of background, needs, or preferences.

True, some education analysts have argued that this healthy competition will strengthen many nonpublic schools, though we also have strong evidence that parochial schools for the poor--perhaps the most important urban schools we have--are overly vulnerable to destructive competition with choice-driven public ones and cannot really compete effectively. Surely, any schools (public or private) that can serve the children from the poorest families and show strong results should be given a chance to survive, as the Kansas City proposal of Coons and colleagues has argued.

TOTAL SCHOOL PRIVATIZATION

Few believe that elementary and secondary schools will be "privatized": that is, made totally responsive to the needs and demands of parents and children.[45] Americans are to date unwilling to rely solely on the private sector provision of schooling, since they have become accustomed to the very ubiquitous public system. Instead, we see and will continue to see public schools only mimicking private ones (competing marginally, being somewhat more aggressively entrepreneurial, seeking some ties with the business community, and extending limited choice within the public sphere).

Shared Resources. Aid to private and parochial schools is limited (though important) in a few states: tax relief as not-for-profit institutions, free bus transportation, loans of publicly-owned textbooks and materials, and off-site provision of remedial assistance. Also, a number of suggestions for direct support have been made, and a few tried with some success.

Local Inter-Sector Transfer Plans. Coons' suggestions for school integration in Kansas City and Williams' efforts in Milwaukee bear watching. These efforts move the private schools into the reform effort in an important way: by allowing limited, local transfer of students from one sector to the other.

Notably, both of these experiments concentrated on the inner-city poor, in part to disarm the usual contention that aid to private schools would line the pockets of the rich. In fact, Coons in the early 1980s advocated a Basic Education Opportunity Grant for poor children. More recently,

Doyle, Cooper, and Trachtman in their book, *Taking Charge*,[46] call for a "Poor Kids Voucher" to extend the same chances and choices to low-income students that the middle class already possesses.

But in the cases of the Coons' voucher and the Williams' transfer plan, the religious nature of nonpublic schools still poses serious problems for policymakers and the courts. We need to know whether the new Supreme Court might overturn bans on public support to religious schools, reversing the *Aguilar* principle of "entanglement" (i.e., that public schools cannot engage their staff on-site in parochial schools).

Justice Antonin Scalia commented several years ago on the rights of religious or sectarian schools to remain sectarian even while receiving public support: "The point is that sectarian schools should be able to remain sectarian without forgoing an educational subsidy for the elements of routine education which are imparted in the course of their programs."[47]

Tax Credits. Perhaps the most important innovation to date is granting public and private school parents a tax break for the cost of their children's education. This scheme, already implemented in Minnesota and proposed elsewhere, has three distinct advantages: 1) it is constitutional since it is accord with the federal court's decision in *Mueller* v. *Allen* regarding "free exercise" of religions; 2) it promotes choice within and between sectors, since public and private school parents alike can file for state tax relief; and 3) it can be implemented without much effort since new bureaucracies or personnel are not needed.

The coalition that passed the tax deduction law in Minnesota might prevail in other states and in the U.S. Congress. This Minnesota tax break permits choice and promotes opportunity but has not "hurt" the public schools. Furthermore, some evidence exists that public schools in Minnesota have become more sensitive to their clients, anticipating that parents have more flexibility in selecting a new school for their children. Also, we have *not* seen a mass exodus from Minnesota's public schools, as some skeptics predicted. Generally, tax policy may be a useful reform in the future for both public and private education.

A SHARED MARKET APPROACH

For practical reasons, strategies should be developed to enable public and private schools to share the responsibility for educating children and to work together for school reform. The practices of implementing Chapter 1 programs between 1965 and 1985 provide cogent examples of such inter-sector cooperation, with 1) the federal government providing the financing; 2) the states distributing the funds to districts; 3) the local public schools hiring and supervising the Chapter 1 teachers and learning specialists; and 4) the private schools supplying the needy and low-achieving students and the "resource room" space for the on-site services in the parochial schools.

It is estimated that between 1965 and 1985 one million poor children attending the nation's nonpublic schools were served by Chapter 1.[48] The concept of shared responsibility and cooperation was a useful one as developed by the Johnson Administration; it included help for private school children without obviously giving direct financial aid to church-related schools. Hence, having public schools provide the teachers and materials (on "loan" to private schools) worked exceedingly well for two decades until the Supreme Court made such on-site provision of these services in the parochial schools illegal.

The current provision of special education also demonstrates again how the two groups can cooperate. When children are unable to gain an "appropriate" and "least restrictive" program within the public sector, for example, they are placed in private facilities in or outside the district (or state). This approach has deep historical roots, extending back to the pre-public school days when most children received their schooling at home or in private schools. Today, society continues to turn to private schools where no public services readily exist (e.g., for pre-school, after-school, summer camps, special education, religious education, tutoring, and advanced music and arts lessons with artists of choice).

These examples of private-public sector cooperation suggest a multiplicative approach (not zero-sum), one in which private resources build upon and enhance the public provision of schooling. This approach relieves the current win/lose approach that seems to be evident in many communities. It seems preferable to work together, rather than to wait for a near collapse of public schools before significant reform can occur.

Perhaps in cities where the public school system has failed miserably and where the states "take over" schools, policymakers might turn to the local private schools to join in the reform process. Desperation may breed innovation. At any rate, private schools now offer many meaningful education choices to inner-city minorities--and can help public schools in this difficult task. The Rev. Virgil C. Bloom, S.J., made this point a decade ago:

Minority parents rightly feel that they have been discriminated against because of their color or ethnicity. They have been denied equal rights in virtually every phase of human existence. Although the battle for civil rights for minorities in the 1960s has changed much of that, the right of meaningful educational choice for minorities [who have become the majority in many cities] is still to be won. State and federal tax policies severely damaged the inner cities, thus leaving minority families with government schools that provide inferior education. Moreover, governments have persistently denied education tax funds to parents who choose high-quality private schools for their children's education.[49]

Private and public schools need each other. They augment each other by illustrating their relative strengths and weaknesses. And they can augment each other by assisting in the provision of a needed but absent educational program or resource. A nation without private provision, or severely limited private access, is truly at risk, as the former Eastern bloc countries learned. A total public monopoly, regardless of its intent and effort, will surely fail to innovate, respond to changing needs, or offer the diverse curriculum that many families require.

Unless the United States helps its struggling urban private schools and their families, the nation shall lose a much-needed resource for children who have so little. Unless we maintain a strong private sector educational option for all children, rich and poor, we lose a valuable resource. Educational choice programs within the public sector cannot do it alone --for programs such as magnet schools and open enrollment do not always illustrate the benefits of small, autonomous, client-driven, and non-bureaucratic education, much as private schools do.

Why not attempt Professor Coons' idea? Permit parochial schools to provide an integrated education for poor, minority children under a court-ordered desegregation effort--as starters, then expand access to private education at government expense for the middle class as well. Have the state pay the children's tuition for parochial schools in inner-city Kansas City, Missouri, for example, and let these willing parochial schools join in the struggle to help desegregate the school experience and educate inner-city students.

Alternately, it also might be useful to follow the Detroit Public Schools' idea of allowing private schools to "join the public system" voluntarily. This would provide these schools with additional financial resources, offer exciting models of autonomous education, and enlist nonpublic schools to help in educating the students in one of America's most hard-pressed public systems? What do we have to lose?

ENDNOTES

1. Samuel B. Bacharach, *School Reform: Making Sense of It All* (Boston, MA: Allyn and Bacon, 1990); Richard Elmore and others, eds., *Restructuring Schools: The Next Generation of Educational Reform* (San Francisco, CA: Jossey-Bass, 1989); Jane Hannaway and Robert Crowson, *The Politics of Reforming School Administration* (New York, NY: Falmer Press and the Politics of Education Association, 1989); Denis P. Doyle, Bruce S. Cooper, and Roberta Trachtman, *Taking Charge: State Action on School Reform in the 1980s* (Indianapolis, IN: Hudson Institute, 1991); and William Lowe Boyd and others, eds., *Choice in Education: Potentials and Problems* (Berkeley, CA: McCutchan, 1990).

2. James S. Coleman and Thomas Hoffer, *Public and Private High Schools: The Impact of Communities* (New York, NY: Basic Books, 1987); James S. Coleman, Thomas Hoffer, and Sally Kilgore, *High School Achievement: Public, Catholic, and Private Schools Compared* (New York, NY: Basic Books, 1982); and John E. Chubb and Terry M. Moe, *Politics, Markets, and America's Schools* (Washington, DC: Brookings Institution, 1990).

3. National Commission on Excellence in Education, *A Nation at Risk* (Washington, D.C.: Government Printing Office, 1983).

4. Carnegie Task Force on Teaching as a Profession, *A Nation Prepared: Teachers for the 21st Century* (New York, NY: Carnegie Forum on Education and the Economy, 1986); and Education Commission of the States, *What Next? More Leverage for Teachers?* (Denver, CO: Education Commission of the States, 1986).

5. The Holmes Group, *Tomorrow's Teachers* (East Lansing, MI: The Holmes Group, 1986).

6. National Governors' Association, *Time for Results: The Governors' 1991 Report on Education* (Washington, D.C.: The National Governors' Association, Center for Policy and Research, 1991); Congressional Budget Office, *Educational Achievement: Explanations and Implications of Recent Trends* (Washington, DC: Government Printing Office, August 1987).

7. Carnegie Task Force, *A Nation Prepared*, 14.

8. Chubb and Moe, *Politics, Markets, and America's Schools*, 180.

9. Barbara Jackson and Bruce S. Cooper, "Parent Involvement: Implications for School Management," *Urban Education* 24, no. 3, (October 1989): 263-286.

10. Coleman and Hoffer, *Public and Private High Schools*, 215.

11. Ibid., 215.

12. Ibid., 222-223.

13. Department of Education, *What Works* (Washington, D.C.: Government Printing Office, 1987).

14. Diane Ravitch and Chester E. Finn, *What Our Seventeen Year Olds Know: A Report on the First National Assessment of History and Literature* (New York, NY: Harper & Row, 1987).

15. Coleman and Hoffer, *Public and Private High Schools*.

16. Ibid., 146.

17. Ibid..

18. Ibid., 213.

19. Robert L. Crain and Christine H. Rossell, "Catholic Schools and Racial Segregation," in *Public Values, Private Schools*, ed. Neal E. Devins (Philadelphia, PA: Falmer Press, 1989), 184-214; Robert L. Crain, "Private Schools and Black-White Segregation: Evidence from Two Big Cities," in *Comparing Public and Private Schools* 1, ed. Thomas James and Henry M. Levin (Philadelphia, PA: Falmer Press, 1988), 270-293; and Edward Page and T. Keith, "Effects of U.S. Private Schools: A Technical Analysis of Two Recent Claims," *Educational Researcher* 10, no. 7, (1981): 7-17.

20. *Aguilar v. Felton*, 105 S.Ct. 3232 (1985).

21. *Grand Rapids v. Bell*, 105 S.Ct. 3216 (1985).

22. Thomas Vitullo-Martin and Bruce S. Cooper, *The Separation of Church and Child: The Constitution and Federal Aid to Religious Schools* (Indianapolis, IN: The Hudson Institute, 1987).

23. Bruce S. Cooper, "The Uncertain Future of National Education Policy: Private Schools and the Federal Role," in *The Politics of Excellence and Choice in Education*, ed. William Lowe Boyd and Charles T. Kerchner (Philadelphia, PA: Falmer Press, 1988), 165-181.

24. Denis P. Doyle and Bruce S. Cooper, *Federal Aid to the Disadvantaged: What Future Chapter 1?* (Philadelphia, PA: Falmer Press, 1988).

25. *Mueller v. Allen*, 463 S. Ct. 388 (1983).

26. Charles L. Glenn, *The Myth of the Common School* (Amherst, MA: University of Massachusetts Press, 1988); Joe Nathan, *Free to Teach: Achieving Equity and Excellence in Schools* (New York, NY: Pilgrim Press, 1983); Henry M. Levin, "The Theory of Choice Applied to Education," in *Choice and Control in American Education* 1, ed. William H. Clune and John F. Witte (Philadelphia, PA: Falmer Press, 1990), 247—284; Joe Nathan, *Public Schools by Choice* (St. Paul, MN: The Institute for Teaching and Learning, 1989); and Mary Metz, "Magnet Schools and the Reform of Public Schooling," in *Choice in Education: Potential and Problems*, ed. William L. Boyd and Herbert J. Walberg (Berkeley, CA: McCutchan, 1990), 123-148.

27. Chester E. Finn, Jr., "Why We Need Choice," in *Choice in Education: Potential and Problems*, ed. William L. Boyd and Herbert J. Walberg (Berkeley, CA: McCutchan, 1990), 14; and Chester E. Finn, Jr., "Are Public and Private Schools Converging?," *Independent School*, 48 (1989): 45-55.

28. David Kearns and Denis P. Doyle, *Winning the Brain Race: A Bold Plan to Make Our Schools Competitive Again* (San Francisco, CA: Institute for Contemporary Studies Press, 1988).

29. Albert Shanker, "The Agenda for Education: Going Forward or Going off Track," *New York Times*, 30 December 1990, *The Week In Review*.

30. Arthur G. Powell, "Stalking the Public-Private School Dualism," *Independent School*, February 1982, 17-23.

31. Coleman and others, eds., *High School Achievement*.

32. Bruce S. Cooper, "The Changing Universe of U.S. Private Schools," in *Comparing Public and Private Schools: Institutions and Organizations* 1, ed. Thomas James and Henry M. Levin (Philadelphia, PA: Falmer Press, 1988), 18-45; and Bruce S. Cooper, "The Changing Demography of U.S. Private Schools: Trends and Implications," *Education and Urban Society* 16, no. 4, (1984): 429-442.

33. James C. Carper, "The Christian Day School," in *Religious Schooling in America*, ed. James C. Carper and Thomas C. Hunt, (Birmingham, AL: Religious Education Press, 1984), 110-129; James C. Carper, "The Christian Day School Movement," *The Educational Forum* 47 (1983): 135-149; and Patricia M. Lines, "Treatment of Religion in Public Schools and the Impact on Private Education," in *Comparing Public and Private Schools* 1, ed. Thomas James and Henry M. Levin (Philadelphia, PA: Falmer Press, 1988), 67-94.

34. John E. Chubb and Terry M. Moe, "Effective Schools and Equal Opportunity," in *Public Values, Private Schools*, ed. Neal E. Devins (Philadelphia, PA: Falmer Press, 1988), 161-183.

35. Chubb and Moe, *Politics, Markets, and America's Schools*, 219.

36. John E. Coons, "Making Schools Public," in *Private Schools and the Public Good: Policy Alternatives for the Eighties*, ed. Edward M. Gaffney, Jr. (Notre Dame, IN: University of Notre Dame Press, 1990), 95.

37. Otto F. Kraushaar, *American Nonpublic Schools: Patterns of Diversity* (Baltimore, MD: Johns Hopkins University Press, 1972).

38. Myron Lieberman, *Privatization and Educational Choice* (New York, NY: St. Martin's Press, 1990).

39. Ibid., 240-241.

40. Ibid., 241.

41. Chubb and Moe, *Politics, Markets, and America's Schools*.

42. Coleman and Hoffer, *Public and Private High Schools*; and Chubb and Moe, *Politics, Markets, and America's Schools*.

43. Powell, "Stalking Public and Private Dualism."

44. Ibid., 18-19.

45. Lieberman, *Privatization and Educational Choice*; *The International Encyclopedia of Education, Supplement* (London: Pergamon Press, 1991), s.v. "The Privatization of Education," by Bruce S. Cooper; Bruce S. Cooper and Grace Dondero, "Survival, Change, and Demands on America's Private Schools: Trends and Policies," *Education Foundations: Journal of the American Educational Studies Association* (Winter 1991); and Bruce S. Cooper, Donald H. McLaughlin, and Bruno V. Manno, "The Latest Word of Private School Growth," *Teachers College Record* 85, no. 1, (1983): 88-98.

46. Doyle, Cooper, and Trachtman, *Taking Charge*.

47. Edward M. Gaffney, *Private Schools and the Public Good: Policy Alternatives for the Eighties* (Notre Dame, IN: University of Notre Dame Press, 1991), 199.

48. Thomas Vitullo-Martin and Bruce S. Cooper, *The Seperation of Church and Child*, 1.

49. Virgil C. Bloom, "Why Inner-City Families Send their Children to Private Schools: An Empirical Study," in *Private Schools and the Public Good: Policy Alternatives for the Eighties*, ed. Edward M. Gaffney, Jr. (Notre Dame, IN: University of Notre Dame Press, 1981), 17-24.

Chapter 11

The Educational Choice Movement in Pennsylvania

David W. Kirkpatrick

THE HISTORIC BACKGROUND

The concept of school choice, an arrangement in which students and their parents select the schools the students will attend, is not only older than the public school system in this country, but it is older than the nation itself. School choice was first suggested by Adam Smith, in *The Wealth of Nations*, published in 1776.

Smith developed this concept and wrote about its possible application because of his belief that the schools of his day were not effective and that they did not prepare students for the world. He also argued that educational arrangements where the student selected the teacher, even with the utilization of public funds, the teacher would be both more responsive and more respected, arguments which seem to have been proven by the subsequent history of more than 200 years. Finally, he was not interested in the issues of parental rights, the separation of church and state, or some of the other arguments about educational choice that are featured today.

As Virginia's Governor in 1779, Thomas Jefferson introduced the New World's first plan for a statewide school system. Within Virginia's school system, Jefferson believed that elementary pupils whose parents were too poor to give them further education as well as bright secondary students who needed financial aid should be given scholarships.[1]

Following the establishment of Virginia's educational system, Thomas Paine addressed the topic of education in the second part of *The Rights of Man*. In this treatise, Paine even delineates the amount of public funding that should be allocated for each child's education.[2]

Temple University Professor Michael Katz has noted that in the early 19th Century it was common for schools to be operated by religious or other private groups and receive funding for the schools from government.[3] In the mid-19th Century, Pennsylvania was among the states that allocated money to private schools that provided education for mentally retarded students.[4] This is a practice that continues today.

In 1859 the drive to establish educational choice was picked up by John Stuart Mill. Mill sets forth the following argument on education:

> A general State education is a mere contrivance for molding people to be exactly like one another; and as the mould in which it casts them is that which pleases the predominant power of the government, whether this be a monarch, a priesthood, an aristocrat, or the majority of the existing generation; in proportion as it is efficient and successful, it establishes a despotism over the mind....An education established and controlled by the state should only exist, if it exists at all, as one among many competing experiments, carried on for the purpose of example and stimulus, to keep the others up to a certain standard of excellence.[5]

Actually, by the time Mill wrote this passage, the option of publicly funded school choice had already been launched in the United States. Educational choice in America was initiated by 1842 in St. Johnsbury, Vermont.

Vermont's action ran against the emerging movement toward government owned and operated schools, led by Horace Mann in Massachusetts and Thaddeus Stevens in Pennsylvania. Vermont's educational system permitted local governmental units to either build and operate their own secondary schools or provide funds to students so they could go to a school of their choice, public or private. This continues to the present day.

Presently, one-third of the school districts in Vermont operate no secondary schools; consequently, about one-quarter of all high school students in that state attend a public or private school of their choice not under the control of their home school district. In fact, Vermont's children chose schools in eight other states and Canada since there are no geographic restrictions on the state's educational choice policy.

Despite public educators' fears about an educational choice program, 75 percent of Vermont students exercising choice select a public school. Many students among the remaining 25 percent would also choose a public school if one had been located within a reasonable distance of their homes.

Although variations of Vermont's educational choice program became available in a few other states, such as Maine and New Hampshire, the idea was generally buried by the movement for government operated schools, despite Mill's warning.

SCHOOL CHOICE AS A CONSTITUTIONAL RIGHT

In the early 1920s the people of Oregon voted in favor of an initiative, partially inspired by the Ku Klux Klan, establishing a mandate that every child in Oregon would have to attend a public school. The motivation behind this initiative was the desire "to mould people to be exactly like one another." This initiative's mandate was appealed through the courts and culminated in a 1925 unanimous ruling by the U.S. Supreme Court that no child in the United States could be legally compelled to attend a public school. The Court argued that "the child is not the creature of the state."[6] Basically, the Court's opinion held that although the state has a fundamental interest in an educated citizenry, it does not have a similar interest in how that education is attained.

The Supreme Court, however, did not rule on the issue of education funding since this question was not under consideration. To this day, the Court has never issued a ruling that stipulates that students, and/or their parents, have any right to public funds in order to obtain their education on their own.

Even though the Supreme Court has ruled that it is constitutionally impermissible to require students to attend public schools, this has become an economic requirement for students from families that cannot afford the tuition at a nonpublic school or the price of residing in an affluent community. These communities have public school systems that are doubly advantaged--in the amount of money they have to operate their systems and in the background of most of their students. These are significant advantages that are denied to many public school districts across the country.

Generally overlooked in considerations of educational choice is the United Nations' *Declaration of Human Rights*, adopted in 1948, which the United States supposedly supports. The Declaration holds that "parents have a prior right to choose the kind of education that shall be given to their children." [7]

THE EMERGENCE OF THE SCHOOL CHOICE ISSUE

The modern revival of school choice in the United States may be dated to 1955. In this year economist Milton Friedman wrote "The Role of Government in Education." In his essay Friedman noted that there has been a "failure to separate sharply the question of what activities it is appropriate for government to *finance* from the question of what activities it is appropriate for government to *administer.*"[8] The government can easily grapple with the first question without addressing the second question. This situation is reflected, for example, when school districts finance school construction but contract with private firms to do the actual work.

Other public policy analysts also embraced the concept of educational choice, such as James S. Coleman. He said the way to finance effective and equitable education would be "a return of resources to each family, in the form of tuition vouchers, so that each family has equal potential for obtaining its child's education, on an open market." [9]

Another advocate for educational choice was Christopher Jencks, of the Center for the Study of Public Policy in Cambridge, Massachusetts. He and a few colleagues received a grant from the federal Office of Economic Opportunity (OEO) to study this educational innovation in December 1969.

Their report, *Education Vouchers*, issued in December 1970, recommended a compensatory, regulated voucher pilot project be attempted. Compensatory, in that it would provide extra funds for students with particular needs, and regulated so it would prevent such things as racial discrimination.

Ironically, especially in the light of subsequent events, one of the first voices for school choice in Pennsylvania, and tuition vouchers in particular, was this writer, while President of the Pennsylvania State Education Association in 1970. Following an attack upon the concept at the 1970 National Education Association annual meeting, the following was written for the PSEA's *Pennsylvania School Journal*:

Public education in the United States is under an ever-increasing attack and is being challenged as never before. To take an ostrich-like view of these challenges, as the NEA Representative Assembly did on some issues at San Francisco in July--issues such as...tuition vouchers...will be to no avail. We should be willing to take part in any educational experiments and be quick to accept those that show value.[10]

Part of the rationale for the above argument, like Adam Smith's, was that this would be advantageous to teachers, as well as to students and public schooling in general.

In 1971, a survey of members of Phi Delta Kappa, a professional educators fraternity, found that 45 percent of the teachers who were members favored educational vouchers. [11]

Attacks by educational organizations, including both national teachers unions, drove support for educational choice among teachers down in succeeding years but did not extinguish it. Every poll of teachers has shown a substantial percentage continue to favor the approach, and some polls, such as one conducted in 1990, found a majority favoring educational choice.[12]

Some realize, as David Rogers has written, that "The frustration that people inside or outside the system feel in trying to deal with the bureaucracy often leads to power-seeking behavior that spreads distrust at all levels. Teachers and parents, both victims of this system, have been taking it out on each other, and the ultimate victim is the child."[13]

Teacher John Holt has also written about some of the consequences that stem from the nature of public education as it is presently organized:

It is because his relation with his patient is based on mutual consent that the doctor can afford to be professional, that is, to say and do what *he* thinks right. Precisely the opposite is true of us. It is because our relationship with the public...is *not* voluntary, *not* based on mutual consent, that we are not allowed to be professional. Because the parents...have to send their children to our classes, because for most of them there is no other option, they are bound to try to make us say or do in those classes whatever they want, whether we like it or not. Only when all parents, not just rich ones, have a truly free choice in education...only then will we teachers begin to stop being what most of us still are...which is jailers and babysitters, cops without uniforms, and begin to be professionals.[14]

One result of introducing an educational voucher-system would be "the relegation of the religious-school problem from the area of political decision to the area of private decision." [15]

THE PENNSYLVANIA DEBATE

The current battle in Pennsylvania over the introduction of Outcome-Based Education, particularly the inclusion of values in the requirements, provides further evidence of the possibility that school choice "would automatically end the fear of state domination of education. It would take the sting out of the issue of giving state support to religious schools. With every parent free to select an institution of his own choice, nobody could complain of forced indoctrination." [16]

One important source of support for publicly funded school choice through the use of vouchers came from the 1971 *Report of the White House Conference on Youth*, which recommended:

> *Educational Vouchers.* Under this plan, a publicly accountable agency would issue a voucher for a year's schooling for each eligible student. The voucher could be turned over to any school which had been designated as acceptable by an Educational Voucher Agency. Each school would then turn in its vouchers for cash...Such a voucher system would certainly promote the development of a more diversified secondary school system and one more related to existing career possibilities. [17]

The Federal Reserve Bank of Philadelphia periodically conducts studies on education, and one such study appeared in 1971 in its publication, *Business Review*. This study maintained that "Voucher proponents have put educators on notice that there is no substitute for individual achievement," it concluded that "the time has come to step completely, albeit carefully, out of the mold of government--operated schools." [18]

Further support for educational choice in Pennsylvania came from Richard Cyert, the former President of Carnegie-Mellon University in Pittsburgh. While his primary interest was higher education, his arguments could apply to basic education as well. By funding students:

> public institutions could escape the political influences of state legislatures....The legislature can effectively transfer its concerns over curricula and similar matters to the control stemming from students' free choice of which school they will attend....At the same time, direct aid to students will provide real accountability for the effective use of public funds. Students will have a strong incentive to make the best use of their money and, despite the problems of making a free choice of a complex product, will do better choosing for themselves than by having others choose for them. [19]

But Cyert was not optimistic. "Though the logical strength of the argument for a market solution is great, there are political forces that discourage optimism."[20]

Even some public school supporters chimed in with support for the concept of educational choice. One such example was Gerald Stroufe, the Executive Director of the National Committee for Support of the Public Schools. He concluded in 1971 that "The special magic of education vouchers is that they offer hope to a society that increasingly doubts the capability of traditional education structures and methods for educating their children....Those of us who would see the institution continue and prosper should address ourselves to alleviating the causes of despair rather than to doing battle with the voucher plan."[21]

During the mid-1970s, there were efforts in the Pennsylvania General Assembly to initiate school choice. Twice bills became law only to be declared unconstitutional by the U.S. Supreme Court because the legislation would have only aided students in nonpublic schools. The Court found that about three-quarters of non-public school students in Pennsylvania attended religious schools, two-thirds of which were associated with one denomination. The Court held that this situation constituted an unacceptable entanglement between church and state and was impermissible. The Court, however, did not say it was ruling on such aid that would go to all students.

Typical of the arguments in the Pennsylvania General Assembly was State Senator John Sweeney who said,

> In my judgment each child who attends an accredited elementary or secondary school in this Commonwealth or any place in this Nation, public or private, is entitled to participate equally in the distribution of the available tax dollars raised for educational purposes. No child should be considered more equal or less equal than another child simply because of the accredited school that he or she attends.[22]

REAFFIRMATION FROM THE U.S. SUPREME COURT

The controversy over giving public funds to private schools would seem to have been resolved in 1983 when the U.S. Supreme Court, in *Mueller v. Allen*, upheld a Minnesota law which allows an income tax credit for certain expenses whether the student is in a public or nonpublic school.

The Court went beyond merely asserting the constitutionality of the law, adding that "there is a strong public interest in assuring the continued financial health of private schools, both sectarian and nonsectarian. By educating a substantial number of students, such schools relieve public schools of a correspondingly great burden--to the benefit of all taxpayers. In addition, private schools may serve as a benchmark for public schools in a manner analogous to the 'TVA yardstick' for private power companies."[23]

The Court followed up this Minnesota case in 1986, with *Witters v. Washington*, in which it ruled that a blind student, receiving public funds to advance his education, was within his constitutional rights to use those funds to attend a seminary to enter the clergy. Notably, this decision was written by Thurgood Marshall.

The judgement of the Supreme Court in both of these cases was centered on the rationale that the money was to aid students, not institutions, and that the funding was distributed in such as way that it available and equitable to all. The fact that some, or even most, of the money might be used to attend a religious institution, or an institution with religious ties, was not relevant and not considered to be a violation of the First Amendment establishment clause.

ACTION IN THE STATES

School choice began to move forward in the mid-1980s. In 1986, Washington State received national recognition for its success in providing vouchers during the previous eight years to dropouts who could use these vouchers at private institutions.[24]

In Hawaii, the League of Women Voters lobbied for school choice as part of school reforms in that state.[25]

Taking the lead among states that hoped to promote educational choice, Minnesota, led by Governor Rudy Perpich, passed a series of laws providing choice for the disadvantaged, dropouts, early admissions to postsecondary education, and among all public school students in the state. Minnesota did not, however, include nonpublic school students among these groups.

In a startling development, statewide civic and educational organizations, such as the League of Women Voters, the Minnesota PTA, and the school principal associations endorsed public school choice.[26] A number of other statewide organizations rose to oppose public school choice, including the Minnesota Education Association (MEA). Nonetheless, a MEA poll, conducted a few years after the Minnesota public school choice plan had been in effect, revealed that the majority of MEA's members favored it.[27]

Subsequent to the establishment of the public school choice law in Minnesota, 12 states have also adopted some form of public school choice.

In fact, Arkansas adopted such a plan in 1989, and it was signed into law by then Governor Bill Clinton.

Wisconsin, led by State Representative Annette "Polly" Williams, in 1991 established a pilot choice program for up to 1,000 of the most disadvantaged youngsters in Milwaukee. This choice program includes nonpublic schools, but not those with religious affiliations.

In late 1990, Arkansas Governor Bill Clinton wrote to Representative Williams to encourage her efforts in promoting public school choice. In his letter he says that he was "fascinated by that proposal" and that he was "concerned that the traditional Democratic party establishment has not given you more encouragement. The visionary is rarely embraced by the status quo." [28] These sentiments, which condone a more inclusive form of educational choice, were missing from Clinton's 1992 presidential campaign.

PENNSYLVANIA: GROWING SUPPORT FOR SCHOOL CHOICE

At the end of the 1980s, the movement for school choice revived in Pennsylvania. A 1989 poll commissioned by the Commonwealth Foundation found that 83 percent of Black Pennsylvanians supported the concept of educational choice,[29] a percentage higher than the public at large and one consistent with many other subsequent national polls such as the Associated Press Poll of 1992. These polls show that minorities have little doubt that school choice would be to their advantage. Ironically, a main source of opposition to school choice in Pennsylvania has been organizations and legislators representing minority groups.

Even the Pennsylvania State Education Association (PSEA), which adamantly opposes full school choice, said it has no official position on public school choice. This statement was made in response to an inquiry by the Chairman of the House Education Committee in September 1990. Later the PSEA issued a publication noting that some educational choice does exist in Pennsylvania. A vocational education student, for example, may ask to take part in a neighboring district's program if the student's home district does not offer it--with both the cost of the program and transportation being covered by the home district.

Another example of educational choice available to Pennsylvania students that was cited by the PSEA is a requirement for a class to be offered if 15 students request it.[30] How many students know they possess these rights; how many school administrators or school board members know this fact? The availability of classes in this manner is not a fact that receives much attention.

Early in 1991, The REACH Alliance was established, a nonprofit corporation specifically geared to making full school choice a reality in Pennsylvania. (REACH is the acronym for The Road to Educational Achievement through Choice.) Its creation coincided with a statement by Pennsylvania's Commissioner of Basic Education that "I'm not concerned with institutional survival; I'm interested in the quality of education received by students." [31]

That may have been true, but the Commissioner's interest did not extend to offering students a choice as to where they may receive that quality education or to opting out of a situation where they believe a quality education is not being offered. And part, perhaps the major part, of his rationale for opposing choice was that it would have a harmful impact on the public school system. Apparently, the survival of this institution has been a major concern.

On the other hand, a columnist for the Harrisburg *Patriot-News* was supportive of implementing school choice in the Commonwealth. He noted that the idea "doesn't sit well with a lot of people running the public schools." His own view was that if people need more than one newspaper to make a choice, maybe they also need more than one choice in education. He concluded with the observation that he hasn't "met anyone yet who is against the right of free choice. Except, of course, when someone else wants to exercise the option." [32]

A few months later, a speaker at a conference on rural education, said that some form of educational choice is already in law in 28 states. [33] While this list and its variations were too long for him to include in his presentation, Pennsylvania might have been included among those 28 states. Not only are there educational provisions such as the ones noted by the PSEA but also there are other practices, such as the existence of magnet schools, that might have mislead this speaker to include Pennsylvania in this category. One wonders how many other states were included in this group because of such meaningless provisions in state law?

Intradistrict choice has been practiced in the Keystone State in the Bethlehem Area School District in its elementary schools since the mid-1970s. The school district has found the results to be sufficiently meritorious to continue the practice.

Like other states, there are many public educators in Pennsylvania who support school choice, but they are hesitant to speak out because of peer pressure. But there are exceptions. One is a Lancaster County elementary school principal, who wrote a newspaper essay stating, "Because choice also provides those parents with money to pay tuition, it is a major change in American education....Will schools' economic competition for students produce superior educations for them? Only the arrogant would say no, only the foolish wouldn't try." [34]

THE LEGISLATIVE BATTLE

The REACH Alliance's school choice legislation was first introduced in the General Assembly in early 1991. Little immediate action was anticipated because of the extensive nature of the reform, the necessity of passing a state budget by June 30, and the legislative summer recess.

In the fall, however, there was increasing interest in the bill, and its prime sponsor in the Senate, Senator Frank Salvatore (R-Philadelphia) urged that an attempt be made to move it. Other supporters finally agreed to do so, and on November 26, after an extended and vigorous Senate debate, the bill passed, 28-22.

An important advocate for the cause of school choice was David R. Boldt, Editorial Page Editor of *The Philadelphia Inquirer*. It may or may not have played a role in the Senate vote, but just two days before the Senate vote he wrote a column which said that his ambivalence on the topic of school choice was waning and that he was becoming an earnest supporter. The reason for his new stance was "in part because of the people who oppose school choice seem to be, in so many cases, such reprehensible hypocrites." In his column Boldt observed that many school choice opponents send their children to private or affluent suburban public schools but would deny less advantaged parents the same option. So, he wrote, "The next time you run into somebody who opposes the choice schools concept, ask him where his children go to schools--and how he arrived at that *choice*." [35]

Boldt's column along with the Senate vote and other pro-school choice activities aroused a surprised opposition. A coalition of all 12 public education groups, with a number of allied organizations, such as the American Civil Liberties Union, was quickly assembled to prepare for the vote in the House.

The campaign conducted by the school choice opponents included a blitz of broadcast ads which, among other things, accused the proponents of a December 7th attack on the taxpayers' pocketbooks. A concern for state finances had not been manifested by these groups a few months before when the state passed the largest tax increase in its history. In fact, much of this tax increase was needed to fund the public schools. The proponents raised funds and responded with an ad campaign of their own. It is not clear how much either side contributed to enlightening the public, or whether the ads had any effect on the House vote a few days later. At the least, these ads raised public awareness of the issue.

The House vote came on December 11, but this vote did not address the substance of the bill. By a tally of 114-89, the House ruled the bill was unconstitutional; therefore, it did not need to be the subject of further deliberation.

House supporters of choice remarked that they had never seen a constitutional vote that was really a question of constitutionality. This procedure was a way to avoid dealing with the school choice issue. The Senate had begun its deliberations the month before the House vote by also considering the constitutionality of the legislation. The Senate had voted that it was constitutional.

Since the House vote was on the entire bill, not on its specific provisions, one can only speculate which provisions the opposing House members believed to be unconstitutional. One of the provisions was for intradistrict choice--that a student could attend any similar school in his district on a space available basis--a practice the Bethlehem School District had been following for years. This is clearly constitutional.

The bill also mandated interdistrict public school choice, a provision that would permit any student in Pennsylvania to attend any public school in the state. As noted earlier, this practice is already in statute in Arkansas, Minnesota, and a number of other states. These programs use state funds in a prescribed manner, and these laws are also clearly constitutional.

These first two provisions alone would affect five of every six students in the state, those attending public schools.

A third provision would have permitted students to attend any nonpublic secular school in the state. While this may be debatable as a public policy, it is also clearly constitutional.

Consequently, the only provision that could pose a constitutional question was the fourth one. The fourth provision of this bill would have permitted students to attend any nonpublic sectarian school in the state and, as with nonpublic secular ones, receive a state grant. This grant would have covered up to 90 percent of the tuition, to a maximum total of $900. This provision was soon called the "GI Bill for Kids," a phrase that President Bush would later borrow for his Administration's school choice legislation.

There is no agreement on the constitutionality of this provision. As noted, the Pennsylvania Senate voted that such support is constitutional. The proponents, of course, argued that it was constitutional, under both the national and state constitutions.

Furthermore, while House opponents cited their oath of office as a justification for voting on the constitutionality of the bill, their oath is to uphold and defend the state constitution, not to interpret it. The legislature has neither the responsibility nor the authority to interpret the constitution; that is a right reserved for the courts.

On the federal level, the constitutionality of this fourth provision is supported by the *Mueller* and *Witters* decisions. These decisions have also been endorsed by Harvard Law School Professor Laurence H. Tribe, a national authority on constitutional law who is not a supporter of school choice. Tribe has said:

> Any objection that anyone would have to a voucher program would have to be policy-based and could not rest on legal doctrine....One would have to be awfully clumsy to write voucher legislation that could not pass constitutional scrutiny....As long as it is a program of aid to parents and not aid as a way of funding parochial schools through the back door, then it would be constitutional.[36]

On the state level, there is a constitutional provision prohibiting grants to individuals. Nonetheless, choice supporters argue that this prohibition does not apply to groups, which, of course, are made up of individuals. Supporters provide examples of the state awarding grants to groups such as welfare grants, unemployment compensation, and workmen's compensation, all of which ultimately go to individuals.

In fact, the *1992 Pennsylvania Abstract*, reporting on state expenditures has a line item for "Grants and payments to individuals." It records that these items grew from $3,333,886,000 in 1987 to $5,045,500,000 in 1991 and exceeded $19 billion for the five-year period.

The crux of the school choice issue in the state is that the House vote on December 11, 1991, was a matter of political power. Some of the legislators saw it as a political survival issue. Unquestionably, the school choice opponents had the preponderance of power and money. A number of legislators on both sides of the issue said that they had never seen such an emotional legislative battle. Hence, the main goal for many legislators was to avoid this issue.

As noted, the measure did bring the school choice issue to the attention of the public and public educators. An earlier public poll by the Lancaster *Intelligencer Journal* had found 55 percent in favor of the REACH legislation, and 45 percent opposed.[37] Some public educators were not as set in their opposition to school choice as their professional organizations. In fact, some districts, like Wallingford-Swarthmore in suburban Philadelphia, have been seeking to recruit students on a tuition basis.

On the day the House vote was scheduled, the Harrisburg *Patriot-News* reported that Northern York School District Superintendent John Allison supported public-school choice and that Carlisle Area Superintendent Robert Stowell said he "would not object to a choice proposal that holds public and private schools to the same mandates and would not eat into existing school financing."[38]

In the western part of the state, Altoona School District Superintendent Dennis Murray told a local Chamber of Commerce meeting that he did not oppose the proposed legislation, providing private and public schools would be subject to the same state regulations.[39]

Speaking in 1992 to 1,700 people in the Harrisburg area, Joe Clark, the former principal of Eastside High School in Paterson, New Jersey, who had received national recognition for his strong actions in a tough school, endorsed school choice. Clark said that the key to improving education is "to take the money from the politicians and give it to the parents." Meeting with the press prior to the speech, he made the same observation as David Boldt:

Many politicians choose to send their kids to private schools, and parents should be given the same opportunity....As it stands now, schools are monopolies, lacking competition....There is no reason for it to change. It's brain dead. It's a dog that won't work.[40]

THE OUTLOOK

A statewide public poll conducted in early 1992 by Mansfield University of Pennsylvania found that 75 percent of the public favored public school choice, and 40 percent supported including private and parochial schools in any educational choice program.[41] One year later, in February 1993, the poll found 63 percent of Pennsylvanians favored full school choice.

In March 1992, a Temple University public survey was conducted in Philadelphia, specifically asking about the Pennsylvania legislation with the $900 grant to help students attend private schools. It found that 55.9 percent favored the idea while only 30.8 percent of the public were opposed. The remainder of the respondents were undecided, did not know, or gave no answer.[42] A 1993 follow-up Temple survey showed support had increased to slightly more than 60 percent.

On June 25, 1992, President George Bush announced a federal initiative for $1,000 grants to 500,000 students to attend a private or public school of their choice. At a meeting a few months later, the Education Task Force of the American Legislative Exchange Council (ALEC) endorsed the Bush proposal. In its news release, ALEC said it "is the nation's largest bipartisan, voluntary membership organization of state legislators, with 2,400 members throughout all 50 states."[43]

In August 1992, the PSEA had 662 Pennsylvanians polled to learn their position on a school voucher program to enable students to attend private or religious schools. The PSEA poll found results 45 percent in favor, with 55 percent opposed.[44] This poll's results are an indication of the growing shift toward full school choice, as also demonstrated by the two Mansfield University polls of February 1992 and February 1993.

In light of the state constitutional question, an interesting letter to the editor appeared in *The Philadelphia Inquirer*, in early November. Its author argued the following:

> The school voucher program that has been proposed in Pennsylvania would provide the children of many poor and middle income families with the financial ability to get a better education, in the school of their choice....The vouchers system is assistance *to all our children* who choose to use it. It does not qualify as direct aid to any school....Thus, there is no entanglement whatsoever between church and state. In fact, the voucher system not only would protect the non-establishment clause of the First Amendment, but actually would promote the free exercise of religion clause of that same amendment.[45]

The writer is a Philadelphia Court of Common Pleas judge.

This letter appeared only days after the November 1992 general election that despite strenuous opposition, showed gains for advocates of school choice in Pennsylvania. The fact that school choice was an issue in many campaigns is significant. In 1990 that was rare, or nonexistent. In 1992 it was an issue, and no House members who voted for the school choice plan were defeated because of that vote. Those House members specifically targeted for defeat because of their support for school choice were all reelected. School choice did not play a major role in the campaigns of those who voted against the measure either, but due to retirements and the outcome of races, there are fewer House opponents than before.

All 28 Senators who voted for choice are in the Pennsylvania Senate for the 1993-94 session while only 20 of the 22 opponents remain. One

Senator retired, to be replaced by a new Senator whose position is unknown. One opponent was elected to the Congress, and his successor will not be chosen until late in 1993. Senate support for school choice is at least equal to the prior session, and one or two votes may be gained.

It is more difficult to gauge support among House members since the House is much larger than the Senate and since votes on school choice will vary with the specific features of any legislation. A review of the December 1991 House votes and statements made during the campaign by newly elected House legislators, shows that any House vote on school choice should be considerably closer than last time. The proponents can list 88 House members, down by only one; the opposition has 97 House supporters, down by 17 votes; and there are 18 new Representatives whose stance is unclear.

New legislation has been introduced in the General Assembly that calls for full school choice, to be phased in over three years, with funding of 90 percent of tuition, up to $700 at the elementary level and $1,000 for high school students. It also provides for the introduction of charter schools in Pennsylvania and a postsecondary enrollment option which would provide state support towards tuition for students attending college during the years they would otherwise be in high school.

The REACH Alliance has become better organized. It has opened an office, established a newsletter, increased its membership, and strengthened its base of support.

The ongoing effort, across the nation as well as in Pennsylvania, has moved the issue of school choice forward. The Gallup organization has polled the public repeatedly on this subject since 1971. Although a Gallup Poll found only 50 percent of the public in favor of school choice in 1991, a 1992 poll found 70 percent in favor. An Associated Press Poll, specifically testing the features of the Bush proposal, found 63 percent of the general public favored its adoption, and other pollsters and analysts have come to similar conclusions. All of these polls continue to show that Afro-Americans, Hispanics, the poor, and other disadvantaged citizens believe that school choice will be of great benefit to them. These groups always support school choice at significantly higher rates than the overall average. Indeed, almost all demographic segments of the national population favor school choice plans that include private schools. This support is seen in all recent national polls on this subject.

Even the National Education Association (NEA) realizes it is losing ground in this debate. It informed its members that a 1980 poll showed 33 percent of the public in support of vouchers, a figure that rose to 44 percent in 1988, and to 51 percent in early 1992.[46]

Former Secretary of Education Lamar Alexander, in a 1992 speech said he believes that by the turn of the century full school choice will no longer be an issue, it will be a reality. [47] In reaching this conclusion, Alexander may be remembering that with the exception of the United States, every major Western democracy provides public money to private (including religious) schools.[48]

In the nations that were formerly part of the Soviet bloc, choice is rapidly emerging, especially in Russia, where President Boris Yeltsin issued a decree calling for independent schools that would be supported from the public treasury. Such schools are emerging all across that nation. It would, perhaps, be the final irony, if the educational system of Russia should prove to be more democratic than the educational system of the United States.[49]

Advocates of school choice are confident that will not happen.

ENDNOTES

1. Pennsylvania School Boards Association (PSBA), "Twelve Major Events that Shaped American Education," *PSBA Bulletin*, September-October 1976, 4-7.

2. Thomas Paine, *The Rights of Man, Part Second*, London: privately printed, 1792, reprinted in *The Complete Writings of Thomas Paine, Volume 2*, ed. Philip S. Foner (New York, NY: The Citadel Press, 1969), 245.

3. Michael B. Katz, Educational Symposium Speaker, Carlisle, PA, Dickinson College, 16 February 1990.

4. Frederick J. Weintraub, "Nonpublic Schools and the Educaiton of the Handicapped," in *Private Schools and The Public Good*, ed. Edward McGlynn Gafney, Jr. (Notre Dame, IN: University of Notre Dame Press, 1981), 49-50.

5. John Stuart Mill, *Three Essays: On Liberty, Representative Government, The Subjection of Women*, (London: Oxford University Press, 1966), 39 and 130.

6. *Pierce v. Society of Sisters*, 260 U.S. 510 (1925).

7. *Educational Choice: A Catalyst for School Reform*, Paper presented as part of the symposium, "A Report of the Task Force on Education" at the City Club of Chicago, IL, August 1989, 13.

8. Milton Friedman, "The Role of Government in Education," in *Economics and the Public Interest*, ed. Robert A. Solo (New Brunswick, NJ: Rutgers University Press, 1955), 143.

9. James S. Coleman, *Private Wealth and Public Education*, with a forward by John E. Coons and others, eds. (Cambridge, MA: The Belknap Press, 1970), XIII-XIV.

10. David W. Kirkpatrick, "The Agony of Relevance," *Pennsylvania School Journal* (September

1970): 71.

11. *Phi Delta Kappan*, May 1971, 512.

12. Pat Ordovensky, "90s Teacher Shortage Is Called a Myth," *USA Today*, 28 August 1990, 1(D).

13. David Rogers, *110 Livingston Street* (New York, NY: Random House, 1968), 110.

14. John Holt, *What Do I Do Monday* (New York, NY: E.P. Dutton and Co. Inc., 1970), 265.

15. Robert L. Cunningham, *Education: Free and Public* (Wichita, KS: Center for Independent Education, n.d.), 7.

16. John Chamberlain, "How About Educational Vouchers?," *Evening News* (Harrisburg, PA), 6 May 1970, 32.

17. *Report of The White House Conference On Youth* (Washington, D.C.: Government Printing Office, April 1971), 53.

18. David W. Lyon, "Capitalism in the Classroom: Education Vouchers," *Business Review*, December 1971, 10.

19. Richard M. Cyert, *The Market Approach to Higher Education,* Paper presented at the meeting of the American Council on Education, San Diego, CA, 10 October 1974, 9.

20. Ibid., 12.

21. Gerald E. Stroufe, "Review of Education Vouchers (The Jencks Report)," *Educational Administration Quarterly*, Winter 1971, 90.

22. Pennsylvania Senator John Sweeney, *Legislative Journal-Senate* (Harrisburg, PA: Commonwealth of Pennsylvania, 2 June 1975), 345.

23. *Mueller v. Allen*, 463 U.S. 388 (1983).

24. David Kelley, "Learning the Hard Way," *Barron's Magazine*, 17 February 1986, 17.

25. *Education Week* VI, no. 39, (24 August 1987): 16.

26. Joe Nathan, "Before Adopting School Choice, Review What Works and What Fails," *The American School Board Journal* (July 1989): 29.

27. Joe Nathan, "Helping All Children, Empowering All Educators: Another View of School Choice," *Phi Delta Kappan*, December 1989, 305.

28. Donald Lambro, "Clinton's Convulted School Choice Record," *Washington Times*, 27 July 1992.

29. William A. Donajue, "Rethinking the Welfare State: A Critical Look at the Underclass," in *Leading Pennsylvania Into the 21st Century*, ed. Don E. Eberly (Harrisburg, PA: The Commonwealth Foundation, 1990), 156.

30. Pennsylvania State Education Association, *Choice in Public Schools* (Harrisburg, PA: Pennsylvania State Education Association, n.d.).

31. Joseph F. Bard, testimony before the Pennsylvania Senate Education Committee regarding vocational education, 12 February 1991.

32. Carmen Brutto, "Sometimes We Get a Choice, and Sometimes. . .," *Patriot News* (Harrisburg, PA), 8 April 1991.

33. Robert E. Stephens, Rural Education Conference Speaker, DuBois, PA, 21 June 1991.

34. Dr. Jacques Gibble, "'Choice' Has Ups and Down," *Sunday News* (Lancaster, PA), 2 June 1991.

35. David R. Boldt, "Opponents Make the Best Argument for Choice Schools," *Philadelphia Inquirer*, 24 November 1991.

36. Susan Chira, "Can Vouchers Hurdle Church-State Wall?," *New York Times*, 12 June 1991, 5(B).

37. "People Poll, School Choice Proposal Supported," *Intelligencer-Journal* (Lancaster, PA), 13 July 1991.

38. "$900 Vouchers Matter Little, Officials Say," *Patriot News* (Harrisburg, PA), 11 December 1991, 14(A).

39. Kay Stephens, "Murray Writes School Prescription," *Altoona Mirror* (Altoona, PA), 8 January 1992, 1(B).

40. Val Walton, "Joe Clark Tells Politicians to Get Out of Education," *Patriot News* (Harrisburg, PA), 22 February 1992, 1(B).

41. Ted Anthony, "Most Back Woman's Right to Chose Abortion," *Patriot News* (Harrisburg, PA), 16 June 1992, 1-2(B).

42. Martha Woodall, "In the Audience Were Those Who Had Fought for Pennsylvania Plan," *Philadelphia Inquirer*, 22 July 1992.

43. American Legislative Exchange Council, *Press Release* (Washington, D.C.: American Legislative Exchange Council, 7 August 1992).

44. "PSEA Survey Says Most Nix Choice," *Patriot News* (Harrisburg, PA), 21 September 1992.

45. Armand Della Porta, "Vouchers Would Save Catholic Schools," *Philadelphia Inquirer*, 8 November 1992.

46. *NEA Today*, May 1992, 13.

47. Lamar Alexander, "A 'GI Bill for Children'," (Ashland, OH: Ashland University, 1992).

48. Ronald H. Nash, *The Closing of the American Heart* (Dallas, TX: Probe Books, 1990), 119-120.

49. Stephanie Simon, "Experimental Moscow School a Lesson in Freedom," *Los Angeles Times*, 9 June 1992.

Chapter 12

Home Schooling: The Oldest Educational Innovation

Howard B. Richman

INTRODUCTION

Home schooling is both the oldest and newest form of education in America today. Although home schooled students still only total about one-half percent of the school student population in the nation and in Pennsylvania, the number of home schooled students in the Keystone State has been doubling every couple of years for the past decade. Pennsylvania's education establishment began its efforts to place a lid on home schooling in 1985, but failed when an act legalizing home schooling was signed by Governor Casey in December 1988.

Where did these home schoolers come from? How did they defeat the educational establishment in 1988? What can be expected from them in the future? In this chapter, I examine the past, present, and future of home schooling in America. I share my perspective as a home schooling leader, who helped organize the effort to legalize home schooling in Pennsylvania, and as the director of an agency that accredits home schooling diplomas.

HOME SCHOOLING IN AMERICA'S PAST

The roots of home schooling go deep into American history. Thirteen presidents were substantially home schooled--Washington, Jefferson, Madison, John Quincy Adams, Lincoln, Tyler, Harrison, both Roosevelts, and Wilson--and those were not the only American leaders to be substantially taught at home. There was General George Patton who began his education at home then went on to prep school and West Point. Clara Barton finished her education at home after developing school phobia, and Thomas Alva Edison was almost totally home schooled.

Home schooling appeared to be gradually dying in the late 1970s when, almost simultaneously, two men on opposite sides of our continent and political spectrum began to advocate home schooling.

In Massachusetts, school reformer, John Holt (author of *How Children Fail* and *How Children Learn*) gave up the idea of reforming the schools and began to look for alternatives. After meeting some home schoolers, he became intrigued with the idea, and founded the first national home schooling newsletter, *Growing Without Schooling*. Many of the same people who would have founded alternative schools a decade earlier decided, "Why spend all of that effort trying to found a school when all we really want is to have a good educational situation for our own children?" Many members of a self-help group of nursing mothers, *La Leche League*, became interested in John Holt's ideas. Some of these mothers, including my wife, had already given up careers in order to stay home and nurse their babies. They wanted to continue to enjoy their children as their children grew older, so they were attracted to home schooling.

On the other coast, in the state of Washington, Dr. Raymond Moore, a conservative Christian psychologist, and his wife Dorothy, a reading specialist, followed a trail of research that led them to conclude that many children would be better off if they began their formal educations later. Their book, *Better Late than Early*, became a Book of the Month Club choice, and they soon founded a newsletter, *Family Report,* and wrote books advocating home schooling. On several occasions Dr. Moore was invited to appear on Dr. James Dobson's "Focus on the Family" radio program. Moore and Dobson saw in home schooling the possibility of renewing the American family. It was already becoming clear that families that home schooled were staying together and raising children who shared their parents' value system. Soon home schooling began growing quickly in the evangelical Christian community and in the professional community.

HOME SCHOOLING IN AMERICA TODAY

All national estimates of home schoolers show growth throughout the past decade. According to the U.S. Department of Education, the best estimate of the total number of home schooled students there were in the nation during the 1970s and early 1980s was John Holt's estimate of 10,000 to 15,000 students. The best estimate of the national home schooled student population during the 1990-1991 school year was about 248,5000 to 353,000 school-aged children (5 to 18).[1]

Throughout the 1980s the legal climate for home schooling improved in state after state. Some states accommodated home schooling by allowing home schoolers to register as private schools. Other states passed new laws to regulate home schooling as a new entity different from private schools. In many states, fierce battles were fought in courts and legislatures before parents could home school their children without fear of being prosecuted.

In 1982, only two states had laws explicitly providing parents with the option of educating their children at home. By 1991, the number of states with such statutes rose dramatically to 33. Eight states (plus the District of Columbia) permit home schooling if programs are "equivalent" to the public schools. The remaining states allow home schooling if the home meets the legal standards of a private school.

Although 33 states now have home schooling "laws," it is more accurate to note that some states have home schooling statutes, while others have home schooling regulations. Maine, Maryland, New York, and Ohio have home schooling regulations, while 29 other states have home schooling statutes. However, both home schooling regulations and statutes deal with the following elements: 1) parental qualifications, 2) required subjects, 3) required days or hours of instruction, 4) notice of intent, and 5) standardized testing.

In many other states with "equivalency" requirements, provisions require home schoolers to obtain "approval" from the local school authorities. "Approval" provisions contained in "equivalency" laws have prompted more home schooling lawsuits than any other kind of law. Because of their former stringent "approval-equivalency" laws, New York and Pennsylvania experienced more lawsuits than most other states.

For the majority of states that require home schools to function under private standards, home schools are essentially unregulated. These states are among the largest in the nation, including California and Texas. The only state in this category which requires all private and home school teachers to possess state teaching certificates is Michigan.

The current debate in home schooling centers on whether home schooled children should be allowed to participate in public school extracurricular activities. Four states now allow home schooled students to take part in such activities. Iowa is the most recent state to permit home schooled children to take part in extracurricular activities centered in the public schools. In other states, such as Vermont, the Vermont Headmasters Association has permitted home schooled youngsters in that state to participate in individual competitive activities (e.g., drama, gymnastics, musical competitions, track, and skiing).

Of the 50 states, only Alaska has a public home schooling option which is financed entirely by the state. The Alaska Legislature realized in 1939 that it had two choices, either build tiny schools in the wilderness or start a correspondence program in which parents would teach their own children with help through the mail. The correspondence program was cheaper and proved to be a phenomenal success. Students in Alaska's correspondence program have achieved at higher levels than students in the state's public schools and at less cost to the taxpayer. In addition, the longer the students have been in the correspondence program, the higher their scores rise.[2]

In 1976 Alaska opened its correspondence program to students who lived within range of school buses, much to the consternation of school administrators. This new option for parents reduced the ability of school administrators to plan on definite student enrollment levels, reduced tax dollars to the schools, increased student achievement, and reduced the total cost of education for the state. Home schooling activity across the nation is predicted to rise into the 21st Century as citizens seek new ways to improve educational quality.

BEGINNINGS OF MODERN HOME SCHOOLING IN PENNSYLVANIA

In Pennsylvania a few support groups began to form in the early 1980s. For example, the first western Pennsylvania support group began early in 1982 when John Holt came to Pittsburgh to be on a Pittsburgh television talk show. Home schoolers were invited to be in the studio audience. Each home schooling family knew about one or two other families. About fifteen mothers gathered and exchanged names. My wife, Susan, was chosen to edit a western Pennsylvania home schooling newsletter (which later expanded to become the state-wide home schooling newsletter,

Pennsylvania Homeschoolers). There were so few home schoolers, that home schoolers learned to put their political and religious differences aside so that their children could go on field trips and play together.

The number of home schoolers began to grow about 40 percent per year throughout Pennsylvania. The state's compulsory school age of eight gave parents the opportunity to get their feet wet without any hassle. But once the oldest child turned eight, then parents had a choice: 1) Go to the school district and try to get permission to be the "properly qualified" private tutor of your children, 2) Found a "school" consisting of just your own children and hope that the Department of Education did not discover you, or 3) Sit tight and hide. All three alternatives were risky. The first option became the most common. Usually the superintendents were curious about home schooling. They were not push-overs, but generally after they had approved one family, they approved others. It seemed that Pennsylvania was going to be a peaceful state.

Towards the end of 1985, when there were about 500 home schooling families in the state, it almost seemed as if a decision was made by the educational establishment in Pennsylvania to try to nip this new "fad" in the bud.

At the Department of Education, the Division of Non-Public and Private Schools began sending out a packet of sample home schooling policies to school districts that were requesting information about how to handle home schooling requests. This packet included policies that restricted home schooling to certified teachers.

MISCONCEPTIONS ABOUT SOCIALIZATION

In December 1985 an anti-home schooling article appeared in the Pennsylvania School Board Association (PSBA) *Bulletin.* William Fearen, PSBA General Counsel, concluded that school districts should establish policies about home schooling based upon their opinion of whether home schooling children were being properly socialized. It was already becoming apparent from reports of home education achievement scores that home schooled students were getting a good education. The new argument of the educational establishment was that the compulsory education laws were there to ensure that children were properly socialized. William Fearen concluded:

Whether home education represents an acceptable and viable alternative to the more conventional school setting involves philosophical considerations beyond the scope of this article and the competence of the writer.

The importance of role models and socialization opportunities, the need for peer interaction in the education process and the question of whether individual parents should have the right to control the scope and emphasis of a child's education are but some of the imponderables. The degree to which these considerations will impact upon the availability of home instruction in any particular district will be determined by the philosophy of the school board as reflected in its policies adopted to deal with this matter.[3]

William Fearen was voicing a popular misconception--that home schoolers are socially deprived. While it is clear that home educated children have a different set of social experiences than school educated children, a case can be made that the socialization of home educated children is actually superior.

Home schooled children socialize more with their family and less with people outside their family. They have much more contact with adults and with children who are older and younger themselves, and have less contact with children their own ages. Three scholarly studies suggest that home school socialization may actually be superior:

1) For his 1986 dissertation at Andrews University, John W. Taylor had home schooling parents, drawn from mailing lists of home schooling newsletters, administer a self-concept questionnaire to their students. He found that the home educated students in his sample had higher, not lower, self-concepts than most school educated students.[4]

2) For his 1991 masters thesis at Eastern New Mexico University, Steven W. Kelley, correcting some of the flaws in Taylor's study, administered Taylor's self-concept questionnaire to home educated students in the Los Angeles area. Like Taylor, he found that home educated students generally have higher, not lower, self-concepts than most school educated students.[5]

3) For his 1992 doctoral dissertation at the University of Florida, Larry Shyers videotaped home educated and school educated children at play, and then had trained counselors observe their behavior. The counselors did not know which children were home educated and which were school educated. After further study, the videotapes showed that home educated students had consistently fewer behavioral problems, were less aggressive, tended to talk more quietly, tended to play well in groups, and tended to take the initiative to invite other children to join them.[6]

In general, the argument that home schooled children are deprived socially comes from people who have not examined and studied the evidence. Nevertheless, Fearen's argument resonated well with many school superintendents and school boards members, many of whom enacted policies to restrict home schooling severely.

THE HOME SCHOOL MOBILIZATION

Across the state, the number of prosecutions of home schoolers was gradually rising. Parents would go to obtain permission to home school from the school superintendents, but would be told that they were not sufficiently qualified. It soon became evident to home schooling support group leaders throughout Pennsylvania that the situation was deteriorating.

Therefore, a meeting was called in Quakertown which formed a coalition of home schooling support groups called *Parent Educators of Pennsylvania* to fight for a change in the law. Two leaders emerged to guide the legislative battle ahead: Tom Eldredge, a West Chester businessman and a leader of the evangelical Christian community and myself, a Jewish school teacher about to receive a doctorate in education from the University of Pittsburgh. For the next four years, we kept our coalition united and led one of Pennsylvania's most successful grass-roots lobbying efforts.

Every grass-roots legislative movement needs a champion in the legislature to help guide it. We found our champion in Representative Joseph Pitts, a strong supporter of religious liberty and the traditional family. He was the chief sponsor of our first and second home schooling bills (introduced in 1985 and 1987), and gradually taught us how to lobby.

A HEARING FROM THE LEGISLATURE

We won over the members of the House Education Committee to our cause when they heard home schooled students speak at our legislative breakfasts and at a December 3, 1987, hearing on our bill. They began to realize that home schooling could be very innovative and its students could be very well educated.

For example, ten-year-old Amanda Bergson-Shilcock let the legislators know that home schoolers are involved in many projects which extend into the community. She described a home cookie and muffin baking business. When she first initiated this business project, she used calligraphy to produce flyers, which she printed and distributed. Then she described a sachet-making business in which she grew, dried, and sold herbs.

Sixteen-year-old Adam Boroughs, who had already begun his path toward a career as a medical doctor, described a medical research project that he had participated in beginning the previous summer. This project induced a disease in rats and tested a method for treating it. He wrote the final paper and was listed as the second author when it was presented at a National Pediatric Association Conference. Adam testified:

> Dr. Ziegler very generously listed me as second author on the project. In fact, the printer listed me as Adam Boroughs, M.D.! I have now been asked back to work on phase two of the project and I begin this week. Being home schooled has allowed me the time to pursue my interest. I could probably spend five years in normal high school science and never receive the education that I received last summer. Being published at age sixteen is something that medical school students and residents would kill for!

Holly Hageman testified about her social life as a sixteen-year-old home schooler. She said that since she began home schooling four years ago, the most prominent question people have asked her is, "What about your social life?" She said:

> My social life has become better and happier for me since leaving institutional school. I've met my best friends at social events such as church, home school support groups, being on community sports teams, and even going camping.

After describing the social life in schools, noting that home schooled children are spared harassment by their peers, and emphasizing the advantage of learning to relate to their parents and other adults on a full time basis, Holly continued,

> In conclusion, my social life is in no way hampered by home schooling. I have many friends of all ages, my own age as well as younger children and older adults. I am very grateful to my parents for their sacrifice of time and energy, to our local school district for their permission and assistance, and to the Lord for using them to train me in the way I should go.

Fourteen-year-old Maggie Smeltzer had an interesting story to tell to the legislators. When her parents had begun to home school her, the local public school superintendent had objected on the grounds that Maggie was not doing well in school and would not be able at home to secure the additional attention she would need. Three years later, he ordered her back to school saying that since she was doing so well on achievement tests she was obviously gifted. He declared that she would not be able to find the opportunity to reach her potential at home. At the hearings she was questioned closely by Representative Joseph Battisto who tried to determine the scope of her education:

Rep. Battisto: Are you a ninth grader now, Maggie?
Maggie: Yes.
Rep. Battisto: Maggie, what are you studying at home?
Maggie: Well, we have the same classes that the regular school has except that we start each morning with Biblical devotions.
Rep. Battisto: Are you taking algebra?
Maggie: Yes, that's one of my favorites.
Rep. Battisto: Are you studying a foreign language?
Maggie: Well, I'd like to study Latin and French, but we have not done it yet.
Rep. Battisto: What are you reading? Do you read any novels, any books?
Maggie: I enjoy reading very much. I like to read mysteries--and novels by Charles Dickens!
Rep. Battisto: Have you written essays?
Maggie: Yes, I've written essays on several Biblical characters and also on Thomas Edison.
Rep. Battisto: Are you studying any science, Maggie?
Maggie: Yes, we're studying about electricity right now, and magnetism.
Rep. Battisto: Are you studying history?
Maggie: Yes, we're studying Pennsylvania history right now.
Rep. Battisto: Are you doing any art work? I noticed Amanda's project. Or are you having music lessons?
Maggie: I've taken piano lessons for about two years right now. I'm not what you would consider an artist, but I do like to draw.
Rep. Battisto: Maggie, so you're about at ninth grade level now. What do you plan to do after you finish your home schooling career?
Maggie: I plan to take the GED and the SATs in order to determine if I can go into college--and I'd like to be a constitutional lawyer!
Rep. Battisto: A constitutional lawyer! No further questions, Maggie!

Many parents also testified at the hearings. One of the most courageous witnesses was home schooling mother Stephanie Wilson since she was home schooling "underground" without the permission of the Pittsburgh Public Schools. Her testimony could have led to her discovery and prosecution by the school district. Although she was married to one of most competent medical doctors in Pittsburgh, she knew that since she did not have a college degree, she would not receive permission from the Pittsburgh Public Schools to home school her children. Nevertheless, she testified clearly that the Pennsylvania home schoolers were not asking for a bill which granted complete freedom from regulation. In response to a question on this issue from one of the legislators, she said:

> When I lived in Kentucky, which is considered to be a totally unregulated state, I saw what I consider to be abuses in home education. I know of two families where the parents were very laid back. They had other things to do and their attitude was, "Well, it will sink in eventually." I realize that there may be children who are not educated. . . .

In response to a follow-up question, Mrs. Wilson pointed out that the evaluation provisions in the home schooling bill would prevent such a situation from happening in Pennsylvania.

The opponents of home education also testified at the hearings. Jack Corbin, representing the Pennsylvania State Education Association (PSEA) said that he did not oppose home education. He simply stated that there was not a need to change the state law.

Three representatives of the Pennsylvania School Board Association (PSBA) argued against the home schooling legislation by using legal theories on the "qualified rights" of parents since judges had ruled it was acceptable to require teacher certification of home schoolers.

A representative of the Pennsylvania Federation of Teachers (PFT), John Fitzpatrick, argued that the home schooling bill was flawed from top to bottom and that home schooling was flawed from top to bottom. His testimony did not appear to be effective since many of the committee members were already committed to the home schooling legislation.

Perhaps the success of the legislative breakfasts conducted by Parent Educators of Pennsylvania and of the December 3rd hearings was best demonstrated in comments that Representative Cowell made to reporter Don Wolf, which appeared in the May 22, 1988, edition of *The Pittsburgh Press*: "Cowell is convinced that most homeschooling parents have 'an exceptional interest in their children and are willing to commit extraordinary amounts of time to their children. . . .The kids are obviously exceptional,' said Cowell."

In the same article Dr. William Logan, state Deputy Commissioner for Basic Education, said that the existing law was "fairly workable," and that he was not disturbed by the differences in home schooling policies among school districts. Douglas Boelhouwer, chief of the Education Department's Division of Non-Public and Private School Services said he believed that home education was just another fad "we'll pass through."

BATTLE OVER THE HOME EDUCATION BILL

From that point, Representative Cowell joined Representative Pitts as a champion of home schooling. He rewrote our bill, and put it into a larger education bill which addressed many issues at the same time. His sponsorship of this bill, as Chairman of the House Education Committee, gave it a much better chance to pass. His bill, however, stalled after it was passed by the House Education Committee on July 28.

Nevertheless, home schoolers in Pennsylvania won a big victory in court on August 24th. Federal Judge Edwin Kosik in Scranton ruled in favor of home schoolers in a Home School Legal Defense Association's civil rights suit (*Jeffery v. O'Donnell*). Judge Kosik declared that the private tutoring provision in the compulsory education law was unconstitutionally vague and that he would overturn it if a new law were not passed or new regulations promulgated by December 31st.

Indeed the judge had left the option for the Department of Education to promulgate new regulations. Our opponents actually saw this case as a defeat for home schoolers because the judge had dismissed as being "without merit" almost all of the claims of the home schoolers that they were being deprived of their constitutional rights.

The court decision spurred the Department of Education into action. Some Department of Education employees wanted regulations or a bill that would protect children so that no child would receive an inferior education; others at the Department of Education just wanted to prevent as many people as possible from teaching their own children.

Representative Cowell chaired several negotiating sessions between opponents and proponents over the next several months and tried to forge a compromise that would be acceptable to both sides. He took Senate Bill 154, a bill which had already passed the Senate, and turned it into a home schooling bill. His bill was laden with requirements. Parents would be required to keep a portfolio of their children's work that would be evaluated by a teacher or psychologist of the parent's choice and turned in to the district superintendent at the end of each year. We liked this bill because it permitted anyone to home school who was willing to put in the effort. Parents' rights were to be protected through an appeal to an impartial hearing officer if the superintendent determined that the children were not receiving an appropriate education.

The Department of Education, the PSEA, and the PSBA, however, were not satisfied. At the least these organizations wanted a law that would put below-average home schooled children in school based on their achievement test scores. Although home educated students do, in general, score higher on standardized tests than school educated students, many home schooled children do score below average. Some children are poor test-takers, some are late-bloomers, some are just not that intelligent. I once facetiously told legislators that we would support such a proposal if the public schools would be subject to the same requirements. In other words, if any of their students scored below average, the schools would send them home to be taught by their parents.

The final drama unfolded during the closing days of the legislative session. On November 14, 1988, the House and Senate came back from the general election recess. They would only have until the end of the month to pass Senate Bill 154. Since the bill had already passed the Senate, once it passed the House it would not be sent to any Senate committee; it would just be brought up for a "concurrence" vote. The House had to pass the bill by November 22nd, just before it was scheduled for Thanksgiving recess. Then the Senate would have to vote on it before the end of the month. Representative Pitts asked us to have a continuous presence in Harrisburg until the bill passed. Each day we assigned a different home schooling leader the responsibility of setting up and manning an information table, as well as organizing the home schooling supporters for effective lobbying during that day.

Over the next three weeks we sent out many phone tree messages through the home school support groups. At one critical juncture we sent out an emergency letter that required support from all of the subscribers to the *PA Homeschoolers* newsletter.

On November 14th, Tom Eldredge realized that our bill was stuck in the Appropriations Committee and it did not appear that it would be released. I spoke to Representative Cowell that day and asked him for advice. He suggested that we attempt to pressure Representative Manderino, the House Democratic Majority Leader who decided whether bills would come up for a vote. That evening, we sent out a general phone tree message for people to call their Representatives and ask them to ask Manderino to move the bill.

The next day, we had about 50 home schoolers in the Capitol for the first day of our eleventh-hour action plan. The home schoolers made it a point to visit Representative Manderino's office. Those supporters who called their representatives from home were also asked to call Manderino's office directly. That day Manderino's office phone rang constantly, and in the afternoon when Representative Manderino was stopped by two home schoolers in the hall, he said, "I'm going to let your bill out of the

Appropriations Committee, but you may not like the way it looks when it comes out."

That morning, Representatives found a "Government Policy Statement" from the PSEA in their mailboxes. The statement opposed several aspects of Senate Bill 154. It concluded:

> PSEA does not oppose the concept of home education. It does believe that the state must live up to its legal and moral responsibility to educate and protect children, especially where the child is kept all day and night in a closed, private setting, insulated from outside observation.

The next morning, the rumor was that the House Appropriations Committee was going to amend the bill. Home schoolers went to the Appropriations Committee members to try to convince them to pass our bill without changes. At noon, five home schooling leaders had a meeting with the Governor's Secretary for Legislative Affairs, Tom Lamb. They were unable to obtain a copy of the amendments. The amendments were even kept secret from Representative Cowell, the Chair of the Education Committee and a member of the same party as Governor Casey.

At one o'clock the Appropriations Committee met. The Committee placed the Department of Education's changes into the bill. Home education programs would be evaluated by achievement tests (not by a teacher or psychologist), and the appeal to an impartial hearing officer was replaced with an appeal to the school board who had hired the superintendent. Requirements for high school graduation were also removed.

Members of the Appropriations Committee told Tom Eldredge that the Appropriations Committee had no choice: either the bill would have been killed in committee or the amendments had to be added. We knew that Representative Cowell was in a difficult position. If he amended the bill again, he would be bucking his party's leadership. Perhaps his future as a party leader would be imperiled. Nevertheless, he stuck with us. Together we drafted an amendment that Representative Cowell could present when the bill came up for the vote. The amendment restored the fairness of the bill and the graduation requirements, but it compromised with the reservations expressed by the Department of Education. This compromise was achieved by accepting some achievement testing, but only in the testing years required of public school students (third, fifth, and eighth grades). On Tuesday, November 22nd, with Representative Cowell arguing for us from the Democratic aisle and Representative Pitts arguing for us from the Republican aisle, the House of Representatives voted unanimously for the Cowell amendment and then unanimously to pass our bill. It passed just before the legislators broke for a Thanksgiving recess.

The next Wednesday, November 30, was the busiest day of the year in the Capitol. Any bill not passed that day would die when the session ended at midnight. That day our total of commitments from Senators increased to 32, out of the total of 50. Still, we knew that even though it seemed as if the bill would be on the calendar, it might not be brought up for a vote. Throughout the day, home schoolers were arriving at the Capitol in small groups. Many others were calling Senators from across the state. Meanwhile, lobbyists for the PSBA were walking the halls urging the Senators to kill our bill. About 7 p.m., the Senate voted unanimously to pass our bill.

At the same time our bill was being voted upon in the Senate, about 50 miles away a school board in York County was listening to a presentation sponsored by the Lincoln Intermediate Unit on how to prepare for the needs of their districts in the years ahead.

The meeting eventually came to the topic of home schooling. The two lawyers making the presentation for the IU said that the Home School Legal Defense Association had wounded its cause. Since the present law had been declared to be unconstitutional, either the Department of Education would not enact regulations, in which case home schooling would be completely illegal in Pennsylvania, or the Department of Education would enact regulations that would make home schooling virtually impossible. The lawyers also claimed to have inside information that our home schooling bill was definitely not going to pass.

It was clear that our victory was not anticipated by the educational establishment. Leaders of this establishment had promised that our bill would not pass, yet on the evening of December 21, 1988, Governor Casey signed Senate Bill 154 into law.

HIGH SCHOOL GRADUATION FOR HOME SCHOOLERS

Home schooling affairs were soon transferred within the Department of Education to the Office of Advisory Services. The attitude of the Department of Education seemed to have changed after the adoption of Senate Bill 154; the Department of Education now helps home schoolers solve their problems with school districts instead of exacerbating those problems.

Perhaps the thorniest issue that was left to be resolved after the home education law passed was the question of who awards home schoolers their high school diplomas. The home education law lists requirements for high school graduation, but it does not state who gives the diplomas.

A January 12, 1989, update from the law firm Curtin and Heefner to their school district clients told the school districts that even though the word "graduation" appears in the home education statute, they would not be under any obligation to award the diplomas. Curtin and Heefner suggested that the Department of Education could award Commonwealth Secondary School Diplomas to home schoolers as they do to people who pass their GEDs.

A March 1989 "Basic Education Circular" sent to Pennsylvania school administrators by Donna D. Wall, Commissioner for Basic Education at the Department of Education, perpetuated the idea that the school districts did not have to give diplomas to home schoolers, but the circular did not provide for any other authority to do so.

After seeing the circular, I wrote to Joseph Bard at the Office of Advisory Services asking who should give the diplomas under the Pennsylvania law. He wrote back on July 11, 1989, that it might be possible for the Department of Education to create a new regulation to award the Commonwealth diploma to graduates of home education programs, but changing the regulations would involve considerable time and effort.

The next step was to contact the office at the Department of Education which deals with the Commonwealth diplomas. I found that this office already awarded diplomas to people who passed the GED (high school equivalency exam) and to people who had completed 30 credits (about a full year's work) at an accredited college. I also learned that it required some sort of transcript to stand behind the diplomas. A diploma is not worth anything unless it is backed by a transcript. For students who had passed the GED, the GED scores functioned as the transcript. For students who had completed 30 credits of college, the college transcript served that function. The Department of Education had file cabinets filled with transcripts for Commonwealth diploma recipients that it sent out when employers or colleges required them.

I began to make plans so that evaluators and parents could issue diplomas to home schooled students. I assembled a home schoolers transcript committee, and this committee developed several alternative forms.

On October 2, 1990, Dr. Philip Mulvihill, the new Chief of the Division of Advisory Services at the Pennsylvania Department of Education, informed me that it would not be appropriate for the Department of Education to award diplomas since home schooling is private education. He wrote, "It is not clear to me how the government could issue a credential for an educational program that was intentionally removed from government control." Instead, he recommended that the diplomas be issued by a home schoolers organization. He concluded:

> It seems more appropriate to me to have the credential for home schoolers issued by a home schoolers organization. The monitoring and evaluation could then be done by individuals familiar with these programs and the quality control could be enforced by those individuals who have a vested interest in maintaining that quality.

Based on this advice and similar advice from the Home School Legal Defense Association, we decided to issue a diploma through *PA Homeschoolers*. We formed a home schoolers accreditation agency to accredit homeschoolers diplomas. The members of the agency consisted of evaluators and parents of high school students and graduates.

Our diplomas were first put to the test when our graduates applied for state scholarship grants for college through PHEAA (the Pennsylvania Higher Education Assistance Agency) in the spring of 1992.

At first, PHEAA was reluctant to award grants to home education graduates. For PHEAA to give a scholarship grant to a student, Pennsylvania law requires that the student must have a diploma that is the equivalent of a Pennsylvania public school diploma. PHEAA and the Department of Education have interpreted this language to include all students who are graduates of non-public schools in Pennsylvania, as well as students who are graduates of foreign high schools. Graduates of correspondence schools or private tutoring, however, must first pass the GED before the Department of Education deems them to have the equivalent of a high school diploma.

After the intercession of Representative Cowell, the new Commissioner for Basic Education, Joseph Bard, wrote a letter to PHEAA recognizing the *PA Homeschoolers* diploma as a valid diploma under the Pennsylvania Home Education Law. PHEAA immediately began to make scholarship grants available to home education families.

Pennsylvania is now one of the first states in the country where one can graduate from high school as a home schooler and have the diploma recognized when applying for state-scholarship grants to college.

HOME SCHOOLING IN PENNSYLVANIA TODAY

Home schooling has been growing steadily in the state, and home schoolers have been doing well as achievement score reports and the testimony of home education graduates indicates. According to statistics compiled by the state Department of Education, there were 3,541 students in home education programs in 1989-90; 4,844 in 1990-91; and 6,450 in 1991-92. These statistics show rapid growth, but underestimate the total number of home schooled children since they do not include many home schooled students who are below Pennsylvania's compulsory school age of eight. The number of support groups across the state has also continued to expand; currently, there are more than 100 of these support groups throughout the state.

An achievement test score study found that home schoolers in the state are achieving excellent results. William Girten, Jay Snyder, and I conducted this study. We administered the Comprehensive Tests of Basic Skills Fourth Edition achievement test to 174 homeschooled students at locations sponsored by support groups throughout Pennsylvania. Tests taken in third, fifth, and eighth grades allowed the students to meet the testing requirement in the home education law. While the students were being tested, we asked their parents to fill out questionnaires which included questions about how they were educating their children. The home schooled students scored on an average of the 86th national percentile in total reading and the 73rd national percentile in total mathematics.[7]

These high scores were obtained even though parents reported that their children only spent a little over 16 hours per week, on average, in formal schooling (structured lessons that were preplanned by either the parent or a provider of educational materials). A similar study in the state of Washington found that home schoolers there also scored above average while their parents only spend an average of about 15 hours per week in formal schooling.[8] One of the main differences between home education and school education is that home schooled children do not spend as much time with textbooks. Home schooled children spend more time reading for their own enjoyment, exploring their specific areas of interest, volunteering in the community, going on field trips, and conducting projects.

Two new studies of homeschooling student achievement in Pennsylvania have been completed, and these studies have also obtained similar high scores.[9] In other states, average or above-average scores have also been obtained by other researchers.[10] While it is always possible to find flaws in a given study, when report after report arrives at the same result, the conclusion becomes inescapable. It is now clear that, on average, home educated students tend to score higher than school educated students on achievement tests.

This conclusion does not mean that homeschools are more effective than schools. Home schooling families have higher average parent-education levels (about 2 to 3 years of college), higher median family income levels ($30,000 to $35,000 even though only one parent works in 95 percent of the families),[11] and higher church or synagogue attendance (about 73 percent attend at least once each week) than the general population.[12] It is likely that children from such families would also score better than average on achievement tests if they attended schools.

HOME SCHOOLING IN PENNSYLVANIA'S FUTURE

In his vision of home schooling, John Holt proposed a "nickel-and-dime-theory" of social change. According to that theory, meaningful social change takes place little by little as people's hearts gradually change.[13] Home schooling may be part of a gradual American renewal.

During a time characterized by family disintegration, home schooling renews the family. Home schooling families are staying together and finding a closeness that can be lost when mothers spend their days working outside of the home and children spend their time primarily with peers at school. In a time of declining values, increasing violence in schools, rising rates of teenage pregnancy and suicide, and rising rates of drug abuse, home schooling families are raising good, friendly, well-adjusted children.

Furthermore, in a time of declining educational outcomes, home schooling families are graduating many students with high achievement levels and deep interest in the fields that they study.

Home schooling has always produced leaders for America, including artists, businessmen, civic activists, mathematicians, presidents, scientists, and writers. Home schooling, education's oldest innovation, is increasingly being used by families throughout the nation to improve the quality of the nation's educational opportunities and provide a new generation of leaders.

ENDNOTES

1. Patricia M. Lines, *Estimating the Home Schooled Population*, OR 91-537 (Washington, D.C.: Government Printing Office, October 1991).

2. Sue S. Greene, *Home Study in Alaska: A Profile of K-12 Students Enrolled in Alaska Centralized Correspondence Study*, privately printed, 1985. ERIC ED 255 494.

3. William Fearen, "It's the Law: School Districts Should Be Prepared to Meet Parental Requests for Home Education," *Pennsylvania School Board Association Bulletin* 49, no.6, (December 1985): 28.

4. John Wesley Taylor, V., "Self-concept in Home-Schooling Children" (Ph.D. diss., Andrews University, 1986).

5. Steven M. Kelley, "Socialization of Home Schooled Children: A Self-concept Study," *Home School Researcher* 7, no. 4, (1991): 1-12.

6. Larry E. Shyers, "A Comparison of Social Adjustment Between Home and Traditionally Schooled Students," *Home School Researcher* 8, no. 3, (1992).

7. Howard B. Richman, William Girten, and Jay Snyder, "Academic Achievement and Its Relationship to Selected Variables Among Pennsylvania Homeschoolers," *Home School Researcher* 6, no. 4, (1990): 9-16.

8. Jon Wartes, "Recent Results from the Washington Homeschool Research Project," *Home School Researcher* 8, no. 2, (1992): 9-19.

9. Howard B. Richman, William Girten, and Jay Snyder, "Math: What Works Well at Home," *Home School Researcher* 8, no. 2, (1992): 9-19.

10. John W. Whitehead and Alexis Irene Crow, *Home Education: Rights and Reasons* (Wheaton, IL: Crossway Books, 1993), 137-159.

11. Richman, Girten, and Snyder, "Academic Achievement and Its Relationship," 11.

12. Maralee Mayberry, Brian D. Ray, and J. Gary Knowles, "Political and Religious Characteristics of Home School Parents: Results of an Ongoing Study in Four Western States," *Home School Researcher* 8, no. 1, (1992): 4.

13. John Holt, *Teach Your Own: A Hopeful Path for Education* (New York, NY: Delta/Seymour Lawrence, 1981), 66.

Chapter 13

Magnet Schools/Charter Schools

David W. Kirkpatrick

MAGNET SCHOOLS

"Magnet school" is a relatively new term for what is a much older practice in education. The idea behind this innovation is the development of a school to which students will be attracted rather than assigned.

Senate Bill 744, introduced into the Pennsylvania Legislature in 1991, defined "Magnet" programs as "Secondary school programs which improve quality in education by offering educationally exciting programs and specialized courses meeting varied educational needs. These courses are designed to go beyond usual school programs by concentrating on topics such as scientific research, creative and performing arts, and international studies."[1] The magnet school concept can also be applied at the elementary level.

The designation of a school as a "magnet" school dates back to the early 1970s when this concept was used to promote desegregation efforts in inner-city schools. The practice of operating magnet schools, however, has been in existence for generations. The concept that magnet schools are based upon was derived from the practices of the European grammar schools. Indeed, it can be argued that the first magnet school in the nation was the Boston Latin School, which was founded in 1635.

The establishment of high quality schools in the inner-city that focused on a specific subject area was one way to maintain and attract additional student enrollment. A prime example is Stuyvesant High School in New York City which has consistently produced the nation's top students in the 20th Century. This fact is not surprising since it had one of the nation's largest school districts from which to draw its students.

Notwithstanding this fostering of excellence, the Stuyvesant environment had its shortcomings. For years, "its students were crowded into an obsolete building with inadequate laboratory, library, and recreational facilities. Classes...typically held 60 students each. Textbooks were out of date and in short supply....Computers were obsolete or broken... (the) teaching staff...came from the same citywide pool that staffed all other public high schools." [2]

What was distinctive, of course, was the student body. Given the environment, it is questionable how much difference the school actually made. It is possible these students would have persevered and succeeded even in their original schools if those schools had possessed a more inviting academic environment.

There is evidence for this argument. In an October 1992 symposium in Washington, D.C., University of Chicago Professor James Coleman reaffirmed conclusions he advanced in the 1960s that showed few differences in achievement by students at magnet and assigned schools when adjustments were made for student characteristics, such as socioeconomic status.[3]

What Stuyvesant did offer the students was a challenging peer group. This large concentration of many of New York City's best students also permitted the city school district to conduct an effective public relations effort. It was far easier for the city to publicize the collective achievements of these talented students at Stuyvesant than if they had been scattered among schools throughout the city.

A DOUBLE STANDARD?

Are magnet schools held to the same standards as other public schools, or is a double standard present for these institutions? This issue is raised because it is common practice among the members of the public school "establishment," like any vested interest, to level charges and criticisms against modifications to the system or what are viewed as threatening alternatives to the status quo that use different standard operating procedures. Indeed, magnet schools within the public system are largely exempt from the close review that is given to similar "outside" programs.

Nationwide, there are between 1,000 to 2,000 magnet schools operating in the largest cities. Magnet school statistics are sketchy at this time because the nation's state and local governments do not have any generally accepted definition for this concept or a mandate to collect data on it. Although the nation may have up to 2,000 magnet schools, the United States possesses approximately 85,000 public schools. Consequently, most public school students never have the opportunity to experience a magnet school.

Magnet schools exist in such Pennsylvania cities as Harrisburg, Philadelphia, Pittsburgh, and York. Pennsylvania legislators have been campaigning to expand the magnet school concept in Pennsylvania. This effort is illustrated by House Bill 436 of 1993. This legislative proposal would provide state funding to school districts in the amount of $200 per student for each school year thereafter if the students are enrolled in state-approved magnet programs.

Historically, most of these special, or narrowly focused schools, in contrast with the comprehensive secondary schools, have been found in one of two categories. These categories have been the academic schools, such as Stuyvesant, which were designed to attract or serve a select school population, and the vocational or technical schools. Many of the latter, have been too often looked down upon by many members of the general public as being less desirable than the comprehensive school, rather than as more desirable, as with the selective, academic Stuyvesant and Central (Philadelphia) high schools.

The double standard that applies to these schools for the gifted, in contrast to a perceived outside threat, is best exemplified by the charge that schools of choice will siphon off the best students and leave the poorest students behind in an even more deprived educational environment than they presently face. Research is showing that, at least for schools of choice, this is not what is happening.

In Milwaukee, for example, the ongoing study of the voucher program, after three years in that district, shows that it was the low achieving students who elected to exercise a choice the first year. During the second year the students choosing to participate possessed even less "academic potential."

This trend was not evident in the public academic magnet schools. They consciously and intentionally select the best students, and leave the rest.

As *The Philadelphia Inquirer* has reported, these schools "siphon off the best students (and) suffer less from oversized classes because they control their admission process." The result is that "'The kids in most need of close academic attention are most likely to get squashed,' said Michelle Fine of the High Schools Collaborative." [4]

These magnet schools not only seek out the brightest students, in terms of native genius, but they also want those who are established achievers. Frequently, it is true that magnet schools select many of their students, rather than the students selecting the school. The magnet schools, therefore, tend to remove from the "regular" schools both their most talented and their most motivated students.[5]

Because these magnet schools are public schools, this recruitment trend seems to be acceptable. One can argue that it might be, if every school were a magnet school, or if, as the slogan of former Pennsylvania Secretary of Education Robert Scanlon (1979-1983) stated it, "Every School a Good School," were a reality.

EAST HARLEM, NEW YORK CITY

One example of a school distict that became a "good school" by adopting a magnet approach is East Harlem District #4, in New York City. This public school district began reforming itself in the mid-1970s, out of the desperation that stemmed from being 32nd among the 32 subdistricts in the city. It has evolved into a district of school choice, where every school has a distinctive purpose. Four schools in this district were closed in the intervening years because they could not attract enough students. These schools were reopened in different circumstances and survived when a clientele was attracted.

This educational experiment demonstrated that a school and a building are not the same thing. The district's 20 buildings now contain 46 schools. Students select three schools they wish to attend; the overwhelmingly majority of students are accepted at the school that was their first choice. Many of these schools are academically oriented, or emphasize the "3 Rs," but other magnet variations include the performing arts and marine studies.

Unfortunately, East Harlem's experience is the exception, not the rule across the country.

MAGNET SCHOOLS AND EQUITY

Even at their best, magnet schools are selective, restrictive, and leave many students outside the realm of educational excellence. The Ben Franklin School in Harrisburg, Pennsylvania, is an example. Established as a magnet school in 1978, its success has led to parents camping out prior to the first Monday in May, which is the school's registration day, in an attempt to ensure that their children are accepted. After 15 years of meeting the purpose for which it was created, "There is a waiting list to gain entrance.... 'Many parents...see standing in line as a must. There's no other way,' said a parent, Cynthia Shikara."[6]

For many students, this small number of available slots in magnet schools is a source of frustration. Why should there be waiting lists for student positions in public education? What is there about public education that makes it essentially impossible to close a failing institution and virtually as difficult to replicate a successful one? If there are too many students for a Ben Franklin to hold, why cannot there be more Ben Franklins?

Some individuals argue, although they would probably not include Ben Franklin High School within this criticism, that magnet schools are specifically created to separate the haves from the have-nots, in a politically acceptable manner, under the guise of "quality education."

Former U.S. Secretary of Education William Bennett brought a lot of attention to the Chicago Public Schools when he said they were the worst in the nation. He backed up this claim with figures showing that a disproportionate number of Chicago's high schools were among the worst in the nation. As a result of his claim, reform legislation was passed by the Illinois Legislature that authorized individual school councils to be involved in each school's operations in Chicago. The city's central school board still exists, but school principals have resisted the change. Their resistance is based on the fact that this new school governance arrangement allows the school councils to replace the principals, and some of the councils have done so. Generally, this school governance reform has fallen short of hopes and expectations. School choice and vouchers are now being advocated as the next step toward better schools in Chicago.

Despite Bennett's evidence of general school failure, there are some children who are not suffering. They are protected by what the city of Chicago calls "magnet" schools.

As the *Chicago Tribune* has observed:

Those with clout who remain in the public system and could have changed it--including journalists, other opinion makers, politicians, and the well-connected--have sent their children to public magnet schools, a quasi-private system supported with tax dollars as a way of isolating their children from the poor.

For years, magnet schools were the dirty secret in Chicago public education, a morally indefensible perk that allowed public dollars to protect the fortunate, at the expense of the poor.

As always, clout was served. Hyde Park and the Near North Side were protected, and the people whose complaints would have been heard were quiet because they had their interests well in hand.

The neighborhood schools in the poor and cloutless black and Hispanic inner-city deteriorated.[7]

In short, many of the magnet schools across the nation have been created for various motives. Some of these schools have consciously sought to improve educational opportunities for students. Some magnet schools have been developed because of a crises situation, such as de facto segregation of inner-city schools, that required drastic measures. Some magnet schools have been created due to public pressure, or due to the leadership of a charismatic individual. Finally, some magnet schools, as may be the case in Chicago, have been established to protect the haves from the have-nots, the affluent from the poor, the powerful from the weak.

MAGNET SCHOOLS AS SCHOOLS OF CHOICE

About one-quarter of all magnet schools are schools of choice as well. But, as stated earlier, the choice in many cases rests largely with the schools and not with the students. About "one-third of these schools base admission on established criteria, such as superior academic performance; the remainder admit students on a lottery or first-come basis."[8] In either case, large numbers of students may be rejected.

Basing admission on academic performance does not assure that even all of the academically qualified will be admitted, any more than all qualified students are accepted at Harvard, Yale, and other prestigious institutions of higher education.

Certainly, determining who is accepted on the basis of whose parents can afford to camp out well in advance of others is not an equitable selection process. Even using a lottery, while equitable in the sense that every student has an equal chance of acceptance, reduces to a matter of luck the opportunity for a student to obtain a better education than might otherwise have been the case.

A somewhat unusual magnet school variation is embodied in a proposal to the magnet school steering committee created by the Metro School Board in Nashville, Tennessee, for operation of a new magnet school by a private company. The company's founders, a nationally recognized Metro principal and two business partners, want to create the "Global School," an international studies school that would emphasize foreign languages and geography.

> The proposed magnet school would begin with 50 to 100 students in fifth and sixth grades and add seventh and eighth grades in the next two years, eventually enrolling about 200 students. It would be open to all students regardless of academic achievement, and the operators would assure a student population representative of the entire community.

> Mayor Phil Bredesen has urged the school board to move quickly into the creation of new magnet schools, suggesting five new ones a year over the next five years....

> ...it represents the kind of fresh thinking that is needed if our schools are to break free of outmoded restraints and find better ways to prepare our children.[9]

This Nashville proposal is out of the ordinary, combining elements of magnet schools, school choice, and privatization, and its performance level will be closely monitored. If this new concept enjoys success, it may serve as a model for other areas that are exploring the idea of establishing magnet schools.

MAGNET SCHOOLS AND SOCIAL CLASS

Nevertheless, until "Every School a Good School," is reality rather than rhetoric, the limitations of the magnet school movement should be recognized. In the best circumstances, magnet schools are an opportunity for a better education for some students; in the worst circumstances, magnet schools may be an opportunity for the advantaged to protect their children from having to associate with, and experience the inadequacies faced by, disadvantaged students.

On a larger scale, it should also be recognized that we have, in effect, "magnet districts." These are areas where the very affluent can afford to live, provide the best educational opportunities for their children, and avoid any responsibility to provide the same educational opportunities for the children of the poor. This form of "clustering" helps to guarantee that the cultural and educational advantages the affluent have, in addition to the monetary ones, will be passed on to their children. Further, their children will not have to worry about competing against disadvantaged youngsters on anything approaching a level playing field. This is not so much a matter of race, although that certainly is a factor, as it is of something Americans do not like to talk about--social class.

As George Gilder has written, "Economic classes will seek out their own kind, whenever possible, and send their children to schools dominated by their own economic class. This ruling applies with near perfect equality to liberals and conservatives, blacks and whites, senators and judges, socialists and libertarians."[10]

This phenomena explains the fact that when *Brown v. Board of Education* was handed down by the U.S. Supreme Court, the majority of students in all but one of the 20 largest school districts in the nation were Caucasian,[11] but today, the majority of the students in all of the 25 largest school districts are minority students.[12]

By themselves, magnet schools will not change this fact.

CHARTER SCHOOLS

By the usual standards of school reform, the concept of charter schools is an educational innovation that is developing with lightning speed. It seems to have been first suggested by Ray Budde in his 1988 book, *Education by Charter: Restructuring School Districts*. The concept was subsequently endorsed by Albert Shanker, President of the American Federation of Teachers (AFT), in a 1988 speech to the National Press Club.

Charter schools are public schools delivering public education and using public dollars, but they are organized by individuals or groups, not school boards, as private, non-profit organizations. Charter schools are created around the concept of a charter or contract between the group that organizes the school and its sponsor--a designated governing body. The charter outlines the school's educational plan, outcomes, and assessment measures. In exchange for this agreement of accountability, the governing body grants the school autonomy.

This organizational arrangement is basically how colleges and universities have been created and operated in this country for centuries. Furthermore, there are thousands of recognized, independent, secular or sectarian nonpublic schools in the nation that utilize this type of organizational arrangement, yet it did not occur to most of the founders of public education in the 19th Century to adopt this arrangement, or authorize it as an option.

A NATIONAL OVERVIEW OF THE CHARTER SCHOOL MOVEMENT

After being developed in 1991 in Minnesota, the charter school movement has continued to grow throughout the nation. Currently, five states have adopted charter school legislation: California, Colorado, Georgia, Minnesota, and New Mexico. In 1992 California adopted this legislation, and Colorado, Georgia, and New Mexico passed charter school legislation during the spring of 1993.

The progress of the charter school movement can be seen below:

PROGRESS OF CHARTER SCHOOLS

State	Year Passed	Number of Schools Eligible for Charter
Minnesota	1991 (revised 1993)	20
California	1992	100
Colorado	1993	50
Georgia	1993	To be determined by state board of education.
New Mexico	1993	5

Source: "Business/Education Insider," The Heritage Foundation, Washington, D.C.: June 1993, p. 2.

At the national level, President Clinton's Administration has not taken any action to promote the charter school concept. Although President Clinton spoke favorably about charter schools during the 1992 presidential campaign, what, if any, action to support this concept will be forthcoming from the national government is uncertain.

MINNESOTA SETS THE PACE

In early 1990, Doug Wallace, a member of the Minnesota State Board of Education, was arguing that "It is time to destruct the district system."

He advocated replacing all of that state's 433 school districts with "individually state-chartered schools, which would be accredited solely on the basis of their students' achievements. All state rules--other than those on safety, affirmative action, and student performance--would be eliminated."

He further suggested replacing reliance on local property taxes with full state funding, through a flat amount per pupil, plus supplements for students with special needs.[13]

He was hoping that his plan would be adopted by the legislature the following year. While it was not accepted in its entirety, a limited version of the charter school part of his proposal became law in Minnesota in 1991. Hence, Minnesota became the first state to implement the charter school concept.

Restrictions the law placed on this arrangement provided an end product that was far from what Wallace, or other charter school advocates, preferred. Compromises, however, were necessary to overcome the opposition that any significant educational innovation will face from most of the public school establishment.

Despite her willingness to agree to the compromises to the charter school proposal, State Senator Ember D. Reichgott, a co-sponsor of the bill, was not endorsed by either the Minnesota Federation of Teachers or the Minnesota Education Association. She was reelected to the state Senate anyway. The enrollment-options coordinator for the state, Peggy O. Hunter, gave her view that some Minnesota educators oppose charters because "The money is more important to them than the kids."[14]

In a state with 433 school districts and some 700,000 public school students, the Minnesota law permits the establishment of only eight charter schools, with no more than two being authorized by any one school district. A charter school may only be proposed by licensed teachers, and the proposal must be approved by the both the local and state boards of education. Finally, a proposed charter school must meet some of the basic requirements of the regular public schools. Minnesota charter schools, for example, may not do the following:

> screen students, have a religious affiliation, charge tuition, or discriminate on the basis of race, religion, or disability....Each school must have a board of directors, a majority of whose members are licensed teachers at the school. All staff members at the school and all parents of children enrolled there must be able to participate in the board's election...beyond those requirements, the law leaves charter schools essentially free from most rules and regulations that apply to public schools. They are to be educationally,

financially, and legally independent--able to hire and fire their employees, devise their budgets, and develop their curriculum.[15]

This innovation may have seemed modest, but it was a start. Interest was immediate. Before mid-1992 about 20 charter school proposals had been made. Only two of these proposals were approved; the remaining proposals were rejected by the local school board.

An example of a charter school proposal being rejected could be seen in the Winona School District. In this school district the teachers' local education association threatened to file a grievance if the Winona school board approved the charter. The association charged that the agreement would violate the school district's master labor relations contract.[16]

Joe Nathan, Director of the University of Minnesota's Center for Policy Studies, who helped draft the legislation, said "The people who are trying to make the law not work are succeeding." This resistance to the charter school concept may have had favorable results since it led to suggestions that the charter school law be amended in the next legislative session to increase the number of authorized schools, to make it easier for the school to be approved, and to bypass local school boards.[17] These amendments were adopted in early 1993.

Amending the Minnesota charter school law yielded a few surprises, such as the realization that this law did not specifically say the new charter school would have to be within the authorizing school district's boundaries. A school board, therefore, could authorize a charter school in some other part of the state, even if that second district's school board had not taken such a step. Indeed, this has already happened.

One of Minnesota's U.S. Senators, David Durenberger, introduced a charter school bill in the Congress on July 31, 1991. This legislative proposal, the Public School Redefinition Act, was based on the new Minnesota charter school law. Under Durenberger's proposal, a first-year sum of $50 million would have been made available to the states. This funding would have been used to support groups wishing to start charter schools. The money could have been used for a number of purposes, such as planning, start-up costs, and the purchase of equipment.[18] Durenberger's bill was not passed before the adjournment of Congress.

THE CONNECTICUT STUDY

While Minnesota was passing a charter school law, the Connecticut Legislature was debating the issue. The lawmakers finally decided to authorize a commission to study the idea.

Encouragement for the charter school concept came from National School Boards Association President, Arlene R. Penfield. She indicated her belief that Connecticut's efforts to investigate the charter school idea might lead to worthwhile changes in the schooling process.

While Penfield was probably envisioning such schools as being within present public school parameters, the superintendent of the New Milford School District, Stephen C. Tracy, articulated a vision that was more ambitious. He argued that in a charter school, "We don't need a school board and superintendent. The charter school concept takes the essence of public education and recasts it in new forms."[19] As one of the state commission's leaders, this was a vision that could not be ignored in the commission's deliberations.

Meanwhile, the Connecticut Task Force proceeded with its deliberations during 1991 and reported its findings in February 1992. It defined a charter school as "a public school or educational program" with a charter from the State Broad of Education, which is staffed and controlled by certified teachers, publicly funded by the student's home district, open to all students, and which attempts to meet the general standards the state sets for other public schools.

Like the Minnesota charter school concept, the Connecticut Task Force viewed charter schools within the public school environment. Despite this view, the President of the Connecticut Education Association, who had served as a member of the Task Force, voted against the adoption of the report.

The Task Force's report contained a number of conclusions. For example, the report concluded that charter schools would do the following: allow for reform and change within the public system; promote professionalism for teachers; focus on outcomes for students; create a more responsive system of public education; provide more active roles for parents and teachers in the creation and implementation of new schools; represent a response to dissatisfaction with the present system; invite all participants in Connecticut's system of public education to try new ideas that may not be possible under the current system; and provide a vehicle for promoting high-quality, integrated education on a voluntary basis." [20]

CALIFORNIA ACTS

In February 1992, the Chairmen of both the House and Senate Education Committees in the California Legislature introduced different versions of charter legislation. Each proposal included the basic idea of teachers creating their own charter schools that would receive public money but be free from most local and state rules. Both state Senator Gary Hart (D-Santa Barbara) and Assemblywoman Delaine Eastin (D-Union City), the Education Committee Chairs and the charter school legislation sponsors, admitted that they hoped such a reform would help defeat the movement for a Parental Choice Initiative to appear on a forthcoming California ballot.

Perhaps because of the educational choice initiative movement--now scheduled to be on the ballot in 1993--and despite the usual strong opposition from both teachers' unions, both bills were passed and were sent to Governor Pete Wilson for final consideration. The Charter Schools Act signed by Governor Wilson was based on the bill sponsored by Senator Hart. Representative Eastin's proposal was vetoed.

California's charter school law is significantly different and stronger than the one in Minnesota. Up to 100 charter schools were authorized, and a district could charter all of its schools if it wished. Charter schools would not only receive about $4,800 per student but would also be eligible for compensatory and special-education payments as well.

Hart's successful bill, unlike the Eastin proposal, does not require the teachers to be certified or tenured. California's charter school law also differs from the Minnesota law since it permits appeals to the State Board of Education and the state Superintendent of Public Instruction, if a local board would reject a request for a charter school.[21] It also allows private sources to give funding and other support to create or operate a charter school. The California law, however, does prevent a private school from becoming a charter school. The manager of California's educational voucher initiative, Kevin Teasley, said he viewed the charter law as a "very good, positive step," but that he still favored competition from the private sector as well.[22]

OTHER CHARTER SCHOOL PROPOSALS

At this time, even individual school districts, such as Detroit, Michigan, are considering the charter school idea. In fact, a reform-minded Detroit school board has considered "chartering" private schools by having them join the public school system. In this manner, students could be enrolled in these private schools at public expense.

One commentator observed that, "It won't happen overnight, but the swing toward private-sector education is under way. The teaching bureaucracy can slow the movement but won't be able to stop it."[23]

In Florida, Dade County is strongly moving toward charter schools. Dade County officials expect to build 49 new schools in the years immediately ahead, and they plan for all of these schools to be charter schools. [24]

Several other states considered charter school legislation in 1991-92, and some, such as North Carolina, came close to passing their own version of such a law. [25]

New Jersey Governor James Florio proposed new charter school legislation, the Quality Education Act, in October 1992. This bill would authorize up to two charter schools in each of the state's 21 counties. [26]

In Tennessee a number of businessmen joined forces to promote charter schools, and these groups were not totally opposed to full school choice using vouchers.

Colorado Representative John Irwin suggested allowing Colorado's schools to withdraw from their local district, as can be done in England, and report directly to the state board of education. These charter school proposals, along with other proposals, led Chris Pipho, a senior staff member of the Denver-based Education Commission of the States, to say, "The idea may catch fire." [27]

Perhaps most startling of all these developments is the possibility that Russia may be developing a more democratic system of education than exists in the United States or virtually any other nation. Under a Russian law that became effective in August 1992, "Each school in the country-- whether 'state, municipal or free institution'--is to operate under a charter that defines its character and mission, how it will operate, and how it will be accountable for results." [28]

Public funds would be provided to all Russian schools on a similar basis. Schools could also have virtually any kind of sponsor: private individuals and groups, religious organizations, or even foreign organizations. This new Russian law is cited below:

> All types of schools--government, private, or church-run--are allowed to have their own bank accounts and are encouraged to supplement their income from public funds by providing additional educational services or engaging in other appropriate activities.

> The role of government is to establish the norms for education and-- through an autonomous assessment organization--determine whether schools are meeting these norms...the new democratic government is committed to decentralization...placing as many decisions as possible in the hands of those who will have to carry them out. [29]

Pennsylvania Charter School Legislation

Pennsylvania has not been immune to this movement, even in the absence of specific enabling legislation.

On November 9, 1991, the U.S. Department of Education presented one of its "A+" awards to Simon Gratz High School in Philadelphia, which features what it terms "charters," or schools-within-the-school. Nearly half of the its 2,000 students are now in these "charter" schools, each of which has its own theme. For example, the Center for Creative Communication stresses creative arts.[30]

Teachers involved in some of Philadelphia's charter schools have indicated that they should select the teachers with whom they will work. The teachers' union, which is supposed to represent the teachers' interests, opposes this proposal, because this selection process might create divisions in the ranks.

A teachers union staff member has said "The thought of only having people in your school who agree with your philosophy is one that we reject, because the whole purpose of restructuring is to give an opportunity [for] ideas to come out and be discussed." His argument is self-contradictory, simultaneously holding that teachers in a school should not have to share a single philosophy while maintaining they have to toe the union line. This prevents teachers from doing anything of which the union disapproves.[31]

In 1992 members of both the Pennsylvania Senate and House of Representatives considered introducing charter school legislation, but time ran out before their legislative deliberations were completed. On February 10, 1993, however, Representative Robert O'Donnell of Philadelphia, a former Speaker of the House, introduced such a bill. His announcement said "Charter schools are publicly-sponsored, autonomous schools which are substantially freed of bureaucratic regulations. They must be approved by the Secretary of Education before their establishment."

O'Donnell said, "Charter schools are a tremendous complement to our public school system. They allow parents and educators to directly define a school's mission and then ensure that its specific goals are met. Charter schools encourage innovation and provide another excellent educational option for Pennsylvania students." [32]

Under his bill, charter schools would have to be nonsectarian but their form of governance could otherwise take any form approved by the Secretary, such as a partnership or cooperative of teachers, or a board of citizen trustees. A charter school could "be established by three or more certified teachers who will teach at the school; six or more parents or guardians of students who will attend the school; and by a college, university, museum or other non-profit organization which the Secretary deems appropriate."

Representative O'Donnell's bill includes some provisions other reformers regard as unnecessarily restrictive, such as the requirement for certified teachers. This is a requirement that nonpublic schools do not need to meet, and its absence does not seem to have a negative effect on their performance. In addition, sectarian schools would not be eligible to participate in this proposed arrangement. This could be a constitutional problem if money would flow directly to the schools, but this proposal should not have this problem if money would be supplied by grants to the students. This latter situation is implied in the O'Donnell legislation. He said his "charter schools legislation will not cost Pennsylvania taxpayers any additional monies since the funding appropriated for the child in his school district would 'follow,' the student to the charter school."[33]

The charter school idea received further impetus in the Keystone State when it was incorporated in school choice legislation introduced in 1993. A provision of those bills would authorize up to 50 charter schools in the Commonwealth.

GROWING ADVOCACY

Educational analysts have said the following of the charter school movement:

It would also represent a response to dissatisfaction with the present system and invite those now in the system to try things they may not be able to do under the current establishment.

Theorists also claim it could result in a more responsive system of public education and be a useful vehicle for promoting quality integrated education on a voluntary basis.[34]

In sum, the charter movement is alive, healthy, and, like the school choice movement, rapidly expanding. Charter schools are an educational innovation favored by the Progressive Policy Institute, which has been called President Clinton's "favorite think tank."[35]

Ted Kolderie, cited as one of the fathers of the charter movement and an early proponent of the idea of educators in private practice, has said:

The "charter schools" idea can also help relieve two serious inequities in American education.

First: it can empower people who don't have time to serve on school or district committees, or who don't get the chance....

Second: it can give us a much more just system of choice than the one we have today. Choice does exist for the fortunate....All it takes is money.[36]

At the March 1993 annual meeting of the American Education Finance Association in Albuquerque, New Mexico, Kolderie also reported that all of the charter school proposals in Minnesota were for small schools. None of the proposals was for "elite" students. The next step to expand the charter school concept, inclusion of not only nonpublic but sectarian schools, may have been taken by Minnesota.

At the same time it passed its charter school law in 1991, the Minnesota Legislature also passed a law that, for the first time, makes church-sponsored schools eligible to receive public funds for educating high-school dropouts and those at-risk of dropping out. Students who are at least 16 years old and who would otherwise qualify for the incentives program may enroll in church-sponsored schools if their local school districts are willing to contract with those institutions. The sectarian schools must not exclude students on religious grounds and must provide "nonsectarian educational services." A separate Minnesota program that allows high-school juniors and seniors to attend college, including religious institutions, at school-district expense was upheld by a federal district judge last year as not violating the establishment clause of the Constitution. The graduation-incentives program provides that 88 percent of the basic state funding received by a district for the participating student--currently about $3,500--be paid to the nonpublic school. The at-risk student's original school district keeps the other 12 percent.

Under the existing program, at least 14 private, nonsectarian schools are participating with public school districts to educate at-risk pupils. Located mostly in Minneapolis and St. Paul, these schools include several innovative, storefront private schools. Statewide, there are 30 private, sectarian high schools in this program.[37]

The schooling system in this nation may at last be reforming. But change will not come easily, if it comes at all. More than perhaps any other institution in American life, schools have resisted reforms and have served as the graveyard of many educational innovations.

ENDNOTES

1. Senate, Pennsylvania Legislature, "Act Providing for School Subsidies and Further Providing for School District Assistance, 1991-92 Legislative Session, *Senate Bill 744*.

2. Peter Shaw, "The Competitiveness Illusion," *National Review*, 18 January 1993.

3. Gerald W. Bracey, "No Magic Bullet," *Phi Delta Kappan*, February 1993, 495-496.

4. Dale Mezzacappa, "A Struggle With Crowded Schools," *Philadelphia Inquirer*, 11 November 1992, 1(B).

5. Gary Putka, "Applied Anxiety," *The Wall Street Journal*, 5 June 1991.

6. Val Walton, "School Pulls Parents Into Children's Educations," *Patriot-News* (Harrisburg, PA), 21 January 1993, 10(A).

7. John Kass, "Back to Classes," *Chicago Tribune*, 6 September 1992.

8. Clint Bolick, "A Primer on Choice in Education: Part I-How Choice Works" (Washington, D.C.: The Heritage Foundation, 1990), 4.

9. "New Mold for Magnet," *Nashville Banner* (Nashville, TN), 16 December 1992.

10. George Gilder, *Wealth and Poverty* (New York, NY: Basic Book Inc., 1981), 91.

11. Edmund Fawcett and Tony Thomas, *The American Condition* (New York, NY: Harper & Row, 1982), 303.

12. *Teacher Magazine*, April 1990.

13. "State Journal," *Education Week*, 11 April 1990, 14.

14. Lynn Olson, "California is Second State To Allow Charter Schools, Law Partly Aimed to Heading Off Vouchers," *Education Week*, 30 September 1992, 1.

15. Lynn Olson, "Chartered Territory," *Teacher Magazine*, March 1992, 28.

16. "Teachers' Union Threatens Charter School," *Education Week*, 19 February 1992.

17. Ellie Ashford, "Charter Schools: Rough Going in Minnesota," *School Board News*, 26 May 1992.

18. Ibid..

19. Ellie Ashford, "Minnesota Teachers Can Seek Charters to Run Their Own Schools," *Illinois School Board Journal* (November-December 1991).

20. Connecticut Task Force, *Report on Charter Schools* (Hartford, CT: Connecticut Department of Education), February 1992.

21. William Trombley, "Law Would Allow Teachers to Create Public Schools," *Los Angeles Times*, 12 February 1992.

22. Lynn Olson, "California Is Second State To Allow Charter Schools."

23. William Tucker, "Foot in the Door" *Forbes Magazine*, 3 February 1992, 50.

24. Theodor Rebarber, *State Policies for School Restructuring* (Denver, CO: National Conference of State Legislatures, April 1992), 7.

25. Ibid., 9.

26. Department of Education, *Issue Brief Update, State Choice Legislation: 1992 Year-End Wrap Up* (Washington, D.C.: Government Printing Office, January 1993), 5.

27. Mary Massey, "Independent Public School Idea Gains Foothold in Some States," *Education USA*, 9 March 1992.

28. Charles L. Glenn, "Organizing the Russian Educational System for Freedom and Accountability," *Network News and Views*, November 1992.

29. "State Journal."

30. Department of Education, *AMERICA 2000* (Washington, D.C.: Government Printing Office, 11 January 1992).

31. Ann Bradley, "Union Blues," *Teacher Magazine*, February 1993, 9-11.

32. House, Pennsylvania Legislature, News Release by Representative Robert O'Donnell, 10 February 1993.

33. Ibid..

34. Dwayne Pickels, "Charter Schools May Be Idea Whose Time Has Come for State," *Tribune-Review* (Greensburg, PA), 14 September 1992.

35. Morton Kondracke, "Education Reform's New Champion," *Washington Times*, 30 December 1992.

36. Ted Kolderie, "Education: The Consumer's View, Charter Schools," *New York Times*, 26 January 1992.

37. Mark Walsh, "Minnesota Law Allows Church Schools To Get Public Funds," *Education Week*, 9 Ocotber 1991.

Chapter 14

Certification Reforms for Teachers and Administrators

Russel M. Sutton

RATIONALE FOR CERTIFICATION

The public school domain fosters a unique relationship between professional persons and the recipients of those services. The teacher-student relationship is of a different nature than the relationship between other professionals and their clients.

For example, in medicine and law, patients and clients are free to seek out and choose the services of their doctor or lawyer. In the public school setting, however, students are not afforded this same opportunity. Rather, they are assigned teachers at the discretion of the school administration. Not only are these students without a choice in teacher selection--they are also required by Pennsylvania law to attend school for a minimum of 180 days a year while of elementary and secondary school age.

The Commonwealth of Pennsylvania has established a licensure or certification requirement for the members of many professions to assure the citizenry that the professionals rendering the services they seek are qualified.

In the education profession, the teaching certificate represents state verification that teachers have met established competency standards. These standards are met by the successful completion of a state

Department of Education-approved college or university preparation program. Certification is a vital assurance to parents that a teacher is qualified as they entrust their children to the public school, hopeful that these students will be afforded every opportunity to realize their full potential.

CERTIFICATION REFORM AMONG THE STATES

According to a 1992 study by the National Center for Education Information (NCEI), 40 states now offer alternatives to the traditional education school route to teacher licensure, up dramatically from only eight in 1983.[1] The center estimates that 40,000 people were certified to teach through alternative means between 1985 and 1992, more than half of them during the past two years.

This study found a growing interest among states in creating ways to augment the teacher force by certifying nontraditional candidates quickly. While the programs vary widely, the newest alternatives require formal instruction in the theory and practice of teaching, along with mentoring arrangements that pair novice teachers with experienced classroom veterans.

Eleven states offer programs with formal instruction and mentoring that allow individuals with bachelor's degrees to become licensed to teach all subjects and grade levels. Eight states offer such programs only for secondary school teaching or for subject areas where a teacher shortage exists.

Although the initial goal of such programs was to help stave off a projected teacher shortage, states are now motivated primarily by a desire to improve teacher quality. The language of legislation creating alternative-certification measures, for example, now typically mentions the need to increase the quality of the teaching force.

While the number of states offering alternative-certification programs has grown fivefold since 1983, the year NCEI began collecting its data, the definition of such programs has changed substantially in recent years. Until 1990, most states had simply utilized their existing provisions for emergency certification, making little attempt to design programs that would offer a coordinated induction into teaching. States, however, are now reserving the term "alternative certification" for new programs designed specifically to bring well-educated and articulate adults who already have at least a bachelor's degree into the teaching profession. The other types of "alternative certification" described by the states were emergency teaching certificates, waivers, and other arrangements that allow people to begin teaching while they complete the standard teacher-education requirements for licensure.

The states that now have "true" alternative programs--with no restrictions on which grades or subjects the candidates for licensure can teach--are Colorado, Connecticut, Kentucky, Maryland, Minnesota, New Hampshire, New Jersey, Tennessee, Texas, Washington, and West Virginia. States that require mentoring and formal instruction, but limit the subjects or grade levels that can be taught by alternatively certified teachers, are Arizona, Arkansas, California, Georgia, Idaho, Mississippi, Missouri, and Ohio.

Legislation under consideration in other states, such as North Carolina, would allow districts to waive any requirements if such rules "inhibit the local unit's ability to reach its local accountability goals." For example, licensure requirements may be waived upon the approval of the State Department of Education.

Among the earliest examples of a state alternative certification approach seeking quality instructors is New Jersey's program. The Garden State, which once faced a drastic shortage of teachers and a declining quality of education, decided eight years ago to open classroom doors to recent college graduates and mid-career professionals who did not possess education degrees. Beginning in 1985, candidates for licensure were required to take several seminars on teaching and, if judged competent after two years, were granted official certification.

Today, New Jersey no longer has a teacher shortage. There were 7,000 applicants under the new program in the first four years, making up 35 percent of the annual intake.[2] Hundreds of qualified would-be teachers are now being turned away.

More significantly, however, the caliber of the uncertified recruits is higher than those who have undergone traditional training, and their drop-out rate is four times lower. According to Saul Cooperman, New Jersey's former Education Commissioner, "We now have two routes competing against each other, and the alternate route is doing dramatically better. They have higher scores on the national teacher exam and better college records."

For school administrator certification, fifteen states required administrators to pass a competency test for initial certification in 1990.[3] Alternatives to administrator competency testing include assessment centers, on-the-job training and assessment, and on-the-job assessment without training. A leader in alternative certification programs for administrators is North Carolina, which has developed a Quality Assurance Program that includes two levels of certification. To attain the second level of certification, two years of administrative experience is required, and during this time, the new principal works with a mentor principal who is also responsible for assessing the novice principal's on-the-job mastery of state-developed competencies.

History Of Certification And Significant Reforms

Pennsylvania has issued teaching certificates since the 1800s. Over the years, the regulatory criteria for issuance has changed periodically to meet the changing needs of schools. The basic composition of certification regulations, however, remained relatively constant through the 1950s. Candidates for certification were required to successfully complete a prescribed number of semester hours credit in both a major academic course of study and a pedagogical sequence.

The beginning of a significant reform movement dawned on July 1, 1969. This movement opened new horizons in Pennsylvania's approach to teacher preparation and certification with the adoption of regulations that incorporated an innovative concept called "Program Approval." In a consortium with a number of other states, Pennsylvania played a key role at the national level in the development of the concept.

To implement the "Program Approval" concept administratively, the State Board of Education delegated to the Secretary of Education the authority to develop standards for approving certification programs to prepare professional educators for the public schools of Pennsylvania. Authority also was delegated by the State Board to develop and implement the procedures used to evaluate each certification program for compliance with the standards and to approve programs based upon that evaluation. Subsequently, Pennsylvania colleges and universities were encouraged to develop teacher preparation programs in accordance with these competency standards and submit their proposals for approval to the state Department of Education (PDE). Institutions that received approval were authorized to recommend successful program candidates for certification to the Department of Education.

The "Program Approval" evaluation method affords college and university faculty an opportunity to develop and implement teacher preparation programs and evaluation instruments and techniques. This method also provides the faculty with an opportunity to observe and screen candidates as they progress toward certification; hence, faculty supervisors are able to conduct subjective evaluations of a candidate. Successful completion of a preparation program culminates in a recommendation for certification. The approach embodied in the "Program Approval" method represents a significant divergence from evaluations conducted under previous certification regulations. PDE certification staff had formerly been confined to a review of paper credentials which resulted in an objective form of evaluation that was primarily limited to collegiate credit counting.

As with all subsequent certification regulations, the 1969 version contained a provision for a decennial review by the State Board of Education. Such a review aims to assure the inclusion of provisions to address the current and future needs of Pennsylvania's schools. It has been the custom to conduct a review of certification regulations in conjunction with or following a review and adoption of new curriculum regulations. As new curricular offerings and social services emerge in the public schools, attendant standards are structured to provide the schools with qualified professional staff. Accordingly, provisions are also made to create appropriate certificates to meet the needs of schools.

Certification regulation reviews have yielded amendments which include improved methods of evaluating the qualifications of candidates prepared by non-Pennsylvania colleges and universities, provisions to voluntarily delete a subject or area from a certificate, and revised procedures for certificate suspension and revocation. Pennsylvania continues to utilize the "Program Approval" method, and it continues to adhere to the premises behind this method.

Regulations issued on June 1, 1989, required candidates for a Pennsylvania teaching certificate to successfully complete a testing program for the first time. Initially, Pennsylvania established its own testing program, but the Commonwealth eventually phased into the National Teacher Examination Program (NTE).

In addition to fulfilling the NTE requirement, teachers who have received their initial Level I Instructional Certificate after May 31, 1987, are required to successfully complete a PDE-approved Induction Program in their school district. This requirement exists in addition to the attendant academic and experience requirements for Level II (permanent) certification. Subsequent to Level II certification, teachers are also required to participate in a PDE-approved Continuing Professional Development Program within the school district where they are employed. Failure to comply with this requirement every five years will result in a teacher's certificate being rendered inactive until this requirement is satisfied.

A Continuing Professional Development Program is also required of administrators. Commissioned school officers who have obtained a District Superintendent of Schools' Letter of Eligibility after May 31, 1987, are also required to participate in such a program.

A CERTIFICATION REFORM PROPOSAL

As of this writing, the Pennsylvania State Board of Education is conducting a review of its certification regulations for teachers and administrators. In response to this review and the forthcoming development of regulations designed to carry Pennsylvania into the next century, this writer has conceived a certification reform strategy. This strategy has been developed into a proposal for consideration by the State Board of Education during its review process.

Furthermore, this proposed certification process could be adopted and implemented by other states. This proposal can best be illustrated by comparing the current and the proposed regulations. Flow charts are used to make the comparison. Since the charts reflect only the basic certification sequences, a discussion of the various aspects of the current process and how the proposed changes will enhance the regulations is presented after the flow charts.

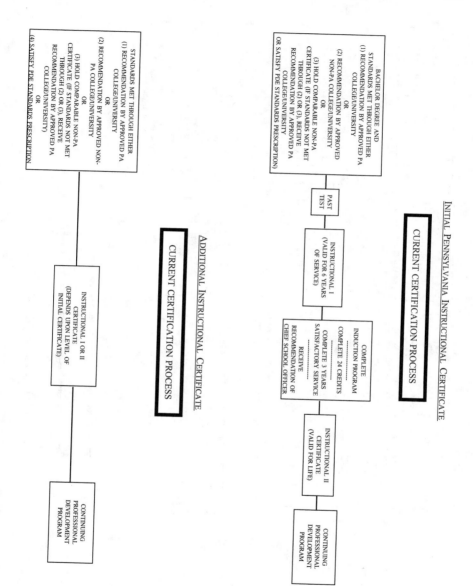

INITIAL PENNSYLVANIA INSTRUCTIONAL CERTIFICATE

CURRENT CERTIFICATION PROCESS

BACHELOR DEGREE AND
STANDARDS MET THROUGH EITHER
(1) RECOMMENDATION BY APPROVED PA
COLLEGE/UNIVERSITY
OR
(2) RECOMMENDATION BY APPROVED
NON-PA COLLEGE/UNIVERSITY
OR
(3) HOLD COMPARABLE NON-PA
CERTIFICATE (IF STANDARDS NOT MET
THROUGH (2) OR (3), RECEIVE
RECOMMENDATION BY APPROVED PA
COLLEGE/UNIVERSITY
OR SATISFY PDE STANDARDS PRESCRIPTION)

PAST TEST

INSTRUCTIONAL I
(VALID FOR 6 YEARS
OF SERVICE)

COMPLETE
INDUCTION PROGRAM
COMPLETE 24 CREDITS
COMPLETE 3 YEARS
SATISFACTORY SERVICE
RECEIVE
RECOMMENDATION OF
CHIEF SCHOOL OFFICER

INSTRUCTIONAL II
CERTIFICATE
(VALID FOR LIFE)

CONTINUING
PROFESSIONAL
DEVELOPMENT
PROGRAM

ADDITIONAL INSTRUCTIONAL CERTIFICATE

CURRENT CERTIFICATION PROCESS

STANDARDS MET THROUGH EITHER
(1) RECOMMENDATION BY APPROVED PA
COLLEGE/UNIVERSITY
OR
(2) RECOMMENDATION BY APPROVED NON-
PA COLLEGE/UNIVERSITY
OR
(3) HOLD COMPARABLE NON-PA
CERTIFICATE (IF STANDARDS NOT MET
THROUGH (2) OR (3), RECEIVE
RECOMMENDATION BY APPROVED PA
COLLEGE/UNIVERSITY)
OR
(4) SATISFY PDE STANDARDS PRESCRIPTION

INSTRUCTIONAL I OR II
CERTIFICATE
(DEPENDS UPON LEVEL OF
INITIAL CERTIFICATE)

CONTINUING
PROFESSIONAL
DEVELOPMENT
PROGRAM

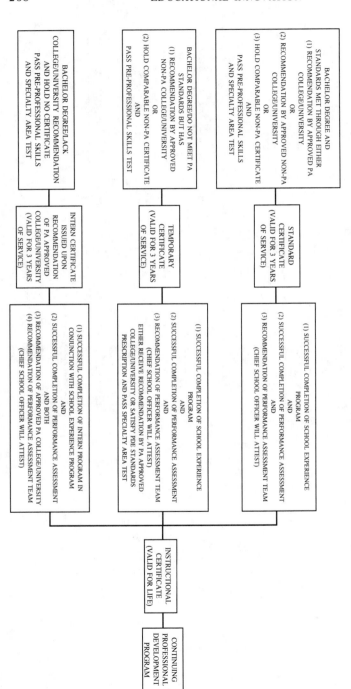

INITIAL PENNSYLVANIA INSTRUCTIONAL CERTIFICATE

PROPOSED CERTIFICATION PROCESS

BACHELOR DEGREE AND
STANDARDS MET THROUGH EITHER
(1) RECOMMENDATION BY APPROVED PA
COLLEGE/UNIVERSITY
OR
(2) RECOMMENDATION BY APPROVED NON-PA
COLLEGE/UNIVERSITY
AND
(3) HOLD COMPARABLE NON-PA CERTIFICATE
AND
PASS PRE-PROFESSIONAL SKILLS
AND SPECIALTY AREA TEST

BACHELOR DEGREE/DO NOT MEET PA
STANDARDS BUT HAS
(1) RECOMMENDATION BY APPROVED
NON-PA COLLEGE/UNIVERSITY
OR
(2) HOLD COMPARABLE NON-PA CERTIFICATE
AND
PASS PRE-PROFESSIONAL SKILLS TEST

BACHELOR DEGREE/LACK
COLLEGE/UNIVERSITY RECOMMENDATION
AND HOLD NO CERTIFICATE
PASS PRE-PROFESSIONAL SKILLS
AND SPECIALTY AREA TEST

STANDARD
CERTIFICATE
(VALID FOR 3 YEARS
OF SERVICE)

TEMPORARY
CERTIFICATE
(VALID FOR 3 YEARS
OF SERVICE)

INTERN CERTIFICATE
ISSUED UPON
RECOMMENDATION
OF PA APPROVED
COLLEGE/UNIVERSITY
(VALID FOR 3 YEARS
OF SERVICE)

(1) SUCCESSFUL COMPLETION OF SCHOOL EXPERIENCE
PROGRAM
AND
(2) SUCCESSFUL COMPLETION OF PERFORMANCE ASSESSMENT
AND
(3) RECOMMENDATION OF PERFORMANCE ASSESSMENT TEAM
(CHIEF SCHOOL OFFICER WILL ATTEST)

(1) SUCCESSFUL COMPLETION OF SCHOOL EXPERIENCE
PROGRAM
AND
(2) SUCCESSFUL COMPLETION OF PERFORMANCE ASSESSMENT
AND
(3) RECOMMENDATION OF PERFORMANCE ASSESSMENT TEAM
(CHIEF SCHOOL OFFICER WILL ATTEST)
EITHER RECEIVE RECOMMENDATION BY PA APPROVED
COLLEGE/UNIVERSITY OR SATISFY PDE STANDARDS
PRESCRIPTION AND PASS SPECIALTY AREA TEST

(1) SUCCESSFUL COMPLETION OF INTERN PROGRAM IN
CONJUNCTION WITH SCHOOL EXPERIENCE PROGRAM
AND
(2) SUCCESSFUL COMPLETION OF PERFORMANCE ASSESSMENT
AND BOTH
(3) RECOMMENDATION OF APPROVED PA COLLEGE/UNIVERSITY
AND
(4) RECOMMENDATION OF PERFORMANCE ASSESSMENT TEAM
(CHIEF SCHOOL OFFICER WILL ATTEST)

INSTRUCTIONAL
CERTIFICATE
(VALID FOR LIFE)

CONTINUING
PROFESSIONAL
DEVELOPMENT
PROGRAM

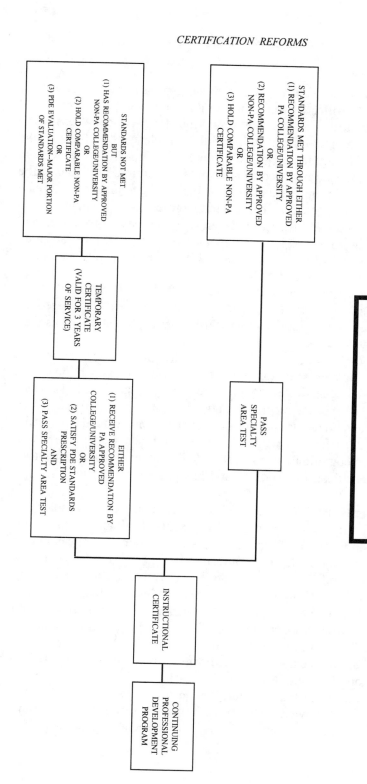

ADDITIONAL INSTRUCTIONAL CERTIFICATE

PROPOSED CERTIFICATION PROCESS

STANDARDS MET THROUGH EITHER
(1) RECOMMENDATION BY APPROVED
PA COLLEGE/UNIVERSITY
OR
(2) RECOMMENDATION BY APPROVED
NON-PA COLLEGE/UNIVERSITY
OR
(3) HOLD COMPARABLE NON-PA
CERTIFICATE

STANDARDS NOT MET
BUT
(1) HAS RECOMMENDATION BY APPROVED
NON-PA COLLEGE/UNIVERSITY
OR
(2) HOLD COMPARABLE NON-PA
CERTIFICATE
OR
(3) PDE EVALUATION--MAJOR PORTION
OF STANDARDS MET

TEMPORARY
CERTIFICATE
(VALID FOR 3 YEARS
OF SERVICE)

PASS
SPECIALTY
AREA TEST

EITHER
(1) RECEIVE RECOMMENDATION BY
PA APPROVED
COLLEGE/UNIVERSITY
OR
(2) SATISFY PDE STANDARDS
PRESCRIPTION
AND
(3) PASS SPECIALTY AREA TEST

INSTRUCTIONAL
CERTIFICATE

CONTINUING
PROFESSIONAL
DEVELOPMENT
PROGRAM

Under the proposed plan, the requirements for issuance of the current Instructional I Certificate would be similar to those of the proposed Standard Certificate. A candidate for the Instructional Certificate, however, would be required to successfully complete all sections of the National Teacher Examination, including the Professional Knowledge Test. A candidate for the Standard Certificate would be required only to pass the Pre-Professional Skills and Specialty Area Tests. The Standard Certificate holder would be expected to demonstrate professional competence to qualify for the proposed Instructional Certificate. Evaluations during and after actual classroom experience would provide a more accurate measurement of an individual's teaching abilities than a paper and pencil test administered prior to a teaching experience.

The Standard Certificate would represent PDE verification that the holder has satisfied the attendant certification standards and has passed the Pre-Professional Skills Test (Reading, Writing and Computation) as well as the Specialty Area Test.

The proposed Temporary Certificate would provide credentials to candidates seeking admission to the teaching profession who 1) possess a non-Pennsylvania certificate comparable to the proposed standard certificate or 2) have the recommendation for such a certificate by an approved non-Pennsylvania college or university, but who do not quite meet the state's certification standards. The Temporary Certificate would represent PDE recognition that the holder has satisfied a major portion of the attendant certification standards and has passed the Pre-Professional Skills Test.

School requests for PDE renewal or extension of a Standard or Temporary Certificate would require the support of and a favorable recommendation from a Performance Assessment Team. These candidates would have to appeal to the Bureau of Teacher Preparation and Certification to undergo a candidate evaluation for the Temporary Certificate. After the Temporary Certificate has been issued, the teacher would have to pursue the Instructional Certificate either by 1) receiving a recommendation from a Pennsylvania-approved college or university, or 2) satisfying a PDE standards prescription.

Candidates for the Temporary Certificate would only be required to successfully complete the NTE Pre-Professional Skills Test. If an evaluation would reveal that a candidate can not meet the specialty area and/or professional knowledge standards, it would not be logical to submit him to those sections of the NTE. Under current regulations, if a candidate does not qualify for an Instructional I Certificate, the only recourse available is the Emergency Certification avenue, which is addressed later in this chapter.

The Temporary Certificate will not only eliminate the need for the Emergency Certificate; it will enrich the pool of potential teachers. Pennsylvania is a teacher-producing state; nonetheless, the state still relies heavily upon other states to provide teachers in order to meet some regional teaching needs. It is imperative that Pennsylvania make the Temporary Certificate available to these prospective teachers entering Pennsylvania with another state's credentials and to Pennsylvania's teacher recruiters who seek out teaching prospects from other states for certain subject and geographical areas in the Commonwealth.

The Intern Certificate is not illustrated in the Current Certification Process diagram, but it has been available for issuance. The requirements to obtain this certificate are similar to those requirements being proposed here for the proposed Intern Certificate. The single difference between an Intern Certificate and the proposed one would be that the current certificate is valid for three calendar years, while the proposed certificate's validity would extend for three service years.

The present Intern Certificate represents PDE acknowledgement that the holder possesses a bachelor's degree; has satisfied the attendant specialty area standards; and has passed the Pre-Professional Skills Test and the Specialty Area Test. After the Intern Certificate has been issued, the recipients are obligated to pursue the Instructional Certificate by completing an approved college or university intern program. Requests for renewal or extension of an Intern Certificate must be supported by a favorable recommendation from both the Performance Assessment Team and the preparing college or university.

Pennsylvania's Intern Certificate was formerly titled, "Interim Certificate," and has been in existence since 1955. This certificate has served the state well as a viable, alternative avenue for entrance into the teaching profession.

The proposed Standard, Temporary, and Intern Certificate concepts for Pennsylvania may receive criticism because individuals who have not met all of the requirements ultimately expected of them are permitted to teach. In essence, however, this practice already exists since the current certification system permits such a practice through the issuance of 1) Instructional I (Provisional), 2) Intern, and 3) Emergency Certificates. This practice can be verified by a simple review of the current eligibility criteria to receive one of these certificates:

1) The holder of an Instructional I Certificate is required to complete 24 post-baccalaureate semester credit hours or in-service credits and to complete the three years of satisfactory service in order to qualify for the Instructional II (Permanent) Certificate.

2) The holder of an Intern Certificate is required to complete an approved teacher preparation program and pass the Professional Knowledge Test to qualify for an Instruction I (Provisional) Certificate.

3) The holder of a regular Emergency Certificate or a Long-Term Substitute Emergency Certificate is required to complete nine semester hours of credit each year in order to qualify for the Instructional I Certificate. The holder of a Long-Term Substitute Emergency Certificate or a Day-to-Day Substitute Emergency Certificate is not required to complete coursework to qualify for certificate renewal.

If one reviews the proposed certificates in their entirety, it is evident that the integrity of the Instructional Certificate would be preserved.

THE PENNSYLVANIA TESTING PROGRAM

The certification reform proposal set forth in this chapter would require candidates for the Standard and Intern Certificates to pass an NTE-developed and administered Pre-Professional Skills Test (PPST) and a Specialty Area Test (SAT). Candidates for the Temporary Certificate would only be required to pass the PPST. Candidates seeking an Instructional Certificate specialty area endorsement would have to pass the Specialty Area Test for *each* endorsement area if an SAT exists for that area.

The PPST would evaluate a candidate's reading, writing and computational skills and abilities. A candidate's professional performance level would be evaluated later during a Structured School Experience Program by a Performance Assessment Team (PAT). Intern Certificate holders would also be evaluated by the preparing college or university personnel. Temporary Certificate holders would be required to pass the Specialty Area Test during the School Experience Program.

The Pennsylvania Testing Program requirement would be waived for an out-of-state candidate for the Standard Certificate who 1) meets Pennsylvania's academic certification standards; 2) possesses a certificate comparable to the Pennsylvania Standard Certificate issued by a state with which Pennsylvania has a reciprocal agreement; and 3) completes five years of satisfactory, certified service.

THE SCHOOL EXPERIENCE PROGRAM

The certification reform proposal would require that each school district provide a state-approved School Experience Program. All candidates for the initial Instructional Certificate would be required to serve successfully in a School Experience Program for a minimum of one service year to qualify for the certificate. Since the first year of teaching is so crucial to a successful educational experience for both the professional educator and the students, the candidate would be required to participate in this school experience in the first year of service.

The School Experience Program should be three service years in length in order to accommodate the varying differences and needs of the Instructional Certificate candidates. During this time, candidates for the Instructional Certificate will be expected to successfully complete the requirements for that certificate. The requirements will vary from person to person according to the type of certificate held, the PDE Standards Prescription, and tests not yet taken or passed. For example, some candidates might qualify for the Instructional Certificate after successfully serving the required minimum of one year of service in a School Experience Program, while others might not qualify until they serve two or three years. Some candidates might never perform competently enough to receive the recommendation of the Performance Assessment Team for the Instructional Certificate.

School Experience Program Plan approval by the PDE would be contingent upon the submitting school district's inclusion of a provision for documented procedures for evaluation and recommendation for performance improvement. Safeguards would also be included to ensure the candidate's right to obtain the Instructional Certificate if his performance is successful, as well as rights to due process if his teaching performance is not successful.

PERFORMANCE ASSESSMENT

Two performance assessment options are offered under this certification reform proposal. Under the first option, the Local Control model, every new teacher would be assessed by a team consisting of an administrator from the employing local education agency (LEA) and a trained, certified teacher. The teacher assessor might or might not be an employee of the LEA, but he must have completed a state-designed and approved training program. Every new teacher would receive at least three evaluations spaced evenly throughout the school year. Each evaluation would require at least three observations by the assessment team, and every LEA would be required to have a state-approved support program to assist new teachers as needed.

The second option would feature the establishment of a network of Assessment Centers by the state to ensure easy access for new teachers. Each center would be staffed with trained, state-approved teacher assessors who would evaluate the documentation for each new teacher in order to determine if he is teaching effectively. Each new teacher would also be required to successfully complete a series of exercises or teaching simulations that would allow the person to demonstrate his teaching skills.

PERMANENT CERTIFICATION AND
CONTINUING PROFESSIONAL DEVELOPMENT

The current Instructional I Certificate in Pennsylvania is valid for six years of service as a teacher. During this time, the holder must complete 24 post-baccalaureate semester credit hours or PDE in-service credits to qualify for a Level II Certificate. Failure to comply with this requirement will render the certificate invalid and the holder ineligible for continued employment.

The proposed Standard Certificate would be valid for three years of service and would eliminate the 24 credit hour requirement. Like the proposed Temporary and Intern Certificates, the Standard Certificate would be valid for three years of service to allow the holders ample time and opportunity to obtain employment and satisfy all of the requirements for the Instructional Certificate.

The current 24 credit hour requirement is not a structured sequence of specific courses which must be completed by a teacher. Rather, teachers may complete courses of their choice. With the advent of the Continuing Professional Development Program, it could be argued that the credit requirement is an unnecessary vestige from the past. The credit requirement enables the Commonwealth to use certification as leverage to force teachers to continue their professional development. If a teacher fails to comply with this requirement, his certification is rendered invalid. Consequently, he must leave the public schools regardless of his ability and success in the classroom.

Teachers who were issued their initial Instructional I Certificate after May 31, 1987, or later are required to participate in a state-approved Continuing Professional Development Program every five years to keep their Instructional II Certificate active. Again in this case, teachers are confronted with the threat of losing their teaching certificates.

Perhaps a different approach to professional development and certification might be fruitful. While Pennsylvania should certainly retain the Continuing Professional Development Program requirement, the state should not use certification to achieve compliance. Continuing professional development should be regarded as an employer-employee issue, as it is in private industry. The requirement that school entities must maintain Continuing Professional Development Programs should allay the concern of the Commonwealth and proponents of professional development.

A Continuing Professional Development Program should be designed to require professional development activities within each five service year period following initial Instructional Certificate issuance for full-time teachers. The program may also be designed to require activities at various times within the five-year limit; however, this would be dependent upon the goals and objectives of the individual school entity's program.

The range of beneficial professional development activities is broader than many individuals might expect. Professional development may include activities such as the following: approved in-service courses, collegiate coursework, community relations, professional conferences, course development, curriculum writing, independent study, performance assessment team membership, research and publication, staff development, and teacher exchanges.

Indeed, the employing school entity may require the completion of post-baccalaureate coursework or the completion of in-service credits during the School Experience Program. This could be done to eliminate any teacher deficiencies detected by the Performance Assessment Team.

The incentives inherent in the School Experience Program should generate the desired level of continuing education activity. The incentives to participate in the program would include the following: self-improvement, self-esteem, salary increases, additional degrees and certificates, and promotions. Failure to meet the expectations of the employer could also jeopardize the status and employment of the teacher. In any case, however, the teaching certificate would remain intact to afford the holder an opportunity to remain in the profession.

This proposed certification process would preserve the integrity of the Instructional Certificate and its standards. Moreover, the intrinsic value of this certificate would also be enhanced by virtue of the fact that it would represent a verification by both the recommending college or university and the employing school entity that the candidate has successfully completed a state-approved teacher preparation program. Further, the certificate under this proposed system would also demonstrate the transfer and application of a number of required competencies from a teacher preparation program into a structured School Experience Program.

INNOVATIVE AND EXPERIMENTAL PROGRAMS AND STAFFING

Under any program of certification reform, the Secretary of Education should be granted the authority to permit school entities to develop and implement innovative and experimental programs. The Secretary should also have the authority to approve the staffing patterns that would be necessary to implement these experimental programs. Pennsylvania's present educational system does not possess a great deal of flexibility in the area of certification. Therefore, when innovative and experimental programs emerge to serve the ever-changing curricular and social service needs of students, the State Board of Education is continually pressed into a catch-up game of certificate creation to match the new roles and assignments.

The Secretary of Education of all states should be given the authority to waive certification restrictions for experimental educational programs. Such authority would eliminate the need for state Boards of Education to create new forms of certification, or grant waivers, for short periods of time. Attempting to educate the large numbers of people who serve on these state boards for such short-term innovations can frequently be an exercise in futility.

EMERGENCY AND SUBSTITUTE CERTIFICATION

School law in the Commonwealth requires that every teacher be appropriately certified to teach in the public schools. Ideally, all such certificates should be Level I or II Certificates. This ideal, however, is not the case. A small percentage of teachers serve on Emergency and Intern Certificates every year. An Emergency Certificate is issued upon the recommendation and request of a chief school administrator to fill a professional vacancy or temporary leave of absence when no fully qualified and properly certified applicant is available.

School administrators cannot realistically rely on an adequately staffed reserve pool of teacher applicants appropriately certified in all of the disciplines for which Pennsylvania issues certificates. A number of variables continually affect the supply and demand of substitute teachers: retirement, resignation, leave of absence, extended illness, death, district reorganization, reduction in force, fiscal resources, contract agreements, school size and geographical location, increases or decreases in enrollment, number of teacher applicants, and the number of teachers certified by the Commonwealth in a particular discipline, for example. Even if every classroom in the state were staffed with an appropriate Level I or II certified teacher at the opening of school, some of the aforementioned variables continue to plague administrators' efforts to maintain full staffing. Temporary leaves of absence, i.e., illnesses, maternity leaves, and sabbaticals, create a need for substitute teachers, who, like all other teachers, are required to be appropriately certified.

Some substitutes will be appropriately certified at Levels I or II; some will possess Level I or II certification, but this certification will not be appropriate to the assignment (e.g., assignment is chemistry and the certificate area is biology); and some will lack certification altogether. For those substitutes who lack appropriate certification, chief school administrators frequently will use the emergency certification avenue. The general public has a right to expect all teachers to be knowledgeable and qualified to teach the subjects they have been assigned. Hence, some members of the general public sometimes criticize school administrators for using the Emergency Certificate. The public, however, is frequently not aware of the previously mentioned reasons which confront administrators and present them with little or no recourse.

If there is an insufficient supply of appropriately certified teachers to meet a specific school's needs, the school's chief administrators select persons they feel to be best qualified to serve the needs of their students. Emergency Certification is then requested.

Due to the constant need for substitute teachers, Pennsylvania should establish a Long-Term Substitute Certificate. Such a certificate would be issued at the request of a school when a teacher is employed by that school as a substitute for a minimum of 100 days in a school year and lacks appropriate certification for the assignment. In addition, chief school administrators should be provided the authority to issue a Per Diem Substitute Certificate when a substitute teacher is employed by the school less than 100 days per school year.

Realistically, there is no way to avoid a limited use of teaching staff who lack appropriate Level I or II certification. Nevertheless, by coupling the Substitute Certificate approach with the Standard, Temporary, and Intern Certificates, the current Emergency Certificate could be eliminated.

This coupling would alleviate the cumbersome and restrictive process chief school administrators must endure to staff their schools. Rather than having to request issuance of Per Diem Substitute Emergency Certificates from the Commonwealth, chief school administrators would possess the authority to issue certificates themselves. These measures would provide staffing flexibility to local schools.

Currently, each school district is required to develop, approve, and provide an orientation program for substitute personnel prior to or concurrent with an assignment within that school district. Invariably, chief school administrators have desirable prospective employees, particularly those prepared by non-Pennsylvania colleges and universities, who do not quite qualify for a Pennsylvania certificate because they lack a course or two toward meeting the state's standards. The adoption of this proposal would provide the flexibility to employ these candidates. Information on the usage of substitute teachers must be provided to the PDE annually for the department's studies on the supply and demand for substitute teachers. A review of these studies illustrates the utility of adopting the proposal set forth in this section on certification for substitutes.

CURRICULUM, CERTIFICATION, AND STAFFING

As state governments study the possibility of creating new certificates to keep pace with the needs of schools, it is imperative that the education community continually abide by the axiom that "Curriculum dictates certification, and certification serves curriculum." Adherence to this basic premise promotes matches between teaching assignments and the competencies required to assure effective teaching, while providing school administrations with staffing flexibility.

If a certificate is created and the criteria for this certificate are defined without consideration for the curricular aspects of particular educational assignments, it is possible that schools will be confronted with certification non-compliance in some situations because the certificate is not appropriate to the assignment.

Certificates should be broad enough in scope to meet the curriculum needs of students and at the same time provide staffing flexibility to school administrators. Caution must be exercised not to "splinter" certificates to the point where the marketability of teachers and the teacher assignment prerogatives of administrators are severely limited. The balance among curriculum, certification, and staffing is delicate and should be given serious consideration when developing curriculum and certification regulations.

Perhaps Pennsylvania and other states should revise the manner in which curriculum is developed, certification established, and staffing set. The philosophy underlying Individual Education Programs (IEPs) is especially relevant here. IEPs are developed for students with special needs in order to help them realize their greatest potential. The establishment of these programs manifests our recognition that not all students learn at the same rate or in the same manner. Despite this recognition concerning special-needs students, the state persists in its practice of applying one set of certification regulations to 501 school districts and 29 intermediate units whose demographies are vastly different. The state attempts to overlay a defined certification grid on curricular activities which are diverse and in a constant state of flux to meet the needs of students in a rapidly changing society. A state's attempts to secure regulatory compliance in the areas of curriculum and certification are often akin to forcing a square peg into a round hole since schools and their students vary so greatly across a state.

Perhaps Pennsylvania and other states should include regulatory provisions to develop Individual Staffing Prescriptions (ISPs) for school entities in recognition of their diversity.

In order to take school district diversity into account, states could establish regional School Evaluation/Improvement Teams. These teams would be responsible for working with schools within certain regions of the state to evaluate and improve them. A team would be comprised minimally of representatives versed in curriculum, certification, special education, social services, vocational education, and fiscal administration. These teams should adopt a proactive advisory role to help schools achieve excellence.

If established, these School Evaluation/Improvement Teams would be authorized to design appropriate ISPs in cooperation with school administrators. Interaction among team members in addressing curriculum, certification, and staffing problems would facilitate the resolution of these items. This proposal would be particularly useful in providing needed assistance to small and rural school districts.

This team-school approach to certification would replace the current school certification audit that seeks school improvement. Under the present system in Pennsylvania, audits are conducted by the State Auditor General's Bureau of School Audits. Certification misassignments or irregularities are identified in a preliminary audit report. This report is subsequently reviewed by the PDE. A final determination of certification non-compliance results in the affected school losing a portion of its state subsidy reimbursement.

In improved certification systems, compliance should not have to rely upon fiscal penalties for enforcement. A team-school approach should be able to secure certification compliance voluntarily and create a new partnership between the schools and PDE. Team members would be able to familiarize themselves with curricular and social service programs offered by schools within their jurisdiction. As brokers, the teams would be able to promote improved communication, increased understanding, and a greater number of partnerships between schools and the PDE, which should culminate in school improvement throughout the state. The teams would evaluate schools and recommend improvements, if warranted. Schools would then be rated on the basis of the evaluation and their implementation of team-recommended improvements. If a school district would persistently disregard team recommendations and compliance with school law, PDE would issue a reprimand or take legal action against the local board of school directors and/or the chief school administrator.

ADMINISTRATIVE AND SUPERVISORY CERTIFICATES

Current regulations in Pennsylvania provide for the following administrative and supervisory certificates: District Superintendent of Schools Letter of Eligibility, Vocational Education Administrator, Elementary Principal, Secondary Principal, Supervisor of Curriculum and Instruction, and Supervisor of Pupil Personnel Services, as well as numerous single-area Supervisory Certificates.

Pennsylvania and other states that possess such an array of administrative certificates might be well served by combining all the letters of eligibility into one administrative certificate. The sole exception to this consolidation would be the certification for the Vocational Education Administrator, which should be retained. Moreover, the scope of the current kindergarten through grade 12 administrative certification should be expanded to birth through grade 12. Additionally, it will be necessary to amend the attendant competency standards. Approved colleges and universities with teacher education programs will be afforded an opportunity to revise their programs to prepare their candidates to meet the amended standards.

These changes would provide schools with greater staffing flexibility, especially small and rural school districts whose resources may be limited. School district administrators have always had the prerogative to select applicants on the basis of their particular area of expertise or experience; however, the comprehensive nature of this proposed new administrative certificate provides even greater latitude to the school in making line and staff assignments. For example, expansion of the administrative certificate's scope would permit the assignment of administrators and supervisors to nursery and preschool programs. Under present certification regulations in Pennsylvania, assignment to such programs is technically improper.

An alternative to the proposal presented above would be to combine all of the administrative certificates into one administrative certificate and combine all of the supervisory certificates into one supervisory certificate. Each of these two certificates would permit assignment throughout a school district.

Another proposal for revising administrative and supervisory certification in Pennsylvania would be to delete experience requirements. The experience requirement is a vestige from pre-Program Approval regulations. Currently, colleges and universities are authorized only to recommend candidates for the academic preparation phase of administrative and supervisory certificates. Acceptable service is determined by evaluations conducted by the PDE. A college or university recommendation should serve as verification that a candidate is qualified for a certificate and prepared to serve in the schools. Again, prospective employers will be free to determine the type and amount of experience they expect an applicant to possess to qualify for specific jobs.

CERTIFICATION RECIPROCITY

Numerous interstate certification agreements exist among states across the country, but a system of true teacher certification reciprocity does not. A true system would automatically issue a certificate to a candidate possessing a similar certificate issued by another state. Pennsylvania is a member of one of these interstate certification agreements, which is comprised of 26 states and the District of Columbia.

Interstate certification agreements are composed of a set of negotiated conditions which facilitate issuance of comparable certificates by other states. Such agreements address factors such as recency of preparation, standards of preparation, recency of certified service, whether the preparation occurred in an accredited certification program, whether the preparation included an academic major concentration, the date of graduation, and certification examination results. Several states are presently engaged in an effort to create a true nationwide reciprocity system and to increase the mobility of teachers across state lines.

An example of an effort to establish a system of reciprocity is the Northeast Common Market Project. This project is a collaborative effort of the Commissioners of Education in the New England states and New York as well as the Regional Laboratory for Educational Improvement of the Northeast, which was founded in November 1987. The impetus for this project was a shared concern about providing a continual supply of highly-qualified educators to teach in classrooms and manage schools throughout this region in the Twenty-First Century.

The Project has undertaken six activities to assure a supply of highly-qualified educators, and three of these activities are oriented toward certification reform. These three activities are listed below:

1) Development, implementation, and evaluation of a Northeast Regional Credential (NRC) that will enhance the employment mobility of educators across state boundaries in the Northeast.

2) Development of regional, visionary, certification standards, and development of a second-generation NRC for special educators so that state certification will no longer be necessary for these teachers after being in this program for two years.

3) Development of regional, visionary certification standards and an NRC for school administrators.

A Steering Committee that consists of one representative from each state, the Regional Laboratory staff, and a number of consultants oversee this project. The proposed date for implementation of the Northeast Common Market Project's efforts has not been set. The NRC was implemented in 1990, but regional standards for administrators and special educators are scheduled for implementation during the autumn of 1993.

These endeavors at certification reform by the New England states and New York will reduce or eliminate many unnecessary bureaucratic obstacles which have impeded not only the mobility of qualified educators but, in some cases, the educational process itself.

CONCLUSION

America's position as the leader of the world is heavily dependent upon its educational system. The nation's leadership must assure that sufficient economic resources, common sense, foresight, and imagination are dedicated to our country's schools so that they can produce the best educated students in the world.

Certainly, the operational efficiency of America's educational system would be improved appreciably if the teacher preparation and certification programs were sufficiently flexible to give professionals mobility throughout the entire system. It is difficult to believe that a nation which has sent men to the moon has not managed to establish national entrance level standards and certificates for teachers among the states. The present system consists of 50 fiefdoms, each with its own set of teacher preparation and certification standards.

Of course each state has the right to determine the manner in which it trains its teachers. Nonetheless, one has to question whether the deviation of standards and certificates among the states serves any useful purpose. Does it justify the retention of a national certification system that impedes progress to higher levels of efficiency and effectiveness in American schools?

Presently, a national certification committee is striving to establish standards for a National Teacher Certificate. This certificate, however, will only recognize master teachers for their outstanding achievements and contributions to the profession.

At the risk of being accused of oversimplification, this writer believes that a sustained effort could produce an agreement on the knowledge and skills a teacher must possess to attain professional excellence. Assuredly, the citizens of all states want their children to receive the best education possible, and all students deserve an excellent education despite their geographical location. Time is of the essence as the nation struggles to improve its schools and forge a consensus on certification before the gates of the Twenty-First Century open.

(Acknowledgement is extended to my former colleagues in the Bureau of Teacher Preparation and Certification, Pennsylvania Department of Education, for their contribution to this proposal. The Northeast Common Market Project information was shared by Dr. Frederica Haas, Director, Bureau of Teacher Preparation and Certification, Pennsylvania Department of Education.)

ENDNOTES

1. Ann Bradley, "40 States Offer Alternative Paths to Teacher Licensing," *Education Week*, 16 September 1992, 8.

2. William Norris, "New Jersey Road Regarded as Best Training Short Cut," *Times Magazine*, 29 September 1989, Education Supplement, 19.

3. Ulrich C. Ritzug, "Administrator Competency Testing: Status, Issues, and Policy Considerations," *Policy Bulletin* (Bloomington, IN: Consortium on Educational Policy Studies, 1990), 1.

Chapter 15

Distance Learning

Dorothy L. Hajdu

Deborah L. Schreckengost

Introduction

The field of distance education has grown exponentially over the last several years. The concept is enlarging the definitions of how students learn, where they learn, and who teaches them. Global competitiveness is increasing the need for the timely access to and delivery of information. Advanced technologies are answering this increasing need by providing a variety of real-time, interactive opportunities. In this rapid, multi-directional expansion, vast amounts of literature are becoming available. It is impossible to provide a detailed coverage of distance learning in a few pages. Therefore, this chapter will attempt to briefly describe what it is, how it is being used, types of applications, and some of the important distance education issues facing the Pennsylvania school system.

In addition to the student population, it is also important to remember that the training our workers receive today will become obsolete within three to five years. Alan Chute, Manager of the AT&T National Teletraining Center, states that as classrooms exist today, they are generally ill-equipped to keep pace with the rate of change and skill

obsolescence projected for tomorrow.
He continues,

> The imposition of time, distance and other constraints on workers will create
> a strong demand for more efficient and expedient ways to distribute necessary
> information. ... The call will be for innovative technological systems that can
> reach great numbers of people with vast amounts of information under a
> variety of conditions. A "just-in-time" approach will enable the delivery of
> critical information where and when it's needed in just the amounts needed.[1]

John Naisbitt in his book, *Megatrends,* states that to stem the anticipated
shortages in skills and qualified personnel, traditional approaches to
training and education will have to be re-engineered.

If our communities are to be competitive, to exist; it is imperative that
they provide growth opportunities for their residents. The proper
implementation of distance education technologies and policies can help
develop solutions to this differential equation.

In the February 10, 1993, edition of *Education Week,* an article entitled,
"Classroom Technology," notes the present status of some distance
education technologies. This essay reported that the number of public
schools with satellite dishes increased by 87 percent, to 8,812 from the
1991-92 to the 1992-93 school years while computer networks increased
by 64 percent. Presently, more than half of the nation's students are in
districts with satellite dishes, videodiscs, and cable television.

WHAT IS DISTANCE EDUCATION?

In Desmond Keegan's 1986 publication entitled *The Foundations of
Distance Education,* distance education is defined as having the following
characteristics:

- Quasi-permanent separation of teacher and learner,
- Influence of an educational organization,
- Use of technical media,
- Provision of two-way communication, and
- Quasi-permanent absence of group learning.[2]

To summarize this academic description of distance education, it should
simply be defined as a method of delivering a learning experience in
which the teacher and the student(s) are physically separated by location.

The method of delivery for distance education may include a variety of formats. These formats should be determined by the intended instructional outcome. For instance, when a class requires exacting visual applications such as found in an anatomy class; some form of video is necessary. This visual presentation may include pre-recorded information or real-time interactive video. When delivering a lecture, the program format becomes less demanding.

METHODS

School districts in Pennsylvania utilize an array of distance education instructional strategies to meet the needs of their students. The type of distance education method used depends on the nature of the course and the availability of equipment. Some of the more common delivery methods are identified and described in the following text.

Two-Way Audio. Audio is a low cost solution when no visual application is needed. Audio "bridges" (a multi-point connection for data sharing), may be used to facilitate conferencing. These electronic devices connect and control multiple telephone lines, allowing many callers to be connected as a group. The advantages of using the audio-only format includes flexibility, low cost, reliability, and portability. The teacher in the classroom would only require a telephone, amplification device, microphone, and regular telephone lines. If more than two sites were on line, an audio bridge would be necessary.

One-Way Graphics. Computer based instruction (CBI) and information retrieval programs are used on an individual basis to augment and complement the classroom lecture. There is a relatively low start-up cost for this method, since the only equipment needed might include a computer, monitor, and software. Some CBI programs also include a laser or compact disc player.

When using the computer to access information at remote sites, a computer modem and telephone lines are also needed.

One-Way Audio, One-Way Video. In a one-way audio, one-way video configuration, students most often receive their learning experience by watching a monitor through the use of cable TV or satellite "downlink" programming. Downlink programs are received through satellite transmission into a standard television receiver. The classroom equipment is simply a monitoring device.

Two-Way Audio, Two-Way Graphics. Audiographics utilizes a computer and modem to provide real-time interaction between multiple sites.

Students and teachers in different locations interact using a speakerphone and generate two-way graphic images on the computer simultaneously. The advantages of this method include cost-effectiveness, ease of use, and multi-functional applications. System equipment includes a computer, monitor, modem, speakerphone, and regular telephone lines.

Two-Way Audio, One-Way Video. In this method students are able to interact with a teacher using a speakerphone and watching the teacher on a screen. The instructor, however, does not see the students. Two-way audio, one-way video instruction in Pennsylvania is most generally delivered using either a cable TV or satellite delivery system. The cost and equipment used in this method varies with the transport utilized.

Two-Way Audio, Two-Way Video. This method is most commonly referred to as interactive video because students and teachers can see and hear each other in real time classes. Both sites are equipped with audio equipment as well as cameras, monitors, and control room equipment. The configuration and operation of this method varies depending upon the type of delivery system available.

The term "video" may be further qualified into compressed video and full motion video.

Compressed Video. Compressed video uses a digital video signal requiring less bandwidth to transmit than broadcast quality or full motion video. Digital technology is used to encode and compress the signal. Picture quality is generally not as good as full motion programming. Compressed video requires transmission speeds between 56 kilobits per second (Kbps) and 2.0 megabits per second (Mbps); a part or whole T1 line, which is a dedicated digital carrier for high-speed transmission. A special coder/decoder, called a CODEC, is also needed to deliver this method of distance education. Since the CODEC will transmit at several different frame rates and resolution levels the integrity of the video may vary. Quick movements often appeared blurred. The lower the resolution and frame rate, the greater the savings, but the poorer the quality of the image.

Full Motion Video. Full motion video uses a standard video signal that can be transmitted by broadcast television, microwave, satellite, or fiber optic lines. As with compressed video, the delivery method may be one or two way video depending on resources. However, unlike the compressed image, the picture quality of full motion video remains constant.

DELIVERY (TRANSPORT)

Transmission systems are continuing to expand capacity. Providers and users of distance learning face growing uncertainty because of the skyrocketing costs. This presents a paradox for the educational administrator who faces tightening budgets and dwindling resources.

On the brighter side, the transmission technologies continue to be readily connectible. Most systems operate with a hybrid of transports which facilitates more efficient and cost-effective usage. It is important that educational administrators are aware of the transports available and their most effective utilization. An explanation of bandwidth is needed to better understand several of the following transports. Bandwidth is the width of frequencies required to transmit a communications signal without undue distortion. The more information a signal contains, the more bandwidth it will need to be transmitted. Televisions signals, for example, require a bandwidth of 3 million hertz (cycles per second), while telephone conversation needs only 3,000 hertz.

A chart which lists and describes various transmission technologies for distance learning has been placed at the end of this chapter. This chart describes the advantages, disadvantages, and trends for each technology. This chart may be a useful supplement to this section.

Plain Old Telephone Lines (POTS). The telephone industry provides several transmission formats for distance education programming. The most basic is copper twisted pair (RJ11) and exists in usable form in every school district, business, and home in Pennsylvania included in the service. This least expensive format can be used for audio conferencing, audiographics, and computer based instruction. The installation costs are minor, and the monthly charge for the service is dependent on the local carrier. The largest cost may be toll charges for long distance calls, which varies from $0.15 per minute to $0.60 per minute. The equipment needed is relatively inexpensive, simple to install and use, and readily available. A standard computer modem and telephone are the basics.

"Switched 56." Telephone companies offer a higher level of telecommunications which brings compressed video into the classroom. The service is switched from a local hub and is commonly called "Switched 56." It originates from a hub and costs $150 plus $1.00 per mile from the hub for the basic line. The hubs in Pennsylvania include Harrisburg, Philadelphia, Pittsburgh, Scranton, and State College. The usage costs are approximately $0.14 per minute plus the long distance toll charge. The toll charge is dependent on the time of day. These switched

lines operate at 56 Kbps and for higher quality visuals users may install two lines and operate at 112 Kbps.

ISDN. Integrated Services Digital Networks (ISDN) allows very rapid, simultaneous high-quality transmission of voice, data, image, and text over a single pair of ordinary telephone lines. ISDN is limited to metropolitan areas.

Due to strict technical rules the service is available up to 15,000 feet from the central telephone office. Also only Centrex users have access to ISDN. A Centrex is a high speed, digital telephone exchange used by central business offices. A single ISDN line contains a pair of 64 Kbps channels. ISDN is less costly than "switched 56" service. The usage fee is $25 per month and is switched from the central point. The hardware necessary for ISDN transmission includes a special terminating modem at approximately $1,500 to $3,000 and the equipment necessary for compressed video transmission. The visual quality is higher under ISDN service than under "switched 56" transmission. ISDN is becoming more available and may at some point replace "switched 56" service. Although an excellent transport, the use of ISDN for distance learning classes in Pennsylvania is infrequent.

T1-Carrier Lines. These lines are a hierarchy of private digital systems designed to carry speech and other signals in digital form, designated T-1 (DS1), T-2 (DS2), and T-4 (DS4). T-1 lines transmit at 1,544 megabits per second (Mbps) in 24 discrete channels. To install a local channel, the cost is approximately $300 and $38 per mile. Pricing plans are now becoming available at lower than the $38 per mile rates for long-term contracts. To utilize T-1 lines, one needs to have at least two local channels to communicate with each other. T-1's operate at 1.54 Mbps and provide high quality visuals. Most users utilize parts of the T-1 bandwidth for video, part for audio, and part for data transmission. Compressed video is most often displayed over a partial T-1 line. The hardware necessary depends on the planned usage. A terminating modem for the basic unit is $1,500. Compressed video equipment varies with the type of CODEC purchased.

Fiber Optics. Fiber optic lines are one of the newest two-way, interactive telecommunications mediums. These fiber lines are made of glass or plastic and transmit light signals instead of electric signals. An optical fiber consists of an inner cylinder called the core, surrounded by a cylindrical shell of glass or plastic called the cladding. The cladding layer keeps light from leaking out. An outside coating provides protection against the elements. Light travels in straight lines, but optical fibers guide light around corners. The number of fibers is unlimited, creating virtually an unlimited capacity. Optical cables are capable of transmitting far more information than coaxial cables of the same size. Digital fiber systems consist of multiplexors, which transmit data from multiple terminals to a central location at high speeds; codec; an optical transmitter; an optical receiver or photodetector, which is a light sensor; fiber cables; and repeaters, which amplify and send signals. The installation costs for a fiber system depend on fiber type, total system design, and location. The major cost considerations include consulting, construction and materials, easements, and terminal equipment. Average labor construction costs range from $0.97 per foot to $1.55 per foot depending on the distance. Material costs may be estimated at $9,672 for rural construction to $15,712 per mile for urban construction. Easement charges vary from city to city, but an average is $1 per foot per year. Terminal equipment costs vary according to the specific program. They range between $25,000 to $75,000 for digital end equipment and approximately $70,000 for digital terminal equipment. Maintenance costs for a fiber network can be very expensive if the fiber is cut. Although fiber optic lines are not yet readily accessible to existing sites in Pennsylvania, several school districts are presently in the process of installing them to deliver two-way, full motion distance education classes.

Microwave. Microwave signals are transmitted electromagnetically through the air. Microwave is similar to broadcasting, except that microwaves use much higher frequencies and are point-to-point. A tower must be constructed to pick up, amplify, and re-transmit microwave signals. For long distance systems, amplification devices are needed to boost the signal from tower to tower. The typical range of 5 to 15 miles is suitable for local communication between two schools. The distance between transmitters depends on topography, antenna size, transmitter size and power, and receiver sensitivity. A good rule of thumb for efficient systems is to link two sites more than one-half mile but less than 20 miles apart. Linking two buildings in a metropolitan area is a good use of microwave. The main components of this type of system include a tower, antenna, antenna feed line, transmitter/receiver, modulator/multi-plexor, and power unit. Microwave systems permit use of two-way, full motion video programming. The video and audio signals are of excellent quality. Maintenance costs of the system are relatively low. Microwave systems carry a large capital outlay for start-up fees. Terrain extremes can increase the cost of the towers and equipment needed. A general cost for a microwave system may be $40,000 to $65,000 plus towers at $25,000 to

$75,000 each. Maintenance costs can be estimated at an average of three to five percent of the system cost per year.

Coaxial Cable. A coaxial cable is a metal cable consisting of a conducter in the form of a tube that can carry multiple signals. Coaxial cable is designed to carry several channels of telephone and TV signals simultaneously. Coaxial cable can carry one-way audio and video signals or two-way live, video and audio signals. The cost for an interactive cable system depends on how much work is required to add two-way capability to the system. Additional equipment needed to bring the signal back "upstream" will increase costs. Initial coaxial cable installation averages $18,000 to $25,000 per mile. Equipment including modulators, demodulators, and reverse flow amplifiers average approximately $9,500. On-going operational costs also vary. There are no transmission costs in broadcasts that use the public or an institutional cable system. Maintenance budgets average between 2 and 5 percent of the system costs. Program subscription rate fees vary according to provider.

Satellite. The age of communication satellites, placed in geosynchronous orbit above the earth's equator eliminated much of the need for land based microwave networks since a single "uplink" can transmit a signal back down to earth. An "uplink" is an earth station that transmits a communication signal to a satellite. Most domestic satellites have a "conus footprint," which means the signal can be picked up by a receiving a dish anywhere in the continental United States. Since it costs the same to broadcast to thousands of sites as it does to broadcast to one site, satellite communications have become the most cost-effective point-to-point mass technologies to date, and many national distributors of live and pre-taped programs to the public schools utilize satellite transmissions to distribute their programs. The system transmits audio, data, and video programming in a point to multipoint configuration. Most sites that wish to receive a satellite course require "downlink" equipment which consists of a satellite dish, electronic receiver, and monitor. Most classes are two-way (limited access) audio and one-way video. In addition to equipment and transmission costs, there is also a fee per student for programming charges. The cost of "downlink" equipment is relatively inexpensive compared to the costs of equipment that is needed to transmit a class using "up-link" hardware.

Cable. One of the largest providers of educational broadcasting in Pennsylvania is cable television. In conjunction with independent and public cable providers, programming is made available to school districts at reasonable rates. The equipment needed by the schools is readily available and affordable. Basic cable television connections for schools are often provided as part of the local cable franchise agreement. Clearinghouses and the cable providers present information to educators about available broadcasting times and dates. This delivery transport is basically a one-way video and audio signal. With more sophisticated and expensive transmission it can become a two-way video and audio method.

LEARNING EXPERIENCES

The learning experience delivered by a distance education class varies according to student needs. There are basically three classifications which cover most distance education applications:

Access. Information retrieval is important to the curriculum and some consider it to be a form of distance education. Computer based instruction, bulletin boards, and information networks all provide needed resources to a student as required. Students access the data they need on bulletin boards and information networks by using a computer and modem connected to the appropriate delivery service. Teachers and administrators also use these services to interact with their counterparts in an on-line format. Examples of information retrieval services include PSInet, Learning Link, and InterNet.

Enhancement. Distance education also provides enhancement or enrichment to the existing curriculum. Students are able to complement their studies with cable, TV, satellite, or audiographic broadcasts. These broadcasts provide added information from subject matter experts on designated topics. The Massachusetts Learn Pike and a shared gifted program in Venango County, Pennsylvania are excellent examples of this type experience. Other sources include interactive laser disc programs, CD Rom programming, and VCR tapes.

For-Credit Class. In addition to the above, students are participating in standard for-credit classes. The subject matter may range from remedial to advanced offerings. Students participate in the curriculum under regular curricular guidelines but receive their information from their instructor who is located at a distance. Examples of this type of activity may be seen in the Satellite Education Resource Consortium (SERC) which consists of satellite delivered courses in science and language or in a calculus course delivered in Southern Tioga School District in rural, northern Pennsylvania.

WHY IS DISTANCE EDUCATION NEEDED?

When questions arise on the need for distance education, a number of answers are available. In the text that follows, seven of these explanations are proffered.

PROVIDE EDUCATIONAL EQUITY

Very often the term "educational equity" brings to mind rural areas, but this problem encompasses a much larger population. As inner-city tax bases erode, so do the educational resources of an area. Since education is a lifelong endeavor, the equality of opportunities to obtain access to information or additional education is vitally significant for the long-term economic health of these geographic regions. The members of the Pennsylvania workforce must have access to timely information about their fields of work to be competitive in the global workplace.

Pennsylvania has the largest rural population in the United States. Its rural students enjoy rolling hills, clean streams, and small school districts. The very nature of many rural students' surroundings, however, creates an educational isolation with limited resources and remote geographical access. Superintendents in these areas sometimes find it difficult to provide mandated courses because of teacher availability or limited class size. Smaller or more isolated school districts may not have the resources available to provide courses in areas such as foreign language, vocational training, and advanced levels of math and science. While students might be bussed to larger areas, the quality of their education may be affected if they must travel long distances each day.

The population shifts of this century have resulted in many American inner-cities losing significant numbers of skilled and professional residents. This exodus has depleted community resources, decreased the tax base, and reduced the educational offerings in many urban schools. Some inner-city students no longer receive state-of-the-art classes as do their student counterparts in more suburban areas.

Many economic development activities in the state are aimed at high-tech industry. An important criteria to these companies in decisions about location and expansion is a trained workforce. Pennsylvania and the other states must continue to find ways to provide its citizens with the latest educational opportunities if strong state economies are desired. Distance education is but one way to address the needs of a state workforce and of our rural and urban students throughout the country and the

Commonwealth.

PROVIDE ACCESS TO SUBJECT MATTER EXPERTS

Since it is very costly or impossible to provide subject matter experts at each educational institution throughout a state, the implementation of a distance learning program provides the vehicle to reach these experts. Students can watch, listen, and ask questions of authors, political figures, or foreign leaders as appropriate to the curriculum.

PROVIDE SOCIAL INTERACTION

Along with educational isolation, "placism" (discrimination based upon where people happen to live) also contributes to social deprivation. Students may now participate with each other in learning situations whether they live in rural, metropolitan, urban, or foreign locations by a simple telecommunications formula. Telecommunications also allow incarcerated students to participate in a wider range of traditional classroom activities. Students whose families have immigrated into the area may interact comfortably with those of similar interests and backgrounds at remote sites. This social interaction provides a learning experience and better prepares students for college entry or job placement.

PROVIDE INCREASED ACCESS TO INFORMATION AND INSTRUCTIONAL RESOURCES

Students and teachers can perform computer searches on various subject-specific databases to obtain up-to-the minute information. Large databases located in university libraries, research foundations, and industry provide technological and curricular resources for school districts on demand.

PROVIDE OPPORTUNITIES FOR TEACHERS TO PARTICIPATE IN STAFF DEVELOPMENT AND IN-SERVICE TRAINING

Due to accessibility and constrained school budgets, teachers may not be able to travel to participate in staff development courses or curricular training. Distance education makes it possible for the teacher or administrator to participate in advanced educational offerings without leaving the school building. Through the use of distance education, this experience can be provided at a fraction of the cost that would be incurred travelling to a conference.

PROMOTE PARTNERSHIPS BETWEEN SCHOOLS, BUSINESSES, COMMUNITY, AND MEDICAL FACILITIES

Distance education can evolve into an information network for the community as well as providing needed adult training courses for the workforce. This sharing of resources with the community members makes the schools stronger and provides much needed educational opportunities to business and community members.

ENABLE STUDENTS TO BECOME TECHNOLOGICALLY LITERATE

Distance education technologies provide a hidden benefit to school districts throughout the nation and the state. Increased awareness of telecommunications by teachers, students, and parents promotes the desire to find new uses for existing technology. The advances that are frequently realized from this empowerment help to alleviate existing isolation.

WHO IS USING DISTANCE EDUCATION?

At the time of this writing, no single source in Pennsylvania had a complete compilation of the users of distance education. The State Library has just hired a coordinator for distance learning who plans to undertake this effort. Mansfield University in Mansfield, Pennsylvania, is presently conducting research on this topic with funds it secured from the Center for Rural Pennsylvania. State Senator James J. Rhoades has advocated legislation which would institute a Distance Learning Commission for the state.

Until this time, distance learning applications have had a proprietary implementation. Those school districts with ample resources have been using technology to provide access and outreach opportunities to their population, while many poor rural and urban districts have been securing programs that demand less expensive transports to supplement their curriculum.

There are, however, several major programs being implemented in Pennsylvania. The following paragraphs will provide a brief description of these projects.

One of the earliest distance education programs to be successfully implemented in Pennsylvania has been the Instructional Television (ITV) network. Typically, these were one-way video television programs which were delivered to the school districts live or were taped by local intermediate units and sent to schools. ITV originally obtained support from the Pennsylvania Department of Education and the Pennsylvania Public TV Network. Although the Department of Education's financial support has been significantly reduced, the Pennsylvania Public TV Network continues to provide financial resources for the program. The Director of Educational Services at the Pennsylvania Public TV Network (PPTN) facilitates program implementation.

In 1984, the Pennsylvania Secretary of Education directed the department to investigate a cost-effective way to deliver otherwise inaccessible courses to students in Pennsylvania. The target audience in this case was primarily rural youth. An audiographic system was initiated and test marketed, or beta tested, at Mansfield University. The project is now housed and administered at the Riverview Intermediate Unit in Shippenville, Pennsylvania. Audiographics, as employed by the Pennsylvania Teleteaching Project, consists of a real-time interactive class delivery system using standard telephone lines and computers. The original project has developed into a user-friendly program which employs a multimedia format of scanners, laser disc players, and curricular software to build its interactive classrooms.

Students in every corner of Pennsylvania have been involved in this network. It has proven to be a cost-effective and readily accessible form of delivery because it uses normal business telephone lines that can be accessed from anywhere. Classes may be delivered from one end of the state to the other; from one end of a district to the other; from one end of the country to the other; and even from one country to another. Some classes which are being taught in Pennsylvania include a course on the Voyage of the Mimi between Central Columbia Middle School in Bloomsburg and its counterpart in Benton; a genetics course between Chadds Ford High School in Unionville and New Brighton High School in New Brighton; a gifted program shared between several high schools in Venango and Crawford Counties; and a Spanish enrichment program being delivered to Moniteau High School in Moniteau from Juarez, Mexico.

The Pennsylvania Teleteaching Project received a grant from the State Library in 1993 to develop a data "bridge" for statewide implementation. Again, a "bridge" provides a multi-point connection for data sharing. The bridge will use single line modems to reach five sites at one time. The program presently delivers courses to one or two sites. Three sites or more can be served by using a daisy chain scenario. A new data bridge will provide a cost-effective, multiple-site configuration which can be implemented by other school districts, intermediate units, or universities. Since classes can generate from one site to five or six receiving sites, even small, poor districts will be able to market special courses and generate revenue for their schools.

Since the spring of 1989, Pennsylvania has been involved in a Star Schools program known as SERC. This program has enabled school districts to purchase satellite "downlink" equipment at discounted prices. SERC is a 22 state consortium which delivers over 1,500 hours of educational programming via satellite to 307 Pennsylvania students in 67 schools. Courses available include Japanese, Russian, microeconomics, probability and statistics, discrete math, and world geography.

"Cable in the Classroom," a non-profit service of the cable industry provides educational programming---from news and documentaries to dramatic presentations--as additional tools for learning. These cable programs come to school districts without commercial interruption. Curriculum-based support materials are provided to assist teachers in using the programs in the classroom. The cable companies provide free installation and basic service to public junior and senior high schools.

There are numerous other applications using microwave, television, cable, and fiber optic technologies to deliver distance education programs. The Office of Technology Assessment (OTA) report, *Linking for Learning,* lists the Philadelphia School District as wiring 16 of its sites for cable television access. In addition, Austin Area School District is contracting with a local cable company to string fiber optic lines in the district for two-way interactive video delivery.

Access to information or information retrieval may be considered a form of distance education in its broadest sense. There are numerous electronic services that provide these services and are available in Pennsylvania. Examples include Penn Link, PSINet, InterNET, Pennsylvania Learning Link, and PREPNet.

Penn-Link is a statewide K-12 computer network offering data exchange, bulletin board services, and electronic mail. PREPNet is the Pennsylvania Research and Economic Partnership Network which links educational institutions, libraries, businesses, and medical and industrial research facilities. PSINet, the People Sharing Information Network, simulates the interactive information exchange that occurs at professional conferences. It enables its users to access and review volumes of research papers and related documents. Learning Link is a regional, computer-based information network which brings many resources from the greater community to area schools by facilitating communications between and among educational professionals. Many of Pennsylvania's schools are also using the Whittle Network to provide news information to its students during morning programming.

During the last two years the State Library has been instrumental in granting over $500,000 to school districts in Pennsylvania for distance education applications. Unfortunately, over $9 million was requested for this same $500,000 allocation. The Distance Education Coordinator for the state has affirmed that he will continue to request these funds from the legislature and will use the overwhelming number of requests as an incentive for additional funding. Further, the Commonwealth's Distance Education Coordinator has also been working with the legislature, the state Board of Education, school districts, distance education providers, and universities in an attempt to develop new policies and programs for statewide application.

The preceding programs were designed for the K-12 environment. Colleges and universities are also using distance learning applications with K-12 schools as well as in their own institutions. Distance learning courses are being delivered to K-12 students and staff. This technology is also being used to connect different campuses of one university and to connect these universities with a wide assortment of government and social service organizations for a large number of purposes.

In southeastern Pennsylvania, West Chester University's Center for Connectivity is actively involved in facilitating an Internet link between school districts and state universities located in the region. As of January 1993, all state owned universities have been provided with Internet capabilities.

Lackawana Junior College in Scranton, Pennsylvania, reports using teleteaching technology to train Literacy Trainers and Literacy Volunteers by linking up to five isolated rural and urban training sites in the northeastern region of the Commonwealth. The college also uses this system of audiographics with complementing technologies to implement a Career Prep Center.

The Pennsylvania Community Learning and Information Network, Inc. (PACLIN) has been formed as a not-for-profit corporation to apply telecommunications technology; to strengthen and expand K-12 education through the Commonwealth; and to make effective, low cost training programs available to educators, business, industry, government, and professional sectors. This corporation reflects the design of a group of

Lehigh Valley educators to begin a national community learning and information network. It is presently seeking schools to participate in its compressed video network across Pennsylvania using a T-1 line.

Penn State University, with the "Mind Extension University," has a full schedule of courses being delivered across the state. PSU also uses public television, cable television, compressed video, microwave, audio, and computer classes to deliver its courses.

Hence, community colleges in Pennsylvania have also been realizing the potential that distance learning programs have to enrich their institutions. Community colleges in the state have formed a consortium to investigate distance education as it might apply to their delivery and training programs.

There are very few institutions training pre-service teachers in distance education delivery. A recently conducted study showed that most technology programs for pre-service teachers mentioned the use of distance education applications, but very few of these programs actually trained or demonstrated techniques in their classes.

Penn State University has a Department of Distance Education which not only teaches the pedagogy, but it also demonstrates techniques by teaching students at branch campuses using audio and compressed video classes. Dr. Michael Moore, Editor of the *American Journal of Distance Education* is responsible for this program.

Two other institutions of higher education in the Commonwealth that have a specific course to train pre-service teachers in distance education implementation include Mansfield University and Marywood College.

HOW IS DISTANCE EDUCATION FUNDED?

Distance learning offers a fresh perspective on how to address major funding concerns. Some awarded distance learning projects display a great deal of imagination in attaining their objectives at reasonable costs.

Distance learning projects have been funded which demonstrate how the technology can be integrated into and become a means to address national concerns such as environmental studies; multiculturalism; and educational programs for preschoolers, at-risk youth, and people with disabilities.

Within the state of Pennsylvania there are several direct sources of funding for distance learning projects. Several creative financing arrangements have also been utilized to conduct numerous distance learning projects.

Much of the satellite equipment in Pennsylvania schools has been purchased with funds awarded from the Satellite Educational Resources Consortium (SERC). Each year since 1989, the Pennsylvania Department of Education has awarded start-up monies to erect "downlink" sites in the state. SERC was an outgrowth of the Star Schools Title IX funding from the U.S. Department of Education's OERI Program for the Improvement of Practice. (OERI is the Office of Educational Research and Improvement.)

For the last two years more than $500,000 has been awarded to Commonwealth schools to assist them with the implementation of distance education programs through the State Library Grant Program. The majority of these funds has been directed to small, rural, poor schools. Projects funded include satellite courses, audiographic networks, interactive video, and cable broadcasts.

The Ben Franklin Partnership, in conjunction with Bell of Pennsylvania, has also provided resources to schools in southwestern Pennsylvania for an audiographic network. Several distance education programs have been operating in part due to Department of Education discretionary funding, legislative initiative grants, and departmental adaptation programs. Other private foundation monies have helped implement production studios, interactive fiber links, and equipment installation.

The State Public School Building Authority (SPSBA) has earmarked $2,000,000 as a revolving loan fund for schools to borrow for purchase or lease of interactive video distance learning equipment. The program is being offered in cooperation with the Pennsylvania General Assembly and the Department of Education. School districts may borrow from $10,000 to $750,000 for a maximum term of five years at an interest rate of 2 percent below prime. These funds may be used for the purchase or lease and installation of equipment used to transmit video, audio, or data by one-way or two-way telecommunications or computer technology while the instructors and learners are in one or more geographically separate locations. These funds may also be used for construction costs and/or renovation costs related to the installation of equipment.

Some other creative approaches to fund the implementation of distance learning programs include equipment loans, reciprocal delivery, and shared programming. Examples of this may be found in sites that obtain equipment on loan from vendors or project equipment banks, in schools that agree to exchange curricular offerings, and in sites that team-teach special topics.

THE FUTURE OF DISTANCE LEARNING

Education and the use of technology are at a point of evolution. Many school districts in Pennsylvania are being forced by shifting or declining population bases and by tightening budgets to re-access how best to meet the needs of students in rural and metropolitan areas. Innovations in distance education may provide answers to these targeted needs.

For the full range of innovations in distance education to succeed, however, educators and policymakers in Pennsylvania and other states must understand the full-range of issues and implications brought about through the implementation of distance learning programs.

In testimony before the Subcommittee on Communications; Committee on Commerce, Science and Transportation; United States Senate on July 29, 1992, Linda Roberts of the Office of Technology Assessment set forth some of the major considerations for this educational innovation:

- Teachers will always be important in distance learning, whether they are the distance learning teachers or the users of these resources;
- The equipment that comprises the delivery system for distance education will become less expensive, but, in the foreseeable future, distance learning's operational and programming costs will remain constant and need funding support; and
- Schools need to acquire information about the growing number and variety of distance learning innovations in order to take advantage of current programs and capabilities as well as to design more effective programs for their own communities.

This attempt by Roberts and the OTA to outline some of the most fundamental developments in the area of distance education innovation provides a starting point for a state strategy to approach this topic. Such a strategy must identify and deal with issues that concern technology, the teaching profession, state policy, and process. The following section attempts to identify and discuss these issues in order to prepare policymakers for creating a strategy to deal with this area of educational innovation.

TECHNOLOGY ISSUES

- No one best model exists for the use of telecommunications technology. There are many delivery systems and many possible uses for existing and planned technology. Schools need to choose the system that is most appropriate for meeting their specific needs.

- Telecommunications providers hold valuable resources which should be tapped by the educational community to achieve cost-effective programs.
- Telecommunications technology encompasses the entire community. School districts should form alliances within the public and private sectors to ensure total access to all community resources.
- Every technology center, whether located in the classroom, the corporate headquarters, or a government building should have access to the resources necessary to make full use of telecommunications.
- School districts should make maximum use of business/education partnerships in order to form a liaison between its students and local employers.
- New school facilities should be designed so that they can take advantage of innovations in distance learning. Electrical outlets and voice, video, and data lines are essential components in today's schools.

PROFESSIONAL ISSUES

- To reduce the need for Emergency Certificates, Pennsylvania might consider the adoption of specific policies for licensing teachers using distance education. Special consideration should be given to the issue of certification   of remote site facilitators.
- With the evolution of distance education, Pennsylvania will need to adopt criteria that will make licenses more accessible and portable.
- Because of the vast choice of telecommunications available to the school districts, higher education institutions must work closely with the school districts in order to assist them identify, implement, and utilize the best equipment and instructional strategies for new and present teachers.
- Teleteacher and facilitator training proves crucial when distance learning and distance learning innovations are introduced. To reduce teacher apprehension and increase teacher skills in order to use distance learning, sufficient resources must be devoted to this area.
- In-service teacher programs should include extensive concentrations on technology in the classroom.
- Since distance education makes additional demands on teachers, distance educators in the classroom should have institutional support. It should not be the sole responsibility of a teacher to create new pedagogical applications, install equipment, arrange scheduling, and maintain equipment.

POLICY ISSUES

Several Pennsylvania legislators have introduced bills to enhance and promote distance education. Senators John E. Peterson, Jeanette Reibman, and James J. Rhoades, along with Representative David Wright have all proposed telecommunications bills in the General Assembly.

To date, no bill has been passed into law. The latest legislative initiative before the General Assembly is Senate Bill No. 2 introduced by Senators Armstrong, Baker, Fumo, Helfrick, Lincoln, Madigan, Musto, Punt, Peterson, Porterfield, Salvatore, Scanlon, Stapleton, Stewart, Stout, and Wenger. This bill would provide alternative forms of regulation for telecommunications services.

Senators Reibman and Rhoades initiated a Distance Learning Task Force in 1992 to meet three goals:

1) Establish a Distance Learning Commission to articulate distance learning policy in Pennsylvania and provide leadership and direction to school districts and other entities in the development of distance education policy;
2) Promote the State Public School Building Authority Loan Program to provide funds to school districts to purchase and/or lease distance education equipment; and
3) Expand PANET, the Commonwealth's dedicated voice and data transmission network, to promote cost savings to Pennsylvania school districts.

It was generally believed that the efforts necessary to reach these three goals would prove to have a significant impact on distance education opportunities in Pennsylvania. Nonetheless, the following points must also be addressed by Pennsylvania's leaders in setting distance education policy for the Commonwealth.

- Legislators are encouraged to provide support for the coordination and expansion of current telecommunications networks (i.e., the expansion of PANET to all school districts) and to develop new, affordable statewide communications networks for education.
- Legislators are encouraged to form multi-state cooperative agreements for distance education teacher qualifications and course specifications.
- Legislators are encouraged to develop a distance education strategy that not only initiates such a program but which also sustains the use of this form of educational technology.
- Legislators are encouraged to establish special rates and policies for

educational purposes so that students and teachers have affordable access to all information networks.

PROCESS ISSUES

The educational benefits of distance education need to be closely evaluated. If a well-designed and properly conducted program evaluation is not conducted, problems related to staffing, logistics, and design might be neglected. Proper program evaluations of a state's distance education program will assist the program's implementation process and ultimate efficacy. Such evaluations also ensure that scarce public revenues are being spent as effectively as possible.

CONCLUSION

Technology has affected every part of our society. Its rapid development produces a wide array of possible applications and uses for the future. These distance learning applications provide an exciting, real-time access to global information. Many Pennsylvania educators, legislators, and community leaders are embracing distance learning innovations and their potential pay-offs with enthusiasm and commitment.

ENDNOTES

1. Alan Chute, "Distance Education Futures: Information Needs and Technology Options," *Performance And Instruction*, November/December 1991, 1.

2. Desmond Keegan, *The Foundations of Distance Education* (London: Croom Helm Publishers, 1986), 49-50.

TRANSMISSION TECHNOLOGIES FOR LEARNING AT A DISTANCE

TECHNOLOGY[a]	CONFIGURATION	ADVANTAGES	DISADVANTAGES	TRENDS
Terrestrial broadcast	One-way broadcast of audio, video, and possibly data; possible audio return	No special receiving equipment or converters; reaches most schools and homes	Limited channels and air time; reception limited by geography; high transmission equipment and production costs	Increased use of data/text transmission
Fiber optic	Two-way audio, data and video	High capacity/speed; channel capacity easily expandable; high quality signal	High installation cost; rights of way may be required to lay new cable	Costs are declining rapidly; fiber deployment is expanding rapidly
Microwave	Two-way point-to-point audio, data and video	Low cost transmission time; no rights-of-way needed	Must be FCC licensed; tower space or location may be difficult to get; difficult and costly to expand channels; crowded frequencies; line of sight required	Use of higher frequencies is expanding
Instructional Television Fixed Service (ITFS)	One-way broadcast or point-to-point audio, data, and video; possibility of audio return	Low cost delivery of video	Crowded frequencies, especially in cities; FCC licensing required; limited transmission range; line of sight required	Digitalization may triple channel capacity; wider coverage areas using repeaters; rebroadcast of satellite delivered programming

[a]Technology systems do not have to operate independently; they are often combined in "hybrid" systems.

Source: Office of Technology Assessment, 1989

TRANSMISSION TECHNOLOGIES FOR LEARNING AT A DISTANCE

TECHNOLOGY[a]	CONFIGURATION	ADVANTAGES	DISADVANTAGES	TRENDS
Public Switched Telephone Network (PSTN)	Two-way voice; limited data and video	Wide coverage; low initial cost; high quality and capacity of fiber optic links; others handle repair and upgrades	Quality is spotty; limited transmission of data and video; cost is distance-sensitive	Expanding fiber installation; digitization of network increasing; increasing intelligence in the network
Satellite	One-way broadcast of voice, data and video; possibility of audio return	Wide coverage transmission cost is distance insensitive	Expensive uplinks; high transmission costs; FCC licensing of uplinks; receive site microwave interference (C-band) or rain fade (Ku band)	More use of Ku band; possible transponder shortage; increased use of data; increased interactive capabilities
Audiographics	Two-way computer conferencing with audio interaction	Low cost; easy exchange of graphics	Visual interaction limited to graphics/still video	More powerful computers; better software and peripherals increase capabilities
Cable television systems	One-way broadcast of two-way point-to-point audio, data and video	Wide availability; low delivery costs	Limited capacity; can be difficult to interconnect; not usually designed for interactivity	Capacity increases using fiber; more addressability and two-way capability

Source: Office of Technology Assessment, 1989

Chapter 16

The Problems of Rural Education

Arnold Hillman

INTRODUCTION

"Improving the lives and futures of rural youths is not a national priority," is the capstone line from Jonathan Sher's 1977 landmark work on rural education.[1] From this profound feeling of a lack of recognition of rural problems, comes a need to examine the basis of the statement and the veracity of its assertion. We have created "Metropolitan educational models that don't work for rural people."[2] In our rush to achieve progress, we have left something valuable behind. Consequently, we must retrace our steps and see what we have done to rural schools in our country and the Commonwealth of Pennsylvania. In this search we may be able to salvage the good practices of rural education that can be applied throughout our educational system before these characteristics are lost forever.

AMERICA'S TRADITION OF RURAL EDUCATION

Our present lack of emphasis on rurality is a historic contradiction. The very basis of our educational system has been the small, rural school. The one room school house, where many of our country's leaders studied and thrived, was the beginning of it all. Even today, former Secretary of Education Terrell Bell recalls with joy and satisfaction, his early schooling in a small building where independent learning, non-gradedness, peer counseling, individual teacher help, and flexible scheduling were the order of the day. The sight of mass produced education did not come into being until the latter part of the 19th Century in imitation of Frederick Taylor's principles of scientific management and Henry Ford's assembly lines. Certainly, rural schooling was the rule until well into the 20th Century.

Lawrence Cremin, author of the recent book *Popular Education and its Discontents,* offers an interesting insight on how the nation and its educational system have evolved. In his three-part examination of American education, he provides a comprehensive, scholarly account of the history of American education. His first two volumes, *The Colonial Experience 1607-1783* and *The National Experience 1783-1876,* describe the development of American education from its Renaissance beginnings to an authentic American edifice by 1876. The third volume, however, departs from the global intentions of the first two tomes and ". . . carries the account to 1980, emphasizing the transformation and proliferation of educative institutions, as the United States became a more metropolitan society and describing the role of those institutions in the export of American culture and civilization to other regions of the world."[3]

A choice made by Mr. Cremin in his third volume to describe metropolitan education, as the "American Way" for the past 117 years, is a popular decision among those who write on educational topics.[4] Even landmark works, such as *A Nation at Risk: The Imperative for Educational Reform,* is almost solely a description of metropolitan education. One has only to review the background and credentials of the commission members, their current positions, their analyses, and their recommendations to see that problems of rural schools have gone largely unattended.

The constitutional battle between the Hamiltonians and the Jeffersonians has been mirrored in the conflict between central and local control of schools. Over the past century, the tendencies toward master plans for educational improvement, consolidation of schools, state and federal mandates, and the creation of the "expert" class in education have led to the diminution of rural education. With the shift of political power to the metropolitan centers and the cementing of the "one man one vote" paradigm, rural America became a heterogenous minority within its own home and history.

Central control mitigated against the once familiar town control of local education. The local school committee, or school board made up of people from the immediate communities, was a bastion of democratic spirit so loved by Jefferson. Children were surrounded by adults of their acquaintance whose morality and ways of life confirmed for them their parent's view of the world. Each book, each scrap of material that was used for instruction in these schools was selected on the basis of local philosophies and local views.

For the "experts," this provincial view of the world did not create an ambiance of progress. As new immigrants came to America in increasing numbers in the 19th Century, schools became a tool for the delivery of nationwide values, rather than the local needs of community residents. At first, the cities spawned a bureaucracy that included specialists in the newest educational philosophies. Rural communities could continue to teach the basic lessons of the past, using materials that rarely changed and methods that had proven effective with children.

As the centralists gained more power and climbed to even higher rungs in the governments of their states, rural people witnessed their way of life change dramatically. The beginning of the 20th Century saw cataclysmic changes in technology, world views, and educational philosophies. Because of the increasing needs of the burgeoning cities, centralist thinking became a view that created the large city high school, at a time when few children in the country were staying in school past the eighth grade. The large gap between the city and country views was exacerbated by the needs of the city to school larger numbers of children in ever larger buildings.

Further, the rate at which children continued on to high school increased. Generally, rural children could leave school at an early age and be employed in agriculture, or obtain jobs replacing their fathers in business, or work in a business that extracted natural resources. For the few, factories sprung up in small towns (a good example in Pennsylvania would be Brockway Glass) taking advantage of the strong work ethic of the local people and their satisfaction with lower wages than their counterparts in the cities. Many a fortune was made in these small towns by industrialists who saw rural people as a labor force that would not be enticed by the new labor movements then becoming prevalent in the more metropolitan areas.

Yes, schooling was essentially one room, single town, one teacher, and the traditional repetitive discipline of teaching. As each state created its own compulsory education laws, it brought with it the conflict between the beliefs of the educational elite and the local form of democratic governance called the school board. The imposition of metropolitan models on rural people was widespread and pervasive. In the name of educational improvement, cost containment, political orthodoxy, and social construction, rural education became a reconstituted mockery of metropolitan schooling.

Opponents of the advancement of this "educational progress" were viewed as "backward" and unable to see the advantages of bringing rural places into the modern era. In a report done in 1895 by the National Education Association (Committee of Twelve on Rural Schools), the advantages of consolidation were proffered by the educational leaders of the day. Those who were opposed were described as either conservative, unknowing, or attracted to "perpetual office-holding."[5]

A current analogous situation can be found in each state administration's response to the many equity suits brought to the bar by poor and rural schools. In their original answers to the plaintiffs' contention that the extant funding system discriminated against poor and rural schools, states are likely to say: these schools are poorly managed, rife with nepotism, inadequately funded because of a lack of tax effort, and not grounded in progressive educational tenets. These attacks are the very ones that were trumpeted by Horace Mann and Henry Barnard, at the onset of public education. A particularly undemocratic view of local people produced an increasingly top-down view of schools that became pandemic across our country. In a quintessential pique of centralist myopia, a national curriculum has been described as a way of improving all schools in the 1990s.

As the 19th Century began to produce an urban view of education, those in authority saw rural schools as archaic, outdated, and unable to move children into the modern era. Those individuals who opposed either the consolidation of schools or the "progressive" curricula were seen as stumbling blocks to a technological future. Even the great John Dewey (who had taught in Oil City, PA) joined the chorus against those who were opposed to this new educational philosophy. Katz refers to the *defenders* of rural schools as "democratic localists."

> The conflicts between the democratic localists and the bureaucrats often assumed the atmosphere of an undeclared guerrilla war of sabotage and resistance as local school districts refused to comply with state regulations and parents refused to cooperate with the state's representative, the teacher. Insofar as most of the resistance came from inarticulate people, it is the hardest and most maddening aspect of nineteenth century educational history to document. That it existed is, however, beyond doubt, as the frustrated testimony of local and state reformers testifies in almost every document they wrote.[6]

These conflicts have not abated, and they continue in 1993. In the Commonwealth of Pennsylvania, central authority still persists in its desire to homogenize the workings of local schools. The statewide antagonism generated by the introduction, by the State Board of Education, of a series of curricular changes known as "Outcomes Based Education" is a resurrection of the struggle between the "democratic localists" and the bureaucrats. The nature of the changes that have been presented may be a positive way of running schools, but rural people see it as yet another way of controlling the minds of school children by central authority. In fact, the new regulations may give local school boards *more* flexibility than previous statutory curricula. There has always been, however, a distrust of central authority in the Commonwealth and during the economically distressed times of the late 1980s and early 1990s, local people are even more apprehensive of the outstretched hand of the state.

Consolidation became a political bandwagon beginning with the 1870s in many states including Pennsylvania. As urban superintendents left to become members of an ever-growing bureaucracy in state capitols around the country, they brought their "bigger is better" philosophy to the entire state. Rural schools were seen as being cost-inefficient, using antiquated educational programs, lacking in the newest materials and technologies, and having poor quality teachers. In our rush to consolidation and metro-modeling, is it possible that we have almost destroyed the beneficial characteristics of rural education?

In a 1934 publication by the Department of Public Instruction in Harrisburg, the reasons for consolidation were enumerated. In a section entitled "Realization of Disadvantages of One Teacher Schools," the authors claim that even rural people knew that consolidation was the wave of the future.

Rural people began to realize that children in the one-teacher schools were not making the degree of progress of those in the graded schools. They also noticed that when their children entered high school, they were more apt to fail or drop out than were the children of the graded schools. In investigating the cause, they found that the one-teacher school practically had become a training department for beginning teachers; that rural teachers were not as well trained as those of the urban schools; that buildings were poor, under-lighted, poorly heated and inadequately equipped; textbooks often were not modern; libraries, supplementary readers and special primary materials were either lacking or had been selected without proper consideration; toilets were frequently in an indescribably, vile condition.[7]

Yet even when rural people "knew" that consolidation was the proper way, they rejected the idea. In 1901, a law was passed in Pennsylvania that made the centralizing of schools available to districts by a referendum. Of all the school districts in the Commonwealth, only two townships, North Shenango in Crawford County and Charlestown Township in Tioga County, voted to consolidate their schools. A change in the school code in 1911 and a separate law in 1919 encouraged districts to consolidate by giving special funds for transportation to the newly centralized districts.

Replicated in many states, the consolidated high school appealed to the centralists as a way of having a more direct relationship with local schools. When federal vocational funds began to flow to schools as a result of the Smith-Hughes Act of 1917, there were even more reasons to group students together in large numbers. Pennsylvania had agricultural programs housed in high schools for many years. As funds for vocational activities increased, vo-ag programs insinuated themselves into more high schools in rural areas. The advantages of these programs were evident to those who saw "farm boys" increase their school attendance across the Commonwealth.

For the many communities that became associated with consolidated high schools across the country , the distance to that institution meant an end to direct community involvement in that high school. The small community secondary school had served as an introduction to higher forms of education to the residents of rural Pennsylvania. As the mechanics of secondary education became more state mandated and less community oriented, suspicion grew that there were "things" going on in that big building 15 miles or more from their home. The suspicion grew even greater when consolidated high schools agreed to form vocational technical high schools that were even further away from the local communities.

Vocational agricultural programs were always community based. Nevertheless, when the federal government began to distribute funds to create vocational-technical schools in the 1960s, centers of learning moved even further from students' home communities. In Pennsylvania, suburban vo-techs, in conjunction with businesses and unions, had little difficulty in developing programs for youngsters. In rural areas, another 45 minute bus ride from the newly consolidated school district brought out opposition and foot dragging. In one county, the vocational technical school was delayed until 1977.

Now, when the worth of vocational schools is being called into question and when these schools are so costly on a per pupil basis and when their return to students is limited by the types of jobs available, rural people wonder why the schools were ever built. In these ways, rural people entertain many of the same questions as city residents. Why is it that we train youngsters, and there are no jobs for them to fill? Why is it that only 35 percent of the Vo-Tech graduates go into fields for which they were trained?

One room schools began to close across the nation. Urbanization and urban modeling became the norm. In the 1930s there were over 128,000 school districts in the United States. By 1972 the number had been reduced to 15,977 operating districts. "These declines occurred at a time when K-12 enrollments increased dramatically, and the net result was significant growth in the average size of school units. Actual schools declined from 231,000 to 91,000."[8] Consolidation continues to be used as a method of bringing rural schools closer to modern educational thought. Those in central authority continue to see consolidation as a way of cutting costs and producing a better educational product.

Pennsylvania has tended to be more conservative than many other industrialized states. One room schools and local school boards were viewed as advantages to local communities. The beginning of a small movement toward consolidation of schools in the 1950s, however, became an avalanche of centralization by 1965. The Consolidation Act of 1965 reduced Pennsylvania's school districts from 2,585 to 505. There has been only one consolidation since then (Woodland Hills became one consolidated school district as a result of court ordered integration of schools). Curiously, there has been a wall of opposition since then. The only action taken by the state in the area of consolidation was to oppose the deconsolidation of the Armstrong County School District. As of this writing, the courts have upheld Armstrong's desire to deconsolidate within its own boundaries (two high schools became six high schools).

Within the law that created the consolidated 505 school districts in Pennsylvania, was a proviso that a test be created that would determine if "Bigger is Better." This test was created and administered from 1969 (on a voluntary basis at first) to 1986. It was called the Test of Education Quality Assessment. However, by the time that the test was administered in earnest, the reason for its existence was forgotten. The EQA was discarded in 1986 in favor of the Test of Learning and Literacy (TELLS), an achievement test created to measure the improvement of individual children, then used to compare schools across the Commonwealth. The thesis that "Bigger is Better" has never really been tested in Pennsylvania.

A number of studies on both school district and high school size and on how size affects cognitive achievement have been conducted during the last 30 years.   Although these studies have yielded some conflicting evidence, there does appear to be a consensus that cognitive achievement tends to increase with smaller numbers of students at each grade level. Nevertheless, national school reform efforts rarely discuss the advantages or disadvantages of size. In Pennsylvania, it appears that the state has forgotten the reason for its efforts to bring youngsters together in larger buildings far from their homes. Recent TELLS scores only show that large city high schools do poorly, wealthy suburban high schools do well, and that medium to small high schools in rural areas fall somewhere between these two performance levels.

In a recent attempt at consolidation in the state of Illinois, a series of studies were completed with the following results:

1) Conclusions about rural schools' inferiority and inefficiency represented a step backward because the data did not support the notion that such schools achieve at a lower rate.
2) Rural schools were the recipients of biased and overly harsh criticism.
3) Data on lower performance were unfairly magnified because small numbers exaggerated otherwise small differences.[9]

CHARACTERISTICS OF RURAL SCHOOLS--THE ADVANTAGES

The domination of the advantages of metropolitan schooling has all but obscured the specific positive attributes of rural schools. The negative mantle of "provincial" ascribed to rural schooling obviates the natural advantages rural schools have over their metropolitan equivalents. Rural schools tend to be the focus of many community activities. In many small rural Pennsylvania towns, such as Brownsville, Coudersport, Ridgeway, and Rimersburg, the happenings at the local schools are a part of everyday adult life.

There is no better demonstration of the basis of our democratic history than a local school board meeting. The direction of community life, cultural, economic, educational, and social can be decided at such meetings. If one has ever witnessed the pull and tug of decisions to build a new building in the community, challenge the authority of the state to mandate new programs, or contract out for a school lunch program, then one can understand how the soul of the community is publicly displayed. Among rural residents there is a sense of ownership of their schools that goes beyond the mere coagulation of "taxpayer groups." On a more subconscious level, community residents are aware of the value of schools to the health of the community in which they live.

This particular characteristic describes the almost personal relationship between the school and each individual child. The teacher is a constant topic of conversation in a home that might have had three generations of students in that teacher's classroom. Certainly, there are disadvantages to this straight line instruction if the staff member is not competent. However, it is a peculiarity of rural society that creates this kind of situation. Pennsylvania has even more of a vested interest in this scene because of the nature of its population. Of all the states in the union, Pennsylvania ranks first in the percentage of its population that is native born, over 80 percent. The chances of a Pennsylvania student going to a school attended by a parent or grandparent is greater than in other states.

The individual attention received by rural students is not just a function of the size of the schools. The entire community interacts with rural children in the school setting. All ancillary staff--administrators, bus drivers, counselors, custodians, cafeteria workers, maintenance people, school medical people, and secretaries--are generally community residents. Problems related to individual students are sometimes ameliorated by the actions of these community residents even prior to their identification by school authorities.

A smaller setting also produces more of a chance to exercise leadership. There are advantages in being the "Big Fish in a Little Pond." In the case of rural schools, there are more opportunities to be part of the activities, more chances to excel, and more opportunities to be part of a successful activity. In these situations, children have many chances to interact positively with their peers and with adults. It may not always be the case that there are fewer students per classroom teacher, but students will know their teachers personally, be able to see them more frequently, and obtain help from them on a very personal level.

Participation rates in all activities, by percentage, are usually higher in rural schools. Although there may not be as many activities, there is greater participation of the student body in almost every phase of student life. The identification with the schools is therefore very high and usually lasts a lifetime. Even for those who leave the area, the memories and lessons of their school's experiences stay with them forever.

Many of the tenants of the "Effective Schools" literature are found in rural schools. These characteristics include a safe surrounding, a lack of red tape, an attention to the basics, a sense of purpose, and a sense of morality. The great danger of state education authorities "equalizing" or "homogenizing" education is that a median school profile will rise from the leveling effort and the positive components of rural schools will be lost forever.

CHARACTERISTICS OF RURAL SCHOOLS--THE DISADVANTAGES

The negative characteristics of rural schools can be divided into size/geographic related variables and wealth/resource variables. The nature of rural schools is that they inhabit large and sparsely populated areas in our country and in our Commonwealth. If one has flown across the heartland of Pennsylvania at night, one would understand that the Commonwealth is a rural state. It comes as a shock to many urban people to learn that Pennsylvania is the most rural state in the nation by population (over 3,700,000 people). It is difficult to portray Pennsylvania to out-of-state residents who believe that Philadelphia and Pittsburgh are characteristic of Pennsylvania's settlement patterns.

Over 200 of Pennsylvania's 501 school districts can be classified as rural. There are as many definitions of "rural" in the lexicon of the federal government as there are federal agencies. For the purposes of this chapter, rural schools are defined as those with a per square mile population of less than 200. The definition of a rural county for the purposes of this chapter is one with more than 50 percent of its population living in any area, town, or municipality that does not have a concentration of more than 2,500 inhabitants and is not contiguous with an established metropolitan area. Under this definition, 42 of Pennsylvania's 67 counties can be considered "rural."

The nature of Pennsylvania both geographically and culturally can be divided into a rural western and northern portion and a metropolitan eastern portion. The area that surrounds Pittsburgh (Allegheny County) considers itself a portion of the Eastern megalopolis extending from Boston to Washington. The people in the rural and western part of the state call themselves "western Pennsylvanians," while the people in eastern Pennsylvania refer to themselves as "Philadelphians" or "Pennsylvanians." The dichotomy between the two regions has some historical meaning for each of the two sections. The settling of the east parallels the early experiences of the original colonies. The populace of the western part of the state, however, assumes itself to be the natural descendants of the pioneers who settled the whole of the United States in the migration to California.

It is not an idle speech by a country politician that calls to mind the "rugged individualism" of his forebearers to make a point to a rural audience. Rural residents are proud of their heritage, their ability to persevere in the face of many hardships, and their dogged determination not to request any help. Rural people, in general, and specifically rural Pennsylvanians, would never think of crying "Uncle." The whole of federal programs were delayed in their distribution to rural areas because of a hesitancy and suspicion of unwanted help.

The economic history of western and northern Pennsylvania is that of extractive industries--agriculture, coal, natural gas, oil, wood, the production of raw materials for the steel mills of Pittsburgh, and one industry towns such as Marienville (glass) in Forest County. It is therefore not surprising that entrepreneurship took a different form in the rural parts of the Commonwealth. Individual fortunes were made in each of the aforementioned businesses. At a time when teachers were earning $4,000 or $5,000 a year in the 1960s, it was not unusual to find youngsters leaving school before graduation to "drive truck" for twice that salary in addition to a Christmas bonus that enabled them to purchase a truck of their own. For example, until 1979 there were more than 30 coal companies in Clarion County, but in 1992 there were only three companies. Moreover, all three companies had "downsized."

The communities that once thrived on natural resources, glass production, powdered metals, and peripheral manufacturing are "ghosts" of their former selves. The families that were responsible for the accumulation of wealth in those communities are long departed, with no intention of returning. The children, grandchildren, and great-grandchildren of the original entrepreneurs have left to live in areas far away from rural Pennsylvania.

The Center for Rural Pennsylvania argues that ". . . over 90 percent of all rural schools can be classified as poor. . . ."[10] The very nature of the failing rural economy has affected rural schools so that there are many rural districts that are on the brink of financial failure. For rural schools, the last 20 years of the 20th Century have highlighted the disadvantages of rural schooling during times of economic deprivation. A lack of choices within the curriculum, a lack of technology, lower staff salaries, a lack of resources, and a low rate of proceeding to post-secondary education create problems within rural communities that only additional funding can cure.

Contrary to rural situations in other states, Pennsylvania has seen to it that poor school facilities are not one of the rural disadvantages. It appears that adequate reimbursement for school facilities enables rural schools to present a pleasant face to the community. In travels around the state, new school building construction can be seen in communities from Northern Tioga to DuBois. The down side of the school construction reimbursement is the lack of local resources to pay even that share of the bond payments that the state does not finance. Some rural schools must cut back on basic educational needs to meet the bond payment schedule. In some cases, balloon payments, foisted upon some rural schools, make budget development and taxation almost impossible tasks.

The lack of resources, as a result of a bimodal spread of wealth across the state, has produced rural schools with an inability to provide the most current technologies for their students. Fewer computers per student, a lack of science laboratories and equipment, and difficulties in securing certified science and mathematics teachers are part of a general trend in rural schools. Add to these problems, fewer advanced placement courses, fewer academic offerings in general, fewer extra-curricular activities, fewer guidance counselors, fewer nurses, and fewer librarians, and the rural education picture darkens considerably.

This lack of logistical support is not particularly an aspect of the geographic/sparsity factor. In fact, the resources that rural and wealthier suburban school districts of the same size have available to them varies greatly. A chart from an award winning series of articles on the discrepancies between poor rural schools and wealthy suburban schools, by Tim Reeves, of the *Morning Call* newspaper in Allentown, Pennsylvania, portrays the differences. In this comparison Northern Tioga School District is compared to Upper Merion, a wealthy district in Montgomery County outside of Philadelphia.[11]

COMPARISON OF A RURAL AND SUBURBAN DISTRICT

	Northern Tioga	Upper Merion
Aid Ratio	.8099	.1500
Enrollment	3,000	3,100
Total Budget	$13.8 Million	$30.7 Million
$ Spent Per Pupil	$2,723	$6,865
Average Teacher Salary	$31,476	$42,352
Superintendent's Salary	$65,000	$98,000
Number of Teachers	156	262
Number of Administrators	9	22
Number of Librarians	4	7
Number of Custodians	25	34
Number of Advanced Placement Courses	3	6
Number of Foreign Languages	3	6
Computer/Student Ratio 7-12	1/14	1/5
Computer/Student Ratio K-6	1/30	1/9
Number of Sports	7	21
Number of Clubs	12	39
Going On To College Rate	46.15	69.7

Source: The *Morning Call*, Allentown, Pennsylvania, September 24, 1990, p. A4.

The results of these distinctions place rural children at a great disadvantage when post-secondary attendance is a consideration. Many rural parents do not see themselves as able to send their children beyond the local school district. There are a number of reasons why this is true. Because of the historical lack of a need for further education, rural parents may not spur their children to seek these experiences. Because of a lack of staffing support within the schools, counseling may not even be available. According to a study done for the Pennsylvania Association of Colleges and Universities in 1984, the most important variable in determining whether a student is going to go on to further education is the philosophy and encouragement of the parent (most particularly, the mother). If there is a lack of educational direction from the adults in the family, then there is a great likelihood that rural students will not be on track for a post-secondary education.

On a purely personal level, the spectre of sending children to a college far away from home is disconcerting for those individuals who have lived in rural areas. Once the youngster leaves a rural home to go to a post-secondary institution, the chances of that youngster returning to his hometown are slim. The rural economy has yet to find room, in its burgeoning low paying service economy, for highly educated, trained, and motivated young people. Jobs and careers are most often found in metropolitan areas far away from rural Pennsylvania. Rural parents are aware of the sacrifices that have to be made if their children leave home to go to school.

There is also a disconcerting lack of information available to rural parents about funds for college tuition via scholarships and the Pennsylvania Higher Education Assistance Agency (PHEAA). Complicated forms that require highly educated people days to complete and that contain sensitive financial information about families are anathema to some rural families. The misconceptions about these available monies and who is eligible for them float through rural communities so that they finally become "folk tales." It is a dogged high school guidance counselor in a school district of 1,000 students or less who has overcome these folk tales to enable eligible youngsters to apply for scholarships and other forms of financial assistance.

THE RURAL ECONOMY

The 1980s were a disastrous time for many rural people. The slow migration of people to rural areas in the 1970s was followed by a massive exodus from rural places to cities, suburbs, and exurbs in the 1990s. Rural America saw the final collapse of the family farm in the 1980s. The march of labor intensive industry to lower cost areas of the U.S. and to modern factories around the world produced a "Rural Welfare State." The description of poverty in rural places has been best depicted by Jim Carroll of the *Erie Daily Times* in a series of articles in 1989 called "Rural Poverty, the Invisible Crisis." Carroll portrays the unseen poverty in rural Pennsylvania created by an economy that has been "dumbed down" and further dismantled.

Rural per capita incomes in Pennsylvania, once close to the state mean in the late 1970s, are now 20 to 30 percent below this standard. The lack of organized economic development has produced "ghost towns" filled with rusting factories and high unemployment rates. Over the past five years--1987 to 1992--the 15 counties with the highest unemployment rates in the state have been rural.[12]

Pennsylvania is comparable to most of rural America with a disproportionate number of the Commonwealth's poor residing in non-metro areas.[13] As in rural areas across the country, Pennsylvania's rural areas have a higher proportion of elderly and young people, under 18 years of age than do metropolitan areas. These two sets of populations are greatly dependent on educational and social programs that have not been adequately funded in rural areas. As wealth leaves the rural portions of the Commonwealth, the needs of these two groups join with the needs of the unemployed to put a great strain on the rural economy. Public expectations have grown across the state for many of these services, and rural areas cannot meet these expectations.

In education, a small rural school district of 1,000 students or less with 50 or 60 teachers and two or three administrators are expected to fulfill all of the state and federal mandates to provide services and programs in the same manner as wealthier school districts with many more resources. As educational needs grow, the rural residents who are least able to provide them and that may have the greatest need for these services face a dark future.

EQUITY

If there is a sense of malaise about the economy of our country, in general, and the Commonwealth of Pennsylvania, in particular, there may be some basis for concern. We have created a large discrepancy between the have and have-nots. From 1983 to 1990 the value of total personal income in Pennsylvania has risen from $85,588,199,150 to $130,265,299,031 an increase of 52.2 percent.[14] The nature of these increases has been particularly uneven. The personal income of the school district of West Chester, in suburban Philadelphia, has risen 92.7 percent from $742,524,836 to $1,464,121,910. The Brownsville School District, in rural Fayette County, has seen its personal income rise only 17.4 percent from $79,873,002 to $93,785,700 during that same time. The same set of numerical statistics are replicated across the state--rural areas, in most cases, show income increases much lower than metropolitan areas. The result of this bi-modal distribution of wealth is an increasing ability of wealthier areas to support their schools with fewer state dollars, while rural areas show a decreasing ability to support their schools even with increased state dollars.

A similar scenario has been played out across the nation during the past twenty years. As early as 1972, poor and rural schools have realized that to accomplish the goals of public education, resources comparable to other areas of the state were needed to provide quality programs for children. The initial state court case that claimed inequitable funding was *Serrano v. Priest* in California. That case has spawned 35 similar cases across the nation. As of this writing, there are 29 extant equity cases proceeding through various state courts.

In 1985, the Pennsylvania Association of Rural and Small Schools (PARSS) was established to work legislatively to counter this growing imbalance of resources among the state's school districts. Although the state significantly increased the financial subsidy for basic instruction, the percentage of school district budgets funded by the state began to decline precipitously. There had been a school code provision that called for the state to fund 50 percent of each school's budget until the early 1980s. In 1992 this figure stood at 38 percent.[15]

Wealthy school districts were able to make up the growing difference between the percentage of their budget funded by local revenues and the percentage of their budget funded by the state because of the massive increases in the value of their real estate and the growing personal income of their residents. At the same time, rural and poor areas of the state were going through cataclysmic economic decline. Local taxes to support schools in rural and poor areas increased to a point that in 1991, "Even if the wealthiest 25 districts and the poorest 25 districts are excluded, the variance is striking. One district would still have to levy taxes at a rate of 35.1 mills on market value to spend $3,751, while another district would need to levy only at a rate of 12.9 mills on market value to spend the same amount."[16]

PARSS efforts, by 1987, produced a Small District Assistance augmentation to the funding of schools in Pennsylvania to help stem the increases in local taxation. Nevertheless, this small pool of funds (never any greater than $24,600,000) spread over many school districts did little to improve rural school funding. Efforts to increase funding for rural schools intensified over a three year period from 1987 to 1990. At the 1990 PARSS yearly conference, Dr. Arnold Hillman, then Executive Director of a rural Intermediate Unit in western Pennsylvania, proposed that PARSS file a class action suit in Commonwealth Court, challenging the funding of Pennsylvania schools. The basis of the suit would be that the system was inequitable to many districts.

The PARSS Board and membership approved the proposal and then hired the law firm of Pepper, Hamilton and Sheetz. On January 10, 1991, the suit was filed on behalf of eight named plaintiffs. The number of plaintiffs (school districts) sponsoring this lawsuit has now increased to 180. Funding for the suit comes from district contributions of $1 per student. Intercessions have been filed, on behalf of the plaintiffs by the

Pennsylvania State Education Association (PSEA) and the Pennsylvania School Boards Association (PSBA) and on behalf of the Commonwealth by a group of wealthy suburban districts led by Abington, the Fox Chapel School District, and the Central Bucks School District. The date for oral argument may be set in the latter part of 1993.

The legislative branch, at first, viewed these attempts at attaining some degree of equity as a threat to the legislative process. After careful consideration and study by the House Education Committee and the House Appropriations Committee during the 1992 legislative session, hearings were held on the subject of equity. At the same time, the two committees employed the National Conference of State Legislatures (NCSL) to study the system, and interview people from all sides of the issue, both in and out of the educational establishment and the legislature. The report was delivered at the end of December 1992 with the following conclusions:

The figures discussed above suggest that while Pennsylvania's school finance system has both strengths and weaknesses, as a whole, the system does not produce equitable results. Equity in school finance can mean a variety of things but, in general, people tend to focus on three aspects, sometimes simultaneously: 1) the variation in revenue/spending across school districts is not attributable to legitimate cost factors; 2) the relationship between revenue and wealth; and 3) the relationship between revenue/spending and tax effort. A system may be considered to be equitable that produces a low variation in revenue/spending; or an equitable system may be one that produces moderate variation in revenue/spending provided that the relationship to wealth is low and the relationship to tax effort is high.

The problem is that none of these objectives are being met: there is an unexplained variation in revenue/spending; there is a systematic relationship between revenue/spending and wealth; and there is almost no relationship between revenue/spending and tax effort   (what relationship exists is negative).

The ESBE distribution system certainly provides more state funds to districts that are comparatively poor, but it also assures that all districts, regardless of wealth, receive some state support. Non-ESBE funds essentially provide a flat grant to all districts; even assuming that the funds are distributed appropriately in response to different needs among school districts, because such aid is not sensitive to the wealth of districts, it neutralizes some of the impact of ESBE. The fact that districts can generate large amounts of local revenue, primarily from property taxes, and that wealthy districts can generate such revenue at relatively low rates, overwhelms the impact of ESBE. If

ESBE did not provide funds to very wealthy districts, if ESBE funds were a higher proportion of all revenues, if non-ESBE funds were wealth equalized, or if local revenues were generated in proportion to tax effort, the results produced by the system, taken as a whole, could be very different.[17]

THE FUTURE OF RURAL EDUCATION IN PENNSYLVANIA

The future of rural education in Pennsylvania is uncertain. Rural schools are particularly tied to the vagaries of economic well-being. Both wealth and social indicators are directly affected by the downturn in the rural economy. The decade of the 1980s was one of "broad rural stress."[18] Slowed job growth, increased unemployment, a widened income gap, and an increased number of low paid service jobs have produced: a decreased quality of rural family life, increased dropout rates, increased child abuse, (rural counties have a higher reported child abuse rate than metropolitan counties), increased divorce rates, and increased poverty.

Education policy as a general concept is uneven, at best. Although the state is responsible for a "thorough and efficient" system, there is a lack of systematic, thoughtful efforts to improve rural education. Individual Department of Education initiatives, such as Outcome Based Education, TELLS, Student Assistance programs, Act 178 (Teacher training), Lead Teacher, and many more are not tailored to rural schools. Too often, rural schools do not have the logistical support to implement and conduct these programs. Further, these programs do not appear to recognize rural schools as a distinct heterogenous entity within the educational framework of the state.

Recently, education has seen its newest panacea--educational choice-- spread from Minnesota to each shining sea. The door to choice has been opened to public school parents. Now families will be able to take tuition dollars from the state along with them when they enter their children in a school of their choosing. These options will force competition among the schools for the consumer's dollar. Second-rate institutions will either close or be forced to improve. Throughout the country many people proclaimed the Minnesota case to be a victory for free choice, the entrepreneurial spirit, and democracy.

Nonetheless, how will the implementation of educational choice improve education in rural areas? There are few, if any, private schools located in these areas, and few, if any, private entrepreneurs are eager to build new facilities in the vast rural expanses of America's heartland. Educational choice will simply remain a concept, an idea, for the majority of rural families in the country. These are the solutions to the problems of education as seen by the "authorities." These experts both governmental and private, are not insincere people. However, when it comes to problems of rural people, they are "sightless."[19]

A program for the comprehensive rehabilitation of rural education should begin with a *revision in the way that schools are funded* within the state. There must be a reduction on the reliance on real estate taxes to provide local funds for schools. NCSL has suggested a statewide real estate tax with exacting assessment values and collections at the state level. It might be more appropriate to look at a personal income tax across the state to equalize funding and make school resources more equitable.

"Schools are often the most significant source of information and leadership within rural communities, but many do not see applying knowledge to community problems as legitimate roles."[20] For those who have viewed rural schools as a way for rural communities to lift themselves by their own bootstraps, the development of rural leadership from within the schools' walls is almost an imperative. *Rural leadership programs should begin with school personnel and expand from there.* A successful model for rural leadership exists at the Pennsylvania State University. RULE (Rural Leadership) has been in operation for four years and can be expanded or replicated.

There is a multitude of solutions to problems in rural areas of the Commonwealth. The following suggestions are just a few that might be part of a comprehensive reform package for rural education in Pennsylvania:

1) Community/School Partnerships,
2) Community Advisory Councils,
3) Service Learning,
4) Spinoff Industries,
5) School-Based enterprise,
6) Specialized teacher training and incentives,
7) Distance Education,
8) Making the connection between education/employment,
9) Awareness of "How the System Works,"
10) Set asides for all grant programs,
11) Rural teacher exchange programs with universities,
12) Programs aimed at parents' views of post-secondary education,
13) Consolidated youth services between agencies aimed at at-risk students,
14) Vocational and adult programs with outreach capabilities,
15) Outreach literacy programs,
16) Local scholarship programs for rural students,
17) Small business outreach programs at universities,

18) Business development centers for individual entrepreneurs,
19) Shadow programs for in-school youth using local service organizations,
20) Programs that expand the role of the teacher in the community,
21) Curricular changes that attend to rural needs,
22) Establishment of community colleges or expansion of vocational schools to community colleges,
23) A rural schools ombudsman within the Department of Education, and
24) Promotion of cooperative efforts among rural schools.

These are just a few of the many ideas that could be incorporated into a comprehensive rural education policy throughout the nation or Pennsylvania. Nevertheless, prior to the implementation of these ideas, there must also be the presence of political courage and political will on the part of the legislature and the executive branch. So often rural endeavors are lost in the act of creating a homogenous solution to problems. If the answer to rural problems is a political one, the rural areas and the cities are natural allies. If it is possible for something positive to come out of the suffering of both rural and inner-city peoples, it is the growing belief that there is more truth than fiction in the parable of the city mouse and his country cousin. Much to their amazement, city people and country people are discovering that their economic and educational needs are similar.

Indeed, the problems of these two areas are similar and are becoming even more similar. There appears to be an awakening to the possibility of a rural/city coalition to bring about changes. It would be difficult to ignore the multitude of people involved in such a coalition. This coalition would represent the majority of the students in all schools in Pennsylvania.

CONCLUSION

Public education has its roots in rural education in the 19th Century. It was not until the latter portion of that century that metropolitan education, fostered by bureaucrats from the cities, began to be the established form of teaching children in the public schools of this country. As those who were metropolitan-trained began to control state education, metropolitan models were used as examples of proper schooling for rural areas. Those who did not agree were seen as "backward."

The great move to consolidation of education in the country and in Pennsylvania did not take into consideration the many advantages of small rural schools. By the latter portion of the 20th Century, rural education became anachronistic in the eyes of the state. Little attention was paid to those 200 school districts in the Commonwealth that fit the rural label. Programs on the state level were prepared for a homogenized population with similar resources.

In the 1980s there was a resurgence of interest in rural schools in the state. Led by some bureaucrats within the State Department of Education and representatives from outside organizations, such as the Pennsylvania Association of Rural and Small Schools (PARSS), and some legislators, some movement was made to produce programs that would specifically attack the problems of rural schools.

As the 1980s produced huge income gaps, most metropolitan communities were able to provide the needed resources for their schools, while most poor and rural communities were not. Because the economy of rural areas is so closely linked to rural education, the sharp increase in unemployment and the closing of extractive industries and peripheral manufacturing, diminished resources for rural schools precipitously.

After entreating the legislature and the executive branch to ameliorate the problems of funding rural schools and failing in their attempts, PARSS went to court, in a class action, to challenge the funding system. The legislature has seen that this is a serious problem and appears to be on the road to devising changes that will make the system more equitable.

The future of rural education rests on the rebounding of the rural economy and the development of a comprehensive policy, at the state level, for rural schools. There are a number of options that could bring rural schools, their communities, and their children into the 21st Century with a fair share of the opportunities that will be available. It will take the force of political will to reestablish rural education to its rightful place in the spectrum of human endeavor.

ENDNOTES

1. Jonathan Sher and others, eds., *Education in Rural America: A Reassessment of Conventional Wisdom* (London: Westview Press, 1977), 1.

2. Arnold Hillman, *There are No Subways in Lickingville* (Shippenville, PA: Riverview Intermediate Unit, 1991), 1.

3. Lawrence Cremin, *American Education-The Metropolitan Experience 1876-1980* (New York, NY: Harper and Row, 1988), ix.

4. Hillman, *There Are No Subwaysin Lickingville*, 4.

5. Pennsylvania Department of Public Instruction, "100 Years of Free Public Schools in Pennsylvania 1834-1934" (Harrisburg, PA: Pennsylvania Department of Public Instruction, 1934), 40.

6. M. Katz, *Class, Bureaucracy and Schools* (New York, NY: Praeger, 1972), 394.

7. Pennsylvania Department of Public Instruction, "100 Years of Free Public Schools," 41.

8. Educational Testing Service, *The State of Inequality* (Princeton, NJ: Educational Testing Service, 1991), 179.

9. David Thompson, "Consolidation of Rural Schools: Reform or Relapse?," *Journal of Educational Finance* 16, no. 2, (Fall 1990): 3.

10. Center for Rural Pennsylvania, *Rich Schools-Poor Schools: Challenges for Rural and Urban Pennsylvania* (Harrisburg, PA: Center for Rural and Urban Schools, 1991), 2.

11. Tim Reeves and Scott Wade, "Pennsylvania School Funding, Aid to the Wealthy," School Funding Series, *Morning Call* (Allentown, PA) 23 September 1990, 4(A).

12. Pennsylvania Department of Labor and Industry, *Civilian Labor Force Series, 1982-1991*, (Harrisburg, PA: Pennsylvania Department of Labor and Industry, June 1992).

13. Rural Services Institute, *Data Report* (Mansfield, PA: Mansfield University, June 1992).

14. Pennsylvania Department of Revenue, "Pennsylvania Personal Income Tax Statistics, 1990" (Harrisburg, PA: Pennsylvania Department of Revenue, December 1992).

15. William Hughes, "Summary of Analysis of Spending, Wealth, Taxes, and Outcomes," (Harrisburg, PA: Pennsylvania State Education Association, August 1991), photocopied.

16. Ibid., 2.

17. John Myers, John Augenblick, and Terry Whitney, "Education Equity in Pennsylvania" (Denver, CO: National Conference of State Legislatures, December 1992), 14-15.

18. Kenneth L. Deavers, "1980s: A Decade of Broad Rural Stress," *Rural Development Perspectives* 7, no. 3, (n.d.): 2-5.

19. Hillman, *There Are No Subways*, 4.

20. Norman Reid, "Risky Futures: Should State Policy Reflect Rural Diversity?," Paper presented as part of a symposium, Louisville, KY, December 1988.

Chapter 17

The Essential Schools Movement

Frederick P. Sample

INTRODUCTION

The foundation for the Pennsylvania Essential Schools Movement, also dubbed the Re:Learning program, rests in an unusual study undertaken in the late 1970s. The study was unusual in not only its scope, but in the partnership of its sponsors. Although both sponsors are engaged in the education of young people, they do not have a history of cooperation in national efforts on the improvement of education. But in this study, the National Association of Secondary School Principals and the National Association of Independent Schools joined hands in commissioning "A Study of High Schools" to determine some bold, new directions for strengthening the school experiences of America's teenagers.

The research team formed to do the study was led by Theodore Sizer, one of our nation's most talented and articulate educators. The team's long, thorough study proceeded into the early 1980s and generated widespread concern about our school programs, led to the formation of the Coalition of Essential Schools (CES), and prompted the writing of three major books.

These three books, all well-written and eye-opening works published in the mid-1980s, are *Horace's Compromise*, *The Shopping Mall High School*, and *The Last Little Citadel*. These works all identified general problems present throughout all schools in our society, and concluded that there was no recipe for quick and universal change.

The Coalition of Essential Schools is a unique formal effort to apply the findings of the Sizer study. It arose from an important recognition that observing and criticizing our schools is not enough. Thought, careful development, and action at every school site are the only routes to new strength and satisfaction in the educational growth of our young people. The CES organization was founded in September 1984 under the leadership of Mr. Sizer and headquartered at Brown University.

Having come to the conclusion that no model of the perfect school exists for all to copy and benefit from, the Coalition advances its work through the formulation of a set of common principles. Membership in the CES requires only that members sincerely share in the group's common principles--a requirement which allows for great diversity in its membership in such areas as governmental control, geographic location, size, wealth, ethnic backgrounds, and others variables.

Before identifying the common principles upon which all CES activities and efforts are developed, and consequently, upon which the activities and efforts of the Pennsylvania Re:Learning program are based, it is helpful to delineate how the CES and Pennsylvania Re:Learning came to be closely related. Early members of CES were from all corners of the nation, and the strengths of the process were communicated widely and enthusiastically. State-level educators became interested and desired some possible involvement. The resources at CES headquarters were called upon to do more than their small staff and budget could manage, while the need to inform and involve states and school districts in a more organized and supportive way grew.

The leaders of the CES and the Education Commission of the States (ECS) held discussions, which eventually produced a cooperative effort and a formal relationship which helped to publicize the process and boost state financial support to schools that would inevitably incur costs for their early involvement. This joint venture of CES and ECS became known as the Re:Learning program, which could be undertaken by any interested state willing to provide the staff and financial support. After many meetings and presentations, Pennsylvania became a Re:Learning state in 1989, and schools in various areas of the Commonwealth became engaged in the program. The participating districts within Pennsylvania are listed at the end of this chapter.

Although a technical difference exists between a Coalition school and a Re:Learning school in Pennsylvania, soon after Pennsylvania became involved, the two terms were frequently used synonymously. While

Coalition schools are members of the CES based at Brown University, Re:Learning schools may or may not be members. It is, of course, desirable for both types of schools to be committed to the nine basic principles underlying their efforts toward improvement. The principles are reprinted and addressed later in this chapter.

The researchers who studied the American secondary school for the National Association of Secondary School Principals and the National Association of Independent Schools concluded that school improvement must have its roots in some widely-held principles about how students learn and how schools should operate. Schools cannot become carbon copies of one another, nor can they adopt a single recipe for operation. Sizer firmly emphasized that:

> No two good schools are ever quite alike. No good school is exactly the same from one year to the next. Good schools sensitively reflect their communities--both the students and teachers within the school building, and the wider neighborhood it serves. A good school respectfully accommodates the best of its neighborhood, not abjectly--playing whatever tune any particular special interest group might demand--but sensibly, balancing the claims of national values with those of the immediate community.

The common principles identified by the researchers, which guide the reforms of participating schools are general, thought-provoking, cohesive, and in many ways, pleasingly familiar. Most educators and parents found them to be very agreeable and easy to discuss, however difficult they might be to interpret and apply. Any interpretation of Pennsylvania Re:Learning, however brief, must contain the full text of these nine guiding principals, listed below:

> The school should focus on helping adolescents learn to use their minds well. Schools should not attempt to be "comprehensive" if such a claim is made at the expense of the school's central intellectual purpose.

> The school's goals should be simple: that each student master a limited number of essential skills and areas of knowledge. While these skills and areas will, to varying degrees, reflect the traditional academic disciplines, the program's design should be shaped by the intellectual and imaginative powers and competencies that students need, rather than necessarily by "subjects" as conventionally defined. The aphorism "Less Is More" should dominate: curricular decisions should be guided by the aim of thorough student mastery and achievement rather than by an effort merely to cover content.

The school's goals should apply to all students, while the means to these goals will vary as those students themselves vary. School practice should be tailor-made to meet the needs of every group or class of adolescents.

Teaching and learning should be personalized to the maximum extent feasible. Efforts should be directed toward a goal that no teacher have direct responsibility for more than 80 students. To capitalize on this personalization, decisions about the details of the course of study, the use of students' and teachers' time and the choice of teaching materials and specific pedagogies must be unreservedly placed in the hands of the principal and staff.

The governing practical metaphor of the school should be student-as-worker, rather than the more familiar metaphor of teacher-as-deliverer-of-instructional-services. Accordingly, a prominent pedagogy will be coaching, to provoke students to learn and thus to teach themselves.

Students entering secondary school studies are those who can show competence in language and elementary mathematics. Students of traditional high school age but not yet at appropriate levels of competence to enter secondary school studies will be provided intensive remedial work to assist them quickly to meet these standards. The diploma should be awarded upon a successful final demonstration of mastery for graduation--an "Exhibition." This Exhibition by the student of his or her grasp of the central skills and knowledge of the school's program may be jointly administered by the faculty and by higher authorities. As the diploma is awarded when earned, the school's program proceeds with no strict age grading and with no system of "credits earned" by "time spent" in class. The emphasis is on the students' demonstration that they can do important things.

The tone of the school should explicitly and self-consciously stress values of unanxious expectation ("I won't threaten you, but I expect much of you"), of trust (until abused) and of decency (the values of fairness, generosity, and tolerance). Incentives appropriate to the school's particular students and teachers should be emphasized, and parents should be treated as essential collaborators.

The principal and teachers should perceive themselves as generalists first (teachers and scholars in general education) and specialists second (experts in but one particular discipline). Staff should expect multiple obligations (teacher-counselor-manager) and a sense of commitment to the entire school.

Ultimate administrative and budget targets should include, in addition to total student loads per teacher of 80 or fewer pupils, substantial time for collective planning by teachers, competitive salaries for staff, and an ultimate per pupil cost not to exceed that at traditional schools by more than 10 percent. To accomplish this, administrative plans may have to show the phased reduction or elimination of some services now provided students in many traditional comprehensive secondary schools.

NATIONAL RE:LEARNING EFFORTS

At this point, it may be useful to summarize and reiterate several points and to examine the extent to which Sizer's nine point philosophy has been implemented by state governments across the nation. Re:Learning is a joint national effort of the CES, ECS, and 11 Re:Learning member states. Formed in 1988, the partnership's goal is to stimulate and support redesign work at the school, school district, state, and national levels. To do this, CES works directly with schools to improve the way students are educated, while ECS works with state departments of education, state policy makers, and school districts to improve the regulatory and policy climate in which schools operate. The purpose of the effort is to reform education through the use of Re:Learning, or more clearly stated, the implementation of CES's Nine Common Principles. Approximately 600 schools nationwide operate Re:Learning programs at an average yearly cost of $50,000 per school.

The Re:Learning effort identifies states that actively use the concept as either exploring, networking, or member.

Exploring status refers to states that: 1) inquire about Re:Learning, 2) express a desire to implement the concept, and/or 3) implement Re:Learning on a trial basis in at least one school. All fifty states have inquired about Re:Learning, and 34 states have expressed a desire to implement the concept. However, only the following five states have tried Re:Learning in at least one school: Alabama, Georgia, Minnesota, Mississippi, and Utah.

Networking status refers to states that: 1) exhibit an expressed willingness on the part of the governor's office, the state department of education, school districts, and schools to adapt Re:Learning to the state education system for at least one year, 2) try to secure state and/or private funding to implement Re:Learning statewide, and 3) apply for networking status. The following six states have been granted networking status: Florida, Kentucky, Massachusetts, Michigan, Ohio, and Texas. In these states, 62 schools actively use Re:Learning.

Member status refers to states that: 1) establish state cooperation between the governor's office, the state department of education, school districts, and schools, 2) form a leadership group to focus on restructuring the state's education system, 3) make a five-year commitment to use Re:Learning, 4) secure state and/or private funding for Re:Learning, 5) implement Re:Learning in at least ten secondary schools, 6) hire an in-state coordinator to assist the Re:Learning schools and correspond with CES and ECS, 7) officially sign-on to a Re:Learning bill, and 8) apply for member status. The following 11 states have been granted member status: Arkansas, Colorado, Delaware, Illinois, Indiana, Maine, Missouri, New Mexico, Pennsylvania, Rhode Island, and South Carolina. Approximately 150 schools actively use Re:Learning in the member states.

THE PROCESS OF IMPLEMENTATION IN PENNSYLVANIA

Although a few Pennsylvanians were aware of the Re:Learning goals before the fall of 1988, it was at this time that efforts were made to promote the program and interact with people across the state. Secondary school principals, superintendents, and professional organization leaders were invited to Harrisburg for an introduction to the meaning and background of the new program with the strange label, "Re:Learning." At the time, the program was identified primarily, if not totally, with secondary schools. This connection was logical because the root study was directed at high schools, and was entitled "A Study of High Schools." Then, as now, most of the problems in American schools were perceived by many people to exist in the high schools alone. It was not long, however, before many educators saw that these principles applied to all schools, and both elementary school and college personnel joined in the reflections and conversations necessary to implement the goals of the program.

Attendance at early meetings on the Re:Learning program was disappointing. Not more than 25 of Pennsylvania's 501 districts were represented. Despite the state's financial support to ease the cost of attending some meetings, the early numbers did not increase, and in fact, actually declined. There was much theorizing about the reasons behind this low number. Some attributed it to lack of publicity, or to satisfaction with the status quo, or to time pressures, or to fear of change, or to distrust of programs promoted by the state, especially without promises of a large guaranteed subsidy.

Others thought the new program would never be attractive to many because it was not in the form of step-by-step procedures which promised a positive and specific end-result for everyone. It appears that all of the above, coupled with recent widespread financial pressures, have limited the number of schools which have adopted the process with enthusiasm, courage, and extra financial support.

In the early Re:Learning discussions for Pennsylvanians, two persons assumed leadership roles by virtue of their positions, enthusiasm, and articulate natures. The educational "insider" who emerged as a leader was then-Commissioner for Basic Education in the Commonwealth, Donna Wall. The "outsider" was Robert McCarthy, the Executive Director of CES and one of Ted Sizer's most trusted associates.

Almost all of the early questions about Pennsylvania's Re:Learning program were directed to these two persons.

One of the most difficult questions for leaders to answer in the early discussions, was and still remains the question about specific timetables and recommended program content. It was unacceptable for many questioners to hear that such answers can come only from within a building and only after the people of that building devoted much time to the nine basic principles. Despite so much evidence to the contrary, many educators seemed to believe that school improvement would come only from a well-packaged and ready-to-implement series of activities. Most people considered the nine principles worthy statements about education, but many needed a recipe attached to them. Many felt some discomfort with a few sentences or phrases within the principles. Many sought and found whatever reason possible to stay out of hard work's way.

Before engaging in the conversations necessary to implement the nine principles, the leaders emphasized the major conclusions from the original study team, reminding educators about the approach to improvement resident in the original nine principles. As time passed, people engaged in the meetings often made no reference to what were sometimes referred to as the five imperatives for better schools incorporated in the original study team's findings. It was a mistake to de-emphasize these findings. Without this emphasis, some people dismissed the principles as isolated idealism; some did not even take the time to read the three major works and became shallow in their comments because of their lack of preparation and foundation.

One of the five identified imperatives for better schools was the directive to give room to teachers and students to work and learn in their own, appropriate ways. Another was to insist that students clearly exhibit mastery of their school work. The third was to get the incentives right, for students and teachers. The fourth was to focus the students' work on the use of their minds. The fifth was to keep the structure simple and flexible. For most discussants, just a simple recitation of these recommendations generated an increased appreciation of the principles. It was a grievous error to reduce the emphasis upon, or eliminate, these essential reminders.

Unfortunately, many other new and good suggestions for education have failed because of the same superficial study they received and their consequent trivialization. No better example can be given in our nation's history than the triviality associated with what people imagined to be the suggestions of John Dewey. Few people who tried to implement school improvement through what they thought were Dewey's suggestions ever took the time to read and study Dewey's original books. From one magazine article or from one short seminar, people tried to practice something they did not really understand. This same practice caused the soured reputation and eventual demise of many well-founded suggestions for improving the educational experience of our young people.

During a seminar in the summer of 1990, a question about triviality was directed to Ted Sizer. It was fundamentally a question asking Sizer how interested parties could prevent the trivialization or prostitution of this process called Re:Learning. "Only with great vigilance" was his response. It is dangerous to implement anything under the heading of "Pennsylvania Re:Learning" if the implementers are not soundly grounded in the content of the three major works which gave birth to this program. Intense and thorough study and conversation about the three works and the nine principles for as much as a year were part of the original understanding for initiating a school's participation in Pennsylvania Re:Learning.

The first school districts to show interest in the Re:Learning returned to Harrisburg for several meetings in 1989. These meetings brought together teams from interested school districts, which included teachers, school board members, interested parents, principals, and superintendents. Representatives from the Pennsylvania Department of Education, the Education Commission of the States, and the Coalition of Essential Schools coordinated these sessions, which helped people to understand the necessary connection between the nine principles and a new vision by all major players in the field of education if school reform was to be effective and lasting. While individual school district teams began to generate discussions at the local levels, individuals began to share in interstate meetings for broadening and deepening the conversation about Re:Learning. It was wise to have higher education involved at this early stage in order to pair each interested school with a representative from a college or university.

Gradually, Pennsylvania's interest, although limited to a dozen school districts, began to take on the signs of a serious undertaking. Funding for districts who dared initiate a serious planning year was arranged. After a period of part-time leadership and coordination, the Pennsylvania Department of Education (PDE) named a full-time Re:Learning coordinator, as did other states before it. The CES staff and the ECS staff continued to help Pennsylvanians make progress. Bringing Pennsylvanians into regional and national meetings was one of the major ways to broaden the conversation and deepen the appreciation of the program.

While the regional and national experiences helped Pennsylvanians grow into the effort, interested school districts spent large amounts of time throughout the 1989-1990 school year engaging in the necessary study, conversation, and planning required for some 1990-1991 implementation. In accordance with warnings and advice, local school districts soon learned of the tremendous amounts of time and effort which had to be invested. Most teachers and principals discovered that they had not been very accustomed to sharing deep thoughts and difficult questions about the real essentials of their school. To invest this kind of energy and time was not in the budgetary thinking of most school districts.

It was not long into the discussions of some school districts that problems surfaced. People began to discuss without the benefit of necessary study. What were to be deep and thoughtful conversations often became similar to the ordinary, monthly faculty meeting. Instead of learning some of the background and processes underlying the activity at other schools in other states and in previous years, some desired simply to copy what another school was doing. Perhaps even worse than the pursuit of a "quick fix" by copying, there was always a group who neither saw nor felt any need for change. By their words and actions it was oftentimes obvious that they were unwilling to take the time necessary to read the background books and think deeply about the nine principles. In the case of one school district, these attitudes were shared by a rather small minority, but the group became very critical of the persons who were willing to undertake leadership roles and invest extraordinary time and effort into working toward a changed school environment.

Reports from other schools in the 1989-90 year of study and planning indicated similar experiences, in which persons emerged who were not only unwilling to participate in the effort, but were also very eager to speak negatively about others who were giving time and effort to the new process. Although no numbers can be reported, the volume of the criticism was enough to dampen the spirits of some persons who were positive and eager to move with a new opportunity.

Despite criticism, many of the schools that were seriously planning, studying, and conversing in 1989-90 readied plans for implementation in 1990-1991. The plans did not place an entire school in a new structure or system, but instead chose some small part of the school as a first step. A change in the combination of courses in a few sections of a grade level; a change in some of the traditional time periods for offering experiences to students; and a short, school-wide common experience for all students were a few of the starting points for school change. This small step (a "school-within-a-school" approach) was consistent with what happened in most early operations of CES schools. It is proper to note here, however, that the ultimate goal has always been identified as a total building operating as a CES or Re:Learning school. The basic principles and the entire process were always intended for use by the entire school. The "school-within-a-school" operation was acceptable only as a realistic recognition of the need for time and resources to change something as complicated as a school.

An example of a "school-within-a-school" is provided in the Commonwealth by McCaskey High of Lancaster. A brief summary of its experience is useful.

This comprehensive high school's involvement with the Coalition of Essential Schools began informally in 1987. McCaskey became an essential "school-within-a-school," in 1991-92 with a team of eight teachers for two groups of students, each approximately 80 in number. The program's main objective has been the implementation of an integrated curriculum and authentic assessment. The school operates under a system of participatory management and follows the guiding principles of CES schools. Two common goals were developed by a team of teachers and district staff to describe the mission of the "school-within-a-school": 1) To provide students with the capacity to use background skills and knowledge to cope with existing and developing conditions and changes in life, and 2) To provide students with a capacity for "personal expansion." These goals, in turn, led the team to agree on the following four essential skills which, combined with the goals, became the impetus for all of the school restructuring and curriculum revision: 1) thinking skills and problem-solving; 2) information processing; 3) information integration; and 4) interpersonal skills. An evaluation of this program will be completed after August 1993.

A year of partial operation provides a great opportunity for all to share and learn while minimizing the fear of change and flexibility. It also provides an opportunity for critics to talk about the most negative consequences accompanying any change. Many verbally expressed comments illustrated that critics were indeed taking advantage of the opportunity to emphasize the negatives about any aspect of the new program. Some people who saw the new environment as a threat to their discipline became extremely negative. So did some who saw the new mode of cooperative efforts as an infringement upon their solo and comfortable style of operation. Some saw the new effort as a disguised plan for the school board to eliminate jobs and save money. Others decided that it was an effort to spend more money in the schools with no assurance of better results.

There seems to be little question about the need for widespread participation in the initial planning year. The more people who own and understand the new effort, the less the changes will be attacked. At the same time, it must be noted that a sound, forward movement will always require people who are daring enough to ignore the inevitable criticisms. One of the reasons for triviality in many new programs is the compromises that are repeatedly being made in order to achieve agreement; these comprises often rob the initially sound suggestion of all its substance. While the nine principles encourage widespread collaboration, they discourage a retreat from the real substance which gives a school its reason for being.

While the first year of implementation caused some bitter controversy in some schools, at least in one school the students and their parents were so enthusiastic about the experience that they became an unstoppable force in moving ahead. Plans for a revised and expanded second year continued, and the second year began with an increased number of new and eager participants, including students and teachers and parents.

In the case of the Pennsylvania experience, the term "Re:Learning" was probably an unfortunate one to use. Similar comments have come from other states. In the Pennsylvania school environment, many people immediately imagined the term to have something to do with special education or tutoring in difficult-to-grasp academic areas. In some cases, even among professional staff, this initial barrier was immovable regardless of explanations.

The term "Re:Learning" was chosen to indicate that the main focus of this national movement was on the learning of our students. It was considered crucial that the focus of the program be on thoughtful changes at every level (national, state, district, and building) in order to greatly improve student learning. Who can deny a school effort which is solely devoted to learning, and to greatly improving the learning of our young people? Although one can argue that the learning of our students is influenced by so many nonacademic influences, such as parent relationships, nutrition, self esteem, and a host of other factors, the term "Re:Learning" was chosen to make it clear that the emphasis was to be on learning, especially learning to use the mind well, and not on transportation systems, food services, budget systems, and a host of other necessary parts of a school operation.

For a number of reasons, it was fortunate that only a few school districts participated in Re:Learning in its first few years. The basic nature of the program, with its absence of specific recipes, required long, supportive conversations among those involved. The resources of the PDE, ECS, and CES were indeed taxed just to help the few districts that were moving ahead. The gradual addition of a few schools each year seems to be an appropriate way to proceed. It will be good for the future of education if this program is one of those very rare ones in which the implementers participate in the foundational study and in the development of the fundamental questions associated with the effort. Too often, educational improvement was expected to happen when the implementers were handed new educational guidelines to follow.

CONCLUSION

The conclusions of a former college president and a former superintendent about Re:Learning might be useful. First and foremost, students have found that Re:Learning is intellectually sound. It can withstand any criticism tossed its way. It requires participants to engage in penetrating thought and collaboration which force them to answer tough questions about learning to use the mind well. This experience enhances the ability to handle essential questions as well as founded or unfounded criticism.

Re:Learning is compatible with much that we know and do. We know what we would like citizens of the 21st Century to be able to do. We are quite aware of what skills will be necessary, and that many of these skills have a very familiar ring.   The attainment of communication and mathematical skills, teamwork abilities, problem solving skills, and many more are hardly new goals for all students.

We also know more than ever about just who our young people are, the peculiarities of certain developmental stages, and the pressures and problems with which they live. Too often we ignore this knowledge. Frequently, we arrive at solutions or panaceas before we really know the problem.

Sometimes we perform in our schools as if we really do not know how people learn. Although much remains to be discovered in the area of how people learn, there is no excuse for failing to use what we already know. Re:Learning is indeed quite compatible with what is already known.

A successful Re:Learning effort requires huge amounts of rethinking, retraining, and restructuring. It is an investment that requires support and understanding from many sources. No one gets off easy. In such an unusual approach, there are many barriers to face, and they can be faced only with great courage. It is not too extreme to say that some people must be willing to put their jobs on the line in order to move ahead. The conversations and the studies and the restructuring must consist of a flow which is constantly both "bottom up" and "top down" in the organization. It cannot be just the faculty's program, or the principal's program, or the superintendent's program, or the school board's program, or the parents' program. It must be everybody's program.

Because of the volumes of work associated with becoming and remaining a Re:Learning school, the chance for large numbers of school districts to become participants in the near future is rather slim. As identified earlier, dozens of excuses for not becoming involved have been offered. These excuses come from almost every source except the students. Administrators, teachers, school board members, union leaders, and parents can all contribute reasons for not engaging in the Re:Learning effort; indeed, significant change of any kind is sure to bring preservers of the status quo to the forefront armed with all kinds of defensive weapons. On the other hand, students from their daily, grinding experiences can explain rather well the benefits of new approaches to education.

Some of the major findings about students in the early study remain the same. Little has changed to cause them to be different. Too many teenage students are bored in school. Large schools, small schools, urban schools, suburban schools, rural schools, wealthy schools, and poor schools all have generated the same result. Generally, students are docile. However, students respect the high school diploma. That fact explains their willingness to spend the time in school. They think of the diploma as a reward for time spent and little else. Teenagers also want to respect themselves and at the same time be respected. This fact, coupled with their respect for the diploma, requires the necessary new school environment to capitalize on what we know. The Re:Learning response simply asks each school to build on a commitment to the nine principles.

It appears that students will be overjoyed with the significant change brought from such a commitment.

Although Pennsylvania's experience is too recent to provide the basis for solid studies on the results of Re:Learning efforts to date, comments by students and teachers indicate progress. More than a few students have indicated that their Re:Learning experience, as they came to identify it from their traditional school experiences, really engaged them in studies for the first time.

Students also report that they undertook a common learning goal in cooperation with other students for the first time. They report a deliberate experience of relating one academic discipline to another. They report, and parents confirm, that parents are more engaged in the students' school learning than ever before. Some students reported that school experiences became the dinner-time conversation for the first time.

Some schools which began early in the CES program have had time to provide more formal results of their work. Some evidence indicates that students are achieving at higher levels, attending classes more regularly, taking greater responsibility for their work, and planning better for higher education.

As Sizer so aptly stated in 1989, Pennsylvania Re:Learning promises no panacea, no quick model that can be put into place. It promises only an honest return to the basic questions about schooling, about growing up, about learning, and about teaching. It promises a hard, but ultimately, liberating, struggle for school folk, not only to advance their work in a setting that squares with the hunches of generations of successful teachers, but also to see ordinary youngsters--particularly those for whom traditional schools seem to have given up--perform in extraordinary ways.

Pennsylvania's Re:Learning schools-in-the-making already signal promises in this regard. Nobody wishes to make strident claims at the present time, but some very capable people are convinced that when the basic ideas and principles are rigorously adhered to, the world of schooling improves both for youngsters and for teachers.

The model of a Re:Learning school is not, of course, one that can be generalized. Rather, it is an approach that leads to an idiosyncratic model for each community, a unique representation of what is best for that setting and its people and which is consistent with some powerful and old-fashioned ideas about learning and teaching. Patience, courage, and an endless sense of humor are required, but the promise is there, rich and increasingly visible.

PENNSYLVANIA RE:LEARNING SCHOOLS BY DISTRICT

Bellefonte Area
Cannon McMillan
Centennial
Central Bucks
Chartiers Valley
Eastern Lancaster County
Franklin Regional
Halifax
Hazleton
Keystone Oaks
Lancaster
McGuffey
New Hope-Solebury
North Hills
Philadelphia
Tyrone Area
Wallenpaupack Area
West Jefferson Hills
York City

Chapter 18

Outcomes Based Education

Judith Witmer

Introduction

Outcome based education (OBE) is not new. Outcome based education is not a curriculum, and it is not a set of rules. Outcome based is one instructional innovation among many that is being considered by schools as they attempt to improve their efficacy, even in the face of large-scale societal changes. Many individuals expect change in the way they conduct their daily lives--from banking to laundering clothes--but are anxious about any changes or proposed changes in the way their children are educated. Nonetheless, our society is evolving at a dizzying rate with major increases in technological capabilities and in man's knowledge of his world and himself. During the last several decades, man has discovered a great deal of new information about the ways by which learning occurs. This new information has led to several new approaches to learning and to the field of education. One of these approaches is OBE.

Outcome based education is a way of organizing educational practices. It is not a single model or program in and of itself. Outcome based education is a way of doing things, a way of focusing and identifying what it is that an educational entity wants to achieve. In its simplest form, outcome based education is a belief that a school community should think about the results of its children's education: What is it that every child should know and be able to do by the time he graduates from high school?

This question becomes a guiding force for all other decisions made by a school district. Such a question is fundamental to all reform.

WHAT IS OUTCOME BASED EDUCATION?

Outcome based education is a procedure whereby the school district, with the community, decides what children should be learning; develops a curriculum or education program accordingly; and teaches the program. Outcome based education is based on the belief that all children can learn, can attain proficiency, and can demonstrate that proficiency. OBE is an approach to education, not curriculum.

Under the student outcomes approach, local schools and their communities will: 1) set specific goals, 2) set student learning outcomes, 3) assess achievement of those outcomes in an "authentic" process (performed by the students through a demonstration or portfolio), and 4) replace the traditional time-based units of promotion with proficiency-based units.

Because outcome based education is a method by which students can approach reform, it is difficult for many laymen, and some practitioners, to understand that there is no one existing model of OBE, which operationalizes outcome based education into practice. Advocates of OBE claim that the framework of outcome based instruction allows for the incorporation of almost any of the best ideas and innovations of the last ten years. For example, OBE could include any or several of the following: strategic planning; site-based management; team teaching; authentic assessment; integrated curriculum; effective schools philosophy; cooperative learning; critical thinking; and, of course, mastery learning. Any or all of these practices become first the springboard and then the guide for schools in the efforts to restructure toward "outcomes of significant or culminating demonstrations of complex role performances in authentic contexts."[1] In such a system, educators select what methods and models they believe will allow all students to learn the competencies they will need to succeed in today's society.

Since 1980, outcome based education has become more widely known and much better understood by both researchers and those educators who have redesigned their schools around its precepts. In an attempt to define commonalities shared by outcome based education programs, Robert Burns, Nikola Filby, and William Spady in *Outcome Based Education: A Summary of Essential Features and Major Implications* (1986) outlined the two fundamental principles they observed:

1) Instructional practice is designed around clearly defined outcomes that all students must demonstrate. Once those defined outcomes have been achieved, then instructional decisions are made about what a student is to learn next.
2) Schools must provide the opportunity for all students to reach learning outcomes. What this means is that teachers are given the flexibility to make instructional decisions regarding use of time, teaching methods, and materials.[2]

In 1986 the work of John Champlin, Executive Director of the National Center for Outcome Based Education, brought into focus an essential dimension of this educational innovation which has had a significant impact on the movement of student based outcomes. Champlin was among the first to articulate that "plugging in" outcome based programs would not be enough to ensure successful educational reform. According to Champlin, if the outcome based approach were to be successful, teachers would have to be involved in every aspect of the change process. Even transforming curriculum and instruction would not be enough. The entire organization would have to change in order to build and support a climate which would allow building administrators, teachers, and all other stakeholders to grow and effect change. This insistence on systemic change (also one of the main elements in Theodore Sizer's Coalition of Essential Schools movement theories which preceded Champlin's theories) is essential for success. No part of the system should remain untouched. Each component of the school system must be examined and aligned with this type of educational approach to ensure a high level of success for all students.[3]

If we further consider what Spady and Mitchell in their work "Competency-Based Education: Organizational Issues and Implications" (1977) term the four functions of schools and classrooms, we begin to see how multi-layered systemic change can be. If we accept the goals of a school to be that youngsters emerge from public education having achieved 1) social responsibility, 2) social integration, 3) personal competency, and 4) formal qualifications for pursuing post-secondary education or employment; we also accept that to accomplish these goals the schools must engage in these functional activities: instruction, acculturation, supervision, and certification. Each function also represents an operational curriculum to be addressed in the pursuit of one of the four above listed goals. Hence, there is an "official" curriculum that is the basis for the instructional system, an "extra"-curriculum in the acculturation system, a "hidden" curriculum in the supervision system, and a "required" curriculum in the certification system.[4]   Add to this curriculum function all of the other elements in operating a school system--facilities, finances, personnel, policy, research, and school-community relations--and the enormity of genuine systemic change becomes clear. What at first appeared to be a simple rearrangement of the delivery of instruction is now seen to be an upheaval of the fundamental way in which schools have "always" operated.

Outcome based education is a movement which can trace its development from student objectives to the push for increased accountability, improved student assessment, clarified school goals, improved teacher evaluation, and elevated community involvement. Outcome based education incorporated the competency-based movement and built itself around the integration of outcome goals, instructional experiences, and assessment devices. Outcome based education (lower case) is the concept upon which many reform practices are built. Outcome Based Education, or OBE, (upper case) began with the organization of the concept into a specialized framework and system established by the work of William Spady as well as the National Center for Outcome Based Education. It is now generally agreed that there are three distinguishing characteristics central to the practice of what is termed Outcome Based Education (OBE): 1) a specific philosophy that embraces success for all students; 2) the alignment of outcomes with assessment, curriculum, and instruction; and 3) accountability for both students and teachers.[5]

The philosophy of OBE contains three maxims: 1) All children can learn; 2) Success breeds success; and 3) Schools control the conditions of success.

Acceptance of these principles leads to a commitment by educators to discover what instructional methods allow each student to succeed. The curriculum content does not usually differ for students.

Alignment of outcomes with assessment, curriculum, and instruction implies that outcomes are determined first. Once the desired outcomes are identified, understood, and accepted; appropriate teaching materials and delivery methods are selected. Therefore, the student will know the destination (the desired outcome) and the route to journey to that destination (material and instruction).

Accountability flows naturally from the alignment of outcomes with assessment, curriculum, and instruction, as the process specifies who is responsible for what. Teachers are held accountable both for providing instructional experiences directly oriented toward achieving the objectives of a particular unit of study and on integrating the instructional experiences with the learning needs of the student. Students are held accountable for achieving a pre-determined goal for that unit of study before proceeding to the next level of proficiency. There is no "seat time" specified. Accountability is shown through a demonstration of proficiency. OBE, however, will only be effective if the outcomes are significant and challenging. This "quality assurance" component is essential to the success of OBE.

At first glance, it may appear that OBE is no different from what good teachers have always practiced. There are, however, differences:

1) *Purpose.* The main outcome of OBE is that students know what they should learn and what they should be able to do by the time they graduate from high school. In an OBE system, students aim for final goals; teachers work with each student to assist them to reach the established goals in ways that can be demonstrated, measured, and performed.

2) *Curriculum.* OBE curriculum is designed and developed from the desired result or outcome to be demonstrated or mastered. The content is viewed as a source for learning experiences; the content is not limited to textbook material. The curriculum should be designed to link it with real-world issues and problems.

3) *Instruction.* Instruction is learner-centered and uses multiple strategies and flexible student groupings. In addition to OBE incorporating a number of approaches to presenting material to students, OBE will also provide students with more than one opportunity to learn material.

4) *Assessment.* OBE assessment measures should include both diagnostic and affirming measures, and should be aligned with instruction and learner outcomes. Diagnostic measures test what a child knows and identifies areas that need improvment; affirming measures test the knowledge that a child displays.

Defining OBE by identifying its differences with traditional classroom instruction, i.e., lectures and discussion, is becoming more difficult as theoretical development of OBE continues. OBE appears to be evolving into three forms. Traditional OBE, uses existing curriculum for curriculum-based objectives. Transitional OBE, draws on subject matter as it seeks to develop higher order competencies, i.e., improved academic abilities. Finally, Transformational OBE, examines all instructional practices and restructures the educational process so that students can achieve their challenging, future-oriented learning outcomes with less time and effort.

HISTORY OF OUTCOME BASED EDUCATION

The question of what every child should know and be able to do, has its origins in educational ideas that were put into practice in the 1950s. These educational beliefs can trace their history to earlier American pioneers in educational philosophy and policy. Ralph Tyler, for example, is recognized as one of the early proponents of outcome based education. His *Basic Principles of Curriculum and Instruction* (1949) stressed the necessity of identifying an objective in order to systematically plan educational experiences. A Tyler objective would include both the behavior that the student should be developing as he engaged in learning and the area or content of life in which the behavior would be applied.

Tyler's pedagogy was further developed in the 1960s by Benjamin Bloom in *Taxonomy of Educational Objectives.* Bloom's work identified objectives that teachers could attempt to realize with their students in academic and attitudinal areas. In 1962, Robert Mager continued this research in his book *Preparing Instructional Objectives.* In this book he laid the groundwork for teachers to design their instructional program to achieve behavioral objectives with their students as well as academic objectives. Mager outlined the three components of behavioral objectives: 1) behavior, 2) conditions, and 3) criterion of performance.

John Carroll of Harvard University in 1963 published his findings in "A Model of School Learning." Carroll's research results showed that student ability for learning is not fixed at birth, and that, given sufficient time, almost all students can learn what typically only the best students learn. Although Carroll clearly stated that learning also depends on the quality of instruction and motivation, the element of time was advanced as the key factor in learning.

Further building on the research work of Carroll, Bloom began to study not only the relationship between time and learning but also the other conditions that affect the instructional process. Bloom's research findings stated that all students can learn well 1) if the instruction is systematic, 2) if help is given whenever students are having learning difficulties, 3) if sufficient time is provided, and 4) if there is a clear criterion to determine, i.e., assess, that material or a skill has been learned.

These beliefs were the essence of what became the strategy for "Mastery Learning," an educational philosophy that assumes almost any student can master a school's curriculum. Supporters of Mastery Learning also believe that students learn at different rates and that they need on-going feedback and reinforcement. In addition, Mastery Learning requires that clearly stated objectives, i.e., outcomes, must be known by both teacher and learner. Adding to this educational theory, James Block in *Building Effective Mastery Learning Schools* (1989) identified five elements which are essential to Mastery Learning instruction: 1) diagnosis (in order not to waste time on material the child already knows); 2) prescription (assigned learning tasks appropriate for each student); 3) orientation (clarifying the learning objective and the performance outcome); 4) feedback (on-going monitoring and assessment); and 5) correction (timely supplemental instruction as needed).

There were major institutional obstacles, however, to the acceptance and implementation of Mastery Learning in the nation's schools. In an attempt to address these obstacles, a small group of national educators, both researchers and practitioners, met initially in October 1979. After a series of meetings, this group outlined four major obstacles to the acceptance of Mastery Learning in the schools. These perceived obstacles included the following: 1) the attitudes and beliefs of the instructional staff regarding themselves and student performance; 2) the need for new instructional techniques and the redefinition of staff roles and responsibilities; 3) the difficulty of changing existing organizational structures and procedures; and 4) the presence of an ineffective, obsolete system of power and incentives governing conditions of staff service, performance, and influence.[6] As the group participants began to address these issues, the group named itself the Network for Outcome-Based Schools (NO-BS), selected a planning committee, and proposed a work agenda. The activities proposed on this agenda were aimed at assisting school districts that used Mastery Learning. This assistance was primarily extended in the area of staff development. By January 1981 the following premises were agreed upon by the planning committee:

1) Almost all students are capable of achieving excellence in learning the essentials of formal schooling.
2) Success influences self-concept; self-concept influences learning and behavior.
3) The instructional process can be changed to improve learning.
4) Schools can maximize the learning conditions for all students by:
    a) establishing a school climate which continually affirms the worth and diversity of all students;
    b) specifying expected learning outcomes;
    c) expecting that all students perform at high levels of learning;
    d) ensuring that all students experience opportunities for personal success;

e) varying the time for learning according to the needs of each student and the complexity of the task;

f) having staff and students both take responsibility for successful learning outcomes;

g) determining instructional assignments directly through continuous assessment of student learning; and

h) certifying educational progress whenever demonstrated mastery is assessed and validated.[7]

In this outcomes based educational system set forth by the planning committee of the Network, students are evaluated by their progress in achieving concrete goals, rather than being compared to other students. The selection and adjustment of instructional approaches in order to accommodate the learning rates of students and the achievement of specified goals become the criterion for success by instructor and the student, respectively. Credit is awarded whenever mastery occurs.

To provide an operational framework for this outcomes based learning system, the Network membership concurs that the following operational components should be present:

1) Publicly determined and stated learning outcomes for all students.

2) Derived from these learning outcomes, a criterion-referenced assessment system which documents, records, reports, and awards credit for student attainment.

3) Derived from these learning outcomes, objectives-based core and alternative curricula.

4) Derived from these learning objectives, a systematic process for planning and providing instruction appropriate to each student and for engaging the student until learning outcomes are attained.

5) A criterion-referenced information management system at the classroom and building levels for coordinating timely instructional planning, student assessment and placement, instructional delivery, and program evaluation.

6) An evaluation/certification system that allows students to demonstrate and receive credit for improved levels of performance at any time.

7) A program evaluation component that guides instructional planning by comparing the learning outcomes of program graduates with the performance demands of post-school roles.[8]

This framework for outcome based education provides only the basic direction for a school. The outcomes established for students should be developed and endorsed by all who have a direct interest in the schools and in the resulting "product"--the educated student. Once the specific goals for a school are established, they should be published for all parents, students, and the community to see. A student and his parents should know what is expected of him in both instruction and assessment.

NATIONAL EFFORTS IN OUTCOME BASED EDUCATION

According to the National Association of State Boards of Education, at least 30 states have identified student learning outcomes. This fact illustrates the growing acceptance of the need to identify and describe what students ought to "know and be able to do" and what level of proficiency they should be able to demonstrate. In addition, professional groups in nearly every subject area are writing outcome standards and are advocating that their membership begin to use these standards. The National Council of Teachers of Mathematics (NCTM) issued its standards in 1989, and other professional groups in the arts, civics, English/language, geography, history, science, and other subjects are expected to follow the lead of NCTM. The establishment of standards by these organizations might push the nation's educational system toward a curriculum of heightened expectations.

Evidence of the growth of outcome based education can be found in the array of schools across the country that have begun to restructure their educational programs to use learning outcomes.

ALHAMBRA HIGH SCHOOL IN PHOENIX, ARIZONA

Eighteen teachers (from a staff of 135) volunteered in 1987 to apply the philosophy and operational principles of Spady's Outcome Based Education to various subject areas. The teachers defined the intended outcomes for their courses and for the units within those courses, aligned performance criteria with the intended outcomes, and allowed students the time they needed to learn and to demonstrate outcomes. They also raised the expectations for minimum acceptable performance from the traditional grading system (A,B,C,D, or F) to an "A" (90 percent competency or above) or "B" (80 percent competency or above) grading system. Students who do not earn an "A" or "B" are given a grade of "incomplete" and cannot move on until an "A" or "B" is earned.

While formal evaluations of Alhambra's program have not been conducted, the participating teachers report increases in student attendance, attention to course work, confidence, motivation, and self-esteem.

GLENDALE UNION HIGH SCHOOL DISTRICT IN GLENDALE, ARIZONA

In 1979, the Glendale Union High School District allowed teachers in its nine high schools to voluntarily implement pure Mastery Learning in core academic areas (e.g., English, math, and science) for students in grades 9-12.   In 1984, OBE was also implemented in the nine high schools, but did not replace Mastery Learning. Instead, OBE and Mastery Learning were applied in all grades and in all subjects, not just core academics. Half of the district's teachers choose to use Mastery Learning, while the remainder used OBE. Under OBE, students will need to meet six exit outcomes to graduate, beginning with the class of 1997. Presently, students must earn a grade of "3" (70-79 percent competency), "4" (80-89 percent competency), or "5" (90-100 percent competency) to pass outcome based subjects.

Since OBE was implemented in 1984, student achievement data in Glendale shows that OBE students achieve a higher percent of desired subject outcomes than Mastery Learning students and non-OBE students. Results from the 1990-91 Student Achievement tests[9] in Algebra I shows that OBE students achieved 83 percent of the desired subject outcomes, Mastery Learning students achieved 69 percent, and non-OBE students 62 percent.   In biology, OBE students achieved 74 percent of the desired subject outcomes, Mastery Learning students achieved 68 percent, and non-OBE students 58 percent. In English I and II, OBE students achieved 78 percent and 88 percent of the desired subject outcomes, Mastery Learning students achieved 77 percent and 87 percent, and non-OBE students 70 percent and 79 percent. OBE students also achieved a higher percentage of subject outcomes in government and world history courses.

LITTLETON HIGH SCHOOL IN LITTLETON, COLORADO

In 1987, Littleton High School implemented an OBE curriculum that has made the school a national OBE model. Graduation requirements are defined not in terms of completing required courses but by students' ability to demonstrate proficiency on 19 different outcomes in such areas as communication, health, and personal ethics (e.g., each student must possess the ability to state why he believes in a certain religion and must develop the ability to question his religion). Students receive traditional grades (A, B, C, D, or F) in core subjects (e.g., English and mathematics), but receive a "complete" or "incomplete" grade in the demonstration of the 19 outcomes.

Formal evaluations of this program will be completed in 1998. Anecdotally, teachers report a heightened student awareness of their accountability for learning.

TOWNSHIP HIGH SCHOOL DISTRICT 214 IN ARLINGTON HEIGHTS, ILLINOIS

In 1985, District 214 implemented OBE in its six high schools. The major focus of curriculum development was the identification and documentation of what students should know, be able to do, and believe. The OBE curriculum has been applied to all subjects and all students in grades 9-12. In addition, students must demonstrate mastery of ten exit outcomes to graduate (e.g., communication skills, problem-solving skills, and value judgment skills). To demonstrate learner outcome or exit outcome mastery, a student must earn a "C" (70-79 percent competency) or higher, using a traditional grading system (A, B, C, D, or F grades).

While formal studies have not been conducted on District 214's OBE program, school officials report that the district's number of National Merit Finalists has tripled under the OBE system even though the district's student enrollment has declined since 1985.

JOHNSON CITY CENTRAL SCHOOL IN JOHNSON CITY, NEW YORK

Johnson City Central School implemented pure Mastery Learning in 1972 in its two elementary schools and its middle and high schools. In 1984, pure Mastery Learning was replaced by an Outcomes-Driven Development Model (ODDM), the creation of the Superintendent of Johnson City, Dr. Albert Mamary.

ODDM is a comprehensive, 20-component program outlining board, district, school, and classroom policies and procedures for reform efforts. ODDM is guided by four questions, which collectively produce what Mamary refers to as a "vision of education": 1) What do you know? 2) What do you want? 3) What do you believe? 4) What do you do?[10]

ODDM's goal for all students is to learn the school's outcomes well and to develop the school's five exit behaviors: 1) Students are to have high self-esteem, both as learners and as persons; 2) They will be able to function at high cognitive levels; 3) They will be good problem-solvers, communicators, and decision-makers; will be competent in group processes; and will be accountable for their own behavior; 4) They will be self-directed learners; and 5) They will have concern for others. To show mastery of an outcome, students must achieve a 70 percent competency level or better.

There is considerable achievement data showing the success of the Johnson City School Model. Data is abundant for this case study because ODDM uses an instructional process that is research-based and all staff development is geared toward continuous improvement of instruction. From 1986-1991, Johnson City students have consistently scored above county and state levels on the New York State Pupil Evaluation Program (PEP) in math and reading; the New York State Regents Exam in the 11 content areas it evaluates; and the California Achievement Test (CAT) in math and reading.[11]

MINNESOTA

In addition to the school districts examined above, the state of Minnesota has been a leader among state governments in considering OBE. Minnesota's Legislature planted the seeds for outcome based education in the 1970s with learner goals. In the 1980s, learner goals evolved into learner outcomes that were developed by a few school districts which chose to practice OBE. In 1983 the Minnesota Department of Education began active study and development of OBE as a part of the state's response to national reports which depicted public education as outdated and ineffective. The State Board of Education approved ten sites as pilot OBE demonstrations across Minnesota.[12] The state Department of Education's Office of Educational Leadership worked with the ten sites to determine the effectiveness of an outcome-based system of education.

During the first year of the OBE pilot project, researchers were asked not to collect test score data because of its association with traditional educational methods. During the second year, however, because of the political nature of project funding, researchers attempted to document the "perceived" effects of the changes brought about by the implementation of OBE. Qualitative research methods, such as case studies and interviews, were used, and the results included two perceived effects on student learning: 1) improved learning and 2) increased student involvement in learning. While limited, this data does provide some initial evidence of the effects of an outcome-based approach to instruction.[13]

In 1991, the Minnesota Legislature expanded this project to 30 pilot sites across the state with a two year grant of $40,000 for each site. Funding for the 30 sites expired in June 1993 and was not re-allocated because the state government hopes to implement OBE statewide for all students enrolled in kindergarten through grade 12. The first class that will graduate under this proposed plan is the class of 2000. Under the state's proposed OBE curriculum, six exit outcomes, such as "communicates effectively" and "works well with others," must be demonstrated by students. Students would be graded on a scale of "1" through "4." A grade of "1" would indicate that the student has not demonstrated the outcome, a "2" would indicate a below average demonstration of an outcome, a "3" would indicate an average demonstration, and a "4" would indicate an above average demonstration. In addition to exit outcomes, students must achieve a 70 percent or higher grade in all subjects to graduate. Even though the Minnesota Legislature has already appropriated $2.2 million dollars in 1993 and 1994 to implement OBE on a statewide basis, the proposed OBE curriculum will only be subjected to public hearings in the autumn of 1993.

OBE IN PENNSYLVANIA

Pennsylvania's state government has been supportive of the state Department of Education's efforts to establish regulations and guidelines that attempt to provide the children of the state with the best possible education. Since the mid-1960s, Pennsylvania schools have operated under the Goals of Quality Education, a comprehensive list of goals to be met by the curriculum of each district. In 1979, these goals were revised and expanded. In the spring of 1989, the State Board of Education undertook a major revision of the State School Code. Those new regulations changed the traditional way that schools can organize and manage their instructional day. These regulations also allow school districts to use students' learning needs to drive the length of time for each class or course.

The change is notable because it placed the learning needs of the students above the usual parameters of time and lock-step schedules. Rather than determining how many minutes or hours students spend in math class, for example, the new regulations establish *what* students should learn. Rather than time being constant and learning being a variable, time will become the variable and learning the constant. "How" and "what" students learn will be determined not by a list of required subjects with allotted times, but by a set of skills and a body of knowledge which all students will be expected to learn.

Pennsylvania, like many other states which are engaged in school reform, began its restructuring plan by supporting a number of programs and projects, both "state-directed preparation activities" and "field organization readiness activities." Examples include projects such as the State Arts Advisory Council, the Pennsylvania Governor's Schools of Excellence, the Pennsylvania Arts Education Advisory Council, the Environmental Education Office, Benchmarks of Excellence, RE:Learning, the Pittsburgh Fund for Arts Education, and the Pennsylvania Geographic Alliance, to name a few. These programs and projects all focus on the state's revised educational goals and direct the attention of community leaders, educators, and parents to what students should be learning and achieving.

From 1990 to 1992 the State Board of Education established a process by which each of the ten Quality Goals of Education would be defined by a set of outcome statements. Specifically, these outcomes would describe the knowledge, skills, attitudes, and habits that students should demonstrate in order to achieve the intent of each goal and to fulfill state requirements for graduation. A concerted effort was made to solicit responses from all persons interested in the revisions to the State School Code. Committees of educators and others with vested interests and expertise were brought together to write the outcomes. Specialists in subject matter and experts on instructional strategies met and crafted initial outcomes. Representatives from professional associations, such as the Pennsylvania State Education Association, were also invited to participate, as were school administrators, teachers, and program specialists from the Department of Education.

After a year's work, the first draft of proposed amendments to the school regulations were ready for review. In 1991, thousands of copies of this first draft of amendments were disseminated with requests for reactions. Public hearings on this draft were conducted in 14 locations across the state and the proposed regulations were published in the *Pennsylvania Bulletin* for public comment. In September 1991, the first draft of 572 student learning outcomes, to accompany the proposed regulation amendments, were disseminated to the public. On March 12, 1992, the State Board adopted the revisions to the State School Code, rescinded the former student learning outcomes, and requested new student learning outcomes. In April 1992, the new revisions to the Code and the proposed student learning outcomes were sent to the *Pennsylvania Bulletin* for publication. In May and June of 1992, these proposed outcomes were then discussed at a series of public hearings, held at various cities throughout the state, in which comments were sought from the public.

Concurrently, the revised versions of the Code, including the proposed student outcomes, were being studied by the House and Senate Education

Committees, as well as the Independent Regulatory Review Commission (IRRC). By July 1992, the original list of 572 student learning outcomes had been refined to 52 through an attempt to remove from the student learning outcomes list outcomes that were the source of opposition to this effort. At this time, the State Board reviewed the hearing testimony and suggestions made by the House and Senate Education Committees and IRRC; then made further revisions in the 52 outcomes. In September 1992, when the State Board met in regular session, it deferred action on the student learning outcomes but encouraged school districts to continue their strategic planning efforts based upon the approved revisions (minus the student learning outcomes) to the Code.

Concerns expressed by opponents of the learning outcomes are said to be the main reason for the Board's delay in voting, as the board discussed ways to accommodate the views of the two education committees and IRRC. The Board's caution was to be expected, as both the Board and state legislators were being contacted by opponents to student learning outcomes. While different points of view were welcomed by the Board, Board members had not expected such a vigorous response from opponents to this effort. Throughout the state, pockets of protesters began to speak out, both at public meetings and in the media. Two groups opposed to OBE were the National Association of Christian Educators/Citizens for Excellence in Education (CEE) and the Pennsylvania Parents Commission. There was also opposition to the Code revisions from members of the House of Representatives, led by Representative Ron Gamble (D-Allegheny). In April 1992, Representative Gamble began issuing a weekly "Gamble-Gram," a newsletter opposed to OBE.

The major criticisms of OBE by its opponents in the state are the following: 1) that there is as much evidence illustrating that OBE does not work as there is that OBE works, 2) that many of the student outcomes call for the teaching and testing of ideas and concepts that are within the "affective" domain (such as attitudes, emotions, and feelings), and 3) that the cost of the program will be much higher than projected by the Pennsylvania Department of Education.

Meetings were organized by various groups (both supporters and detractors) and held throughout the state. Some of the meetings were held by the State Board as part of its public hearing process, some by school districts in reaction to questions from their citizenry, some by parent-teacher organizations, and some by interested civic and educational support groups, such as CEE.

On November 2, 1992, in the midst of this public controversy, the State Board of Education's committee on revisions approved the student learning outcomes with recommendations to the Board for two changes: 1) highlight the prohibition on requiring students to hold or express particular attitudes, beliefs, or values by moving its placement to a more prominent section (at the beginning of the first section), and 2) give districts additional time to submit their strategic plans. The committee's report to the Board also addressed some of the major issues raised as a result of three public hearings held in response to recommendations to do so by the House and Senate Education Committees and IRRC. In brief summary, five major issues were raised:

1) Clarity of language. A request to more precisely specify the outcomes.
2) Benchmarks and state assessments. Addition of a new subsection to specify state assessment benchmarks and to strengthen the language to include a description of how local school districts will measure transitional outcomes and address the needs of students who have difficulty in meeting them.
3) Outcomes required for high school graduation. A proposal to drop some outcomes and to express others in more clearly measurable terms.
4) Attitudes, beliefs, and values. Addition of the following sentence to the revisions was proposed: "Achieving the outcomes in this section shall not require students to hold or express particular attitudes, values, or beliefs."
5) Specificity. Belief that the outcomes as written allow for school districts to adapt the regulations with local control meeting state expectations.

On January 14, 1993, the State Board of Education approved "student learning outcomes," the final section needed to complete the revision of regulations governing assessment, curriculum, and vocational education approved by the Board in March. Prior to its final vote, the Board adopted some changed in the regulations as suggested by Governor Robert P. Casey. The Board eliminated an outcome requiring that "all students know and use, when appropriate, community health resources" and one dealing with the historical and social development of families. The Board also honored the Governor's request to require that student outcomes and criteria for state assessments be reviewed annually. The Board, however, did not delete all of the outcomes which had generated controversy. The Governor responded by expressing his reservations about this action and by noting that a consensus on the educational reforms would be more difficult to achieve.

On March 31, 1993, Governor Casey announced a revamped version of the regulations. He stated that he and education leaders had been working for weeks on the revision, and he stated that the changes would help students reach their highest level of academic achievement. Some of the changes included the deletion of the goals "appreciating and understanding others" and "personal, family and community living" from the regulations. OBE opponents contend that most of these affective outcomes were simply reworked and shifted to another section. One of the biggest changes called for dividing goals into two sections: academic and common core. In order to graduate, students would have to master goals such as "communications," "mathematics," and "career education and work and citizenship." Teachers would be asked to help students develop "common core" goals, such as adaptability to change, ethical judgment, and self-worth. "It is time to close ranks and move forward in a spirit of mutual cooperation and understanding to build an educational system which concentrates on the primary goal of public education: superior academic achievement for all of our children," said Casey. On April 14, 1993, the revisions were reviewed and approved by the State Board of Education.

The approved revisions were then sent to the education committees of the House and Senate where the revisions were approved. These committees then sent the revisions to the IRRC, the final approval needed before the regulations became law. IRRC followed suit by approving the revisions. Finally, the Attorney General provided his reluctant approval to OBE in July 1993, when he certified the new regulations were legally in order. Several legislators within the General Assembly plan to continue their fight against OBE through legislative measures, such as a bill to allow schools to "opt-out" of the OBE plan.

OPPOSITION TO OBE IN PENNSYLVANIA

The introduction of OBE as an educational reform has spurred widespread opposition during a time when a majority of citizens are demanding improvements in the performance of the nation's schools. Nine arguments against OBE are heard most frequently in the state. These arguments are set forth below. Through the process of compromise between OBE proponents and opponents, some of these arguments have been eliminated or mitigated to some degree.

MISLEADING JARGON

OBE opponents contend that OBE is packaged in deceptive language that misleads parents. Opponents insist that public school administrators have an obligation to present "reform" plans in plain English, allowing parents to easily understand the objectives, the methods, the contents, and the differences between OBE and traditional schooling.

The Argument. OBE advocates continually use double-entendre expressions that parents assume mean one thing but really mean something different in the OBE context. When they talk about "new basics," for example, OBE supporters are talking about attitudes and outcomes, not such academic subjects as arithmetic, reading, and writing. The following statement from OBE literature is typical: "OBE schools are expected to become 'success based' rather than 'selection orientated' by establishing the instructional management procedures and delivery conditions which enable all students to learn and demonstrate those skills necessary for continued success." "Success" for all children means success in demonstrating only the "dumbed-down" outcomes that the slowest learners in the class can obtain. OBE means success in mediocrity rather than excellence.

LACK OF PROVEN OBE SUCCESS

OBE opponents object to extensive changes in our education system in order to adopt a system that has not conclusively proven to be effective. OBE advocates are not able to produce any replicable research or pilot studies to show that the system works.

The Argument. The best test of an OBE-type system was Chicago's experiment in the 1970s with professor Benjamin Bloom's Mastery Learning (ML) concept, which is arguably the same as OBE. This experiment proved to be a failure and was abandoned in 1982. The test scores proved to be low, and the illiteracy rate rose.

LACK OF ACCOUNTABILITY

OBE opponents contend that OBE offers no accountability to parents, students, taxpayers, or teachers.

The Argument. Because OBE includes no objective standards of achievement that are measurable the state might invest years of effort and millions of tax dollars before educational authorities will truly know if students are being effectively educated.

At present, secondary schools are structured on a measurable grid called "Carnegie units." The traditional high school curriculum includes four units of English; three units each of mathematics, science, and social studies; two units each of arts and humanities; a unit of health and physical education; and several electives. After a certain number of these units are completed, normally 21, a high school diploma is awarded.

Outcome based education replaces these units with vague and subjective "learning outcomes" that cannot be measured objectively by standardized tests and for which there is no accountability to parents and taxpayers. Because of the vague language used in student learning outcomes, OBE will make it virtually impossible to conduct any kind of tests that allow comparisons with students in other schools, other states, or prior years. Under OBE, grades have no relation to academic achievement and knowledge. Colleges will have no criteria by which to judge whether students are ready for admission.

OBE PROMOTES MEDIOCRITY

OBE opponents contend that OBE will promote mediocrity and stifle individual potential for excellence and achievement by holding the entire class at the level of learning attainable by every child.

The Argument. OBE is based on the unrealistic notion that every child in a group can learn to the designated level and must demonstrate mastery of a specific outcome before the group can move on. The faster learners are not allowed to progress, but are given busy work called "horizontal enrichment" or told to do "peer-tutoring" to help the slower learners, who are recycled through the material unit until the pre-determined behavior is exhibited.

In order to master all outcomes, children with a particular talent are required to forfeit time in their area of strength. Because no child moves ahead until all students demonstrate mastery, the inevitable happens: the faster learners quickly learn to slow their pace in order to avoid extra work, and they give the answers to the slower learners so the group can move forward. Incentive and motivation are reduced and boredom and resentment increased. The final result of OBE is that all students demonstrate "mastery" of mediocrity and none can aspire to excellence. Every child loses under this system.

VAGUE/SUBJECTIVE OUTCOMES

OBE opponents contend that in an OBE system, academic and factual subject matter is replaced by vague and subjective learning outcomes.

The Argument. In an OBE system, the traditional subject-based curriculum disappears. New OBE report cards substitute check marks for grades, focusing on attitudes, behaviors, and general skills instead of individual subjects. Additionally, many outcomes are heavily layered with such "Politically Correct" themes as training for world citizenship and government (instead of patriotism), population control, radical environmentalism, and government "solutions" for every problem.

VALUES/ATTITUDES OUTCOMES

OBE opponents object to the fact that a high percentage of OBE "outcomes" concern attitudes, opinions, and values rather than objective information, and a large number of OBE's goals are affective (concerned with emotions and feelings) rather than academic (concerned with knowledge and skills).

The Argument. OBE requires students to meet vague psychological objectives relating to adaptability to change, ethical judgments, and self-esteem. Moving from one level to the next, and even graduation, is dependent on meeting outcomes containing behavior-change requirements and government-mandated attitudes.

Many of the outcomes are affective, which means that they concern attitudes, emotions, feelings, and values rather than academic achievement. "Self-esteem" is a major attitudinal outcome demanded by OBE. "All students understand and appreciate their worth as unique and capable individuals, and exhibit self-esteem." Many of the techniques used to change a child's self-esteem or his adaptability to change are psychotherapeutic, a practice normally reserved for licensed psychologists.

OBE thus involves a major change in the school's avowed mission. Henceforth, its mission is to conform student attitudes, behavior, and beliefs to prescribed school-mandated social norms, rather than to provide an academic education. Parents are concerned about what methods will be used to change behaviors that are deemed incorrect.

Parents who are trying to rear their children with strong religious values are concerned that a willingness to go along with the crowd is taught by OBE as a positive rather than negative attitude. Since "tolerance" is a major attitudinal outcome demanded by OBE, parents are concerned that this includes requiring children to give their stamp of approval to all types of lifestyles imaginable. Many OBE critics question whether children are mature enough to make decisions about issues of this sort.

Some tests in the OBE system include many questions of attitude and opinion for which there are no right or wrong answers. What is the correct answer, for example, to questions about whether the student "understands others" or "applies good consumer behavior"? Nevertheless, the student is required to conform to the government-mandated outcomes, whatever they are.

OBE raises the fundamental question of who should decide what attitudes, beliefs, and values a child should be taught. Should it be the parents or the state? Should the public schools be allowed to teach values that may be controversial or contradictory to values taught to children by their parents?

"BIG BROTHER" COMPUTER TRACKING

OBE creates a computer file on each child to track the child's efforts to master the learning outcomes. OBE opponents are concerned about who will have access to these files and how this individual student data might be used in the future.

The Argument. These "electronic portfolios" will take the place of traditional assessments and test results will become the basis for the school's effort to remediate whatever attitudes and behaviors the school deems unacceptable. The portfolios will include all medical, psychological, and school records, and they might be available to prospective employers after graduation.

The computer portfolio on each child plays an essential role in the tracking of individual students. The computer records how the child responds to behavior modification, his threshold of resistance to remediation, and his final attitudes vis-a-vis the mandated outcomes.

An OBE system, with its computer base will still jeopardize student privacy. This privacy certainly would be violated if these computer files would be made available to employers or prospective employers.

HIGH COST

OBE opponents contend that OBE will be costly to implement and administer.

The Argument. OBE entails higher educational costs for new computer capabilities, administration, and the retraining of teachers in an entirely new approach to education. These costs will be reflected in higher school taxes.

LOSS OF LOCAL CONTROL

OBE opponents also object to the loss of local autonomy in the education of their children.

The Argument. OBE involves increased state control of education at the expense of local control. Although OBE proponents claim otherwise, the new system increases the control of state and federal education officials because they write and approve the required outcomes, develop the curriculum, train the teachers, and judge the performance of the students. Even though local school districts may be told to develop their own plan for achieving the designated outcomes, the plans must be approved by the state Department of Education.

Although the process of compromise has eliminated or reduced many of the points of contention between OBE opponents and supporters, the debate on OBE has not been completed. To a large extent, the debate of Pennsylvania's OBE system has evolved into an argument as to whether OBE works, specifically whether Pennsylvania's OBE, as proposed, will work.

OBE Efforts At The Local Level In Pennsylvania

There are at least 30 states that have identified some form of essential student outcomes. Pennsylvania, however, is the first state to pull away from the system of amassing Carnegie units as a prerequisite to graduating, replacing it with a plan that requires students to demonstrate their attainment of desired outcomes.

As a result of some other state sponsored educational initiatives, such as Re:Learning, a number of schools in Pennsylvania have experience working with outcomes. This experience has enabled them to proceed in implementing the new OBE regulations.

The following schools in Pennsylvania have designed their instructional program, to some degree, around an outcome-based approach. This enumeration does not list several other schools in the Commonwealth that may be using performance as a criterion, but do see themselves as using OBE. Following this list is a closer examination of a few of the OBE programs currently being used across the state.

PENNSYLVANIA SCHOOLS USING OUTCOME BASED EDUCATION

Ambridge Area SD	Jenkintown SD
Altoona AVTS	Kane Area SD
Berks County AVTS	Lancaster SD
Boyertown SD	Lancaster County AVTS
Burgettstown SD	Lebanon County AVTS
Crefeld School	Mars Area SD
Daniel Boone SD	Mercer County AVTS
Dauphin County AVTS	Monessen City SD
Ellwood City SD	North Allegheny SD
Fox Chapel SD	Rochester Area SD
Greenville Area SD	Shade-Central City SD
Hatboro-Horsham SD	South Side Area SD
Hermitage SD	Trinity Area SD
Jefferson Morgan SD	West Mifflin SD

AVTS = Area Vocational Technical School
SD = School District

JENKINTOWN SCHOOL DISTRICT IN JENKINTOWN, PENNSYLVANIA

In 1987, Jenkintown School District's staff developed a consensus to adopt and utilize a system of outcome based education. This innovation was to be implemented over a three year period between 1988 and 1991, and orientation and training in OBE was to be provided for the teaching staff during this time. Following the training, the staff developed learning outcomes and then proceeded to differentiate affective and cognitive outcomes. The staff believed that affective outcomes should not be used as criteria for graduation and the awarding of a high school diploma. While the teachers recognized that they can have some influence on students' beliefs and values, they believed that they should not be held accountable for the attitudes and the values that students manifest because many other sources outside the school also affect attitudes, beliefs, and values.

Jenkintown follows the OBE model endorsed by the National Network for Outcomes Based Education, and its staff believe that all of the following principles must be in place in an OBE system for students to succeed: 1) Clarity of Focus--students know what they must learn and be able to do; 2) Expanded Opportunities--students do learn in different ways and at different speeds; 3) High Expectations--students can all achieve at high levels; and 4) Design Down/Deliver Up--students learn more efficiently if instructional programs are tailored to specific objectives or learning outcomes.

Since no evaluation has been conducted of the Jenkintown OBE program, no data is available on the success or failure of this program.

THE CREFELD SCHOOL IN PHILADELPHIA, PENNSYLVANIA

The Crefeld School is a small (66 students), private prep school that systematically began rebuilding itself in 1987. It operates as a performance based school guided by the common principles of the Coalition of Essential Schools. There are no grade designations at Crefeld. Courses are scheduled in two-hour blocks of math/science, humanities, and electives, and the curriculum is designed around conducting systematic inquiries into a few key issues. At Crefeld, teachers assume the role of coaches and students assume the role of workers who learn that hard work is an element of the school's culture. There are criteria for graduation, and a student must apply for graduation with a plan a year prior to that event. In order to graduate, a senior must successfully complete six exhibitions; these "exhibitions" are seen as the culmination of a student's school career. Undoubtedly, the size of this school permits OBE theories to be implemented more easily.

CONCLUSION

Four questions persist in the debate over the merits of outcome based education as an educational innovation:

1) Does OBE increase student achievement?
2) Will OBE teach values to students at variance with the beliefs and values of their parents?
3) Is OBE more expensive than traditional instruction?
4) Will OBE hinder students' opportunities to obtain admission to college?

These four questions will be addressed in this final section, and some final observations on OBE will be offered. In regard to the first question, it may be useful to examine an independent study of Jefferson County, Kentucky, by the Kyle Group of Boston. This study examined scores from this county's schools on a standardized basic skills test from 1988-1991. Since some Jefferson County schools had been attempting to reform teaching and learning there since 1983, these schools had five years of experience with learning outcomes. In the study, the county schools were divided into three groups. Group I schools were those which had made a long-term commitment to reform and restructuring. Group II schools were those that shifted from one short-term educational improvement project to another. Group III schools were those that believed that reform was not necessary.

The Kyle Group's results showed that the Group I school students scored two times higher than students from Group II or III on a standardized test. There were also increases in student attendance, parent and student satisfaction, and parental involvement as well as a decrease in grade retention and discipline problems. These differences in student behavior were seen in the Group I schools 83 percent of the time, in Group II schools 44 percent of the time, and in Group III schools 50 percent of the time. Within the Jefferson County schools, 81 percent of the students in restructured grades at Pleasure Ridge Park High School had no failing grades as compared to 73 percent of the students in traditionally organized grades.[14] Similar studies yield the same results.

The second question addressed the issue of teaching values. Indeed, research shows that it is possible to teach values[15], and one of the intents of an OBE approach is to do so. There has been a great deal of misunderstanding of the "values" issue throughout the process of revising the Public School Code in Pennsylvania. The citizens of almost every nation have some common values, values shared by all of the citizens. Although citizens of a specific nation may share a set of values, these common values will vary among nations. In the United States, the common values comprise the American character, which is comprised of values such as charity, freedom, honesty, responsibility, and self-discipline.

Because the school is a reflection of and preparation for society, the school cannot divorce itself from the issue of values. Schools, like all other social institutions, are a creation of society, and, as such, they reinforce its values. The Pennsylvania State Board of Education, established by the General Assembly to be the principal administrative regulatory body for elementary/secondary and higher education in the Commonwealth, has the statutory authority to "adapt broad policies and principles and establish standards governing the educational program of the Commonwealth." In its 1991 Annual Report, "Approaching a New Century," the Board took the position that the intellectual and social abilities of the child, not simply the child's knowledge of facts, is a concern of the schools. Reflecting that position, it adopted outcomes that deal with values. It was not the intent of the Board to usurp the right and responsibility of parents to instill moral values in their children. Rather, its intent was: 1) to reinforce the common values Americans share and 2) to teach those values to students whose parents have abdicated that responsibility.

Under Pennsylvania's OBE regulations, students will not be required to hold or express particular attitudes, beliefs, or values. The wording of the regulations states that schools "should teach students to improve the importance of making ethical judgements for the common good" and "convey to students the need for honesty, integrity, individual responsibility, and tolerance."

The third major issue raised by OBE is finances. The costs for outcome based education may or may not exceed the costs of the traditional schooling. This will depend on the plan adopted by each district. The costs involved with OBE are for staff development and curriculum revision. Staff development and curriculum revision, however, are necessary parts of annual school budgets. Therefore, the new school district needs created by the adoption of OBE might be able to be funded with the normal school budget in this area.

In seven of Pennsylvania's school districts where outcome based education is being implemented, three districts reported no net increase in costs for staff development and curriculum revision; one district showed a net increase in costs of two-tenth of one percent; and three districts reported small increases (of $7,000, $10,000, and $40,000). Of the 169 school districts that are in Phase One of Strategic Planning for OBE, 33 of those districts were surveyed by the Department of Education to discover what additional funding they plan to include in their budgets for OBE. Fifty-one percent of these districts say there will be no increase in these costs when they begin implementing the new regulations. The remaining 49 percent of the school districts that responded an increase in costs would be necessary, reported an average of $15,000 in additional estimated expenses. As in any program, additional costs will depend upon what each community includes in its strategic plan to improve its own schools, such as computer technology for tracking purposes.

The final major question raised by OBE is whether high-caliber, competitive colleges and universities will readily admit students from educational systems that utilize OBE. Providing a portfolio of achievements should be a distinct advantage to the student. In addition, the skills and knowledge of Pennsylvania students will be more completely stated through the use of portfolios and more detailed high school transcripts. As a result, students graduating from outcome based programs will be able to present more complete documentation of their achievements than will students from traditional programs. Many major universities and smaller private colleges welcome a "student profile," for it gives the applicant a more personal "showing." This system may lead to a better "match" of a student to a college which will meet his needs.

Based on the answers to the four major questions posed by OBE, it appears as if there is some merit in a system of outcome based education. There is evidence that schools that have struggled with school restructuring support a student learning outcomes approach because of improvements in their students' academic performance. Although these schools have not had an outcomes based system long enough to do quantitative longitudinal studies, the local test scores have, thus far, been promising enough for the schools to continue this approach. Additionally, the schools profiled in this chapter are convinced that they made the right choice in adopting the process of outcome based learning.

What must be addressed, however, is the need for assessment, which is both valid and reliable. That may not be an easy task, but it is a necessary one. Many OBE critics have good reason to be doubtful of exhibitions, performances, and portfolios; these individuals question whether or not these are just new terms for what they remember as "reports" and "projects." Teachers need additional training in the use of these new methods in order to better understand portfolio assessment. With valid and reliable assessment, the OBE system will take on a much greater degree of accountability.

Most importantly, OBE will only improve education if *all* of the outcomes are stated in clear, measurable terms. Outcomes must be clear so that parents, students, and teachers alike will know what is expected of the students. Further, the outcomes must be measurable so that the parents and teachers can see if the schools are performing their job. Outcomes must be established that are challenging and appropriate so that a "dumbing-down" process does not occur. Outcomes cannot be limited to exit outcomes (for graduating from high school). Benchmarks must also be established to assess student performance throughout school. Without benchmarks there can be no accountability.

Gifted students must not be held back, but must be permitted to progress at their natural speed. In addition, an OBE system should have a process to evaluate students on a continuum. The "GAP Report" strongly calls for performance standards with respect to each outcome and a process by which to revise outcomes and expectations in light of experience.[16] This continual self-assessment is a necessary component in any successful educational reform movement.

Certainly, the concerns expressed over the question of values teaching must also be addressed. The fears expressed by parent groups are real. Schools must devise a system of open and on-going communication with parents. Parents and other interested community members should feel comfortable in dialogue with teachers and school officials, and they must be afforded an opportunity to help decide what will be taught. Educators know that values are implicit in everything they teach and in the way they teach. In addition, teachers model values by their own interaction with students. There are, of course, also values which may be taught explicitly through case studies, lessons, and simulations. These values are the ones which must be agreed upon through dialogue with the community, which must be reassured of the fact that outcome based education is a localized, grassroots, "bottom-up" approach.

Change and innovation in schools is an especially difficult task since there are as many preconceived notions as to what a school should look like as there are citizens in the state. Pennsylvania will soon be followed by other states, such as Virginia, and other individual school districts that are attempting to improve their educational system's performance by implementing outcomes based education. Although its establishment of challenging minimum standards will be a useful addition to American education, will educators and parents be able to resolve the problems posed by OBE? Only the passage of time will disclose the answer to this question.

ENDNOTES

1. Karen M. Evans and Jean A. King, "The Outcome-Based Education" (San Francisco, CA: American Educational Research Association, April 1992).

2. William G. Spady, Nikola Filby, and Robert Burns, *A Summary of Essential Features and Major Implications*, in *OERI Models of Instructional Organization: A Casebook on Mastery Learning and Outcome-Based Education*, ed. Robert Burns (San Francisco, CA: Far West Laboratory for Educational Research and Development, April 1987), 1.

3. John Champlin, "A Powerful Tool for School Transformation," in "Revisiting Some Foundational Concepts of Outcome-Based Education," *Outcomes*, ed. William J. Smith, Spring 1992, 8.

4. Spady, Filby, and Burns, *A Summary of Essential Features*, 33.

5. Karen M. Evans, "An Outcomes-Based Primer" (St. Paul, MN: University of Minnesota, February 1992), 5.

6. Carol Murphy and others, eds., "Outcome-Based Instructional Systems: Primer and Practice" (Washington, D.C.: National Institute of Education, May 1984), 2.

7. William G. Spady, *Outcome-Based Instructional Management: A Sociological Perspective* (Washington, D.C.: National Institute of Education, January 1981), 7.

8. Ibid., 18-20.

9. C.J. Kyllo, "OBE: Finance and Achievement Summary" (St. Paul, MN: Minnesota Department of Education, February 1992), 6.

10. Tom Rusk Vickery, "Learning from an Outcomes-Driven School District," *Educational Leadership*, February 1988, 52.

11. Kyllo, "OBE: Finance and Achievement Summary," 9-13.

12. Wayne Erickson, Gilbert Valdez, and William McMillan, "Outcome-Based Education" (St. Paul, MN: Minnesota Department of Education, February 1990), 2-4.

13. Evans and King, "The Outcomes of Outcome-Based Education," 11-13.

14. *Education Week*, n.d..

15. Judith T. Witmer, "The Case for Testing Educational Administrators in Making Ethical Decisions" (Ph.D. diss., Temple University, 1989), 233.

16. Christopher Edley, Jr. and Sarah Robinson, *A World-Class School for Every Child: The Challenge of Reform in Pennsylvania* (Harrisburg, PA: Business Roundtable, November 1992), 29-30.

Chapter 19

Business Support for Education

Leonard S. Koshinski

INTRODUCTION

Forcefully, the cutting edges of the long-wall mining machine move across the face of a 100 foot seam of coal. Mists of water suppress dust which is potentially explosive and definitely damaging to a human's lungs. The operator sits in a reinforced cab of the long-wall miner orchestrating the process that would have required a score of miners a few decades ago. Along the entire coal seam, a series of roof-support machines creep forward to keep the mining area safe from cave-in. The noise near the cutting area is deafening. Fifty students let out a collective sigh of relief when the machinery is turned off and the guide asks for questions.

Are they a thousand feet underground? No, they are not in a mine at all, but in a building that covers approximately three football fields. The six foot coal seam is a prepared material of coal and concrete that simulates, as closely as possible, seam coal.

This is all part of the U.S. Department of Interior's Bureau of Mines facility located in Bruceton, Pennsylvania about twenty miles southeast of Pittsburgh. The students from seven school districts are part of an ongoing Partnership In Education brokered by the Mon Valley Education Consortium (MVEC). The MVEC is a public, nonprofit education fund with multiple educational initiatives serving twenty public school districts.

The creation and maintenance of school/business partnerships is one of these initiatives. In addition to the partnership with the U.S. Bureau of Mines, the MVEC has over 100 business partners linked with numerous school districts in western Pennsylvania.

Once the tour is complete, the students will select from ten project areas and return to the Bureau of Mines for a nine week internship, once each week for a half-day. Each student is assigned a mentor for the duration of the internship and work at a specially designed project in his chosen area. The menu of educational choices includes computer programming, destructive testing, ecology, electrical engineering, ergonomics, fire and explosions, geology, office skills, and robotics in addition to the long-wall mining area.

General Motors, Harbison-Walker Refractories, and the Pittsburgh Energy Technology Center are a few of the other intern sites that MVEC offers. High school basics are put to the test in the real world of work. Problem-solving, team building, and cooperative education are all part of this partnership. Unfortunately, the classroom to which these students and many students like them across the nation will return will be limited to "sit in your seat, open your book and do your own work." Is it any wonder that kids say "school is boring"; "it doesn't relate to life"; "it doesn't teach you to do anything"?

THE NEED FOR AUTHENTIC EDUCATION

By the year 2000 the United States will need 750,000 more biologists, chemists, engineers, and physicists. Everyone agrees that something must be done in our classrooms. As American education spirals downward by global comparison, nearly one million American students drop out of school each year according to the U.S. Department of Education. Dropouts cost the economy $147 billion in 1986 according to a report by the National Alliance of Business.

The Hudson Institute predicts that the majority of new jobs over the next 15 years will require some form of education beyond high school. At the same time the number of young workers entering the labor force will decline by 10 percent. To fill job openings, industry will have to dip into the pool of traditionally less skilled and underutilized population groups-- minorities and immigrants. "The hidden time bomb," says Apple Computer Chairman John Sculley, "is that in the 21st Century we won't be able to maintain an affluent middle-class lifestyle. We can't keep flipping hamburgers and making fried chicken for the rest of the world. We need skills for the information economy."[1] The same opinion is expressed in the *Suggested Action Plan for Business/Education Cooperation in Pennsylvania*, a study and series of recommendations by the Pennsylvania Business Roundtable.[2] Schools, however, continue to operate on an agrarian calendar preparing students for industrial competency in an information age.

Business and education are two vital but different streams that feed our American culture. Typically, business methods and values are more tangible--product oriented--while education is concerned with less tangible goals such as helping students become good citizens.

Motivated by the need for an improved labor force, businesses in Pennsylvania and across the nation are working with schools in a broad array of partnerships that affect every aspect of the education process. Nonetheless, there is no single state or national plan that coordinates these partnerships. Educators, prompted by increasing conflicts between resources and goals, have encouraged this involvement.[3] One company aiding public schools is RJR Nabisco Inc. through its five-year "Next Century Schools" project. This initiative will give away $30 million in grants to 45 schools with innovative reform proposals. The grants run for three years, though RJR is planning to extend some aid to schools whose reforms inspire copying and to give small replication grants of $100,000 to other schools. [4]Champion International, a Stamford, Connecticut paper manufacturer, was impressed by a 1989 Carnegie Council on Adolescent Development report, offered a partnership to a school board that was planning to create four middle schools. Champion offered an investment of two million dollars through the hiring of a full-time consultant, financing a summer school for low achieving students, and a bi-weekly training session for every middle-school teacher.

Many business organizations such as the Conference Board, the Business Roundtable, the U.S. Chamber of Commerce, the National Association of Manufacturers, the National Alliance of Business, and others have undertaken to mobilize resources and conduct programs aimed at external resource development and the education reform effort. This theme was underscored in an address by John H. Croom, Chairman and CEO of the Columbia Gas System before the National Association of Regulatory Utility Commissioners:

> The concern of business is the serious problem of maintaining the quality of the work force needed to operate our systems efficiently, safely, and dependably. The issue is as simple as that....Jobs are more and more high

tech, and more frequently they call for employees to be decision makers. Required skill levels are rising. The prospective employees who come through the door today should be better equipped in the three R's then their older siblings, and those we see five years from now should be even better. As we are finding, such is not the case; far from it.[5]

A need for a literate workforce goes beyond the workplace. Can customers understand their bills, comprehend safety messages, and grasp communications directed at them? Will the public generally be sufficiently literate to consider, much less comprehend, business-related issues that come before them?[6]

Students in authentic education settings within the business world are one part of needed national school reform. These are numerous well conceived programs with small or large business backing that are very effective. Some of these programs are outlined below:

Sanborn, NY. Eighty-two percent of participating students in the Harrison/BOCES Co-op Program, have continued their education for careers in business administration, computers, or engineering. Harrison Division, a major manufacturer, provides a work environment divided into a four-part exploration series which focuses on different departments, as well as involves employees to give one-on-one guidance and supervision for students. The two-year program involves students from 14 high schools. Of the 106 students who have graduated from the program through 1991, all have gone to college. Forty-two of 44 students who applied to the General Motors Institute were accepted into the program. In addition to gaining career knowledge, the students learn communication skills, organizational skills, study skills, and the importance of working with others to accomplish goals and objectives.

Southington, CT. A community, multi-level nursing facility and a school system bridged a gap between senior citizens (residents) and students so curricular, interpersonal, and citizenship goals could be realized. The Southington Care Center made sure that its residents continued to be part of the community.

Louisville, KY. The Louisville Gas and Electric Company and the Jefferson County Public Schools formed a unique partnership to ensure that capable young people will enter occupations relating to environmental research and technology.

Seattle, WA. The Boeing Company joined with other businesses, the local school district, and the local institutions of higher education to form the

Rainier Beach Teaching Academy, which nurtures students interested in teaching. Specifically, minority students were encouraged to enter the Academy to investigate the teaching profession and determine if it was for them.

Lincoln, NE. The law firm of Rembolt Ludtke Parker & Berger work with inner-city, multi-ethnic, high-need, elementary school students to increase their chances for high school graduation.

Austin, TX. With a ten year commitment and staff from IBM Corporation, Austin Independent Public Schools, along with numerous volunteers, created the "A+ Coalition," which seeks to improve public education and to increase parental involvement in the community.[7]

To be competitive in an increasingly global marketplace, Pennsylvania business needs a motivated, well-educated workforce prepared to cope with continuing economic and technological change through lifelong learning.[8]

A Historic Look At Partnerships

Rapid industrial changes in the 1800s necessitated the creation of education programs and institutions that could respond to the changing needs of the work force. Public schools were not without partners. Institutions of higher learning have conducted long-standing relationships with public schools to provide student teachers, pilot various curricula, and provide expertise. Most of the partnerships were forged from the mutual concerns of teaching and learning. Perhaps the oldest school/business partnership is the partnership between the Future Farmers of America (FFA) and young farmers.

Education partnerships began their growth in earnest in the 1970s stemming from the country's rich history of volunteerism. Social pressures of the late 1960s and early 1970s led both universities and businesses to address public school concerns. At the college and university level, partnerships addressed development of multi-cultural curricula, trained teachers to respond better to diversity, and worked on quality education issues for an increasingly disadvantaged school population. Pennsylvania college/university partnership initiatives ranged from the West Philadelphia Improvement Corps (WEPIC) to Clarion University's outreach to rural school districts. This outreach effort was led by the Center for Educational Leadership headed by Dr. Claude Perkins, now Deputy Superintendent of the Richmond School District in Virginia.

The early business-sector partnerships with public schools were motivated primarily by public relations concerns and the desire for corporations located in or near urban communities to be good neighbors. The substance of these early business partnerships focused on financial donations, write-offs of equipment, or purchasing awards for various student incentives for improved grades or attendance.[9]

The movement gained momentum in 1981 when Dr. Ruth Love of the Oakland, California School System pioneered the Adopt-A-School Program.[10] Businesses, large or small, were asked to adopt a school and provide external resources such as expertise or financial support. Similar programs sprouted in other cities. The Sara Lee Corporation propelled the adopt-a-school program to national attention with its support and other major corporations soon followed.

A national volunteer organization having more and more of its members engaged in school adoptions became the National Association of Partners in Education Inc. (NAPE) based in Alexandria, Virginia, since 1982. NAPE has become the official spokesperson for 200,000 education partnerships and school volunteer programs involving 2.6 million volunteers. It convenes various regional groups and hosts the annual Symposium on Partnerships in Education in Washington, D.C. The Symposium itself is a partnership sponsored primarily by the McKee Foods Corporation.

On the national scene the Association of School Business Partnership Directors, (ASBP) a group of practitioners in school/business partnerships offers expertise and collaboration with those individuals administering partnership programs. The ASBP meets twice each year, once as a conference strand of the NAPE Symposium.

Between 1983 and 1992 the number of school/business partnerships increased dramatically from 42,200 to over 250,000. For example, in 1988 more than nine million students, 24 percent of all public school students, were directly involved in education partnerships. Activities varied enormously, from small-scale projects which provided a school-to-work transition for selected high school students to city-wide partnerships such as the Pittsburgh Promise, a New Futures initiative grant from the Annie E. Casey Foundation, that features a jobs component. The Pittsburgh Promise is modeled on the Boston Compact that developed long-term goals for school improvement in exchange for business' pledge of employment opportunities for graduates.[11]

Partnership is the buzzword of the 1990s. While it was once the sole province of the education and business communities, partnering is increasingly used as a catalyst to stimulate and encourage reforms within and between a whole spectrum of service delivery systems. Today, we use the term "partnership" to describe any number of relationships.[12]

The growing partnership movement produced a wide array of initiatives among various partners as the agenda for school reform and innovation became more ambitious. Multiple partnership projects began to include the human service sector, community-based agencies, labor unions, health organizations/hospitals and city/county/federal government.[13] A number of public education funds in Pennsylvania and across the country have also been engaged in education partnerships either through grant programs or working on more systemic educational change. Many of these funds have been represented by the Public Education Fund Network (PEFNet) based in Washington, D. C.

Partnership arrangements are legion. No two look exactly alike, in part owing to the needs, resources, and abilities of the partners. One definition suggests:

> ...successful partnerships are characterized by an exchange of ideas, knowledge and resources. Partners form a mutually rewarding relationship with the purpose of improving some aspect of education. The relationship must be based on identification and acceptance of compatible goals and strategies. In addition, the partners should respect the differences in each other's culture and style, striving to apply the best of both worlds to achieve established goals.[14]

In most cases partnerships begin through individual or institutional relationships and grow as collaboration increases. Many are driven by the needs of resource-poor schools such as the partnership between Clairton City School District and USX Clairton Coke Works; other partnerships are driven by an interested business or parent. Given the variety of partnerships, it is almost impossible to categorize them. There are agreed upon steps toward a mutually rewarding partnership, however, which shall be addressed later.

WHAT IS HAPPENING IN PENNSYLVANIA?

Across the Commonwealth the involvement of business in education is growing. The process gained a significant profile in June 1991 during a governor's conference. This conference was entitled, the "Governor's Conference on Business/Education Partnerships: Building a Coalition for

Educational Excellence and Reform." A joint effort of the Pennsylvania Economic Development Partnership, the Pennsylvania Department of Education, the Allegheny Conference on Community Development, the Lehigh Valley Business/Education Partnership, and the Committee to Support the Philadelphia Public Schools. This two-day conference featured presentations by U.S. Secretary of Education Lamar Alexander, Governor Robert P. Casey, and Paul O'Neill, Chairman and CEO of ALCOA, who is concerned with national education issues.

The conference attracted a broad cross-section of educators and business leaders from across the state for the purpose of organizing a Pennsylvania Business/Education Coalition. Guidelines for the Coalition included:

- Ensure non-duplication of existing effort, fill voids, and extend needed reinforcement;
- Identify common barriers facing local partnerships and develop solutions;
- Act as an advocate for public policy reform;
- Assist in establishing and strengthening local partnerships; and
- Act as a communications network to build public awareness that there are problems and develop a consensus related to expectations.

The Coalition was not perceived to be a "super partnership" or to be a regulatory body. A board, reflecting strong business involvement, was appointed by the Governor .

The Coalition became the Pennsylvania 2000 movement and is presently addressing the National Education Goals. Governor Robert P. Casey and Edward Donley, Chairman of the Executive Committee of Air Products and Chemicals, jointly chair Pennsylvania 2000. It has received the support of an array of business and corporate interests across the state.

Currently, a significant number of school/business partnerships exist and thrive at various levels of development throughout the state. The overview that follows describes selected partnering efforts of business, higher education, and public schools.

SOUTHWESTERN PENNSYLVANIA

Pittsburgh and Allegheny County. Southwestern Pennsylvania is recognized nationally for its ability to form public and private partnerships to solve community problems, institute change, and promote progress. The economic redevelopment of Pittsburgh and its downtown renaissance are evidence of the collaborative effort of the Allegheny Conference for

Community Development and local government.

The Allegheny Policy Council for Youth and Workforce Development, a new organization formed May 12, 1992, is designed to help achieve the national education goals in Pittsburgh and Allegheny County. The Policy Council is a consolidation of activities by the Pittsburgh New Futures, the Allegheny County Commission for Workforce Excellence, the Education Fund of the Allegheny Conference on Community Development, and Partnerships In Education. Each of these efforts has pursued separate education and workforce development activities that will be merged into the new organization.

Business support for the Policy Council is seen by the representation of Allegheny Ludlum, ALCOA, PPG Industries Inc., Giant Eagle Inc., Duquesne Light Company, Miles Inc., American Micrographics, and WPTT-TV on the Council's Board of Directors.

The new organization's plans include the formation and implementation of long-range strategies aimed at solving community-wide problems in education and human development. It is also seeking to develop and advocate public policy to implement the National Education Goals; develop comprehensive education training, health care, and human service strategies; utilize funds more efficiently and develop new funding; and increase public awareness and understanding of community needs.[15]

The Allegheny Policy Council, an outgrowth of New Futures, will seek to develop public policy strategies that result in long-term systemic institutional change which will positively affect the quality of life and delivery of services to all children, youth, and families, particularly those who are at risk.[16] The structure and mission of the Policy Council builds upon the experience of the Pittsburgh New Futures: that systemic change occurs only with the active involvement of the community's stakeholders, the collaboration of existing service providers, and the rational redeployment of resources. The transition is supported in part by the Annie E. Casey Foundation.[17]

To date, three task forces have been named by the Policy Council: Early Childhood, School-Age, and Adult Workforce Development. Composed of community representatives from the fields of education, health, the judicial system, public housing, small business, social services, and youth services, the Task Forces are charged with identifying and recommending public policy strategies relating to the Allegheny Policy Council's mission.

While not a funding agency, the Policy Council's intent is to develop systemic public and policy strategies at the local and state level, to promote and facilitate the reallocation of resources, to highlight and consolidate effective programs throughout the county, to provide opportunities for strategic collaboration between city and county, and to reduce duplication and proliferation of programs.

The Policy Council is designed specifically to function as an agent of change. The Executive Board, made up of individuals and institutions with the power to formulate and influence policy, is informed by the broad-based Task Forces representing all sectors of the community and the institutions that serve populations at greatest risk. The Policy Council is neither a study panel nor a police force; it is a proactive model for collaboration and problem-solving.

The Mon Valley Education Consortium. The rapid demise of the steel industry affected the Monongahela River Valley in cataclysmic fashion. Robert Gleeson, director of the Center for Economic Development at Carnegie Mellon University, showed through his economic studies of the region from 1979 to 1989 that over two billion dollars annually was lost to the region's aggregate income. Communities and families were shattered. Out-migration of younger people numbered about 130,000 leaving behind "gray" or aging communities. The tax base of most municipalities was eroded.

In 1986 the Allegheny County Commissioners appointed the Mon Valley Commission to prepare a plan for revitalization of the Valley. The idea for an expanded version of the McKeesport Education Consortium, which was formed in October 1985 by the Allegheny Conference on Community Development and modeled after the Conference's Education Fund, was advanced. The Commission's Education and Labor Task Force recommended the formation of the Mon Valley Education Consortium.

The MVEC was established with the primary goal of creating a new spirit around public education. Today, the Consortium is a private, nonprofit corporation, independent of the 20 public school systems it serves. It acts as innovator, catalyst, and broker to deliver programs and opportunities to its member districts. It is supported by a mix of corporation, foundation, state, and federal money. Corporate and local business support for the MVEC are critical.

Since its formation in 1987, MVEC has leveraged more than $5.5 million for Mon Valley public schools located in four counties: Allegheny, Fayette, Washington, and Westmoreland. It is working with a group of corporate interests, governments and school districts and hopes to provide services to economically distressed Greene County in the near future. The MVEC has focused its energies on developing a broad network of partners--corporations, small business, colleges, universities, government, agencies, and foundations. [18]

The Consortium began modestly with a mini-grant program for teachers and with a determination to restore and build public confidence in schools. Gradually, school/business partnerships, college/university collaboratives, post-secondary education expectations, cooperative learning, strategic planning, and school renewal through teacher leadership initiatives were phased in to support and enhance school improvement strategies. Financial and non-financial resources were leveraged on behalf of schools. Businesses and communities were encouraged to become involved in the critical task of education.

The MVEC efforts closely parallel those of the Public Education Fund Network (PEFNet), a national association that has grown into a movement for rebuilding communities around their public schools. The Consortium is one of the Local Education Funds in the Network which has affiliates in 26 states.[19] Encouraging support and involvement of all community stakeholders--93 communities and 20 school districts--the MVEC initiatives are far-ranging because of the diverse area served and the focus on public school districts. Its business support numbers in the hundreds.

Business support on behalf of the MVEC is broad-based. This fact has been repeatedly demonstrated through the provision of external resources for the schools by the various corporate foundations and businesses of all sizes. Furthermore, this business support for MVEC can be seen in their support of the Great Idea Grants Program

When the Consortium was established, it was assumed that the local economies would eventually rebound. There is little evidence to date that this has occurred or that it will occur to any significant degree in the near future. The problems facing public schools now are just as daunting as they were five years ago. Shrinking resources complicate the issue. How can financial equity in education be achieved in the face of declining tax bases and complex legislative issues affecting children? How can exciting environments be created for learning when gross inequities in salaries, in per pupil funding, and in physical plants demoralize professionals and entire school systems? How can an aging population on fixed incomes be convinced of its stake in the success of its public schools?[20]

MVEC has attempted to address these issues through a series of programs. These programs are presented below:

Great Idea Grants (GIG). A mini-grant program for teachers and administrators to initiate quality learning projects outside the school budget. The GIG Program is supported by a grassroots network of School Action

Committees (SAC) in each district. These SACs have proven successful in bringing new people to the schools and in increasing community awareness and involvement. Local small businesses have been prominently represented on these SACs.

School-Business Partnerships. Business partners share their expertise in the classroom or provide a chance for students to experience the world of work firsthand, through on-site internships, mentoring, or shadowing activities. As the program has evolved and changed, several Consortium districts have progressed to become active partners in the enterprise, rather than simply recipients of services. Fifty-two businesses are in significant partnerships with multiple school districts.

Horizons/University Collaboratives. The goal of this program is to bring the resources of the college and university to member districts. "Horizons" was developed to help remove barriers that keep students from a post-secondary education experience. The University Collaborative put Mon Valley faculty members and students in the vanguard of new program development in both curriculum and technology. The MVEC became a single point of contact for brokering of college and university programs, beginning as early as middle school to focus student attention on existing opportunities.

Educator In Residence. This initiative brings well-known national and state figures in the field of education to the Mon Valley for one-day programs on a variety of issues as in-service educational opportunities for teachers and administrators.

Restructuring. A demonstration project, the School Restructuring Project begun in 1990, centers on the improvement of the quality of teaching and learning. Change is implemented through five major themes: collegial teaching, cooperative learning, integration of computer technology, parent/family involvement, and site-based management.

School Renewal. Formally known as the "School Renewal Through Teacher Leadership Project," this program develops a "critical mass" of teacher leaders in each school to maximize the talent and expertise. Another goal is to break the isolation that historically has existed in education by providing a forum for the exchange of ideas and information. This program is one of nine such programs funded by the Commonwealth. The School Renewal Program has laid a foundation for the strategic planning now ongoing in 14 of the 20 member districts.

Strategic Planning. Five years of partnership building have linked the

Consortium to a wide network of businesses, community-based agencies, governments, and cultural organizations. This network has engaged key personnel to work toward systemic educational improvement in the region. Instead of emphasizing the classroom or special student populations, these business, community, and education leaders are focusing on more substantial restructuring issues. Fourteen districts are presently in the strategic planning process. A Regional Planning Group is at work identifying additional student learning outcomes valued by business. This task force is composed of CEOs or their representatives from heavy and light manufacturing, retail business, high technology business, banking, medical, human service agencies, economic development groups, the arts, and higher education.

Even Start and Family Foundations. Two demonstration projects are under the MVEC umbrella. Event Start is a family literacy effort funded by the federal government. The program is designed to break the cycle of intergenerational illiteracy by strengthening the literacy skills of adults so that they can help their children. Family Foundations is a comprehensive child development program. It is part of a national demonstration project that coordinates existing agencies such as health, housing, and social services resources to serve low-income families with integrated, sustained support services moving them from welfare to self-sufficiency.

City of Washington, Pennsylvania. A grant from the Howard Heinz Endowment launched an intensive planning effort in 1989 for the formation of the Washington School Community Coalition. The Coalition's membership is demographically representative of the city. Local businesses have responded to the call for partnerships and have formed a number of meaningful authentic education experiences for students. The Coalition continues to assist in renewal and reorganization efforts to improve academic, technical, and vocational preparation of students.

NORTHWESTERN PENNSYLVANIA

Erie. Several years ago Erie County initiated a community-wide program to focus the attention of its citizens on the importance of excellence and quality. The effort attracted broad-based interest and support in an effort to affect every aspect of community life. In its infancy it was called the Northcoast Business League, but it is now known as the Excellence Council. Various corporations and small businesses are involved in the Council.

The education component of this quality program is directed by an

Academic-Industrial Committee. Single education issues are brought before a community forum where all aspects of the issue are addressed by knowledgeable spokespersons. The proceedings of the forum are videotaped and distributed through the community for further review and discussed by community groups. The Committee has achieved support by a consensus for change in the education delivery system.

Another part of this program that attempts to improve educational quality is the creation of an "Education Day." "Education Day" is sponsored by the Northwestern Tri-County Intermediate Unit in cooperation with the Erie Chamber of Commerce, IBM, Lord Corporation, Marine Bank/PNC, National Fuel, PENNCREST, WSC Weidenhammer Systems Corporation, and Xerox Corporation. Teachers and administrators of the Intermediate Unit are the guests of the business community for a series of keynote speakers and "breakout" sessions featuring various aspects of the business community.

Clarion. In the Clarion region of northwestern Pennsylvania, The Center for Educational Leadership is working with seven school districts to develop systemic partnerships among public schools, businesses, and Clarion University. Working in a rural area, educators frequently discover that it is often difficult to create business partnerships due to the great distances between many homes, businesses, communities, and schools in this rural part of the state combined with the fact that few large businesses are present with which to establish a partnership. The outreach in this case was to a wide variety of smaller businesses such as banking, home builders, local health care institutions, and resorts and motels.

The Center was assisted in its early efforts by the Mon Valley Education Consortium. It conducts numerous school-business partnerships, brings needed resources to schools, and convenes an annual Superintendents' Roundtable for businesses and educators.

The 1992 school year will conclude in the Clarion area with a business partnership arrangement that has 43 businesses sharing 882 hours of volunteer service by their personnel. An evaluation of the Consortium for School Business Partnership revealed that the partnership had five buildings in three school districts involving 110 teachers, 110 employees, 1,561 students, and 158 residents; moreover, the financial commitment was sizable.

Crawford County. The Crawford Central School District is collaborating with a Community Advisory Council. Composed of members representing business, industry, and higher and secondary education, the group uses an interdisciplinary approach to prioritize issues particularly those of school restructuring. The district's long-term objective is school restructuring.

CENTRAL PENNSYLVANIA

Harrisburg. The Council for Public Education, a private, nonprofit corporation, is in the process of strategic planning to identify its role in development programs to enhance quality education in the 26 school districts serving three counties (Cumberland , Dauphin, and Lebanon) of Central Pennsylvania. The Council is headed by a Hershey Foods executive and comprised of members of business, industry, and higher and secondary education.

The Council continues to lead in the Capitol Region 2000 initiative to meet the National Education Goals. It has completed its strategic plan and is in the process of project development. Other initiatives include a math and science alliance and a modified mentor program that targets students who may lack necessary skills for post-secondary education. An innovative program assisted by two local health facilities, the Polyclinic Hospital and Medical Center and the Capitol Health System, focus on pre-natal mentoring in a confined residential area, like the block parent program.

The Council continues to channel the interest in education of business partners directly to local schools for partnership formation. Business leaders in school involvement include: AMP Inc., EDS, GPU Nuclear, Hamilton Bank, Harsco, Hershey Foods Corporation, IBM, Mellon Bank, Pennsylvania Power and Light, and United Telephone.

Another program in the Harrisburg region that is sponsored by the Council is the Total Quality School Initiative. This is a partnership with Penn State University's Center for Total Quality Schools. Local businesses sponsor school teams for training and provide support and follow-up. One district completed its training this year, and five additional districts will receive training during the next school year.

Finally, a workshop on learning standards is planned on the regional level to address the issues of learning outcomes. Business and educational leaders will be invited to the forum.

Bradford County. In 1988 a business development survey conducted in the Bradford region by the Valley Economic Development Association (VEDA) indicated a need to improve the academic and technical preparation of high school graduates. VEDA is a voluntary, nonprofit organization serving the two state area of Waverly, New York and Sayre and Athens, Pennsylvania. A series of meetings between businessmen, educators, and community agency leaders resulted in the formation of an Education for Industry Program. The goals developed for this program are below:

- promote effective communication between industry and education,
- develop a cooperative program designed to meet the needs of industry for adequately prepared job applicants and help prepare students for careers in the vocational/technical field, and
- present opportunities for students to become familiar with a workplace environment through shadowing and internships.

The program seeks to demonstrate the relationship between academic subjects and their relevance in the work place. Offered to all tenth-grade students in 1991, each year a new class is added to the program with the inclusion of the new sophomore class. An evaluation is schedule to be conducted after the first three-year cycle.

SOUTHEASTERN PENNSYLVANIA

Delaware County. The Delaware County Chamber of Commerce delivers a variety of specific education programs to local school districts such as career guidance materials; economic education materials; energy materials; international trade seminars; a resource directory of mentors, plant tours, and speakers; and science fairs.

Philadelphia. Much of the present business support for education in Philadelphia began in the spring of 1985. At that time, The West Philadelphia Improvement Corps (WEPIC) emerged from the research of University of Pennsylvania undergraduates in an honors history seminar on urban university-community relations. The research resulted in a proposal to create a better and cheaper youth corps, one that would utilize existing resources.

The plan revolved around the premise that middle school and high school students who, up to then, had encountered academic difficulties in the traditional classroom might find success academically if the education process was integrated with real-world employment skills.[21] Joining into a partnership to implement this plan were the University of Pennsylvania; the Philadelphia School District; the Private Industry Council; the U.S. Department of Labor; the Philadelphia Urban Coalition; the Philadelphia Area Labor Management Committee; the state Departments of Education and Labor and Industry; the Philadelphia Housing Development Corporation; and unions representing the city's teachers, sheet metal workers and plumbers. [22]

After receiving financial support, the project was to begin with 50 youths in five West Philadelphia neighborhoods in July 1986. The MOVE fire--a fire that enveloped over a city block as a result of a standoff between city police and MOVE, a militant Black group--on Osage Avenue in Philadelphia dramatically changed the scope and schedule of the program. WEPIC was asked to involve *all* the young people affected by the fire and begin in the first week of June. The high profile and success of the project led to its implementation in other local schools.

The centerpiece of this project involves organized labor. A U.S. Department of Labor National Demonstration Housing Rehabilitation Project is run by a retired union carpenter and the chair of the Industrial Arts Department at West Philadelphia High School. Students learn construction skills and improve their academics in this after-school program. A wide variety of union members participate: carpenters, cement masons, electricians, plumbers, roofers, and sheet metal workers. In fact, this program has been driven by the Philadelphia building trades, specifically the carpenters union, as they joined the Philadelphia Federation of Teachers to help at-risk youth and revitalize the community. The partnership has broadened during the last few years to include a number of other schools and programs.

LEHIGH VALLEY

Educators and business leaders in the Lehigh Valley have been active for a number of years in forging business support for education. Early partnership efforts of the business/school community grew into LEHIGH VALLEY 2000. Task forces identified 18 areas of education reform, of which seven became a priority in a report issued by the group. These priority areas included streamlining regulations that impair educational improvement, avoiding duplication, raising the graduation age to 18 years of age (combined with an agreement not to provide working papers for failing students), and encouraging technology actively.

Businesses throughout the Lehigh Valley encourage employee involvement in education issues and make time-off work allowances for employees to serve on school boards and on other educational projects.

School Works is a project of the Allentown-Lehigh Valley Chamber of Commerce. This initiative is the formation of a liaison between schools and business that encompasses nine school districts in Lehigh County and two school districts in Northampton County. In true partnership fashion, business provides needed resources, and schools provide business with services and expertise.

Lehigh Valley Business/Education Partnership focuses primarily on vocational education with 30 business partners preparing students for the world of work. Students move through a series of vocational-oriented internships with businesses such as Daytimers (appointment books), M. W. Wood (institutional food caterers), and Rex Roth (hydralic and numatics).

NORTHEASTERN PENNSYLVANIA

Scranton. As a prelude to establishing greater business support for education in the greater Scranton area, the Chamber of Commerce conducted a membership survey of business and industry. It determined that 80 percent of the high school graduates in this region lacked the academic and technical skills to qualify for entry level jobs. Collaboration among business, community agencies, and education resulted in the formation of the Skills in Scranton Program. Chaired by Al Graft, president of Akzo Salt International, this collaborative effort organized six committees to address specific areas to improve the preparation of high school graduates for employment. More than 125 volunteers, 75 representing business, are engaged in committees that include: basic education, business speakers, higher education, employer workshops, job fairs, and mini-grants for teachers. The long-term goal of the Skills in Scranton Program is to produce a well trained workforce that can compete and meet the challenges of a global economy in the 21st Century.

WHAT MAKES A GOOD PARTNERSHIP?

Committed partners seems the obvious answer between business and education! The perfect medium in which to grow a partnership is a "learning community," one in which all citizens are committed to lifelong learning.

Becoming a partner is an investment in the future. Good schools produce knowledgeable citizens, informed consumers, skilled and marketable workers, and inspired leaders. Creating good schools, producing an environment that values learning, and rewarding hard work is not the sole responsibility of educators. Achieving these ends requires the cooperative effort of the community. Partnerships pay dividends to everyone involved.[23]

While there are many ways to establish a successful school/business partnership, most professionals in partnering programs agree that several elements are necessary for the full potential of a partnership to be realized.

TOP LEVEL COMMITMENT

There must be a commitment by the business or agency CEO and the school superintendent, between the business manager and the school principal. It is also very useful to have the active backing of the business' board of directors and the locally elected school board. This indicates a philosophical buy-in, as well as a commitment of employee time and resources.

Normally, it is helpful to have a third party act as a "facilitator or broker" in the partnership formation. A public education fund or Chamber of Commerce may play this role as a neutral convener, knowledgeable about several organizational worlds, and able to help partners bridge differences and set common goals. Few partnerships survive if leadership is not expanded beyond a single individual.[24]

GOALS AND OBJECTIVES

Enrichment and support of the educational environment in both the school and the business becomes the summative goal of each partnership-- an important step in creating a "learning community." Working goals of the partnership may address widely shared needs. Each partnership is unique and should be free to develop its resources in order to address its needs. Roles and responsibilities should be clearly defined, keeping in mind that their goals can only be reached through a joint effort.

COMMUNICATIONS

Effective communication makes for successful partnerships. In addition to the participants being aware of partnership developments, it is necessary to have a good public relations program to keep the varied "publics" of the community informed. Recognition and shared credit keep partners involved; they will feel that their efforts are appreciated. Acknowledgement of achievement is critical.

CLEAR ROLE RESPONSIBILITY

A clear understanding of roles and responsibilities at the outset of the partnership is vital. Roles and responsibilities should be clearly defined. Partnerships are simply the development of reciprocal roles and sharing of resources in order to achieve a goal that cannot be realized alone.

STRATEGIC PLANNING

The best partnerships follow the rules of strategic planning. Take time to plan well. A mission statement, goals and objectives, strategies to meet objectives, timelines, responsibilities, monitoring, and evaluation lead to better defined programs.

INVOLVE AS MANY AS POSSIBLE

Partnerships should be inclusive. They should involve every segment of the community that will be affected by them. Local ownership is important for success. As a variety of partners are drawn into the planning process, they begin to take ownership of it. As the project meets the community needs, it takes on a life of its own.

CRITICISM OF BUSINESS IN EDUCATION

The movement of business into education is not applauded by all. Critics are concerned about schools becoming the training base for particular industries. Some suggest that much of business' concern with education is really an attempt to rationalize business' failures.

American firms spend about $30 billion a year on improving the skills of employees. Corporate training devotes about 8 percent of that total to provide remedial classes in arithmetic, reading, and writing. Most of this training budget is used for high-level managers. Employees with college degrees are 50 percent more likely to receive training than are non-college graduates; executives with post-graduate degrees are twice as likely to get training as those with college degrees.

While the number of school-business partnerships has risen dramatically in the last decade, corporate giving to American education declined markedly in the 1980s, even as the economy boomed. In the 1970s and through the beginning of the 1980s, corporate giving jumped an average of 15 percent a year. In 1990, however, corporate giving was only 5 percent more than 1989; and in 1989, it was only 3 percent over 1988.

Where do corporate education dollars go? Most of the money rarely finds its way to public primary or secondary schools. Of the $2.6 billion that corporations contributed to education in 1989, only $156 million went to support American grade schools. The remainder went to private schools or to colleges and universities.

Critics also point to the economic development packages used to entice businesses to locate or to remain in an area. This competition for business among states and among local governments has grown more intense in the 1990s as businesses throughout the industrialized world engage in "downsizing" or "rightsizing." Consequently, the tax base of many schools is shrinking.

Other critics of business say that US firms are too eager to look abroad for workers. For example, a few years ago the nursing shortage was mitigated by importing 10,000 temporaries from Ireland and the Philippines on temporary work visas. A recent amendment to immigration laws strongly supported by American business, creates a new category of skilled immigrant to whom a visa will be issued annually. If an ample supply of foreign workers is available, why be concerned about a skilled work force at home?

BUSINESS NEEDS TO GET SERIOUS

To be competitive in the global marketplace, Pennsylvania business needs a motivated, well-educated workforce prepared to cope with continuing economic and technological change through life-long learning. Both the fast growing service sector and slower growing manufacturing sector will require better skilled employees to remain competitive.[25]

School-Business Partnerships offer an opportunity to acquaint students with career paths, offer strong role-models, deliver needed external resources, and build community support for education. Through "authentic education" students obtain realistic information about the world of work. Teachers' skills are upgraded and improved. A quality educational system benefits employees and employers.

In a society where traditional family structures and values have been eroded in the last two decades and where we are becoming multi-racial, multi-cultural, and multi-ethnic, education needs collaborative partners to meet the challenges of the 21st Century. Pennsylvania business has much to offer and gain by joining this education partnership to build learning communities.

ENDNOTES

1. Nancy J. Perry, "The Education Crisis: What Business Can Do," *Fortune Magazine*, 4 July 1988, 72.

2. Pennsylvania Business Roundtable, *Suggested Action Plan for Business/Education Cooperation in Pennsylvania* (Harrisburg, PA: Pennsylvania Business Roundtable, August 1990).

3. Alan Baas, "The Role of Business In Education." ERIC EA 47 990.

4. "Saving Our Schools," *Business Week*, 14 September 1992, 74.

5. John H. Croom, "Public Education Reform: A Business Necessity," Paper presented as part of a meeting of the National Association of Regulatory Commissioners Committee on Administration, Washington, D.C., 27 February 1991.

6. Ibid., 5-6.

7. "National Symposium on Partnerships in Education," at the meeting of the National Association of Partners in Education, Washington, D.C., 16-22 November 1992.

8. Pennsylvania Business Roundtable, "Suggested Action Plan."

9. Ibid., 2.

10. David Smallwood, "Business Adopts A New Approach to City's Schools," *Dollars and Sense*, February-March 1987, 12.

11. National Alliance of Businesses, *America's Leaders Speak Out on Business Education Partnerships: Proceedings and Recommendations* (Washington, D.C.: National Alliance of Business, 1989).

12. Terry Grobe, "Synthesis of Existing Knowledge and Practice in the Field of Educational Partnerships" (Washington, D.C.: Government Printing Office, December 1990).

13. Ibid., 5.

14. Regional Education Laboratory, *Business Education Partnerships: Strategies for School Improvement*, privately printed, 1986, 5.

15. Chuck Glazer, *Press Release* (Pittsburgh, PA: Allegheny Policy Council for Youth and Workforce Development, 12 May 1993).

16. Ibid..

17. Ibid., 4.

18. Mon Valley Education Consortium, *The First Three Years, 1987-90* (McKeesport, PA: Mon Valley Education Consortium, 1990).

19. Mon Valley Education Consortium, *Five Year Report, 1987-1992* (McKeesport, PA: Mon Valley Education Consortium, 1993).

20. Ibid., 1.

21.　University of Pennsylvania, *Annual Report 1987-1988* (Philadelphia, PA: University of Pennsylvania, 1988), 5.

22.　Ibid., 6.

23.　Mon Valley Education Consortium, "Partnerships In Education: A Guide" (McKeesport, PA: Mon Valley Education Consortium, 1989).

24.　Grobe, "Synthesis of Existing Knowledge," 30.

25.　Pennsylvania Business Roundtable, "Suggested Action Plan," iii.

Chapter 20

The Total Quality Movement in Education

John A. Leuenberger

Seldon V. Whitaker, Jr.

Historical Perspective

Over the past decade, Americans have become painfully aware of the challenges we face as a nation in a fiercely competitive global marketplace. There was a time not so long ago, that the label "Made in the USA" was an international symbol of quality. That is no longer the case. Rather, our trade deficit serves as an almost constant reminder that many of our goods and services are no longer as competitive as they once were in the international arena. We now stand toe-to-toe with nations whose workforces and work processes are simply better than our own.

The total quality movement began as a result of a visionary's dream to permit the American economic system to maintain its edge in what he perceived as a growing global market. This man was W. Edwards Deming, an American statistician who trained under Walter Schuhart, an American economist selected by President Roosevelt to head the Office of War Time Quality Control. Unfortunately, the reality is that no one in the American business community heeded Deming's warnings or responded to his teachings.

Directly following World War II, Deming was called to Japan to conduct a post-war census for the Imperial Japanese Government. It was during this period that Deming introduced his theories of "Total Quality Management" to the Japanese industrial leadership. He envisioned that the key to the success of any organization rests with the optimization of its systems. System optimization assures that everyone within the organization gains. The success of any organization depends totally upon its ability to know and fulfill the needs and expectations of its customers; a customer being defined in its external and internal context.

In Deming's view, top management is responsible for the success or failure of any organization. Contrary to traditional thinking, Deming's view perceives that the worker has little control over the destiny of an organization. In fact, the great majority of workers want to succeed at what they do, and it is the inefficiency of an organizational structure that frequently prevents success from occurring. If workers in a organization are permitted to have a say in their destiny, the organization has a greater opportunity for success.

If total involvement is an indicator of quality, it becomes incumbent upon the structure of the organization to allow for staff participation in the decision-making process. This concept allows the complete staff to have a say in the shaping of their destiny. This view corresponds to Deming's belief that intrinsic motivation is a key stimulator and that extrinsic motivators, while important, have less impact upon the efficiency and productivity of the worker.

There is widespread agreement that the essential components of "the quality strategy" are best illustrated through the statement: ...*listen to your customers; develop products and services that are better than your customers expect them to be; and, continuously improve organizational processes that lead to customer satisfaction.*

W. Edwards Deming illustrated his beliefs related to Total Quality Management through the publication of his now famous Fourteen Points or Principles. The Fourteen Points deal with specific behaviors and environments that must be present for a quality organization to succeed. These points are listed below:

1) Create a constancy of purpose toward the improvement of products and services.
2) Adopt a new leadership philosophy for the new economic age.
3) Cease dependence on mass inspection to achieve quality by building quality into the product or service in the first place.
4) End the practice of awarding business on price tag alone. Instead,

minimize total cost, often by developing a long-term relationship with a single supplier.

5) Improve constantly the system of production or service to improve quality and reduce costs.

6) Institute training on the job.

7) Institute leadership to help people to do a better job.

8) Drive out fear so that everyone can work more effectively.

9) Break down barriers between departments.

10) Eliminate slogans, exhortations, and targets for the employees.

11) Eliminate quotas and management by objective.

12) Remove barriers that rob all employees of their right to pride in workmanship.

13) Institute a vigorous program of education and self-improvement.

14) Put everyone in the organization to work to accomplish the transformation. Transformation is everybody's job.[1]

Deming's fourteen points have recently been adapted to the field of education. It is true that one may question the relationship between Deming's industrial model and its adaptability as a tool for educational reform. When studied in depth, however, the total quality model has major implications and profound possibilities. For the first time in the search for educational reform and innovation, the quality movement has brought forth a plan that is all inclusive.

In order to demonstrate the impact of total quality upon the complete educational system, we have opted to utilize the following graphic for illustrative purposes.

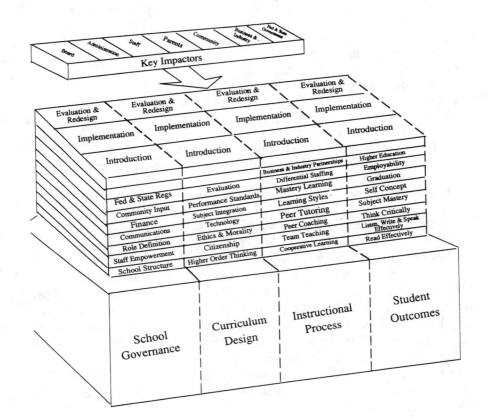

As the graphic illustrates, the success of the quality movement begins with its relationship to the key players affecting the system. This includes the school board, administration, staff, parents, community, business and industry as well as federal, state, and local governments. Each must understand the philosophy and beliefs which drive the quality program as well as the methodologies and tools which allow quality to evolve. Without this basic commitment and understanding on the part of the key players, the quality movement, like so many of the other well-intentioned reform movements, will fail.

If you look at past education reform efforts, most have concentrated on one or, at the most, two of the "educational impactors." The quality movement concentrates its efforts and energies upon all of these impactors: school governance, curriculum design, instructional practices, and student outcomes or expectations. Deming's philosophy of management, his desire to systemize the process, his belief in the involvement of the participant, his desire to work in cooperative groups, and his insistence on satisfying the customer all take on new connotations for educators.

Dr. Deming is uncompromising in his assertion that it is time for bold leadership and systematic change. It is his belief that "Transformation" is required in government and industry as well as education. Management is presently in a stable state. Transformation will be required to move management from this state of stability to one representing a new metamorphism. This transformation process cannot represent a mere patchwork on the present system of management, but must encompass a complete change of state. While we must continue to solve problems and stamp out fires as they occur, such activities do not change the system.

TOTAL QUALITY MANAGEMENT EXAMPLES IN OTHER STATES

Educational organizations throughout the United States are re-creating their work processes, systems of human interaction, mission statements, and their long-term vision and strategies. For example, in Glenwood, Maryland, the middle school has instituted New England-style town meetings for the student body. Before attending the meeting, every student works in one or more quality circle "S-Teams" with fellow students. S-Team (or Support Team) is a play on the word "esteem." In the teams students discuss how their work, individually and collectively, can be improved. They pledge specific efforts to help bring about the planned results in their "house" or grade, or even the entire school.

S-Team projects take the students into the community as well, for public service and town improvement efforts at nursing homes and hospitals, at home to improve family life, and at school for campus beautification.

Schools in Virginia's Rappahannock County have implemented TQM in virtually every aspect of the district's functioning. Reports cards have been designed by a parent-teacher-student team. Serious disciplinary problems on bus runs have been solved as a result of the efforts of a Quality Improvement Committee, composed of administrators, bus drivers, parents, students, and the transportation supervisor. In addition, results of district-wide customer satisfaction surveys have shown remarkable gains in the three years since the district began implementing Total Quality principles and practices.

Redwood Middle School in Napa, California, is solving its new problems generated by a growing population, such as impersonalization by creating cohort groups of teachers and students. Teachers are given time every day to meet with their student groups, to discuss the progress of students, to monitor their individual and collective learning processes, and to plan additional learning opportunities for the students. Learning at Redwood is a team project.

TWO EXPERIMENTS RELATED TO QUALITY REFORM IN PENNSYLVANIA

THE ERIE EXPERIENCE

In July of 1987, the Erie Excellence Council was founded to bring the concept of Total Quality Management to the Greater Erie Region. As a result of this decision, Erie, Pennsylvania become the model for other Pennsylvania communities to emulate. Erie area businesses, governmental entities, and educational institutions designated the 1990s as the "Decade for Excellence." The groundwork was laid for what was expected to lead the greater Erie community toward a higher quality of life. In essence, the movement represented a total community revolution.

Over 20 committees representing every phase of community life were established to work toward quality achievement. One of the most active committees has been the Excellence Council on Quality Education. The committee was given the assignment of developing a written plan to be entitled "Vision for Education," with implementation by the year 1999.

Five major goals were established to guide the committee forward in its mission. The first goal establishes that by 1999, the schools within the Erie Quality Region will be recognized as national leaders in the teaching and practice of quality. Goal two states that each institution will have developed and implemented a continuous quality improvement program at all organization levels. Goal three provides that small project teams will be utilized in the schools to address specific opportunities for improvement with emphasis on process improvement rather than problem-solving. Goal four states that schools will develop a system for quality assurance. Staff members will be trained in basic team dynamics, data utilization, and team processes. Goal five specified that all students graduating from area high schools will be knowledgeable about and be able to demonstrate application of continuous quality improvement concepts.

The Erie educational community has accepted the quality challenge with unprecedented enthusiasm. All of the 17 school districts within the Northwest Tri-County Intermediate Unit have agreed to participate in this experiment in quality. A number of projects are already off the ground and more are being planned for the future.

The educational quality movement for all 17 districts was officially launched in 1992 as a part of the celebration of the North Coast Quality Week sponsored by the Erie Chamber of Commerce and supported through the cooperation of business, education, and government.

Over 1,200 educators representing the 17 school districts within Pennsylvania's Intermediate Unit 5 assembled to celebrate the Greater Erie Area's move toward quality. The program consisted of a keynote presentation in the morning session and over 50 program selections during the afternoon. The evaluations which were returned at the conclusion of the day indicated that the program was a huge success.

As an added incentive, such eminent personalities in the quality movement as Joel Barker, Stephen Covey, W. Edwards Deming, and Myron Tribus made major presentations. The preparation for the 1993 celebration is already underway with planned return visits by Barker, Covey, and Deming and possible guest appearances by President Bill Clinton and Peter Senge.

Participation of the school districts in the quality movement continues with frequent updates on the progress of the Educational Excellence Committee and the development of its "Vision" document. Technical seminars also continue to be held to train school administrators in the use of quality tools.

Several districts now have trained teams in "Total Quality Teaching" (TQT) and will use these internal teams to train other personnel. In practice, many of the school districts have developed their training to the extent that the entire staff is heavily involved in the process. The remaining are continuing to explore the concept of quality, but have as yet to begin implementation at the building level.

THE CENTER FOR TOTAL QUALITY SCHOOLS

The Center for Total Quality Schools (CTQS) at Penn State University is the first university-based project devoted exclusively to providing K-12 teachers and administrators with the training, support, and research base needed to implement Total Quality Management principles and practices in the public schools of Pennsylvania. Housed in the Department of Educational Administration in Penn State's College of Education, the CTQS is well positioned to serve the training requirements of practitioners throughout the Commonwealth.

The CTQS evolved over a very short period of time during the 1991-92 academic year due to confluence of seven key factors:

A strong community quality council. TQM envisions systemic change in organizatons. School districts are arguably among the purest practitioners of the traditional or "Taylorist" management style, which enphasizes striving for higher levels of efficiency through strong managerial direction. School administrators who aspire to fostering systemic change can expect to encounter resistance and must have allies in the community who understand and support the change to TQM. Therefore, linkages with progressive business leaders can provide the foundation for developing community support for the successful implementation of TQM in the public schools.

Founded in 1990 in State College, the Total Quality Council of Central Pennsylvania has had a significant impact on the development of a community-wide understanding of, and appreciation for, the importance of TQM in all kinds of organizations.

Active participation. Both Penn State and the State College Area School District were founding members of the Total Quality Council of Central Pennsylvania. From the outset, representatives of both organizations shared in the efforts to develop the fledgling quality council. And, teams of employees from both organizations participated in comprehensive training programs offered by the Quality Council. Thus, educators from basic and higher education found themselves learning about TQM side-by-side with their counterparts from the private for-profit and non-profit sectors.

It became clear early in the development of CTQS that the business community views the educational community primarily as a "supplier" of human resources for their organizations. Hence, these businessmen do recognize the importance of ensuring that graduates enter the workforce already aware of the vital importance of quality issues. These linkages were vital in promoting the CTQS when funding was needed to "jump-start" initial activities in the development phases.

Strong commitment. An absolutely vital ingredient in TQM is leadership from top management. At Penn State, the university provost assumed leadership of the university-wide TQM effort. His previous experience with TQM while serving as dean of the College of Engineering has allowed him to move ahead decisively. The superintendent of schools for the State College Area School District was part of the initial school district team to be trained in TQM. He continues to play a leadership role in bringing the principles and practices of continuous quality improvement into the school district through direct training of employees. Also, two members of the State College Area District School Board received training in TQM through their role as employees of Penn State University.

Innovative in-house training programs. During the 1991-92 school year, the State College Area School District developed a prototype monthly training program for 85 first-line supervisors. The training group included: all members of the administrative team; subject area coordinators, most of whom are also part-time classroom teachers; physical plant supervisors; and cafeteria managers. In addition, the nine members of the school board were invited to attend and did so as their schedules permitted. The training series was led jointly by the superintendent and the president of the State College Area Teachers Association.

Close working relationships. Given the geographic proximity of Penn State and the State College Area School District, a history of positive working relationships has been cultivated between the school district and numerous sectors of the university. An especially close partnership exists between the district and the Department of Educational Administration. The superintendent holds an appointment as adjunct associate professor of educational administration. And, members of the department have worked as consultants to the district administration on numerous management projects. It was natural, therefore, that the Department of Educational Administration would be willing to assess the implications of TQM for the effective administration of public schools.

Positive Reputation. Penn State University enjoys a positive reputation for excellence throughout the state of Pennsylvania. Therefore, as the CTQS project began to take shape, the development team received a cordial and supportive reception from corporate partners and educational administrators alike.

IBM Grant Initiative. Perhaps, the single greatest catalyst for the creation of CTQS was the announcement by IBM of its TQM grant initiative for higher education. After deciding to develop a proposal, Penn State created a cross-functional team that included members of the Colleges of Business, Education, and Engineering. A unique feature of the Penn State proposal was the development of special working relationships with its "suppliers," K-12 school systems.

Within the context of this project, the decision was made to move ahead aggressively with the creation of the Center for Total Quality Schools in the spring of 1992. With funding and/or in-kind support from The Total Quality Council of Central Pennsylvania, IBM, Supelco/Rohm and Haas, Hershey Foods, the Pennsylvania League of Urban Schools, the Harrisburg-based Council for Public Education, the Philadelphia Area Council for Excellence, and Penn State's Continuing Education division, an initial two-day introductory conference on TQM in education was held in State College.

In the fall of 1992, IBM announced that Penn State had been selected from among over 200 applicants as one of eight recipients of the IBM grant. The distinguishing feature of the proposal was the inclusion of K-12 education as the "supplier" of higher education.

Taken together, these elements provided the foundation on which the Center for Total Quality Schools was built.

The initial activity of the CTQS was the Leadership Training Program offered during the 1992-93 academic year. Participants included teams from 15 school districts and intermediate units. The typical team of trainees included the superintendent or assistant superintendent, the president of the teachers' association, a building principal, and a classroom teacher. Each month the teams traveled to Penn State's University Park campus for a full day of training in Total Quality Management. The modules in the training series included:

September	Quality: The Challenge of the 1990s
October	Transformational Leadership
November	The Customer-Driven Organization
December	Systems and Variation
January	Continuous Quality Improvement
February	Teams and Teamwork
March	Quality Schools and Classrooms
April	Quality Measurement and Assessment
May	Planning for Quality
June	Partnerships for Quality Improvement

Also, in cooperation with the CTQS, Penn State's Department of Educational Administration conducted a graduate level course entitled "Total Quality Management in Education" during the spring term of 1992-93. The course followed the same basic thematic structure of the Leadership Training Program.

Plans are underway to expand the training efforts of the CTQS in future academic years to include regional TQM training programs. Additionally, the CTQS will provide logistical support for the school districts and the state's intermediate units (IUs) in the "first wave" of training as they implement TQM principles and practices in their school districts. Another facet of CTQS efforts is a research and publication campaign to document "what works" among the various TQM techniques in the school district setting. Finally, members of the CTQS staff are actively pursuing corporate support to provide a solid foundation for the operations of the center over the next five years.

CONCLUSION

There is litte doubt that in the 1990s that the character of public education for the 21st Century will be forged. While the Quality Movement has gained momentum and has acquired its share of profits, there are many concerns that must be addressed by the educational community if its place in the new order is to be assured.

If "Quality" is to be a major player in the reform movement, its message must be applied throughout the entire educational program. In simple terms, if school governance is not addressed, if curriculum design is ignored, if the instructional process is not redesigned, and if student outcomes are minimized, the impact of the Quality Movement as a driving force for reform will be negated.

As public educators, we cannot afford to continue in the vein of business as usual. We must take bold and dynamic steps to redirect this massive institution called public education. We are convinced that within the parameters of this movement called "Quality" that such new and bold possibilities exist.

ENDNOTE

1. W. Edwards Deming, *Out of the Crisis* (Cambridge, MA: Massachusetts Institute of Technology, n.d.), 23-24.

Chapter 21

Educational Outreach Programs

Charles E. Greenawalt, II

INTRODUCTION

In recent years the conditions of childhood in America have changed dramatically. Many children are subject to the ravages of health problems, mental illness, poverty, substance abuse, teenage pregnancy, and unemployment. Family structures have shifted and become more fluid, and schools, built on earlier notions of "family" and social problems, are simply not equipped to help.

Illustrations of the changed conditions of childhood can be found in numerous national statistics. About 25 percent of American children under the age of six live in poverty. Approximately 60 percent of mothers are employed, including half of those mothers with babies less than one year of age. Many of these mothers have little time to give their children the support they need; too many of these mothers lack the skill and inclination. Although estimates vary, 7 million school-age children return from school to an empty home and fend for themselves during business hours. An even more serious disadvantage has befallen the estimated 220,000 to 750,000 homeless children in the United States.[1]

Throughout the country many innovative education programs strive to help these vulnerable children and their families through educational outreach. This chapter will review a few of these programs and their progress.

NATIONAL EFFORTS

As America's social problems become more burdensome and children more vulnerable, states have recognized the need to assist and encourage schools to provide a wide variety of services beyond education. The following summaries briefly describe a sample of state activities that focus on educational outreach through partnerships with families, the community, the schools, and/or state agencies.

ARKANSAS

The Arkansas Home Instruction Program for Preschool Youngsters (HIPPY), serving more than 1,000 families each school year since 1987,[2] provides a better start for the state's educationally disadvantaged four-and five-year-olds by teaching parents how to help their child at home. Paraprofessionals provide in-home instruction, through the use of role-playing, to teach mothers to use educational materials at home with their children for 15 minutes a day, five days per week, 30 weeks per year for two years. Originally, this program was developed in Israel about 20 years ago to prepare immigrant children for that country's high pressure school system. HIPPY has had a ripple effect on participating parents who have enrolled in literacy classes, obtained their GEDs, pursued continuing education, and participated more frequently in parent/teacher conferences and school programs.

FLORIDA

Florida forged an interagency collaboration between its Departments of Education and Health and Rehabilitative Services when its legislature passed 1990 legislation that established the Full Service Schools Program. A $7 million state appropriation in 1992, derived by combining previously independent funded categorical programs, the Full Service Schools Program allowed more than 70 participating schools to offer a variety of services to children of all ages and their families.[3] Some services offered include day care, health care, AIDS education and prevention, substance abuse intervention, and dropout prevention programs.

HAWAII

Meeting statewide demand for affordable, quality day care, Hawaii's A+ After-School Program, established in 1990, served more than 22,000 children in its first year.[4] The A+ program is designed for children of parents who are employed or enrolled in a job training program. There is no income restriction for eligibility. During the school year child care is provided at elementary school sites until 5:30 p.m. for all children enrolled in grades K-6. Students also receive help with their homework and participate in enrichment and recreational activities. Parents must pay $28 per month for the services. These payments provide approximately $2.7 million each year for the program, while the state contributes more than $15 million annually.[5]

KENTUCKY

Initiated in 1988, Kentucky's Integrated Delivery System (KIDS) was developed in collaboration with the state's Department of Education and the Governor's Cabinet for Human Resources (e.g., the Departments of Social Services, Health, Mental Health and Mental Retardation, and Employment) to avert problems that might prevent students from staying in school. KIDS coordinates existing state services (e.g., health and mental health care, parent and child education, employment counseling, and job training and placement) and makes those services available at 30 school sites through employment counselors, social workers, mental health counselors, public health professionals, and teachers. New funding is not required for KIDS, since the program restructured the existing social service delivery system.

MARYLAND

Maryland's Family Support Centers are community-based, drop-in programs providing counseling, child care, parenting classes, peer support, educational and vocational training, and health screenings to adolescent parents and their children. The centers are administered by the state's Department of Human Resources and participating community foundations. Funding for the centers varies for each site, based upon the revenues collected by local fund-raising activities.

MICHIGAN

Located in or near rural and urban high schools, Michigan's 19 Teen Health Centers provide free medical care including general medical support, chronic disease management, substance abuse counseling and treatment, health promotion, and preventive services to approximately 20,000 teenage students. Each center receives around $150,000 in funding from the state and community.[6] The state annually contributes $2 million to the centers and each community contributes the remaining funds through cash contributions and "in-kind" services.[7]

In addition to the innovative programs outlined above, it is useful to review two larger educational outreach programs that have attracted much national attention during the last few years. These two programs initiated on the state level that attempt to reform education and schools through outreach are Missouri's Parents As Teachers (PAT) and New Jersey's School Based Youth Services (SBYSP) programs.

MISSOURI'S PARENTS AS TEACHERS PROGRAM

Missouri's Parents As Teachers Program (PAT) is a home-school partnership designed to give children under age three the best possible start in life and to support parents in their role as their child's first teachers.

DESCRIPTION AND BACKGROUND

The Parents As Teachers program was initiated in 1981 as a pilot project. The goal of the project was to enhance the development of the participating children through the education of their parents and the provision of support services. Participating families were enrolled shortly before the birth of their first child, hence the pilot project was named New Parents As Teachers (NPAT).

NPAT was organized and implemented by the Missouri Department of Education and Secondary Education (MDESE) in four school districts representing metropolitan and rural communities. Each of the four school districts received $30,000 per year for four years to serve 380 selected NPAT families from all socioeconomic strata, parental age groups, and familial configurations.[8]

Beginning in the third trimester of pregnancy and continuing until the age of three, each NPAT family received timely information on child growth and development; periodic health, developmental, hearing, and vision screenings; a monthly home visit by specially trained parent educators; and assistance in accessing needed services that were beyond the scope of the program. In addition, NPAT families attended monthly group meetings at parent resource centers located in neighborhood schools.

The NPAT concept was mandated on a statewide basis in 1984, when the Missouri General Assembly enacted the Early Childhood Development Act. The Act required the delivery of parent education and family support services via the state's 543 school districts to the parents of all children under the age of three. Since program services were no longer restricted to first-time parents, NPAT was retitled Parents As Teachers (PAT).

A legislative appropriation of $2.8 million in the 1985-86 school year allowed statewide implementation of the PAT program to begin, providing services to ten percent of Missouri's families with children under age three.[9] PAT enrollment and funding has steadily grown since its first year. During the 1991-92 school year, PAT served 30 percent (over 60,000) of Missouri's families with children under age three on an allocation of $10.8 million, an average operating cost of $20,000 for each of the state's 543 school districts.[10] During the 1992-93 school year, PAT served 35 percent of Missouri's eligible families on $13.1 million, an average operating cost of less than $25,000 per school district.[11]

Participation in PAT is free and voluntary. The basic goals of the program are to increase parental knowledge of child development to do the following: allow parents to understand their child's emotional, mental, and physical development and progress; increase parental confidence in child-rearing activities; and identify conditions that might inhibit a child's normal development. To accomplish these goals, the program provides the following services: home visits by specially trained parent educators to create individualized programs for each child and family; information and guidance to parents at each stage of their child's development, including pre-natal services; periodic health screening and testing of children to check language and motor development; and group visits with other participating parents to help parents share experiences and gain insight into their child's behavior and development.

Parent educators are field workers who recruit families, go into homes, and provide family education services. Briefly, qualifications for parent educators include at least a two-year degree and certification in education, home economics, or nursing that focuses on child development and two to five years experience in a program working with children and their parents. In addition, parent educators must complete a four-step MDESE-approved training program that consists primarily of in-service training.

The following are descriptions of four school districts that are participating in Missouri's statewide PAT program and offer tailored services to meet the needs of the communities they serve:

Kansas City School District. More than 100 parent educators, 10 area managers, and a central office director serve a mostly black and Latino population of approximately 7,000 urban families per year. The Kansas City School District, in collaboration with the city's housing authority, has set-up PAT offices, family resource centers, and lending libraries for project residents in one apartment in each of the city's seven low-income public housing projects.

New Madrid County School District. This rural school district employs four parent educators to serve over 500 families. Because most mothers in this district do not work outside the home, the district holds PAT meetings during the day and provides child care and transportation services for each meeting. In addition, the district works closely with the Women, Infants, and Children (WIC) nutrition program to ensure that WIC participants are enrolled in the district's PAT program.

Springfield Public Schools. This urban school district employs 52 parent educators to provide services to more than 5,000 families who comprise a diverse, but more homogenous population than the Kansas City and St. Louis school districts. In addition to providing basic PAT services, the Springfield Public Schools have developed special programs for teenage mothers and mothers of preschoolers. The teenage mothers program provides child care in both of the city's two high schools. The program for mothers of preschoolers provides preschool classes to toddlers, while their mothers attend special parenting classes.

St. Louis City School District. Comprised of a diverse population of mostly black and new immigrant families from Southeast Asia and Central America, this urban school district employs 35 parent educators to work with approximately 2,500 families of children under three and 16 parent educators to provide limited services to another 2,000 families with three- and four-year-old children. Also, the district works closely with a local international institute, which provides interpreters to aid communications between parent educators and non-English-speaking families.[12]

EVALUATION

A total of three independent studies have been conducted on Missouri's Parents As Teachers concept by the Research and Training Associates of Overland Park, Kansas. The first two studies, released in 1985 and 1989, evaluated the New Parents As Teachers (NPAT) pilot project that was initiated in 1981. The third study, released in 1991, evaluated the Parents As Teachers (PAT) statewide program that was implemented during the 1985-86 school year.

The first study, released in 1985, indicated the following outcomes of the NPAT project:

1) At age three, NPAT children demonstrated more advanced achievement and language ability than did comparison children;
2) NPAT children demonstrated significantly more positive aspects of social development than did comparison children; and
3) NPAT parents were more knowledgeable about child-rearing practices and child development than were parents of comparison children.[13]

These 1985 findings were further substantiated by a follow-up investigation of NPAT and a comparison group of children in 1989. The 1989 evaluation found that NPAT children scored significantly higher than did the comparison group on school-administered, standardized measures of reading and math achievement.[14] In addition, it found that parents of NPAT children were twice as likely as parents of comparison children to be involved in their children's school experiences.[15]

The third study or "Second Wave Study," released in 1991, assessed the impact of PAT following its statewide implementation during the 1985-86 school year. The study, funded by the Ford Foundation and conducted by the Research and Training Associates, included a randomly selected sample of 400 families enrolled in 37 school districts across Missouri. The study investigated child, parent, and parent-child interaction outcomes among one- and two-parent families of varied socioeconomic status. The study also included a substudy of 150 families residing in the St. Louis and Kansas City metropolitan areas. The substudy focused on parent-child interaction and parent effectiveness as a teacher.

Major findings of the Second Wave Study and its substudy include:

1) *At age three, children in PAT scored above national norms on measures of school-related achievement.* Notably, the study group included above-average numbers of families with traditional "risk" factors such as poverty, minority status, single-parent households, and mothers with less than a high school education.
2) *PAT helped children overcome delays in their early development.* More than half of the children observed to have delays in development, including language development, overcame these delays by age three. Problems of developmental delay and parent-child communication were

found to be highly related.

3) *Parents in nearly all types of families showed significant gains in knowledge about child development and child-rearing practices.* The greatest gains in parent knowledge were achieved by white mothers with less than a high school education.

4) *Parents in PAT became more active in their child's education.* All types of parents actively participated in the PAT program during the three-year period, and parents were consistently eager for information and assistance. Eighty-three percent of all participants rated their home visits as "very helpful." Parents who had children with developmental delays participated in significantly more home visits than other parents.[16]

NATIONAL EFFORTS

In 1987, the non-profit Parents As Teachers National Center was established by the Missouri Department of Elementary and Secondary Education to provide information about PAT, plus training and technical assistance for those interested in adopting the program. To date, the PAT National Center has assisted in the implementation of more than 1,000 PAT programs in the following 39 states: Alabama, Alaska, Arizona, Arkansas, California, Colorado, Connecticut, Delaware, Florida, Georgia, Illinois, Indiana, Iowa, Kansas, Kentucky, Louisiana, Maine, Maryland, Michigan, Minnesota, Mississippi, Nebraska, New Mexico, New York, North Carolina, Ohio, Oklahoma, Oregon, Pennsylvania, Rhode Island, South Carolina, South Dakota, Tennessee, Texas, Virginia, Washington, West Virginia, Wisconsin, and Wyoming.[17] In addition, the PAT National Center has helped the Federal Bureau of Indian Affairs and the nations of Australia, England, Ireland, and New Zealand to establish PAT programs.[18]

Of the states that have established PAT programs, Kansas is the closest to implementing PAT on a statewide basis. Since 1988, PAT pilot projects have operated in five Kansas communities. The enrollment, success, and parental response regarding the pilot programs prompted the Kansas Legislature to enact House Bill 2218 in 1990. The bill not only secured state funding for PAT, but it also provided for a three-year statewide phase-in for the PAT program in Kansas. Currently, PAT programs operate in 200 of Kansas' 300 school districts.[19] The three-year phase-in process will be complete in 1994 when all of Kansas' 300 school districts will offer PAT programs. Other states that are planning PAT implementation on a statewide basis are Oklahoma and Texas.

NEW JERSEY'S SCHOOL BASED YOUTH SERVICES PROGRAM

New Jersey's School Based Youth Services Program is a social services-school partnership designed to enable adolescents, especially those with problems, to lead a mentally and physically healthy life by guiding them to complete their education and obtain skills that either lead to employment or additional education.

DESCRIPTION AND BACKGROUND

Established in 1988, the primary goal of New Jersey's School Based Youth Services Program (SBYSP) is to prevent at "risk" students from "falling through the cracks." The program assists young adults, ages 13-19, who have problems that delay or prevent their development as productive individuals. These problems include: substance abuse, suicide, teenage pregnancy, mental illness, unemployment, health problems, and high drop-out rates.

Essentially, SBYSP functions as an umbrella organization that augments and coordinates support services and programs provided by the New Jersey State Departments of Education, Health, Human Services, and Labor with those provided by community entities. SBYSP is a collaboration between community organizations, local government, school boards, parent and teacher organizations, the business community, unions, the employment and training community, non-profit social service agencies, and health care providers.

SBYSP was organized and implemented by the New Jersey Department of Human Services at 29 sites with at least one program operating in each of the state's 21 counties. Every program site is housed in or near a junior high, vocational, or high school that is located in primarily low-income urban and rural areas and is managed by a school, hospital, social service agency, and/or a community based organization. SBYSP serves all students, not only students identified as having problems, to encourage teens to use the services without feeling any stigma. Parental consent, however, is required for the receipt of all SBYSP services.

While the New Jersey program does not impose a single statewide model on individual sites, every site must offer certain core services and must operate program activities not only during school hours, but after school, on weekends, and during vacations to facilitate student access. Each of the 29 sites offers "one-stop shopping" for employment and training services; mental health and family counseling; substance abuse services;

information and referral services; and recreation. In addition to these core services, many sites also provide day care, transportation, family planning, and hotlines.

SBYSP is funded by state appropriations and host communities, which must contribute 25 percent of program costs through direct financial participation or "in-kind" services, materials, or facilities. In 1988, SBYSP received $6 million in state funding to deliver over 35,000 services to more than 10,000 adolescents.[20] In 1992-93, the program received $7.1 million in state funding to provide un-duplicated services to over 19,000 teenagers at a cost of approximately $245,000 per site.[21]

The following are three examples of the 29 SBYSP sites operating in New Jersey:

Bayonne, Hudson County. The Bayonne SBYSP, called "Project Connect" is administered by the Bayonne School Board and housed in a Police Athletic League building adjacent to the urban community's high school. In addition to providing core services, the site offers a "peer-helping" program to improve student self-concepts and communication skills; tutoring in reading and math by certified teachers; preparation courses for taking the GED; and assistance with the juvenile court system to provide alternative probation to some offenders.

New Brunswick, Middlesex County. Housed in the New Brunswick High School, this SBYSP site is managed by New Brunswick Tomorrow, a non-profit community agency involved in the revitalization of the city. The New Brunswick site offers the following services to inner-city teenagers: core services; health fairs; dental, health, and psychological screenings; a program aimed at bringing dropouts back to school; a program that helps pregnant teens find child care services; museum outings; and fashion shows.

Plainfield, Union County. The Plainfield program, housed in and administered by the Plainfield High School, serves an inner-city community. The Plainfield SBYSP offers core services plus dance and theater programs in the summer; child care while teenage mothers are in school and during summer months; play and parental-skills classes for teenage parents; life-skills classes; and employment training with the local office of the American Telephone and Telegraph Company (AT&T).[22]

EVALUATION

Although the New Jersey School Based Youth Services Program was first established in 1988, the program has not formally been evaluated due to insufficient funding from private sources. Generally speaking, the program seems to have improved the attendance, behavior, and grades of the participants.

In 1991, the New Jersey Department of Human Services conducted a survey of all school personnel employed at the 29 SBYSP sites about their views of SBYSP. Results indicate that over 90 percent of school personnel found the program to have a positive effect on students (93.4 percent) and school environment (90.4 percent).[23] School personnel also found SBYSP helped them to be more effective in their own jobs (86 percent) and allowed them to assist more students (88 percent).[24] In addition, school personnel reported perceptions that SBYSP had a positive effect on the following: decreasing and assisting teens who are substance abusers (87.6 percent); increasing academic performance (81.3 percent), decreasing the dropout rate (79.7 percent), increasing the graduation rate (76.6 percent), increasing school attendance among students (75.9 percent), and decreasing pregnancy rates (64.1 percent).[25]

Other than the 1991 survey, results released by the Pinelands and Hackensack sites indicate that SBYSP is effective in decreasing dropout rates, fights, pregnancy rates, and suspension rates. The Pinelands site (a rural and poor area) reported that SBYSP reduced the pregnancy rate from 20 students in the 1988-89 school year to 13 in 1989-90 to 1 in 1990-91; suspension rates from 322 students in 1989-90 to 78 in 1990-91; and dropout rates from 73 students in 1989-90 to 24 in 1990-91.[26] In addition, the Hackensack site (an urban area) reported that the number of student fights decreased from 123 in 1989-90 to 72 in 1990-91 due to aggression control and conflict resolution programs.[27]

NATIONAL EFFORTS

New Jersey's School Based Youth Services Program has been replicated on a statewide basis in Iowa, Kentucky, and to some extent, California.[28]

In 1989, the Iowa General Assembly appropriated an annual sum of $800,000 for four years to provide school-based youth services programs in four school districts.[29] The Iowa SBYSP sites are located in or near schools and serve middle and high school students. Services provided by the Iowa sites include mental health care, primary health care, job training, and employment services.

The provision of school based youth services was mandated in Kentucky when the state's General Assembly enacted the Kentucky Education Reform Act of 1990. Kentucky's Youth Services Centers provide services to all middle and high school students that are enrolled in schools in which 20 percent or more of the students qualify for the free lunch program. Established through a $9 million state appropriation in the 1991-92 school year, 133 centers provide the following services to 232 eligible schools: health care; employment counseling, training, and placement; summer and part-time job development; and mental health and substance abuse counseling.[30] By the 1995-96 school year, Kentucky's Youth Services Centers will be established on a statewide basis.

PENNSYLVANIA'S EFFORTS

Pennsylvania has established two programs that link schools with homes and/or other programs to ensure that children are receiving the services and attention that they need to be healthy and productive members of the Commonwealth. The two programs, Family Centers For Child Development and School-Based Health Service Pilot, are discussed below.

FAMILY CENTERS FOR CHILD DEVELOPMENT

Pennsylvania's Family Centers For Child Development Program, modeled after Missouri's Parents As Teachers Program, is a home-school partnership that collaborates with local Head Start programs so that children from birth until their entrance in school are given the best possible start in life and parents are supported in their role as their child's first teachers.

DESCRIPTION AND BACKGROUND

Established in 1991, the primary goal of the Family Centers Program is to enhance the emotional, mental, and physical development of the participating children through the education of their parents and the provision of support services. The Family Centers aid all young children from 0-5 years of age and their families, but priority is given to families that are at "risk": the homeless, disabled, poor, limited or non-English speaking, single parents, teenage parents, and those with less than a high school education. Participation in the Family Centers Program is voluntary for those who are eligible.

The Family Centers Program collaborates with several Pennsylvania-funded programs to ensure that children and their families receive a "seamless network" of services and to benefit the state by avoiding the costly duplication of services. The Family Centers coordinate services provided by the following state-funded programs: Head Start, Healthy Beginnings Plus, Chapter I Preschool and Early Childhood, early intervention services, Homeless Children and Youth Education, teen parenting programs, special education programs and services, family focused drug and alcohol prevention, foster parent programs, Even Start as well as other adult literacy programs, inter-generational programs, and in some cases School-Based Health Services Clinics.

The centers, managed by the Pennsylvania Department of Education, are located at 26 sites across the state. The first Family Centers were established in 1991 at 13 sites and the remaining 13 centers were established in 1992. The centers are housed primarily in elementary or high schools that are located in mostly low income urban and rural areas. Staffed by parent educators who are trained in child development, each Family Center must offer the following core services to children and families:

1) Group meetings to provide informational and educational programs on topics such as employment, health, literacy, nutrition, and parenting skills, as well as allowing parents to share experiences and gain insight into their child's behavior and development;

2) Home visits by parent educators to create individualized programs for each child and family and to help parents understand each stage of their child's development, while receiving practical tips on ways to encourage their child's learning;

3) An information and resource network that ensures families are referred to state agencies or community-based organizations that can meet the needs of children and their families which cannot be met by the Family Centers; and,

4) Periodic overall developmental, health, hearing, language, motor, and vision screenings to ensure early detection, prevention, and/or treatment of problems.

In addition to core services, some centers offer services, such as a book and/or toy lending library, lead screenings, transportation to group meetings, and demonstrations. The following are examples of Family Centers established in 1991 and 1992 that provide core and additional services to children and their families:

Benton Family Center. Established in 1991, this center is the only Family Center located in rural Columbia County. It employs four parent educators to serve approximately 75 families with children ages 0-3 and children 3-5 years old who are not eligible for Head Start. The Benton

Family Center offers core services; on-site WIC services three times a month; conducts lead screenings; provides child care; and allows faculty volunteers, student teachers, and interns from Bloomsburg University to instruct and interact with children and their families.

Central Fulton Family Center. Serving rural and relatively poor families in Fulton County, this center offers core services, school age child care, summer child care, family literacy programs, and a pre-kindergarten program for four-year olds. Established in 1991, the center employs two parent educators to provide its services to over 60 families with children ages 0-4.

Duquesne Family Center. The Duquesne Family Center, established in 1991, is one of nine Family Centers that provide core and additional services to the people of Allegheny County. Duquesne, located 12 miles southeast of Pittsburgh, is an urban and poor community. Five parent educators provide services to more than 150 families with children ages 0-5. Additional services provided by the center are prenatal health care, parent-child play groups, a toy and book lending library, Head Start Home Base services for three year olds, Head Start Health and Nutrition, Head Start Disability services, and Intergenerational Training for the elderly to provide child care.

Allentown Family Center. One of two Family Centers in Lehigh County, the Jefferson Elementary School site, established in 1992, serves approximately 120 families in the center city and surrounding urban areas of Allentown. Three parent educators provide core services to children ages 0-5 and their families. In addition to core services, the Allentown Family Center operates a toy and book lending library, holds parent-child play groups at homeless family shelter sites, offers personal development workshops for parents, and provides immunizations and lead screenings through a school-based health clinic housed in the elementary school.

Greater Nanticoke Area Family Center. Located in Luzerne County, this center serves urban and rural communities in Nanticoke, Newport Township, Plymouth Township, and Conygham Township. Established in 1992, the center employs four parent educators to provide core and additional services to over 100 families with children ages 0-5. Additional services include transportation to and from group meetings and center activities and child care. While the main center is located at John S. Fine High School, two fully-equipped satellite centers are located in Nanticoke City's largest housing authorities.

Reading Family Center. Established in 1992, the center employs five parent educators to provide core and additional services to more than 130 families with children ages 0-3 that live in Reading, Berks County. Parenting, nutrition, and health workshops; transportation to and from group meetings and center activities; child care; teenage parenting programs, and adult literacy classes are some of the additional services provided by the Reading Family Center.

The Family Centers Program is funded entirely under the U.S. Department of Health and Human Services through the Child Care and Development Block Grant Act of 1990.[31] In 1991, the grant provided $1.5 million to establish the first 13 Family Centers and an additional $755,000 to provide services to over 1,100 families.[32] In 1992, the grant provided $1.8 million to establish another 13 centers and an additional $967,000 to provide services to slightly under 2,500 children and their families.[33]

EVALUATION

The Family Centers For Child Development Program has not been evaluated since its establishment in 1991, primarily because the program is relatively new. Generally, the program has increased parental knowledge of child development, improved parental confidence in child-rearing, improved cognitive and language development in children, enhanced social development in children, and has decreased undetected incidences of disabling conditions, particularly in hearing and vision.[34] In addition, parents and children report positive attitudes about the program and school.[35]

SCHOOL-BASED PRIMARY HEALTH SERVICES PILOT PROJECT

Pennsylvania's School-Based Health Services Pilot Project is a school-health care partnership designed to provide basic health care for children in under-served areas of the Commonwealth so that their health is improved.

DESCRIPTION AND BACKGROUND

Initiated in 1992 and in the process of being established at six sites, the primary purpose of Pennsylvania's School-Based Health Services Pilot Project will be to ensure that elementary school children do not "fall through the cracks" of health care programs. The pilot project will do this by integrating and coordinating school-based services with services that are provided to children who are eligible for Medical Assistance and those who are uninsured or underinsured.

The pilot project, administered by the Pennsylvania Department of Health and the Department of Education, will operate six sites located in three rural and three urban areas of greatest need. High need is defined as districts with an average daily Aid to Families with Dependent Children (AFDC) membership of over ten percent and/or a district eligible for designation as a Family Center for Child Development. The receipt of services from the project is free and voluntary for all children who are enrolled in the selected high need districts.

Housed primarily in elementary schools, the Health Clinics will coordinate all health service programs that presently serve children. In conjunction with at least one local health care provider, each Health Clinic will ensure that all health care services are provided on a community-based level, mostly at the clinic. In addition, each Health Clinic will act as gateway to services that are provided off-site.

In 1993, the three urban and three rural Health Clinics received $400,000 in Federal ($350,000) and state ($50,000) grants to offer physical examinations, immunizations, growth and developmental assessments, diagnosis services, and treatment for common illnesses.[36] In addition to the above services, each Health Clinic is expected to provide services tailored to the needs, conditions, and resources of the community it serves. The following is a brief synopsis of each of the six selected sites:

Allentown School District, Lehigh County. This urban school district will provide primary health services to all students enrolled at Jefferson Elementary School in Allentown. In cooperation with three community-based health care providers (Lehigh Valley Hospital, Sacred Heart Hospital, and the Allentown Health Bureau), the district's health clinic will expand its primary health services to include preventive and treatment services.

Central Fulton School District, Fulton County. In cooperation with the Fulton County Medical Center and the Fulton County Center for Families, this rural school district will provide comprehensive primary health services to all students attending the McConnellsburg Elementary School.

Farrell School District, Mercer County. Farrell School District, a rural district, will cooperate with the Shenango Valley Primary Health Center to provide primary services to pre-school children at the John Herta Child Development Center in Farrell. Pre-school children include Head Start participants, four-year old half-day kindergarten students, and children enrolled in the school's day care program. Expanded school-based health services will also be offered to all students who attend the Farrell Elementary School.

Lancaster School District, Lancaster County. In 1993, this urban school district will expand its school-based health services in conjunction with the Family Center at Burrows Elementary School in Lancaster, which serves low-income parents and preschool students. In 1994, the district will establish a school-based health clinic in its Martin Luther King Elementary School.

Philadelphia School District, Philadelphia County. The Philadelphia School District, a large urban district, will establish a school-based health clinic at the General George Meade Elementary School in partnership with Quality Community Health, a non-profit community based health care organization.

Towanda School District, Bradford County. In cooperation with the Guthrie Medical Center, this rural school district will establish a primary health services program at the Early Learning Center in Towanda for children enrolled in the full-day kindergarten age four program.[37]

EVALUATION

A detailed evaluation of the School-Based Primary Health Care Services Pilot Project is planned for the future, after the pilot program has been properly established.

According to the Pennsylvania Department of Health, future evaluations of the pilot project will involve both process and outcome measures. Process measures will focus on the needs of the community and whether or not the pilot site and community health care provider have tailored their services to and if they are meeting the needs of the community. Outcome measures will focus on demographic criteria, the frequency of health care use, the type of medical care provided, and the number of children served.

CONCLUSION

With growing societal problems, school districts have become a place where more than education must be provided to students. Indeed, schools are being asked and mandated to do more than at any previous time. Alone, school districts simply do not have the resources to effectively provide all of the services that are needed by children. Other agencies and families must work in conjunction with school districts to provide children with the necessary services and education they need, as well as to prevent children from "falling through the cracks."

Missouri's Parents As Teachers (PAT) and New Jersey's School Based Youth Services (SBYSP) programs are two successful examples of innovative state policies that engage in outreach to at "risk" students to prevent them from "falling through the cracks." Although PAT serves children from birth to age three and SBYSP serves adolescents ages 13-19, each provides the necessary services for the age group it serves. Each program has increased academic performance among participants, provided participants with a support system to deal with the adversities they face, improved school attendance or parental involvement, assisted at "risk" participants and/or those with early developmental delays, and increased positive behaviors and emotions among participants.

Initiatives such as the Family Centers for Child Development and School-Based Health Services Programs demonstrate that Pennsylvania is making an effort to link schools with families, the community, and state agencies. While these state programs provide PAT-like services to children ages 0-5 and their families and health services to elementary school children in high-need areas of the state, the majority of Pennsylvania's children enrolled in elementary, middle, and high school grades and their families remain unserved or underserved. To serve all of the Commonwealth's children, the state should consider the following:

1) *Expand the Family Centers for Child Development and the School-Based Health Services programs on a statewide level.* This will ensure that PAT-like services are provided to all children ages 0-5 and their families and that health care services will be provided to all elementary school students.

2) *Establish a program similar, if not identical, to New Jersey's SBYSP on both the middle and high school levels.* Such a program would provide a variety of services necessary to keep high-school aged students in school and middle-school aged students away from drugs and alcohol and prevent teenage pregnancies. Pennsylvania's School-Based Health Services Program could also be expanded to the middle and high school levels to provide the health care component that New Jersey's SBYSP offers.

3) *Foster more collaboration between schools and the business community.* By doing so, the business community could not only provide funding or "in-kind" services for school programs, it could offer job training, stress the importance of a quality education, and supplement school curriculum by offering guest speakers, and tours of businesses.

4) *Encourage inter-agency collaboration.* By combining all state

programs that benefit children and families and offering them on a community-based level, preferably through the schools, the state could ensure that children and families receive the services they need without the hassle of bureaucratic "red tape" and without the duplication of services or funding.

During the last 20 years, psychologists have gathered conclusive evidence that the preschool years are critical to the formation of a child's personality. By the age of two or three the process is well underway. At age five, when children reach kindergarten, it is almost too late to make a significant difference with any action short of intensive therapy. By the fifth grade, at age ten, dropouts-to-be are already scoring lower on standardized achievement tests than their classmates who will finish school--the result of problems unnoticed in earlier years.[38] Clearly, educational outreach programs are a valuable innovation that enables intervention to occur with at-risk students and their families. These efforts will frequently change the direction of a child's life and prevent him from reaching the point of failure. This will be an increasing role for tomorrow's schools.

ENDNOTES

1. Marvin Cetron and Margaret Gayle, *Educational Renaissance: Our Schools At The Turn of the Twenty-First Century* (New York, NY: St. Martin's Press, 1991), 12 and 57.

2. David Ensign, *Innovations: Missouri's Parents As Teachers* (Lexington, KY: Council of State Governments, 1989), 9.

3. National Health and Education Consortium, *Creating Sound Minds and Bodies: Health and Education Working Together* (Washington, D.C.: Policy Studies Associates, Inc., 1992), 36.

4. Sally F. Sachar, *From Homes to Classrooms to Workrooms: State Initiatives Meet the Needs of the Changing American Family* (Washington, D.C.: National Governors' Association, 1992), 30-31.

5. Ibid., 31.

6. Ibid., 32.

7. Ibid..

8. Parents As Teachers National Center, *Parents As Teachers History* (St. Louis, MO: Missouri Department of Education, 1990), 2.

9. Ibid., 5.

10. Children's Defense Fund, *Helping Children by Strengthening Families: A Look at Family Support Programs* (Washington, D.C.: Children's Defense Fund, 1992), 48.

11. Patricia A. Holman of Parents As Teachers National Center, interviewed by author, April 1993, St. Louis, MO.

12. Children's Defense Fund, *Helping Children by Strengthening Families*, 48-51.

13. Parents As Teachers National Center, *Parents As Teachers History*, 3-4.

14. Ibid., 6-7.

15. Ibid..

16 Research and Training Associates, *Second Wave Study of the Parents As Teachers Program* (St. Louis, MO: Missouri Department of Education, 1991).

17. Holman, interviewed by author.

18. Ibid..

19. Ibid..

20. Kathleen Sylvester, "New Strategies to Save Children in Trouble," *Governing The States and Localities*, May 1990, 34-35.

21. Edward Tetelman of New Jersey Department of Human Resources, interviewed by author, April 1993, Trenton, NJ.

22. New Jersey Department of Human Services, *Linkages* (Trenton, NJ: New Jersey Department of Human Services, 1989), 1-3.

23. New Jersey Department of Human Services, *Linking Systems Together: New Jersey's School Based Services Program* (Trenton, NJ: New Jersey Department of Human Services, 1992), 3.

24. Ibid..

25. Ibid..

26. Ibid., 2.

27. Ibid..

28. Joining Forces, "Bringing Services to Schools" (Washington, D.C.: Joining Forces, 1991), 4-5.

29. Ibid..

30. Sally F. Sachar, *From Homes to Classrooms to Workrooms: State Initiatives Meet the Needs of the Changing American Family* (Washington, D.C.: National Governors' Association, 1992), 31.

31. Pennsylvania Department of Education, *Family Centers for Child Development: Program Profiles 1992-1993* (Harrisburg, PA: Pennsylvania Department of Education, 1993), Cohort I and II.

32. Ibid..

33. Ibid..

34. Pennsylvania Department of Education, *Investing in Good Beginnings* (Harrisburg, PA: Pennsylvania Department of Education, 1993).

35. Ibid..

36. Pennsylvania Department of Health, *School-Based Primary Health Services Pilot Project Description* (Harrisburg, PA: Pennsylvania Department of Health, 1993), 4-5.

37. Ibid..

38. Cetron and Gayle, *Educational Renaissance*, 59.

Chapter 22

Reform at the Local Level: Roadblocks on the Road

Ann K. Monteith

INTRODUCTION

In November 1992, an article by John I. Goodlad, director of the Center for Educational Renewal at the University of Washington, appeared in *Phi Delta Kappan* magazine under the title "On Taking School Reform Seriously." In it, Goodlad contends that without grassroots support, education reform is doomed to fail and the current "America 2000" national movement is understood by only a tiny fraction of citizens, parents, and teachers across the land.

The America 2000 initiative, which grew from the national summit on education convened by President George Bush in 1989 in Charlottesville, Virginia, calls for national goals and national tests as a means to achieving world-class schools. According to Goodlad, these tests are to be the measure of individual achievement, individual achievement is to be the instrument that creates educational excellence, and educational excellence will create a robust nation.[1]

In addition to America 2000, Goodlad cites the existence of grassroots education reform movements, which he calls "homegrown school improvement activities," taking shape under the leadership of such reformers as James Comer, Howard Gardner, Henry Levin, and Theodore

Sizer. "It becomes increasingly clear," he says "that there are two sets of school reform movements operating in the U.S. and that they are not joined."[2] About these two movements, Goodlad says:

> Top-down, politically driven education reform movements are addressed primarily to restructuring the educational system. They have little to say about educating. Grassroots reform efforts, on the other hand, have little to say about restructuring. They are virtually all about educating our young. Perhaps it is time for political leaders to take stock of this second education reform movement and to buy tickets for trains that require no endorsements from governors and mayors.[3]

The key question addressed in Goodlad's article is the following: "We have an educational movement that claims to be sweeping the country though it seems at best to be known only vaguely to parents and educators—those who must ultimately buy in if it is to be successful. Or must they? Or do those promoting America 2000 care? Or should we take the effort seriously at all?"

Certainly the same question can be raised with regard to the Pennsylvania State Board of Education's attempt at public school reform via the controversial Outcome Based Education (OBE) plan which it passed in January 1993. The initiative began in 1990, when the State Board was scheduled to review existing regulations for curriculum and assessment under Title 22, Chapters 3, 5, and 6 of state law. At that time, the Board decided to reform the entire system, mandating a change from how many credits the student accumulates to how much the student knows through the mastery of "outcomes." Originally, the Board proposed 575 such outcomes, as part of Chapter 5, but had to retreat when the plan came under heavy criticism. Critics said that the outcomes lacked clarity, were redundant, could not be assessed or implemented, and overemphasized *affective* matters that intruded on behaviors and values[4] such as "wellness and fitness," "personal, family and community living," "citizenship," and "appreciating and understanding others."

As soon as the State Board passed the plan, Governor Casey asked the legislature to remove the remaining provisions he opposed, and the Pennsylvania Parents Commission, a citizens group opposed to OBE, opposed the regulations in the legislature. Despite this criticism, the General Assembly adopted OBE, and it did comply with the Governor's wishes. Critics and supporters have continued to exchange barbs, the Department of Education remains silent, and the public—including teachers—generally is uninformed as to the substance of the regulations which will reshape its public schools. In light of John Goodlad's prescription for successful "grassroots" school reform, the prognosis for OBE as a school reform cure-all is poor at best.

Long before the State Board of Education became embroiled in the effort to reform the public schools, there existed a Pennsylvania grassroots network of citizens, parents, and teachers who hoped to implement educational innovations and reform in the public schools. In 1986, I joined with like-minded leaders of concerned citizens to form BEST for PA (Better Education/Sensible Taxation), which today exists as the education division of the Pennsylvania Leadership Council (PLC). By the primary election of 1991, a record number of citizens affiliated with BEST for PA had succeeded in winning a large number of seats on school boards throughout the state. In spite of these victories, these would-be reformers have found the educational system to be virtually reform-proof. In the midst of our frustration, however, we have learned much about what set the Pennsylvania public school system on the road to decline and what it will take to bring it back.

The Decline Of Pennsylvania's Schools

The mid-1960s appears to mark the beginning of the decline of public education in America in general, and in Pennsylvania in particular. Prior to that time, education was accomplished in small, neighborhood schools. Having evolved from the simple one-room school of pioneer America, the neighborhood school system served the nation effectively as it grew from a fledgling democracy to the acknowledged leader of the free world. The system was teacher-based, community-directed, and focused on the need to provide students with a sense of common heritage, a knowledge of the world in which they live, and a practical level of literacy and numeracy. It was in the smallness of these schools that we find a heritage of success: the small size gave students a sense of belonging and nurturing, where opportunities for educational involvement were considered paramount. Parents, too, felt a sense of belonging to these neighborhood schools. They were involved in the school process and, thus, aided and abetted the cause of quality education.[5]

In 1965 there were more than 2,500 local school districts or "union" school districts in Pennsylvania, the latter resulting from a voluntary joining of two or more districts. A movement to consolidate Pennsylvania school districts was born in the post-World War II era. The need for change was based largely on the experiences of young men and women who served in World War II and in the Korean War, who discovered that their better educated comrades had the advantage when it came to promotions. The concept of the "shopping mall" high school--schools which offer a large number of elective courses for students to enroll in if they wish--also was considered at that time to be the solution to a lack of student interest and a problem with student retention.[6] The movement picked up steam in the 1960s when "redistricting" was proposed to solve the following three problems that were considered serious at the time: 1) one-room or very small schools; 2) differences in the educational offerings between wealthy and less affluent districts, although state allocations were supposed to equalize the costs per pupil; and 3) poor physical facilities that provided students with few educational resources, especially at schools in rural and poorer urban areas.[7]

Rooted in the premise that "bigger is better," The School District Reorganization Acts of 1963 were imposed on the public schools. These acts were passed against a backdrop of organized opposition from local citizens' groups, which wanted their school systems to retain their autonomy. In the years since consolidation, Pennsylvania's economy, employment needs, and demographic characteristics have changed dramatically. One such demographic change, for example, has been the increase of older retired property owner. on fixed incomes. No arm of government has suggested the need for an updated report on Pennsylvania's public education system since its redistricting. No arm of government has investigated its consequences.[8]

In 1977 a solitary, but important, voice warned against the continuing trend toward consolidation. It was none other than Dr. John C. Pittenger, Pennsylvania Secretary of Education under Governor Milton Shapp. In his final report in office, Pittenger said, "The school consolidation movement is an unhappy example of what happens when the American infatuation with size and efficiency gets out of hand... . There should be no more consolidation; the movement toward bigness has gone far enough. . . . Districts should think twice about doing what some have already done—closing several 'obsolete' schools and building one large central school serving the whole district."[9]

Pittenger's warning, however, has gone unheeded, and by 1991 a record number of school construction projects—some 1,500 buildings—were in the works, many of which involve neighborhood school closings for the purpose of consolidation.[10]

In 1988, BEST for PA released a study on the effects of redistricting. The report concluded that the consolidation of Pennsylvania's public school system has done the following: 1) adversely affected the financial and political structures of many communities, 2) caused a duplication of educational and recreational services, and 3) done nothing to improve education in Pennsylvania.[11]

Indeed, Pennsylvania's poor showing in education relative to the other states, makes it reasonable to conclude that consolidation is the single most compelling reason for the decline of public education in Pennsylvania. (In 1992, Pennsylvania ranked 46th among the states for combined SAT scores.) Three precepts support that conclusion:

1) Largeness has destroyed children's sense of belonging and limited their opportunities for participation, two of the most important elements for school success. In lieu of belonging and participation, school time now is dominated by "programmatic instruction" which de-emphasizes the teacher as the primary facilitator of learning.

2) School consolidation has contributed to the growth of a bureaucracy that does not contribute to the processes of teaching and learning. This bureaucracy thwarts educational innovations and obscures accountability for educational failure.

3) The growth of bureaucracy has created a system of school governance that concentrates the power for financing education at the state level and away from local citizens who support the public school system with their taxes. This shift has resulted in a public which is increasingly hostile to the school system and, consequently, less supportive of its mission.

Any plan for educational progress, then—whether it is America 2000 or Outcome Based Education—must confront these three issues.

REMAKING THE PUBLIC SCHOOLS

REVERSING THE EFFECTS OF LARGENESS

The most notable effect of consolidation in Pennsylvania has been the creation of large school structures which house great numbers of children. In fact, ten elementary schools in the Commonwealth now contain over 1,000 students. For example, an elementary school expansion program in the Derry Township School District in Hershey, Pennsylvania, has created a building with a student capacity of nearly 1,800 pupils in grades kindergarten through five.[12] High schools and middle schools routinely count pupils in the thousands.

Among the reasons commonly stated for building these huge new facilities is to ensure quality education, allow for the equal delivery of services, and achieve administrative efficiency. No attention is being paid to the growing body of research which suggests that the cause of education is best served when schools are made smaller rather than larger.[13] The widely-heralded Carnegie Foundation's 1988 Special Report, *An Imperiled Generation*, for example, acknowledges that school size is crucial to educational success or failure. It maintains that the large size of urban schools has resulted in a sense of student isolation, the logical extension of which is truancy and dropping out. In a section entitled "Small Schools: A Sense of Belonging," the report states that, "Most city schools are too big and anonymity among students is a pervasive problem. There is a feeling of isolation among teenagers at the very time their need for belonging is most intense....Therefore, we conclude that large schools should be divided into clusters with no more than 450 students each so that all students can be well known to each other and to teachers. ..."[14] Among the problems the report laid at the door of largeness are truancy, dropping out, parental indifference, violence, and the defacing of property.[15]

Two negative effects of large school structures on student learning are readily observable and easily understood. The first is the loss of a sense of belonging to a "school family" which is prevalent in smaller neighborhood schools. Teachers and parents alike mourn the loss of this type of nurturing environment which they believe is the best possible atmosphere in which learning can flourish, particularly at the elementary school level. Many parents report feeling alienated from the bureaucratic atmosphere which pervades large school structures. According to studies by James Comer and Herbert Walberg among others, the single most important factor to learning success is the involvement of parents in the learning process.[16] Parents intimidated by the school atmosphere are less likely to participate in school activities or learning situations. This, then, gives rise to the misplaced conclusion and complaint of teachers that parents "just don't care about the education of their children."

The large size of middle schools is also of concern to education researchers. In June 1989, a task force of the Carnegie Council on Adolescent Development stated that most middle schools make an already difficult period of life even harder and may create an "arena of casualties" for students and teachers alike. "Most young adolescents," says the report, "learn from unconnected and seemingly irrelevant curricula, know well and trust few adults in school, and lack access to health care and counseling....The chances that young people will feel lost are enormous."[17] The second most obvious failure of large schools is the inability, simply because of the logistical problems associated with largeness, to provide students with opportunities for full participation in school and extra-curricular activities. Long recognized as one of the most important factors for school success, participation is limited because of many factors. Busing to consolidated schools means that many children have 90 minute rides one-way and, consequently, cannot take advantage of after-school activities. Furthermore, large numbers of students in school discourage less aggressive students from the competition required to participate. Having observed and analyzed the process and results of school consolidation throughout the state, former Pennsylvania school superintendent and educational consultant, Dr. John F. Magill, Jr. concluded that consolidation "has resulted in a tragic inverse proportion—the percentage of students 'involved' in the school has decreased as the number of students in the school has increased." He adds that teachers cannot "retain and maintain an interest in school with this kind of eroding involvement."[18] Teachers burdened by the administrative and bureaucratic needs created by large structures are less inclined to muster the creativity needed to engage children in the kinds of activities which encourage learning through participation.

The most serious obstacle to educational improvement in today's school environments is not so readily recognized. Instead of the kind of natural learning that comes about through participation under the loving guidance of a qualified teacher, today's schools have come to be dominated by a system of learning that relies on elaborately designed and slickly marketed pre-packaged tests and "teaching materials," usually worksheets or workbooks which require the student to fill-in-the blank or indicate the correct one-word answer. Such packaged learning supports an educational theory which has grown up around the "behaviorist" theories of B.F. Skinner. Skinner's theories assert learning can be guaranteed if instruction is delivered systematically, one small piece—or skill—at a time, with frequent tests to ensure that students and teachers stay on task.[19] The problem with this "programmatic" theory, according to Dr. Frank Smith, a pioneer in the study of how children learn to speak, read, and write, is that it conflicts with the manner in which the human brain functions. A one-time colleague of B. F. Skinner during his Ph.D. studies at Harvard, and now a leading figure in the "Whole Language"[20] movement, Smith condemns programmatic instruction for four reasons. His objections are listed below:

1) The programs do not reflect the way that anyone learns about language or about anything worthwhile. Programs control teachers and assume they are incapable of making educational decisions.

2) The language arts programs do not reflect normal reading, writing, or language generally. Filling in the blanks is not the way anyone uses language, spoken or written.

3) Programs are usually designed by people who know how to write instructional programs rather than by people experienced in teaching children.

4) The programs—whether in print or on computer screens—deny children opportunities to learn in more meaningful ways or to see any sense in what they are learning. Instead of reading or writing, they merely fill in the blanks.[21]

Smith maintains that, "There is nothing in the real world that is like any of the pedagogical treadmill (of programmatic instruction). Nobody learns anything, or teaches anything, by being submitted to such a regime of disjointed, purposeless, repetitive, confusing, and tedious activities. Teachers burn out, pupils fall by the wayside, and parents and administrators worry about the lack of student 'progress' or interest."[22]

Even worse, says Smith, "The brains of children are frequently blamed for the failure of programmatic instruction at school. It is taken for granted that something must be wrong with children who are confused or discouraged by school activities." He describes these activities as "ritualistically dull."[23] Consequently, the failure of such students to learn is attributed to a "disability" or a "minimal brain dysfunction." "This," says Smith, "is like arguing that a child who cannot jump a certain height must have a special kind of defective leg, even through there is no direct evidence of fractured bones and the child is perfectly able to walk, run and swim." The minimal brain dysfunction diagnosis says, in effect: 'We have decided that there must be something wrong with the child's brain even though we can't detect where or what the disorder is. We just assume that any child who fails to take advantage of the instruction provided at school, must be short of something in the head.'"[24]

The issue of programmatic instruction which Smith defines, sets in historical perspective, and evaluates in his 1988 book entitled *Insult to Intelligence: The Bureaucratic Invasion of Our Classrooms*, is essentially a political one. It is a question of who will control how students are taught: teachers or curriculum controllers?[25] Today in Pennsylvania, as in most states, the curriculum controllers are in charge, and the consequences for students continue to be devastating. Because programmed learning has become so embedded in large, bureaucratically-oriented school systems, banishing "packaged learning systems" and restoring the responsibility for teaching to teachers will be a challenge of the highest order.

Smith also worries about the reluctance of teachers to rely on their own creative abilities rather than on programs, which stress the teaching of skills in rigidly presented increments that are easy to test. Many teachers, he says, have known nothing else in their training; consequently, they have come to believe that programmatic instruction *is* education. "Programmatic instruction," he says, "has become entrenched in countless textbooks, course outlines, and curricula, from kindergarten to college ....Programs are credited with any learning that students and teachers are able to achieve, and students and teachers are blamed for the failures of programs."[26] And those who wish to get away from the tedium of "teach and test, drill and kill," are reluctant to confront the bureaucratic structure which imposed the systems in the first place.

The unspoken assumption behind the production and promotion of all programmatic instruction is that someone outside the classroom can make better decisions than the teacher in the class.[27] Implicit in this curious scenario is that teachers either cannot be trusted or do not have the skills required to make students learn. Even when teachers are proven to be inadequate, Smith reminds us, "Programs cannot be the solution. Programs are not an alternative, they will not do the job that good teachers are supposed to do."[28]

Dr. Smith is only one of a host of researchers who have concluded that the logical alternative to programmatic instruction is competent teachers who enjoy autonomy in the classroom. He finds good teachers easy to identify:

> Good teachers respond instinctively to the way in which children—and adults—learn, without direction from outside authorities. Good teachers never rely on programs or tests, and they resist external control when it is thrust upon them. They do not allow themselves or their "apprentices" to engage in pointless ritualistic activities. Instead, these teachers manifest attitudes and behaviors that learners become interested in manifesting themselves, and then these teachers help learners to manifest such attitudes and behaviors for themselves. Such teachers attract and indenture apprentices

without knowing they are doing so; they initiate learners into "clubs." The two essential characteristics of all the good teachers I have met is that they are interested in what they teach and they enjoy working with learners. Indeed, they are learners themselves.[29]

BATTLING THE BUREAUCRACY

The consolidation of public schools in Pennsylvania has given rise to an immense bureaucratic structure, witnessed by an increase in the ratio of administrators to teachers needed to cope with the complexities of the larger school systems.[30] The emergence of this looming bureaucracy has been facilitated by the General Assembly empowering the state Department of Education to control virtually every facet of local school administration. As a result of these changes, the Pennsylvania State Education Association has become one of the most formidable interest groups in the state. Not surprisingly, as the bureaucracy has grown, the autonomy of the classroom teacher and building principal has diminished. Decision-making has become centralized—far from the classroom where the effects of teaching can best be observed—in the office of the school district superintendent and in the halls of Harrisburg. Indeed, Pennsylvania's educational bureaucracy has succeeded in establishing authority while at the same time obscuring accountability.

For school boards, which traditionally have served as the focus of accountability to the voting public, the growth of bureaucracy has, according to former school superintendent Dr. Magill, significantly altered their function. The school board, he says, "has become overwhelmed with just the four 'B's'—buildings, bonds, budgets, and buses. Its meetings and its thrust are devoted to these things; consequently, the real reason for schools is lost in the shuffle and the hassle."[31]

To an extraordinary degree, the entrenchment of programmatic instruction, with its emphasis on repetitive testing of isolated skills, has aided and abetted the cause of bureaucratic control of education. "The people who try to assert every detail of what teachers should teach are not really in the business of helping students to learn at all," says Dr. Frank Smith. "Their business is the control of education, and their method is...testing."[32] Professor W. James Popham, an expert on educational testing at the University of California, Los Angeles, has written, "In an evidence-oriented enterprise, those who control the evidence-gathering mechanisms control the entire enterprise."[33]

There is only one reason why any bureaucracy insists on controlling the educational process. Implicit in its mania for control is the tenet that teachers cannot be trusted to teach. Accordingly, teachers are given the responsibility to teach by the bureaucracy, but teachers are denied the autonomy to do so. When they fail, it is not the bureaucracy that is blamed for creating a "Catch-22" situation. Rather it is the teacher who is deemed ineffective, the children who are termed dysfunctional, the parents who are labeled as disinterested, or the society, which has forces that have crippled the learning process. Dr Smith defines accountability as:

> . . . the standard term for the belief that teachers will teach better if they are constantly and publicly confronted with the consequences of their teaching, in the form of numerical test results. Through tests, teachers can be controlled without anyone ever entering their classrooms. And ironically, the procedures that are supposed to ensure that teachers teach effectively prevent them from doing so....Control through tests is lowering standards and reducing expectations. The deterioration is clouded by an educational jargon that is literally doublespeak, saying one thing while meaning another....Making teachers accountable means taking responsibility away from them.[34]

Former Pennsylvania Secretary of Education John C. Pittenger was mindful of the "accountability dilemma" faced by teachers in bureaucratically-controlled schools dominated by programmatic instruction. "I don't think it is accidental," he said, "that the years of school consolidation have been years of increasing teacher militancy. Bigger schools mean teachers who feel they have less and less influence over the conditions under which they work. Hence, they have turned increasingly to unions for the improvements and protections they could no longer achieve individually."[35]

Surely, the growth of union power over the Pennsylvania educational enterprise is the most stunning example of transferring power in education from the taxpayer to a bureaucratic entity, in this case one whose primary focus is on the wages and prestige of its members. This transfer of power was assured in 1970 by passage of Act 195. This legislation gave public school employees the right to strike without, in most cases, the loss of wages or benefits. Since that time, more than 800 school strikes have occurred in Pennsylvania, thus making the Commonwealth the national leader in school strikes. During the period between 1970 and 1988, one strike in four in the U.S. took place in Pennsylvania.[36] In spite of the fact that Act 195 clearly states that "public employers shall not be required to bargain over matters of inherent managerial policy," the State Supreme

Court, in a 1975 decision, significantly broadened Act 195's scope by making all public school policy subject to collective bargaining. Their decision thus empowered teacher unions to bargain on management issues ranging from class size to quantity and quality of classroom materials to timing of parent-teacher conferences.[37]

Teacher unions further tightened their grip on public education in 1988 with the passage of Act 84, which permits "negotiable agency shop," whereby a government employer must bargain on the subject of agency shop if the employee union so desires. Agency shop is the means by which unions seek authorization to force all non-union workers to pay representation fees to the union as a condition of continuing employment. To date over 167 Pennsylvania school districts have imposed involuntary union dues on teachers.[38] In 1992 the Pennsylvania State Education Association (PSEA), the statewide teachers union, succeeded in inserting language in Act 88 that prohibits school boards from hiring substitute teachers to replace strikers unless these substitutes had been on the payroll during the preceding 12 months. This provision effectively prevents school boards, during a strike by teachers, from fulfilling its constitutional mandate to "provide for the maintenance and support of a thorough and efficient system of public education."

An organization which monitors the forced union situation in Pennsylvania is the Concerned Educators Against Forced Unionism (CEAFU) of Springfield, Virginia, a division of the National Right to Work Committee. Former CEAFU director Jo Seker, a Pennsylvania resident, warns that meaningful education reform is not possible as long as unions dominate the educational landscape. "The reality is," she says, "that union officials intend to make education reform only on their terms. Education reform to them means local contracts giving them veto power over merit pay, innovative programs, length of school day, calendar schedules, class size, teacher evaluation, management of the schools, curriculum planning, textbook selection, and worst of all, who shall be hired or fired."[39]

PENNSYLVANIA SCHOOL GOVERNANCE: RECLAIMING RIGHTS FOR CITIZENS

In recent years, the escalation of confrontations between taxpayers, teachers, and school boards are symptomatic of the fact that citizens in Pennsylvania enjoy less control over their schools than the citizens of any of the other 49 states. Only in Pennsylvania are school directors given independent authority to both raise taxes and incur bonded indebtedness.[40]

This power was granted to school boards by the legislature with its passage of the Local Government Unit Debt Act (LGUDA) of 1972, which broadened the concept of "local government units" to include schools boards. Prior to that time, school boards were governed by the Pennsylvania School Code that stipulated that the people must provide their consent through an election of any school board action that proposes to incur bonded indebtedness in excess of 5 percent of the assessed value of real estate deemed taxable for school district purposes. Under the LGUDA, local government units can borrow up to 250 percent of their borrowing base (the average of total tax revenues for the previous three years) without a referendum, which, for all practical purposes, removes borrowing restrictions.[41]

In the absence of borrowing restrictions, school boards may undertake elaborate school building programs, often involving the closing of neighborhood schools for purposes of consolidation, without regard to the wishes of local taxpayers. The recent history of school building and remodeling projects throughout the state has been one of confrontations between schools boards—led by the powerful special interests of architects, bond counsels, attorneys, and union contractors—and citizens who oppose either the closure of their schools or the scope of the school projects. School building projects involving as much as $49 million for a single school are not unheard of,[42] and outraged citizens stand powerless to prevent either the closing of their schools or the assault on the public purse. In view of the fact that the Pennsylvania Constitution offers no provision for the recall of school directors, and that school directors are not even required by statute to allow public comment at school board meetings, the lot of Pennsylvania citizens is to pay the bill without comment.

Without exception, every special interest group, including the various arms of the Pennsylvania educational bureaucracy, has gone on record as opposing referendum for school building projects based on the assumption that Pennsylvania citizens would never vote to tax themselves for school improvements. They cling to this notion although citizens in the other 49 states operate this way, and, in several instances, have voted for more costly building plans than those supported by the local school board. Ironically, citizens from several school districts in recent years have demonstrated, by way of non-binding referenda, that they would favor a more costly building plan that would retain neighborhood schools, but their wishes were denied by an all-powerful school board which preferred the less costly route of consolidation.

So too, the recent history of school building in Pennsylvania points to a growing number of huge, new, closed buildings falling victim to "Sick Building Syndrome," in which ventilation systems are inadequate to filter out impurities in the air, causing children to suffer from a host of respiratory ailments.[43]

Adding to the already contentious environment which tends to surround school building and remodeling projects is the manner in which the legislature makes funds available for these projects. School districts are prohibited from receiving any state funds for routine or deferred maintenance projects. State money comes only for new school building projects or projects in which existing schools are literally rebuilt. Consequently, school boards which are caught between unions demanding and getting higher teacher pay and citizens demanding stable tax rates simply do not fund school building maintenance. Thus, under Pennsylvania law, taxpayers are virtually doomed to a system of "throw-away schools" which are routinely replaced or rebuilt every twenty to thirty years because of the "prescribed neglect" of Pennsylvania's peculiar system of school governance. What the legislature has done, in effect, is to provide an "automatically-renewable" source of building projects for the trade unions and other special interests in the form of public school buildings. They have done so at the expense of local taxpayers and of the educational system itself.

The frustration created because citizens have no say in controlling the spiraling costs of public education or to influence the structure and content of schools is not likely to subside amid reports of the declining performance of Pennsylvania school students. Without radical innovation in both the classroom and in the way in which schools are governed, perpetual turmoil is virtually assured, and it will become even harder to find qualified people to serve as school directors.

THE GRASSROOTS AGENDA FOR REFORM

Despite the array of problems on the educational landscape, some stout-hearted citizens do step forward with the hope of bringing about change through school board service. Reform-minded citizens who have been elected to school boards across the state have embraced most, if not all, of the following goals for educational progress:

> Reverse the trend toward large, consolidated schools in favor of a system of smaller, decentralized, community-based schools. Wherever possible, large schools should be broken into small units that

encourage full participation by teachers and students and a sense of belonging for all.

- Strive for educational accountability by restoring to teachers and school principals the responsibility for learning success or failure, giving them the autonomy to decide how learning can best be achieved, and allowing them to develop more reasonable measures for evaluating student progress than those defined by programmatic instruction systems and standardized tests.

- Assist teachers in improving their performance when it becomes evident that learning is not being achieved. Should the teacher fail to improve, the administration must be empowered to remove him from the classroom.

- Amend Act 195 to restrict the right of teachers to strike with impunity and to limit the scope of issues subject to collective bargaining to wages and hours only.

- Repeal Act 84 (agency shop) which is used to force non-union teachers to pay union dues as a condition of employment.

- Restore the right of citizens to take part in the process of school governance by enacting legislation to do the following: require a vote of the people when school directors propose to borrow funds in excess of 10 percent of the borrowing base; require a vote of the people when neighborhood schools are closed or consolidated, and allow the use of state funds for routine and deferred maintenance of school buildings.

As reform-minded school directors have learned, implementing their goals for educational innovation and reform clearly are not an agenda shared by Pennsylvania "educrats." From the day that would-be reformers take their school board seats, they are confronted at every turn by interest groups who are not happy with having their boat rocked and who will defend the status quo with all of their considerable might.

First are the architects, bankers, contractors, and lawyers who want their slice of the multi-billion dollar school construction pie. No sooner does a reform-minded school board succeed in halting a lavish building scheme, then squads of architects, bankers, builders, and lawyers return with new plans and all kinds of alarming data suggesting that the school district sky is falling, and the only thing that will save the children is a bigger and better construction plan. Their strategy is simple: it is the "victim-savior syndrome." Their goal is to convince the board that the school district has some particular, vexing problem, which will hinder effective education, and then the special interest groups come to the rescue with their services. The second assault wave on the school board consists of parents who have been traumatized by the special interest groups into believing that the very survival of their children is threatened unless the building project comes to pass.

Next to oppose change is the statewide Pennsylvania State Education Association teacher union. When a school board locks horns with the PSEA, they are pitted against a group which has 129,000 members, 12 regional offices, 60 full-time field representatives,[44] a central staff of 200, and an annual budget of almost $25 million.[45] Every time a new teacher contract is negotiated, the PSEA increases its financial resources, because union dues are calculated as a percentage of teacher salaries. Knowledge of this fact makes it easy to understand why the issue of agency shop is so important to the teacher unions; it is the union's most important, non-salary bargaining goal.[46] If the PSEA succeeds in making Pennsylvania a "closed shop," it will add an additional $10 million to its war chest. [47]

What does all of that union money buy? The PSEA uses its funds to elect its supporters to school boards and to the General Assembly so that the union can secure laws such as agency shop in order to harness even more power. PSEA money paved the way for the passage of Act 195, which gave teachers the right to strike and which paid for the 1975 court fight that resulted in broader bargaining powers. With as much as 85 percent of the school district budget now subject to collective bargaining because of Act 195, education policy is today fashioned behind closed doors without any input from citizens. If Pennsylvania becomes a closed union shop because of Act 84, and school boards cannot even hire substitutes for union teachers on strike because of Act 88, then the process of reforming schools will rest squarely in the hands of the PSEA bureaucracy which was not elected by the public and has no statutory accountability to parents or citizens. Even the toughest reform-minded school board will be powerless to implement educational innovations that might improve our children's education or to stress accountability through new merit pay plans.

Another important bureaucratic player is the Pennsylvania Department of Education. The mandates, regulations, and rules of the state are legion. School board reformers report that when they attended their first board meeting, they were presented with a stack of manuals and regulations measuring some four feet high. "You'll have to learn all about this," they were told by the district superintendent who quickly added, "Don't worry, I'll be there to explain it all to you." Reformers agree that this is just another variation of the "victim-savior syndrome." Overwhelm the new school directors with red tape, so that they will feel relieved to let the superintendent take charge.

So far, most pro-reform school directors who have achieved majorities on their boards have not been able to withstand the pressure of this extraordinary bureaucracy that dominates Pennsylvania education and school governance. In nearly every case, one or two school directors have been targeted for "re-education" by the superintendent, other board members, and/or "friends of the bureaucracy." These "educrats" know that it usually takes only one vote to swing the majority in order for their side to have its way. When this happens, there are devastating consequences to the community. The citizens who worked so hard to get the pro-taxpayer slate elected feel betrayed. They begin to perceive, and rightly so, that it does not make any difference whom you elect, because nothing changes. Most likely this is why Pennsylvania and other states suffer so profoundly from what could be called "programmed apathy." When citizens perceive that they cannot affect the operation of their schools and the manner in which their taxes are spent, they simply drop out of the system. As this happens, the bureaucracy becomes stronger.

School board members who favor grassroots reform will be powerless to act meaningfully without changes in the law. How likely is this to happen? More than a few state legislators are candid about their reluctance to tackle issues that are opposed by the PSEA. When one confronts the breadth and depth of power wielded by the state's largest union, one can better understand why neither major political party has stepped forward to take up the banner of education reform and give it the attention it deserves as a public issue of the first order. Providing lip service to educational reform and supporting legislative reform proposals that will meet a certain death in the legislature's Education Committees is not enough to secure the quality education children deserve.

THE CONSEQUENCES OF CONTINUED SCHOOL FAILURE: A CALL TO ACTION

The failure of public education in Pennsylvania poses a significant threat to the state's economic fabric. Each year the public schools produce increasing numbers of illiterate graduates whose inability to function in unskilled, entry-level jobs has forced employers to restructure those jobs so that literacy and numeracy are not factors affecting employment.[48] In order to find the workers needed to fill higher-level jobs, Pennsylvania business and industry is forced to spend millions of dollars to re-educate workers toward levels of acceptable literacy.[49] The burden that illiteracy will continue to place on already overburdened social welfare and penal institutions is worrisome to contemplate because of both economic and humanistic considerations.

The 1990 census confirmed that individuals are leaving Pennsylvania in record numbers. A recent study by Penn State's Population Issues Research Center found that two million residents left the state since 1940.[50] What is particularly disturbing about this study is that it shows Pennsylvania to be losing the cream of its crop. It reveals that the largest group of people leaving the state is 20 to 24 years old, the age when most in that group are finishing college. More than 12,000 people in that age group leave the state each year. The second largest group of individuals leaving—about 5,500 each year—is comprised of people aged 25 to 29. Penn State analysts further determined that the loss of workers is greatest among the most skilled people, including administrators, executives, managers, and professionals. The only group of workers not declining in numbers is blue-collar manufacturing and assembly workers. Finally, the study discloses that from 1980 to 1985, 44 of the state's 67 counties suffered net population losses in which the people moving out of the state are generally better educated and earn higher incomes than the people moving into the state.[51] The negative implications of this migration for business and government are fairly obvious.

It is apparent that few public policy issues speak more directly to the fulfillment of personal potential or the achievement of economic stability than the issue of reforming our schools. One would expect that with reform efforts such as America 2000 and OBE pending, the legislature will no longer be able to avoid examining and implementing reform. We at the grassroots level can only hope that state legislators will be guided by the one point about which virtually all education reformers agree: the schools will not improve until citizens, government, parents, and teachers can work on the problem together. It is hoped that any reform efforts will consider the "Grassroots Reform Agenda" cited in this chapter. Unless and until the legislature acts to empower citizens to become players in   education reform, public resentment toward the public schools will continue.

The politicians who so singularly control the mechanisms by which the schools are to be reformed would be well advised to heed John Goodlad's admonition that true reform can be accomplished only if it comes from the grassroots up, and not from an effort that is mandated from "on high." As he says so wisely,

There can be positive progress toward school improvement when the ideas perceived by thoughtful, inquiring educators are endorsed by policy makers. These ideas are implemented successfully when teachers and parents see eye to eye on their merit. But when parents and teachers are largely on the sidelines, this coming together will occur only by chance and only occasionally.[52]

ENDNOTES

1. John I. Goodlad, "On Taking School Reform Seriously," *Phi Delta Kappan*, 2 November 1992, 232.

2. Ibid..

3. Ibid..

4. Pennsylvania School Boards Association, "1992 Year In Review," *Information Legislative Service* (Harrisburg, PA), 31, no. 1, (January 1993): 6.

5. John F. Magill, Jr., *About Public Education in America: A Cause for Panic, A Recipe for Its Revival*, (Millersburg, PA: Turkey Valley Publishers, 1989), 1.

6. Irma E. Zimmer and Ann K. Monteith, "School Consolidation in Pennsylvania," Better Education and Sensible Taxation for PA, Annville, PA, privately printed, September 1988, 7.

7. Ibid..

8. Ibid., 8.

9. John C. Pittenger, "Progress and Problems in Education-A Report to the People of Pennsylvania" (Harrisburg, PA: Pennsylvania Department of Education, 1977), 71-72.

10. Pennsylvania Department of Education, "PLAN-CON Projects" (Harrisburg, PA: Pennsylvania Department of Education, April 1991).

11. Zimmer and Monteith, "School Consolidation," 6.

12. Better Education and Sensible Taxation (BEST) for Pennsylvania, "When is Bigger Too Big?," *BEST Report* (Annville, PA) 3, no. 2, (October 1989): 2.

13. Zimmer and Monteith, "School Consolidation," 15-22.

14. Carnegie Foundation, *An Imperiled Generation - Saving Urban Schools* (Princeton, NJ: Princeton University Press, 1988), xiv and 21-24.

15. Ibid..

16. Pennsylvania School Boards Association, "NSBA Report Stresses Need for Parent Involvement in Schools," *Information Legislative Service* (Harisburg, PA), 18 November 1988.

17. Carnegie Council on Adolescent Development, *Turning Points: Preparing Youth For the 21st Century* (New York, NY: Carnegie Corporation of New York, 1989), 13.

18. Magill, *About Public Education in America*, 3.

19. Frank Smith, *Insult to Intelligence: The Bureaucratic Invasion of our Classrooms* (Portsmouth, NH: Heinemann, 1988), ix.

20. "Whole language" is the term given to a language arts theory which stresses the need for teaching language in an "integrated" fashion, using real books rather than incremental "skills-based" exercises which stress testing following the teaching of each skill.

21. Smith, *Insult to Itelligence*, 10-11.

22. Ibid., 7.

23. Ibid., 50.

24. Ibid., 51.

25. Ibid., x.

26. Ibid..

27. Smith, *Insult to Intellegence*, 125.

28. Ibid., 127.

29. Ibid., 171.

30. Zimmer and Monteith, "School Consolidation," 9.

31. Magill, *About Public Education in America*, 5.

32. Smith, *Insult to Intelligence*, 128.

33. Ibid., 130.

34. Ibid..

35. Pittenger, "Progress and Problems in Education."

36. Pennsylvania School Boards Association, "Pennsylvania Claims Strike Record After 20 Years of Act 195 Bargaining," *Information Legislative Service* (Harrisburg, PA), 18 July 1989, 1-6.

37. Dr. Charles W. Baird, "Pennsylvania's Act 195: Twenty Years of Folly" (Harrisburg, PA: Pennsylvania Department of Education, 1990), 9-10.

38. Concerned Educators Against Forced Unionism, "Agency Shop Districts," Springfield, Va, privately printed, January 1993.

39. BEST od Pennsylvania, "When Is Bigger Too Big?," 6.

40. Maj. Gen. Bruce E. Kendall, "Fifty-State Taxation Study" (Annville, PA: Annville-Cleona Taxation Advisory Committee, 1986).

41. Zimmer and Monteith, "School Consolidation," 24.

42. Pat Land, "Hempfield Plans High School," *Sunday Patriot-News* (Harrisburg, PA), 14 October 1990, 19(A).

43. Marcia Reecer, "Sick School Syndrome: What To Do When Buildings Threaten Students' Health," *American School Board Journal* (August 1988): 17-21; and Ann K. Monteith, "The Agony of a Sick School," *BEST Report* (Annville, PA), April 1989, 4-5.

44. Wythe Keever and Joseph J. Serwach, "PSEA Does Political Homework," *Patriot-News* (Harrisburg, PA), 23 February 1992, 1(B).

45. Pennsylvania State Education Association, *Operating Budget Report* (Harrisburg, PA: Pennsylvania State Education Association, September 1990).

46. National Education Association, *NEA Handbook* (Washington, D.C.: National Education Association, 1991-92).

47. Jo Seker, former director of Concerned Educators Against Forced Unionism, interviewed by author, 18 February 1993, Annville, PA.

48. Iris Lefever, Paper presented at the workshop of the Lebanon/Lancaster Intermediate Unit, East Petersburg, PA, 18 November 1989.

49. "Employers Wrestle With 'Dumb' Kids," *Industry Week*, 4 July 1988, 47-52.

50. Ibid..

51. Ibid..

52. Goodlad, "On Taking Schoo Reform Seriously."

Chapter 23

The Unionization Movement in Pennsylvania Education

G. Terry Madonna

James W. White

INTRODUCTION

The need to develop a public policy toward public sector collective bargaining emerged in Pennsylvania after World War II. Concern over the growing number of strikes led the Pennsylvania Legislature to approve an anti-strike law in 1947. This law applied to all public employees, including school teachers whose numbers had grown to more than 100,000 working in 742 school districts by 1968. Under the terms of the 1947 Act, striking teachers had their employment terminated automatically. While a school district could reappoint a terminated teacher, it could not give a reappointed teacher a salary raise within a three year period, and a teacher served a five year probationary period.[1]

Teachers were permitted to join labor unions, and the changing nature of the post World War II economy, particularly the demand for increased educational services, a more highly educated teacher force, and a growing demand by teachers to have greater control over their professional livelihood, led to increased membership in the two national organizations representing teachers: The National Education Association (NEA) and the American Federation of Teachers (AFT). Eschewing strikes and organized labor, the NEA considered itself an educational organization, permitted school administrators to join its ranks, and prided itself on advancing the interest of teachers through conciliation and professionalism. The AFT, on the other hand, was an integral part of the nation's labor movement and part of the American Federation of Labor, and primarily concerned itself with securing enhanced economic benefits for teachers.[2]

Both organizations had mutually co-existed as more or less friendly rivals between World War I and 1960. This changed in 1961. In that year a brutal bargaining agent campaign in New York City, won by the AFT, led to bitter rivalry at the national level. In Pennsylvania the AFT affiliate, the Pennsylvania Federation of Teachers (PaFT), became the dominant force in the state's two largest cities, Philadelphia and Pittsburgh; and NEA's Pennsylvania organization, the Pennsylvania State Education Association (PSEA), enrolled substantially more teachers into membership in the vast majority of the other school districts.[3]

By the 1960s a set of fairly clear legal principles existed regarding teachers' labor relations. They were permitted to join labor unions, a right not barred by state law (and probably protected under the First Amendment to the Federal Constitution), and upheld by a Pennsylvania Supreme Court decision, *Broadwater vs. Otto*. School boards could, at their discretion, recognize a teacher organization as a bargaining representative for teachers, though some doubt existed as to whether such representation could be exclusive. Complicating the question of exclusive representation was the fact that each teacher had a separate contract with his school district. In brief, though the law was reasonably clear, the labor environment for teachers was inconsistent and unstable.[4]

Some school districts, like Philadelphia and Pittsburgh, had granted to teacher representatives *de facto* exclusive bargaining agent status during the 1960s; others, mostly suburban and rural school districts, simply would not bargain at all. The Pittsburgh School District was a notable example of the former. In May 1968 the Pittsburgh Federation of Teachers (PFT) was recognized as the bargaining agent for a "majority" of the teachers of the district. The election of a bargaining agent was conducted by the Allegheny Court of Common Pleas, following a federation called 11-day strike enlisting more than 1,200 teachers. Negotiations between the PFT and School Board representatives led to a "Memorandum of Accord," formalizing negotiated economic agreements and a list of professional concerns identified by the Federation. The more common practice in many districts, however, was for teachers to present their positions on wages and working conditions to school districts which unilaterally decided, as long as they were consistent with state law, salary, and working conditions.[5]

In many instances, when a teacher organization's request to bargain was opposed by a local school board, county judges ruled that bargaining violated state law. But, when strikes occurred, county judges generally did not dismiss striking teachers, largely because they believed the loss of employment was too severe a penalty for a teacher to pay for participating in a strike. In the midst of substantial labor chaos in the schools, a growing number of policymakers believed the time was ripe for the passage of a public sector collective bargaining law.

By the late 1960s external factors also helped make the passage of a collective bargaining law possible in Pennsylvania, as well as a few other states. Several factors contributed. First, President John F. Kennedy in 1962 had issued Executive Order 10988, granting collective bargaining rights to federal employees. Second, in the same year, Wisconsin passed the first comprehensive public sector bargaining law, providing both a model and a cause for other teachers contemplating collective bargaining. Third, the Pennsylvania Legislature in 1968 adopted a collective bargaining law, Act 111, for police, firefighters, and public safety personnel, which provided for binding arbitration in a negotiations impasse and outlawed the right to strike.[6]

Nationally, the onset of collective bargaining and teacher unionism in public education in the early 1960s led to numerous strikes in the 1970s. According to the U.S. Bureau of Labor Statistics, public school teachers struck 25 times between 1960 and 1965. Between 1975 and 1980 there were over 1,000 strikes that involved more than a million teachers.

In many respects, the year 1968 was the turning point in Pennsylvania. The lobbying and public relations activities of the teachers' organizations plus the work of other public and private sector unions brought about a changing dynamic in the state. Following a two month teacher strike in Pittsburgh, a strike which culminated in arrests, fines, and enjoinment, Governor Raymond Shafer appointed a commission to study public sector employee relations, with the expectation that a recommendation for a collective bargaining law would be forthcoming. Commonly known as the Hickman Commission, named for Leon E. Hickman, an attorney and Vice President of Alcoa, the group first met in May 1968 and issued its report in late summer.[7]

The Hickman Commission's report was divided into four general categories, many of which were eventually enacted into law. First, the Commission believed that special legislation should be enacted to govern the public sector. Second, all public employees, with a few exceptions, were to be covered by the new law. The Pennsylvania Labor Relations Board (PLRB), given expanded jurisdiction, would administer the new law. The PLRB would determine appropriate bargaining units. Additionally, wages, hours, and conditions of employment would comprise bargainable subjects. Third, both parties were required to bargain in good faith, and all negotiation agreements had to be reduced to writing. State mediation and appointed fact finders were to be utilized in resolving bargaining disputes. Police and firefighters would use binding arbitration to resolve bargaining deadlocks. The most controversial area broached by the Commission was its position in favor of the limited right to strike, which could be used by employees after a series of other impasse procedures had been exhausted. Any strike endangering public safety could be enjoined.[8]

The Commission saw its limited strike right proposal as balancing employer and employee rights:

> The collective bargaining process will be strengthened if this qualified right to strike is recognized. It will be some curb on the possible intransigence of an employer; and the limitations of the right to strike will serve notice on the employee that there are limits to the hardships that he can impose.... In short, we look upon the limited and carefully defined right to strike as a safety valve that will in fact prevent strikes.[9]

A lively debate in the legislature followed the introduction of the Commission's report into draft legislation, which became Senate Bill 1333. Several competing bills were introduced into the Pennsylvania General Assembly incorporating various aspects of the Commission's report along with the ideas of the sponsors. One such bill, House Bill 1443, an employee rights version supported by numerous unions, passed the House in July 1969 but died in a Senate committee. Finally, a Senate bill, encompassing compromise language and most of the Hickman Commission's proposals, passed the legislature in July 1970, by a vote of 32-13 in the Senate and 157-34 in the House. It was signed into law by Governor Raymond Shafer as Act 195 of 1970.[10]

The passage of Act 195 ushered in a new era in public sector labor relations. No one emerged completely satisfied with the legislation finally enacted. Governor Shafer had preferred binding arbitration to resolve negotiations disputes. The unions had lobbied for, but did not get, agency shop, the right to collect fees from non-union members. The School Boards Association had argued for a separate independent agency to administer the new collective bargaining act. Yet most of the major participants in the public sector looked to the future with a sense of optimism and with an expectation that the new labor law would work well.[11]

THE NEW BEGINNING

Act 195 went into effect on October 21, 1970, and within ten weeks the PLRB's offices were flooded with representation petitions. The teachers' unions, the PSEA and the PaFT, were out of the starting blocks fast, organizing teachers and other professional school personnel. Some 651 representation cases were filed with the Board; in 514 of them the employer was a school district. By 1972 most of Pennsylvania's teachers were organized. Cooperation between the teachers' unions and school boards was widespread in the halcyon early years. In more than 65 percent of the early representation cases, certification requests were jointly requested by the unions and the school districts. Teachers organized in bargaining units separate from all other employees. In only two school districts were teachers and nonprofessionals placed together in the same bargaining unit. PSEA organized and negotiated contracts in 560 school units, including school districts, vocational-technical schools, and intermediate units. The PaFT's strength, since the inception of collective bargaining, has been largely confined to urban areas; it represents the teachers in Philadelphia and Pittsburgh.[12]

The first several years of bargaining were characterized by ceaseless organizational activities by teachers' unions, expanded administrative work by the PLRB, hundreds of successfully negotiated collective bargaining agreements, and finally by a number of strikes, mostly of short duration. A Carnegie Mellon University study of the first phase (1970-1975) of collective bargaining described an environment in which "inexperience," the contrary expectations of the various parties, and commonly held beliefs that negotiations equated necessarily with win-lose positions by the various sides largely predominated. With important exceptions, few local unions or school boards had any practical experience in formalized collective negotiations. Initially, teachers received crash courses in various aspects of the negotiations process and were "modestly" trained, while managers in school districts received little or no instruction.[13]

A widespread sense of exhilaration existed among teachers who now found themselves able, through their teacher leaders and union representatives, to place negotiable demands before their employers and not have them dismissed out-of-hand. These feelings ran highest in regard to salary increases and the desire to be dealt with as professionals. School boards naturally feared that salary demands would ultimately lead to higher property taxes and a loss of the unilateral management of local schools.[14]

COLLECTIVE BARGAINING AT WORK

No part of Act 195 has been more hotly debated than the section granting employees the limited right to strike. Little known is the fact that certain categories of employees may not strike: prison guards and court employees, for example. Also, no employee may strike during the fact finding period of the collective bargaining process; secondary strikes are banned as well as strikes generated by an employer's unfair labor practice. Teachers must cross picket lines and go to work unless they are themselves engaging in a nonprohibited strike. Act 195 contains only one nonprohibited type of strike: one that occurs after the parties have bargained to impasse and a collective bargaining agreement has expired.[15]

Given the inexperience of both employees and employers, the first year of collective bargaining produced surprisingly few teacher strikes. In many districts, a congenial and professional approach led to collective bargaining agreements, but in others the process broke down. In 1971, the first full year of bargaining, 71 work stoppages took place; 36 of them in school districts. PSEA represented employees in 35 of the 36. The following year, 60 strikes occurred, 30 of them involved school districts, of which 29 were called by PSEA. Many of PSEA's strikes were in small and medium size school districts. The strikes involving the largest number of teachers, however, took place in Pittsburgh in 1971 and Philadelphia in 1972 and 1973. Teachers in both districts were represented by AFT affiliates.[16]

The longest strike in the first year was the 19-day strike in the Brockway Area School District; while Osceola and York Suburban school district teachers struck for only a single day. Most of these strikes were first contract strikes, and seven of the first year's work stoppages resulted in lost classroom instructional days because the school year was not extended sufficiently to replace the lost school days. The Public School Code, which sets the operational parameters for school districts, requires that each school district offer 180 days of schooling or lose state funds. The seven districts, which did not make up missed school days, lost a total of 11 instructional days.[17]

There were 29 strikes in 1972, 36 in 1973, 30 in 1974, with lost instructional days numbering, 29, 116, and 71, respectively. In a few districts, long, bitter, and publicly unpopular strikes introduced a new aspect of labor relations. The Philadelphia Federation of Teachers struck in 1973 for 54 days, then the longest strike to-date under Act 195. All told, the 36 strikes in 1973 produced 525 days of work stoppages.[18]

Most of the strikes in the 1971-74 period lasted fewer than 10 days. This did not, however, negate their unpopularity with the public and parents. Most authorities believed the causes of these strikes lay in the novelty and inexperience of those participating in bargaining for the first time, and the desire of the parties to prove their toughness and resolve.[19]

Teacher expectations ran quite high in the initial round of negotiations. Leading on the list of concerns was salaries. Teacher salaries lagged behind the pay of other similarly educated professionals. Classroom teachers salaries averaged $8,858 in 1969-70 and rose to $11,400 by 1974-75, an average annual increase of approximately five percent. But a PSEA assessment of the teachers' average salaries, when adjusted for inflation in 1991 dollars, showed teachers losing ground to inflation, with salaries dropping from $32,000 in 1972 to below $30,000 in 1975. A Carnegie Mellon University study indicated that teachers were relatively pleased with what they considered to be a "modest" bargaining beginning.[20]

EARLY LEGISLATIVE REVIEW

A Special Joint Legislative Committee was created in 1973 to examine the operation of Act 195. After holding hearings throughout the state and taking the testimony of all the principal participants, the Committee issued its report in November 1974. Teachers were represented in the inquiry by PSEA and PaFT leaders; school board members by representatives of the Pennsylvania School Boards Association (PSBA). Fred Heddinger of the PSBA testified that Act 195 was "more comprehensive and explicit than other collective bargaining laws." He said, "Despite some shortcomings.... Act 195 is a sound law, with proper administration and with certain shoring up of obvious shortcomings [it] can function as it was designed to do." The PaFT, in the testimony of Marvin Ginsburg, argued strongly for no change "in any way at this time," insisting that Act 195 met its major purpose of promoting more harmonious relationships." The most significant conclusion reached by the Legislative Committee was to term the period of collective negotiations under the Act a qualified success. The Committee found that no adverse relationships had developed in the public schools, summarizing that, because public sector collective bargaining was still new, it opposed any changes in Act 195.[21]

While a consensus emerged on the big question of whether to recommend modification to Act 195, naturally the various collective bargaining participants viewed the developments of those past few years differently. PSEA favored a separate administrative board to administer collective bargaining affairs for public education; an expanded bargaining unit to include additional professionals, such as building principals; and the enlargement of bargainable subjects (mindful of the State College Education Association Case). The PSBA weighed in with its agenda. Its spokespersons defended bargaining units that excluded first-level supervisors, preferred guidelines clearly spelling out inherent managerial policy, and wanted assurances that collective bargaining agreements would never contravene state laws.

THE PLRB AND THE LAW

The Pennsylvania Labor Relations Board is responsible for administering Act 195. The PLRB existed before Act 195, but it primarily dealt with private sector labor relations. The PLRB's functions were expanded tremendously as part of the Act 195 collective bargaining process. Its rulemaking authority permits the PLRB to adopt rules and procedures to implement Act 195; it also monitors representation elections, certifies bargaining units, appoints fact-finding panels, decides unfair labor practice disputes and, on occasion, petitions various courts for restraining orders to resolve unfair labor practices. The Board consists of three members, chosen by the governor, whose appointments require the approval of the State Senate.

In the first three months of the operations of Act 195, the Board handled 666 public sector representation and unfair practice cases, with school district filings totaling about 78 percent of the caseload. By the end of the first full year, school district cases had fallen to 54 percent of the public sector caseload.[22]

By far the most substantive school issue taken up by the PLRB in the early years concerned the bargaining demands of teachers that related to "inherent management policy." Act 195 requires management to negotiate wages, hours, and terms and conditions of employment, but not any "matter of inherent management policy." Teachers in the State College Area Education Association filed an unfair labor practice with the PLRB contending the school district would not negotiate over 21 separate items placed on the bargaining table by the union. The case was initially decided by the PLRB and then reviewed by the appellate courts before being remanded to the Labor Board, paving the way for a legal interpretation regarding the nature of management policy. As resolved by the courts and the PLRB, management was required to engage in "meet and discuss" sessions on those matters of management policy that had an effect on teachers' working conditions. Specifically, when in 1975 the Supreme Court ruled in the State College case, it provided a standard for determining what subjects required bargaining. The High Court said that certain items were not precluded from mandatory bargaining just because they might impinge on subjects customarily perceived as management prerogatives. The critical part of the balance test was the degree to which the items in question related to legitimate employee interests in wages, hours, and conditions of employment.[23]

When remanded to the PLRB, it found that five of the 21 questionable items were required subjects For bargaining: timely notice of teaching assignments, cafeteria duty for teachers in the senior high schools, chaperoning athletic duties, access to teachers' personnel files, and school closings prior to certain holidays.[24]

Another crucial area where a legal precedent was established dealt with an aspect of the limited right to strike. Act 195 allows an employer to seek an injunction halting a work stoppage, if the strike "creates a clear and present danger or threatens the health or welfare of the public." The Armstrong School District had obtained an injunction against its striking teachers from the Armstrong Court of Common Pleas, basically for three reasons: 1) the strike had caused disruption of the school district's sports and extracurricular activities; 2) public officials were harassed by individuals not involved in the strike; and 3) state funding would be lost should missed instructional days not be made up. The Armstrong Education Association sought and won relief from the Commonwealth Court, which ruled that "clear and present" meant a "danger or threat [that] is real or actual and that a strong likelihood exists that it will occur." Subsequent appellate court decisions strengthened the right of teachers to strike.[25]

A Second Comprehensive Review

In 1976, Governor Milton Shapp established a nine-person commission to conduct an evaluation of Act 195 (and Act 111), making it the second comprehensive review of the law. This particular study was headed by Benjamin R. Jones, a retired Chief Justice of the State Supreme Court. The Commission conducted 13 days of public hearings, heard from more than 100 witnesses, some of whom testified on behalf of 20 organizations. Issued in 1978, the Commission Report reaffirmed the efficacy of the right of public employees to engage in collective bargaining.

Of the Commission's many deliberations the most relevant for the education community: 1) reaffirmed the State College balancing test; 2) asserted the need for a new bargaining timetable, especially a shortened and compressed schedule; 3) proposed strengthening fact finding; 4) regarded the right to strike as worthy of continuance, but wanted several forms of arbitration available to the parties; and 5) recommended maintaining 180 days of minimum instruction and full state subsidy but with important alterations. Any rescheduled days should be the subject of permissive bargaining. Any lost instructional days should penalize both teachers and school districts, the former would lose a day's compensation for each day on strike, the latter would have their state subsidy reduced by 1/180th for each day of instruction less than 180 days.[26]

The Commission was optimistic the legislature would adopt at least some of the proposed changes as amendments to Act 195, but it did not. The decade of the 1970s ended without any modifications to the state's basic law for public sector labor relations.

Increased Conflict, 1975-1983

One major study has called the second period of public sector collective bargaining the "adversary years," largely on the basis of the increased number and length of teacher strikes in the period. The Carnegie Mellon Study of *Teacher Labor Relations in Pennsylvania Public Schools* compared the length of first and repeat strikes from 1975-76 to 1982-83:

School Strikes, 1975-76 and 1982-83

Incidence	No.	Average Length	10 Days Or Less	20 Days Or More	30 Days Or More
1st Strike	155	14.9	34.2	41.9	15.5
2nd Strike	77	21.7	20.3	61	27.3
3rd/4th Strike	15	24.9	13.3	60	26.7

The authors of the study concluded that 60 percent of the second and third strikes were of 20 days duration or more, and one in four lasted 30 days or more. These data compared unfavorably to the majority of first strikes which lasted fewer than 20 days, while one in three lasted fewer than ten days.[27]

A close examination, however, indicates a degree of unevenness in both the number and the duration of strikes occurring during the period. In 1975-76, there were 37 work stoppages, lasting 282 days collectively. The number of work stoppages dramatically jumped to 54 in 1976-77, with a total of 682 days of strikes, followed by a decrease to 41 in 1977-78, but with more days lost, 739. In 1979-80, work stoppages slipped to 20, with 333 days lost; climbed again during the 1980-81 school year (573 days struck); stayed about the same in 1981-82, 33 and 631, respectively; fell to 25 and 358 in 1982-83; and shot up in 1983-84 to 38, with 934 struck days.[28]

Rarely examined, however, is the relationship between the number of contracts being negotiated and the number of strikes. In 1976, a year in which 54 strikes occurred, there were 377 open contracts; while in 1979, a year with 20 strikes, there were only 256 open contracts.[29]

Certainly the late 1970s was marked by an increase in labor hostility. Several factors help explain the deteriorating environment. The high inflation of the late 1970s had eroded teachers' salaries. PSEA points to the period as one in which "increases in inflation again greatly exceeded teacher salary increases." Teachers demanded salary raises commensurate with or higher than inflation. Some school boards, faced with a set of dynamics different from the early 1970s, refused teacher salary demands. The first new dynamic was the decline in the proportion of state funds school districts received. There was the commonly held assumption within the education community that the Commonwealth should pay for approximately 50 percent of the instructional cost of public education.

The proportion of state to local support declined precipitously between 1970-71 and 1980-81, as the state share fell below 40 percent. A second consideration was declining pupil enrollment and the belief by some school boards that fewer students, which meant a declining support base and state subsidy, should translate into a more conservative bargaining position.[30]

The PLRB expressed no surprise that teacher bargaining agents struck more than any other group of public employees. By 1975, 56 percent of all the existing bargaining units under Act 195 consisted of units representing school personnel. The PLRB cited the "economy of the times" as the chief reason for the increase in strikes. As the PLRB put it, "Here were the public employees, some emerging from multi-year contracts, hounded by the inflationary erosion of their past economic gains at the bargaining table. But just across the bargaining table sat public officials facing ballooning costs, limited revenues, reluctant taxpayers, and an already squeezed tax dollar."[31]

A THIRD REVIEW OF ACT 195

The increase in strikes led to a third major review of Act 195. In 1984, the State Senate directed a five-member task force to examine two major aspects of the labor law: first, what changes should be made to prevent strikes; and second, what steps could be taken to shorten the length of strikes and to reduce the disruption to the education community. During the hearings, an array of arbitrators, legislators, and labor lawyers wanted the Act amended to require the arbitration of negotiation disputes in certain situations. The PSEA and the PaFT opposed modifying Act 195. Their leaders, in vigorous testimony, insisted that surrendering the right to strike would mean an end to collective bargaining. They also opposed substituting binding arbitration for the right to strike. The PSBA saw dangers in continuing the right to strike and in requiring binding arbitration. According to PSBA's position, Act 195 had not "built a stable labor environment [describing] arbitration... as even more destructive to an environment of agreement."[32]

No issue was more difficult for the State Senate Task Force to resolve than the so-called 180 day rule, requiring each school district to provide 180 days of instruction each year. Critics of the rule, which is in reality a state law, pointed out that it permitted striking teachers to stop working, go on strike, and return to work after the strike. Most school districts amended their school calendars mandating the completion of 180 days of instruction, allowing teachers to make up the lost days. In effect, most striking teachers lost no salary as a result of work stoppages.

A former member of the original Hickman commission, Judge Emil Narick of Allegheny County testified that the Hickman group expected strikers, similar to the private sector, would lose compensation when on strike, and school districts would forfeit 1/180th of their school subsidy for each struck day. Narick argued that once a school district established its yearly calendar no adjustments should be made to extend the school year. The immediate ramification for both the school board and striking teachers would be economic loss: the school board would lose state funding for failure to provide 180 days of actual instruction while teachers would lose salary for work days missed while on strike. Narick believed that without penalties for both parties the limited right to strike provisions in Act 195 would be thrown out of balance by advantaging one side or the other. In their testimony, school superintendents wanted flexibility to make up the missed days, based on each school district's own special circumstances. They also believed most make-up days were unproductive, with both student and teacher absenteeism unusually high.[33]

One new element was added to the strike controversy by William Caldwell, a professor of education at Penn State University, who entered the debate with an argument that school strikes had a deleterious effect on learning. Caldwell seemed to provide support for what many nonacademic critics of the right to strike had been saying for almost a decade: school strikes had a negative effect on student learning. Caldwell had previously published the results of two research projects, which were widely available within the education community. His testimony summarized his research. He essentially made three points: 1) differences in standardized test scores increased after strikes, with the students of non-striking districts scoring better in mathematics tests in the fifth and eighth grades and in reading tests in eighth grade than did their counterparts in districts not on strike; 2) lower standardized test scores in reading and mathematics were recorded by students in struck districts in the first two academic years after a work stoppage, though academic achievement did rise in later years; and 3) the longer a strike, the more significant the decline in achievement scores.[34] Caldwell, who was joined by legislators and school officials, urged the retention of the 180 day requirement.

After six-months of deliberation the Task Force issued five recommendations. They wanted to accomplish the following items: condense the collective bargaining time-table; strengthen the mediation process; permit either party to initiate fact finding, limiting the ability of school districts to extend the school year to make up days lost because of strikes; and continue to assess the option of amending the constitution to allow for arbitration as a substitute for the right to strike, if strikes remained at an unacceptably high rate and duration.[35]

Perhaps the most significant proposal for change dealt with the 180 day rule. The Commission's majority concluded that there was simply no economic incentive to resolve strikes, as school districts extended instructional days in order to receive full state funding and teachers recouped their lost wages. In some cases, but not the majority, county courts enjoined strikes (usually in late October) only when it appeared unlikely that school districts could succeed in completing 180 days of instruction before the end of the Commonwealth's fiscal year. The Task Force members were especially cognizant of this concern. They wanted to prevent school districts from extending the school year beyond their original date for ending the school year or June 15th, which ever was later. Also, no classes would be scheduled over the Christmas and New Year holiday.[36]

The task force consisted of five senators: three Republicans, D. Michael Fisher, who chaired the group, Ralph W. Hess, and Robert C. Jubelirer, and two Democrats, Jeanette F. Reibman and James Lloyd. The Democratic members issued a strong dissent from the Task Force's Majority report. They believed the Act was "functioning well," the right to strike should be retained, the fiscal penalties for not completing the required minimum school year should be continued, and "The prohibition against rescheduling days [over the holiday season]... which was recommended in the [Majority] report should be rejected unless it is coupled with a requirement that districts expand the school day in order to provide students with the equivalent 180 days," a modification that should be made in the public school code and not in Act 195.[37]

The task force report hit the legislature with all the weight of a feather. Over the years since 1970 a plethora of analysis and amendments to Act 195 have appeared. Some have been studies conducted by academics, some have been analyses by legislative committees, some have been assessments by various elements within the education community, but no amendment to the law has been approved by the General Assembly. The legislature has certainly dealt with collective bargaining issues, but in doing so has changed other statutes.

Post 1983 Period

For a variety of reasons, the number of school strikes in Pennsylvania declined after 1983, as the following table indicates:

School Strikes, 1984 - 1991

	1984	1985	1986	1987	1988	1989	1990	1991
Number of Strikes	11	22	14	22	16	23	19	19
Duration of Strikes (in days)	236	302	269	381	318	372	284	268

A few of the strikes, however, were lengthy, such as the 84 day strike in 1984 at Greater Nanticoke Area School District, the 99 day strike in 1988 at Turkeyfoot Valley Area School District, the 62 day strike in 1989 at West Greene School District, and the 54 day strike in 1991 at New Castle School District. But overall, strikes were fewer in number than in the late 1970s and early 1980s. The Carnegie Study found several reasons for the decline in strikes. One was the development of a new "sensitivity" on the part of both teacher unions and school boards to the growing public apprehension over the number and severity of strikes in the state. A second factor of significant consideration was the increase in real salary gains made by teachers.[38]

Salary data compiled by PSEA confirms the Carnegie assessment. In 1983-84, the average teaching salary in Pennsylvania was $22,703, ranking the state's teachers 18th in the country but by 1990-91 salaries had risen to more than $36,000, 11th best in the nation, and $3,000 more than the national average of $33,041. Also, by 1991 teachers' salaries adjusted for inflation had risen to their highest point since the passage of Act 195. The easing of inflation in the post 1982-1983 recession period was also a contributing factor in the willingness of negotiators to reconcile salary impasse differences. A third factor was related to the maturation and sophistication of everyone involved in collective bargaining. Each side realized that collective bargaining was in the state to stay, and no change in Act 195 would be enacted into law materially helping one side or the other.

Therefore, having to "live with one another," the parties cooperated more; teachers realizing that strikes had their limits and managers realizing that teachers had a legitimate concern over their professional and economic livelihood. The Carnegie University study provides an excellent summary of the changing relationship:

> From our interviews with union and management teams, it is apparent that collective bargaining is becoming characterized less by conflict and more by mutual problem solving. Both parties have gravitated toward this kind of approach since there has been a mutual recognition that it is better to reach an agreement, although one might have to give up something, than to resort to a strike. Strikes have tarnished the image of teachers and contributed to negative feelings about public education. Further, as communication between both parties improves, there has been a realization that they share many of the same concerns and that cooperation on issues of mutual interest and compromise in areas of disagreement serves the interest of both parties.

Naturally not all of the participants saw the process as beneficial. In some districts tension still exists, sometimes because of lingering effects of a strike or because the personalities of those involved proved to be too combustible to resolve the problems.[39]

THE RECENT YEARS

During the late 1980s, the teacher organizations, along with other public sector unions, made a major push to win legislative approval for the right to collect fees from non-union members, a concept referred to as fair share or agency shop. Under the provisions of a state law adopted in 1988, Act 84, public unions won the right to negotiate contract provisions requiring non-union members to pay the union representing the employee a fee for the collective bargaining services provided by bargaining agents. The agency fee law, a complex piece of procedural legislation, had long been a goal of teachers' unions. Originally supported by the Hickman Commission, but not enacted into law as the compromise that became Act 195, fair share had proved elusive to the unions. Union leaders viewed as unfair the fact that non- union members received the negotiated benefits and that unions were required to represent those without union membership in virtually every aspect of collective bargaining, even though they received no financial support from the non-members. The opponents of fair share viewed the law as punitive and coercive, insisting it violated their constitutional rights. Act 84 was subsequently challenged, but upheld in various courts.

As the collective bargaining process evolved, so too did some of the practical bargaining techniques. The emergence of early-bird negotiations is an example of both the evolution and maturity of public sector collective bargaining. Conceptually, an early-bird contract is one completed substantially prior to the end of a bargaining year. Early-bird negotiations began in the late 1970s largely to correct contract salary inequities brought about by inflation. They were used in the recent past, however, as a means to achieve an early settlement as opposed to eliminating salary disparities. Both management and labor has viewed them as a way to promote more harmonious relationships, particularly when they have been employed after a strike or bitter contract negotiations.[40]

Efforts to bring about significant change in public sector collective bargaining had failed for more than twenty years, 1970-1992. Two major evaluations of Act 195, the Jones Commission and the 1984 State Senate Task Force, went unheeded and ignored. Then in 1992, without the benefit of a lengthy study, the state Legislature approved the most sweeping alteration of Pennsylvania's basic labor law since 1970.

The genesis of the reform lay in the use of the selective strike by the state's largest teachers' organization, the PSEA. A selective strike is one that takes place on a day-to-day basis, often with little or no public notice. This type of strike may be utilized building-by-building within a school district for a partial or a complete day. Selective strikes have an aspect of unpredictability about them, often angering parents, students, community members, and typically creating an atmosphere of confusion. Even organized labor's friends were unhappy over their use. The PaFT, PSEA's union counterpart, publicly opposed the use of selective strikes, refused to use them, and was openly critical of their employment. PSEA employed the selective strike as a major negotiations impasse tool in the late 1980s and early 1990s.

In 1991, one proposal pushed in the state Senate called for the use of binding arbitration to settle negotiations disputes actually made it to the floor of the state Senate. This was the first bill amending Act 195 to reach the floor of either legislative chamber since the passage of Act 195. A series of complex negotiations took place over the next year with the teachers' unions and PSBA lobbying hard for their respective positions. PSBA continued its historic opposition to compulsory binding arbitration, "contending that the granting of authority to third party arbitrators to establish salaries and benefits--and, effectively, local tax rates--constituted a cure worse than the strike 'disease'." The unions' natural inclination was to keep the right to strike as it had existed for the past 22 years. The pressure was heavy, however, because as PSEA put it "vocal taxpayers" were demanding substantive changes in Act 195 to limit the right to strike and to subject striking teachers to severe penalties.[41]

As approved by the Legislature in the summer of 1992, Act 88 became a legislative milestone and ushered in a new era in collective bargaining for public education. Act 88 did not amend Act 195, but it modified the Pennsylvania School Code and its provisions applied only to school districts. Under its basic terms: 1) a 48 hour notice is required before any strike may commence; 2) an advisory arbitration is required if a strike would prevent a school district from completing a 180 days of instruction before June 15th or the final day of the scheduled school year, whichever falls later; 3) a strike must end when the parties agree to arbitration and it may not begin until the arbitration award is rejected by one of the parties; 4) the use of selective strikes is banned; 5) during the first strike, a school district may not use employees who have not been employed by the district for at least 12 months, but if a strike resumes after the rejection of an arbitration award, strike breakers may be used; 6) the Secretary of Education is given legal standing to seek an injunction if a strike may prevent the completion of the 180 day school year requirement; and 7) a more compressed and vigorously enforced bargaining timetable is established.[42]

Passage of Act 88 was secured essentially because of a major compromise reached between the contending lobbying forces. The unions wanted to prevent the use of strike breakers and management's goal was to eliminate the selective strike. In the end, the law was passed with the support of PSEA, PaFT, and PSBA. During the first year in which Act 88 was operational, teacher strikes in Pennsylvania declined from 36 to 17, even though Pennsylvania still led the nation in school strikes. Though the law's implementation is relatively new, there exists high hopes and solid expectations that labor relations in Pennsylvania school districts will be substantially enhanced.

ENDNOTES

1. John Schmidman, "Collective Bargaining in Pennsylvania's Public Sector: The First Thirty Months," *Labor Law Journal* (1973): 755-756; and Hickman Commission, "Minutes of Organizational Meeting" (Harrisburg, PA: Hickman Commission, 9 May 1968).

2. Otto Davis and Ben Fischer, *Teacher Labor Relations in Pennsylvania Public Schools A Research Study,* (Pittsburgh, PA: Carnegie Mellon University, 1987), 29-31; and Ross Engle, "Teacher Negotiation: History and Comment," *Journal of Law and Education* 1, no. 3 (1972): 487-489.

3. Engle, "Teacher Negotiation," 487-492.

4. *Broadwater v. Otto,* 370 Pa. 611 (n.d.); and *Philadelphia Teachers Association v. La Brum,* 370 Pa. 212 (n.d.).

5. Al Fondy, "Current Facts and History of the Pittsburgh Federation" (Pittsburgh, PA: Pennsylvania Federation of Teachers, August 1992); Saul Diamond, "The PFT in the 60's, 70's, and 80's - Times of Strife and Strength" (Pittsburgh, PA: Pennsylvania Federation of Teachers, 1985), 28-29; and Edward Smith, former President of Pennsylvania State Education Association, interviewed by authors, 15 March 1993, Pittsburgh, PA.

6. Davis and Fisher, *Teacher Labor Relations,* 33-34; and Pennsylvania School Boards Association, *Public School Negotiations A Complete Guide To Collective Bargaining in Pennsylvania's Public Education* (Harrisburg, PA: Pennsylvania School Board Association, 1993), 20.

7. Hickman Commission, "Minutes of the Organizational Meeting," 6-8.

8. Ibid.; and Pennsylvania Labor Relations Board, *Annual Reports 1970-1973* 34-37, (Harrisburg, PA: Pennsylvania Labor Relations Board, 1973), 6-8.

9. Hickman Commission, "Minutes of Organizational Meeting," 7.

10. Pennsylvania Labor Relations Board, *Annual Reports,* 8-9.

11. Ibid., 3-5.

12. Ibid., 79-81.

13. Davis and Fisher, *Teacher Labor Relations,* 34-36.

14. Ibid..

15. Schmidman, "Collective Bargaining," 762.

16. Pennsylvania Department of Education *Summary of Public School Work Stoppage Activity 1970-71 through 1991-92* (Harrisburg, PA: Pennsylvania Department of Education, 1992), 15-16.

17. Ibid..

18. Ibid., 16-18.

19. Ibid., 16-19; and Schmidman, "Collective Barganing," 762.

20. Davis and Fisher, *Teacher Labor Relations,* 35.

21. Pennsylvania Senate Task Force, "Report on Act 195" (Harrisburg, PA: 1973-74 Legislative Session, November 1974), 8 and 12.

22. Pennsylvania Labor Relations Board, *Annual Reports*, 79-88.

23. Ibid., 162-163.

24. Ibid., 19-21; and *Pennsylvania Labor Relations Board v. State College Area School District*, 9 Commonwealth Court 229 (n.d.).

25. Pennsylvania Labor Relations Board, *Annual Reports*, 22; and *Armstrong Education Association v. Armstrong School District*, 5 Commonwealth Court 378 (n.d.).

26. Hickman Commission, "Minutes of Organizational Meeting."

27. Davis and Fisher, *Teacher Labor Relations*, 37.

28. Pennsylvania Department of Education, *Summary of Public School Work Stoppage Activity*, 19-32.

29. Pennsylvania State Education Association, *Two Decades Later - The History of Act 195* (Harrisburg, PA: Pennsylvania State Education Association, January 1991); and Pennsylvania State Education Association, *Act 195 - The Third Decade* (Harrisburg, PA: Pennsylvania State Education Association, January 1992).

30. Ibid., 12; and Davis and Fisher, *Teacher Labor Relations*, 36-38.

31. Pennsylvania Labor Relations Board, *Annual Reports*, 198.

32. Pennsylvania Senate Task Force, "Report on Act 195."

33. Ibid..

34. William Caldwell and others, eds., *The Effect of Strikes in Pennsylvania Public Schools on Student Achievement and Attendance* (University Park, PA: Pennsylvania State University, 1981), 21-22; and Peter Zirkel, "The Academic Effects of Teacher Strikes," *Journal of Collective Negotiations* 21 (1992): 134.

35. Pennsylvania Senate Task Force, "Report on Act 195."

36. Ibid..

37. Ibid..

38. Davis and Fisher, *Teacher Labor Relations*, 41-44; and Pennsylvania Department of Education, *Summary of Public School Work Stoppage Activity*, 33-41.

39. Pennsylvania State Education Association, *Act 195-The Third Decade*, 10-12; and Davis and Fisher, *Teacher Labor Relations*, 43.

40. Pennsylvania State Education Association, "Early Bird Negotiations and Early Abbreviated Bargaining" (Harrisburg, PA: Pennsylvania State Education Association Collective Bargaining Committee, 25 June 1986).

41. Pennsylvania School Boards Association, *Public School Negotiations*, 7; and Pennsylvania State Education Association, *The Voice For Education* (Harrisburg, PA: Pennsylvania State Education Association, January 1993), 6-7.

42. Ibid., 7-11; and Ibid., 6-7.

Chapter 24

The Viewpoint of Teachers on Educational Reform

Annette Palutis

WHY RESTRUCTURE SCHOOLS?

In the view of the Pennsylvania State Education Association (PSEA), public education must change to meet the new demands of an emerging age. Rapid growth of scientific and technological developments; the proliferation of alternative sources of information; and changing political, social, and personal values have dramatically affected public education's role. Societal, technological, economic, and global forces make our current education model obsolete. Prussia's schooling model of bureaucratic efficiency and simplicity was designed to meet the needs of urbanization, industrialism, immigration, and the democratization of politics. Age-graded grouping and direct, whole-group instruction met the need to inculcate large numbers of students. Later, uniform textbooks aided the standardization. In turn, an examination system was instituted to screen students to serve the needs of the industrial society. High levels of education were available to just the few needed to run industry. This basic structure for schooling, which worked so well in the past, is used across America today. But, it is no longer appropriate.

The Need For Change

Today, the U.S. confronts a clear choice. We can remain competitive with the rest of the world by either lowering our standard of living so that we produce cheaper goods and services or by improving our productivity. The choice is obvious. Our future economic well-being depends on the skills of everyone in the work force. Most children in our public schools today will change careers, not just jobs, several times in the course of their work life. We must place greater emphasis on learning skills. By 2030, the proportion of our population over age 65 will nearly double, and the number of persons supporting each retiree will drop from 3.3 to just over 2. America will need a well-educated and competent work force with the capacity to achieve high earnings and to regularly adjust to change.

Our nation's inability to dominate the global economy is propelling the external drive toward school reform. The interest of business and community leaders is fortuitous. They now join educators in demanding that schools provide all students the opportunity to become competent learners.

Unfortunately, some of the proponents of change have adopted a strategy that includes undermining confidence in public schools. They believe that their ideas for change will only be accepted if people think the public schools are failing.

The public schools are not failing. Nevertheless, this is not an endorsement of the status quo. Teachers and their unions are not in favor of the status quo; however, all change is not created equal. Some of the reform ideas for change, for example vouchers, would cause irreparable damage to our public schools. This chapter will discuss the threat to public education of vouchers and also outline specific reform ideas favored by teachers and their unions.

Desired Changes

The National Education Association (NEA) has articulated two central tenets of school reform: 1) Fundamental changes in schooling must emerge from the school site rather than be imposed externally or unilaterally, and 2) The direction of change should be drawn from a research base rather than prompted by political expediency.

Based on these tenets, the following nine principles of educational excellence drive NEA's activities in school reform:

1) Students must master what is taught.
2) Students must be active participants in learning.
3) Full learning opportunity must be available for all students.
4) Learning should occur throughout life.
5) Authority must be vested in the local school faculty.
6) School staff must be professionally compensated.
7) There must be high standards for teacher preparation and practice.
8) School/community resources must be coordinated to benefit students.
9) Adequate financial support for education is essential.

So what must change? Public education must be democratized in order to educate successfully for a democracy. School must prepare students to participate in the decision making processes inherent in the responsibilities of democratic citizenship. We must rethink pedagogical methods, the range of instructional services, and how to organize schooling. Active student participation in learning, with opportunity for all, accommodates diversity and cultivates commitment to a common national purpose.

Parents and other stakeholders must actively participate in determining the broad goals of schooling and in providing for a range of optional approaches to achieve those goals. Then business and citizens within the community must provide the political leadership necessary to support the goals, and parents must be active in selecting the program most appropriate for their children. If reform efforts of Pennsylvania's State Board of Education are successful, all school districts will be required to involve students, teachers, administrators, parents, and citizens in the creation of a strategic plan to guide the mission of their schools. The new reforms would also institute a system known as "outcomes-based" education, shifting the emphasis from how much *time* is spent in learning to demonstrating what has actually been learned. Pennsylvania is embarking on a bold new venture by inviting its citizens to reshape public education.

In conjunction with these reforms, the entire school staff must receive the necessary training to be successful, and the parents and community must be educated about the changes. Schools will be most effective when the authority of the school staff is expanded to include all decisions related to the teaching-learning process. Specifically, the staff must have the latitude to remove identified barriers to learning like tracking (which channels students into restrictive learning environments), rigid grade structures, or bureaucratic, top-down administration.

Too often today's schools are characterized by student learning and teaching practices, which are confined within the parameters of an inflexible hierarchy; externally determined goals and objectives; and a measurement driven, highly fragmented curriculum. Other conditions typical of these schools are high dropout rates; teacher isolation that prevents collegial support among educators; no professional development outside of the classroom; and unclear linkages between student needs, curriculum objectives, and evaluation strategies.

The role of staff within tomorrow's schools anticipates the many facets of instructional responsibility--namely, student instruction; research and curriculum development; induction of new staff; time to reflect, write, and plan; time for collaborative exchanges with colleagues; and access to professional development opportunities. The school is interactive with the community. It may be a site for delivery of essential services which support the educational, health, and social needs of the families and individuals within the community served. Some schools have already begun to pilot such programs. For example, the Farrell School District in Mercer County, Pennsylvania offers primary health services to pre-school children and expanded health services for its elementary children. Schools will have to reach beyond the traditional school-age group they have traditionally served. In the future, schools will offer "womb to tomb" programs, beginning with services for infants and ending with inter-generational programs for adults.

Professional discretion to change learning conditions as required to support good practice is necessary to achieve educational excellence. Those who set education policy must provide authority for school staff to develop and implement appropriate instruction rather than prescribe standardized solutions for all schools to follow. Bilateral decision making at the school site, between management and employees, is the essence of professionalism. Collective bargaining is the process to be used for attaining this bilateralism; although restructuring takes place in individual schools, the entire school system must be involved.

Democratized schools will display the following characteristics:

- Inspire all students with a belief in their ability to learn.
- Establish teaching-learning objectives and conditions which meet the demands of new and different goals and tailor practice to accommodate the rich diversity among students.
- Use the skills, talents, and potential of every person employed in the school in an effort to provide the highest caliber service to students.
- Measure school outcomes broadly, through teacher-designed accountability plans which include information such as dropout rates, attendance patterns, participation in co-curricular and extra-curricular

activities, and academic achievement.
- Establish a school environment amenable to change.
- Encourage experimentation based on a careful consideration of viable options and with the capacity to act on findings.
- Reshape elements of school management and decision making in a manner that provides for cooperatively determined school goals and budget.
- Link the school, higher education, and the community in a partnership to meet the full range of student needs.

ACCOUNTABILITY

The responsibility for student success must be equally shared by students, parents, administrators, school board members, legislators, taxpayers, and professional staff. A system of accountability will be complex, consist of several indicators, and require a phase-in period. A sufficient period of time must be allowed for the articulation of expectations, the development of programs designed to meet them, and creating and implementing a fair and adequate system of assessments of the achievement of the expectations. Any consequences of failure and/or success would be activated upon completion of the final phase.

Educators are responsible for the implementation of practice which meets the needs and learning outcomes of their students. Therefore, they must be responsible and accountable for the diagnosis, analysis, and evaluation of student learning needs and opportunities. Educators must know how to revise practice as indicated by that professional review. Further, educators must assume responsibility for bringing conditions which do not support best practice to the attention of those with the capacity to address the problem.

PSEA recognizes that evidence of learning is not always available upon request or demand. Performance criteria are not always uniformly or universally applicable to a given population. Therefore, PSEA will resist any attempt to transform an assessment system into a single test. Such an approach would seek to measure all students, teachers, or school systems by a single set of standards and thereby impose a single program. We will oppose the use of pupil progress, standardized achievement tests, or student assessment tests for purposes of teacher evaluation.

Vouchers Are Not The Answer

We have endured 12 years of concerted attacks on the public schools for the purpose of persuading the public to accept privatization of education. The attacks have not been fair or accurate. Researchers taking a fresh look at the mountain of education data have begun to speak out against this disinformation campaign. Those responsible for providing public education should take pride in the recent conclusions of several major educational studies. One researcher, for example, writing in the *Phi Delta Kappan* concludes:

> So many people have said so often that the schools are bad that it is no longer a debatable proposition subject to empirical proof. It has become an assumption that turns out to be false. The evidence overwhelmingly shows that the American schools have never achieved more than they currently achieve. And some indicators show them performing better than ever.[1]

Critical demographic and economic trends are affecting public education in Pennsylvania. Today's students are racially, ethnically, and linguistically diverse, and increasingly poor. They face complex social phenomena such as the impact of changes in the family structure, poor child care options for working parents, and the lack of meaningful options for recreation and adult supervision outside of school. The role of the public schools has changed dramatically over the past three decades. Schools are being asked to perform functions traditionally fulfilled by parents. We now must teach and counsel our students about AIDS, teen pregnancy, drugs and alcohol, and crime and violence on our streets and even in our homes. Breakfast and latchkey programs have been instituted to watch and care for children during non-school hours.

As if this was not enough, fewer children are ready to learn when they enter our schools. Eight percent of Pennsylvania's families live in poverty. The poverty rate doubles for families with children under five, and most alarming of all, six of every ten female-headed families with children under five years old live in poverty.

Children who are hungry and/or deprived of educational resources at home have a distinct disadvantage in the classroom. We must work to ensure that the very youngest in our state receive the necessary attention in Harrisburg, as well as Washington, D.C. Rather than focusing on the costs of programs such as Chapter 1 and Head Start, we must adopt an "investment mentality" and understand that these programs are not only morally correct, but also fiscally enlightened.

Opponents of the public schools rarely acknowledge these pernicious trends when they seek to undermine public confidence in our educational system. We can and must improve our public schools. PSEA favors education reform ideas which recognize the crucial role of teachers and which seek to give teachers greater say in how schools are run.

For the most part, there are not "good" schools and "bad" schools as proponents of choice would like us to believe. The assumption of choice advocates is that the free market will reward the "good" schools and punish the "bad" ones. The reality is that school districts vary widely in their resource base and in their socioeconomic composition. The truth is that some schools are rich and others are poor; some educate children who come from stable, wealthy, highly educated families; and others must deal with children who come from dysfunctional, abusive, poor, and poorly educated families.

Handing out vouchers to parents to spend on private, religious, and public schools is a grave threat to public education. As *The New York Times* stated in an editorial this past October, "At its worst, choice becomes a cruel hoax, allowing the best students to escape weak schools but leaving behind ever-greater concentrations of students from the poorest, most embattled families." These "weak" schools must then educate the neediest students with even fewer resources.

Choice proponents are often heard promoting their ideas as a solution for inner city, poor families. Yet, the 1992 Carnegie Foundation for the Advancement of Teaching report on choice questions the effectiveness of choice programs. The report concludes that choice benefits children of better-educated parents. It also found that choice programs have the potential of widening the gap between rich and poor school districts. Privatizing education would undermine the very fabric of our society.

UNION ROLE

As teachers unionized in Pennsylvania during the 1970s and 1980s, they began to gain some professional rights. Freedom to speak; increased wages; reduced sexism, favoritism, and nepotism by management; rewards for professional training; rewards for career teaching; and encouragement of assertive behavior all represent advances achieved through collective bargaining. At the same time, bargaining also locked in a factory model through contractual processes--union leaders talked to management leaders, standardized procedures, and defined management rights. We have found, however, that a strong contract does not preclude good working relations between teachers and administrators.

PSEA is moving into a fresh examination of how union processes can increasingly complement professionalism. We have attempted to bargain professional issues at the table, but a Pennsylvania court decision allows school boards to avoid such topics. We have been told that class size, the selection of curriculum material, and the ongoing professional needs of teachers are not appropriate topics for a teachers' union to discuss at the table.

Our members continue to share a collective value system. Therefore, we will continue to utilize formal organizational structures that generate collective behavior reflecting the values and mission of our members. We will seek to protect children by maintaining high standards for those allowed in the classroom. As in other professions, we want the freedom to practice free from external control. We will promote the growth of professional knowledge and develop public trust through competence and accountability. PSEA will work to ensure that education reform ideas be legitimate and properly implemented so that children are not harmed in the rush to appear as though something is being done.

We will help meet the ongoing professional concerns of teachers. PSEA annually holds a two-day Education Conference covering such topics as student portfolio performance assessment, issues and trends facing special education, changes occurring in Russia, present and future concerns of vocational education, dealing with pregnant teenagers within the schools, and how to write outcomes for Pennsylvania's new outcome-based education system.

CONCLUSION

The nation is confronting the awesome challenge that the potential for human learning is unlimited. Our understanding about how learning occurs continues to grow. Schools must be structured in ways that permit educators to capitalize on that knowledge and apply it in practice. Organizational, instructional, curricular, and assessment issues are all involved.

Researchers tell us that higher order thinking is the hallmark of successful learning at all levels--not only the more advanced. While good thinking depends on specific knowledge, many aspects of powerful thinking are shared across disciplines and situations. Further, the elements of thinking are teachable.

Recent research on cognition shows that: schoolwork is much more complex than long assumed; real life presents ill-structured, not well-structured, problems; efficient learners possess specific learning strategies; solving problems requires a mix of social and cognitive skills; and the basic units of education are tasks, not information.

PSEA is like the rest of the world. We want progress, but the necessary changes are uncomfortable at first. We grapple with preparing our members for participatory decision making, for collective accountability, and for shaping professional development. We question our communication means and our use of time. We are evolving.

Teachers and their union would be the first to suggest that public education must change. The challenges for public education are great. The obstacles are many and difficult. The cost of failure is steep. Yet, this is also a time of enormous opportunity. If we are successful, we will produce a public education system destined to create valued citizens of all children. We will ensure that future generations will continue to enjoy a high quality of life.

ENDNOTE

1. Gerald W. Bracey, "Why Can't They Be More Like We Were?," *Phi Delta Kappan*, 73, no. 2, (October 1991): 106.

Chapter 25

The Viewpoint of School Boards on Educational Reform

Thomas J. Gentzel

Overview

Education is a birthright of every American, an entitlement extended regardless of creed, income, race residence, or scholastic ability. This is the philosophy of the Pennsylvania School Boards Association (PSBA), the state-wide association for school board directors. PSBA's view of educational reform is presented in this chapter.

The doors of public schoolhouses open just as wide for all who enter. Once inside, students are offered a range of courses tailored to satisfy varying interests and learning styles. New instructional techniques and technology are used to enhance the delivery of subject matter. Tests are given frequently to measure progress, and remediation is provided to assist those who are falling behind. Sports and other extracurricular programs are made available to help sustain interest in school and enable youths to be well-rounded, fit in mind and body. In addition to furnishing an education, public schools increasingly are expected to administer numerous supportive services to meet the emotional, physical, and social needs of the children they serve.

No other country in the world attempts to fulfill such an ambitious agenda. The United States stands alone in its national commitment to the education of all children, including those with even the severest mental and physical impairments. The public schools perform well in the face of numerous obstacles, many of which are the product of a rapidly changing society.

DEMOGRAPHICS

For example, fewer than 10 percent of homes today are of the once-typical "Ozzie and Harriet" model: a working father, homemaker mother, and two children. More than one-half of all children are raised by a single parent for at least a year before they reach age 18. Especially troubling is the reach of poverty, which touches one in every five children. For minorities, the statistics are even more staggering; nearly one-half of all black youth are from poor families. Children below age six are more likely to live in poverty than any other age group in America.

The changing demographics of our society are extensive and overwhelming. They dramatically affect how schools operate. One measure of those changes can be found in a comparison of leading school discipline problems, compiled by the National School Safety Center. Its research notes that while talking, chewing gum, and making noise were the top three discipline problems in the 1940s, drug abuse, alcohol abuse, and pregnancy were the primary school problems in the 1980s, in addition to suicide, rape, robbery, and assault.

Such changes have not diminished expectations for our schools. In fact, Americans seem to demand even greater achievement from our schools as the problems of society grow. Remarkably, the public schools have responded. For instance, in just three generations, the high school completion rate literally has soared: 22 percent in 1920, 64 percent in 1960, and 87 percent in 1985. Nonetheless, when the nation's governors and the president met several years ago to identify needed changes in the public schools, graduation rates were targeted for improvement.

No one has proposed that the goals of public education be scaled back to recognize changes in the American family, shifting demographics, or the increasingly limited resources available to support this enterprise. As a society, we simply have raised our sights further, expecting even more.

SEEKING CHANGE

Many changes in public education have been conducted in the name of "reform"--a suggestion that the major impediment to reaching lofty goals is the institution of public education itself. Calls for educational reform and innovations are not new and typically occur every 20-30 years. This latest reform cycle has been underway since 1983. It initially called for more state mandates such as additional courses of study, more credits required for graduation, or a longer school year. Today, the emphasis has shifted from imposing new "inputs" to clarifying the expected "outcomes" --that is, what we expect children to know and be able to do when they complete 13 years of education. This focus has produced renewed interest in measuring student performance along with affording a greater degree of local flexibility in designing the programs that will enable schools to produce the desired results.

The debate on "educational reform" taking place in Washington, D.C., the 50 state capitals, and in communities across the country, is a healthy one. Americans rarely, if ever, are completely satisfied with their schools; there is always some improvement that can be implemented. In this search for educational improvement and innovations, perhaps a consensus about what we truly expect of public education can be reached.

Pennsylvania school boards, created nearly 160 years ago as local agents of the General Assembly, are vital participants in this dialogue. The 4,500 people who serve on those boards are as different as the communities they serve, representing a genuine cross-section of the Commonwealth. Their diverse views need to be heard by policymakers at the state and national levels, particularly since they are the closest elected officials to the people they represent and the children served by our public schools.

NEW GOALS, HIGHER EXPECTATIONS

Education is one of the few topics on which virtually all Americans are qualified to offer an opinion. And they do. Whether their views are based solely on personal experience or that of their children or are shaped by conversations with neighbors over the backyard fence, most people are willing to offer thoughts on the public schools--occasionally about what they do right but, more usually, about what should be changed.

Given the importance of schools to our everyday lives, this should come as little surprise. In many communities, the school district is one of the largest employers and imposes the highest taxes of any local jurisdiction. Schools, too, are natural centers of community activity; nearly everyone has at least some contact with them. They also serve to drive the economic potential of an area or region, since many companies weigh quality schools as an important factor in locating their business.

Such widespread exposure inevitably makes schools, at best, open to suggestions and, at worst, vulnerable to criticism. That is as it should be. If the system of public education is to meet its fundamental charge of preparing children for a productive role in society, then it must know how society defines that role and how it might change over time. Neither pollsters nor experts in pedagogy are qualified to perform that task; the public at large must.

Since most people no longer have children in school, and, therefore, have little direct exposure to what is actually taught, such public input sometimes can have little bearing on reality. Those who offer suggestions based on their personal experience of 20 or more years ago, for example, might be shocked to learn how much our schools have changed over that time.

Still, the more dialogue, the better. Public education needs a clear vision of its mission and of the expectations for which it will be held accountable. Given the diversity of input, such a vision may be difficult to achieve.

NATIONAL EDUCATION GOALS

In 1990, former President Bush and the nation's governors charted an ambitious agenda to improve the schools, selecting six major goals to meet by the year 2000:

- Readiness - All children in America will start school ready to learn.
- Completion - The high school graduation rate will increase to at least 90 percent.
- Student Achievement and Citizenship - American students will demonstrate competency over challenging subject matter.
- Mathematics and Science - U.S. students will be first in the world in mathematics and science achievement.
- Literacy and Lifelong Learning - Every adult will be literate and able to compete in a global economy.
- Disciplined and Drug-Free Schools - Schools will be free of drugs and violence and will offer a disciplined environment for learning.

These goals dictate the implementation of some sweeping societal changes, not only on the part of the public schools but by other agencies in both the public and private sectors. For example, ensuring that all children enter school ready to learn suggests a major commitment to provide needed educational, medical, and social services for all children. A drive to achieve literacy and lifelong learning among the general public will necessarily include the active involvement of many entities, particularly the business community in retraining workers for the numerous jobs they will hold over their lifetimes.

In a 1991 report, *National Goals for Education: A Pennsylvania Progress Report,* the Pennsylvania School Boards Association noted that most school districts in the Commonwealth already are well along in the effort to achieve the goals established by former President Bush and the nation's governors. Based on surveys of local school directors and school administrators, PSBA reported strong local support for the direction that has been established. That direction may be strengthened by President Clinton who, as Governor of Arkansas, led Democratic governors in the discussions that facilitated development of the national goals.

The major obstacle to meeting these national education goals, according to the local officials most directly responsible for the daily management of public schools, is money--the persistent underfunding of education at the federal and state levels.

Therein lies the paradox for our public schools: As expectations for schools rise, the level of financial support (measured as a percentage of school costs) actually provided by federal and state governments has been declining. The result has been enormous public pressure on local school officials to produce greater results with fewer resources. Fundamental change in the public school system requires, first of all, a significant new commitment to funding education. That becomes the starting point for any meaningful discussion of school reform.

RESTRUCTURING

Much of the school reform debate is driven by sheer necessity. Neither the economy nor the workforce of the future will bear much resemblance to what we know today.

For example, a majority of all new jobs created by the year 2000 will, for the first time in history, require postsecondary education. Economic growth will be directly linked to the skill level of workers, with the fastest-growing jobs requiring greater language, math, and reasoning abilities than the ones available today. Even those who fill lower-skilled positions will be expected to be able to read and comprehend directions, perform basic math, communicate clearly, and use some kind of equipment based on new technologies. Workers of the future will need to possess advanced skills just to have access to needed training.[1]

In short, the days when society could afford a large number of students who drop out of school, or just "go through the motions" to collect a diploma, are gone forever. The American economy of the future no longer will have many relatively high-paying but low-skill jobs available to fill. Indeed, such jobs already are disappearing by the millions. The ability of people with only a high school education to find stable employment at adequate wages is becoming increasingly difficult.

Such trends have enormous implications for public education, which will need to change as dramatically as the society it is expected to serve. This must be reflected not only in what schools teach but in how they are organized to deliver that material.

VOCATIONAL EDUCATION

An early casualty of these coming changes is likely to be the "general" track in many schools, where students prepare neither for college nor a vocation. All students in the future will need to take full advantage of their time in school and to graduate with a solid education and meaningful skills.

Also directly affected will be the vocational education programs which have developed over the past several decades. School districts, on their own or through joint-operated area vocational-technical schools, will have to "re-tool" those programs extensively. Training no longer can be limited to meet immediate labor market needs, because jobs in any given area will change rapidly and students cannot necessarily be expected to stay in the communities where they grew up in order to pursue job opportunities.

Perhaps most importantly, vocational education must shed its image as a step-child of the public school system--a place where less talented students are sent until they graduate. Courses of study must be revamped and made useful for, and available to, all students. For example, young people contemplating engineering as a career should be encouraged to take drafting courses while still in high school. In addition, students enrolled in vocational programs should be encouraged to take challenging courses which once were considered appropriate only for those headed for college. Algebra and geometry, for instance, provide skills needed for numerous jobs, yet those courses often are not available to vocational students.

In short, there needs to be a real and meaningful integration of the now separate academic and vocational programs. Artificial barriers, intended to corral students into convenient groupings, should be removed as much as possible in an attempt to challenge all children and enable them to benefit from courses of study wherever they may be offered.

A REVISED APPROACH TO REGULATION

Ultimately, the state's interest in regulating public schools ought to be what students learn, and not the titles of courses in which they learn it. Pennsylvania, like most states, traditionally has directed its state oversight to controlling the course offerings and graduation credits required in local districts. These inputs are easily regulated and become a relatively simple means of assuring the public that all schools are achieving at least a minimum degree of consistency in how they operate.

In fact, the reform movement that swept the country in the mid-1980s, following publication of *A Nation At Risk*, really constituted more of that same kind of thinking. New mandates were added, more courses required, and additional credits demanded for graduation. The emphasis on basic skills caused classroom teaching to adapt accordingly.

Such change was accompanied by a renewed emphasis on standardized testing, a readily accepted and understood measure of student achievement and school performance. Such assessment, however, typically only reveals knowledge of limited information. Schools effectively were forced to modify their curriculum to ensure that necessary subject matter was covered before such tests were given.

The fixation by state governments on regulating courses of study and measuring knowledge of facts came at the expense of what today generally is regarded as a far greater imperative: ensuring that students attain mastery over challenging subject matter and are able to communicate and solve problems. In essence, parents, the business community, and the public at large are demanding not that students become warehouses of data but competent, thinking adults, ready to contribute meaningfully to society.

Appropriately, this perception by the public of what is needed matches much of the recent research in the field of education. Such respected experts as John Goodlad and Theodore Sizer have concluded that a fragmented curriculum emphasizing rote learning, teachers overwhelmed with paperwork, and generally disengaged students are unfortunate characteristics of many American schools. They found in too many schools that students and their teachers make an "unspoken deal": Children agree to "go through the motions" if teachers do not demand much of them.

The prescription for this malaise is for state government to be less involved with what is taught and more interested in monitoring what is learned. That concept is driving Pennsylvania's regulatory efforts. The Commonwealth's legitimate interest is in ensuring that children have attained a level of achievement in critical academic areas; how each of the 501 school districts provides for such instruction is best left to them.

PSBA welcomes this approach, which clearly enables school boards, administrators, and teachers to work far more closely than in the past to design courses of study and modify instructional techniques to raise student achievement to the desired levels. This approach to education also entails that the Department of Education would become less of a regulatory agency, concerned primarily with compliance monitoring, and more of a source for advice and technical assistance for local school officials.

PUPIL ASSESSMENT

Almost inevitably, this fresh look at the state's role in regulating school curriculum also involves a re-examination of how performance is measured. If students are expected to possess problem-solving and critical-thinking skills, then new means of measuring the performance of these skills are needed as well.

While alternate assessment measures are welcome, the dangers of a single test are that it would unduly influence local curriculum--thereby restricting the very flexibility that the emphasis on outcomes seeks to promote--and that its results would be vulnerable to misuse. These concerns could be mitigated if, instead of a single examination, schools participate in a system of assessment which provides a variety of testing instruments and other means of evaluating performance, including portfolios and projects.

Most importantly, such assessments must be designed to enhance instruction--to provide useful feedback to teachers. In turn, teachers need to be provided adequate training in the interpretation of test results, so that they are equipped to use the data they receive to improve student learning and to design better assessment measures in their own classrooms.

Comprehensive assessment systems also can provide a more meaningful measure of school performance to be shared with the general public. Such reassurance that the schools are meeting or making progress toward achieving intended results is an essential element of school reform. Assessment systems, however, need to be carefully developed and well understood by all concerned if their results, in fact, are to be accepted as reasonable measures of performance. Those who monitor the results of these assessments--particularly state policymakers anxious for quick results--will need to display patience, because change will take time.

ROLES AND RESPONSIBILITIES

Teachers are vital to the process of restructuring schools. They need to be more actively engaged in the development of courses of study, to feel a sense of ownership of what is being taught, and to be willing to adapt instructional techniques to ensure that mastery is realized. In exercising greater responsibility for the improvement of school performance, teachers must accept increased accountability as well. Career ladders and performance pay plans could be a significant means of enabling that to happen.

Teachers also should be required to participate in extensive in-service education, regardless of their certification status or current legal obligation to engage in such training. The notion that "experienced" teachers do not require further professional development directly contradicts the call for greater local leadership in meeting the instructional needs of students and in taking advantage of new findings in research on how learning occurs.

School administrators, too, must accept the challenge to improve student learning with equal enthusiasm. Principals and others at the school building level in particular will need to adapt to the coming changes. This means a different operating style than the school system has demanded in the past, with less attention to paperwork and building operations and more emphasis on instructional leadership, working closely with teachers.

Finally, school boards must recognize that these changes likely will require funding allocations and policies which enable their personnel to fulfill important new duties.

Other actions are needed as well. Agencies in both the public and private sectors must better coordinate services for children, adopting a holistic approach which addresses the full range of needs of young people and their families. Schools should actively support these efforts.

State and federal governments should offer financial incentives and technical assistance to help school districts provide services for at-risk youth and early childhood education programs, as well as to enable the appropriate use of technology in the classroom. The business community must make a long-term commitment to improving public education, forging active partnerships with schools which permit valuable expertise to be shared with the schools, encouraging and enabling their employees to devote time to work with schools (including service on school boards), and recognizing academic achievement of students, to name a few.

Such changes will strengthen the public schools. They build on the solid foundation of local control of education by encouraging the necessary leadership to ensure that all children learn.

CHOICE

Still, in so doing, state officials need to avoid taking action which could undermine public education.   One such proposal would create an open enrollment program in which students could select the schools they wish to attend.   Such attempts to enact choice pose enormous logistical questions, offer no guarantee of improved school performance, and threaten to undermine the funding needed for public schools. In truth, for a variety of reasons, many children still would be unable to move; they would be left to learn in schools that others have abandoned.

The experience in other states with choice programs raises serious doubts about the effectiveness of the concept.   Choice needs to be carefully weighed before being enacted in any far-reaching way. In no event should the federal or state governments mandate such programs or provide funding in the form of vouchers to parents. Choice cannot be allowed to become a means for vital financial support for public education to be diverted to other uses or as a disguise to use public tax funds to support private schools.

On the other hand, local school officials ought to consider means of further expanding choice models already available within their systems. Programs such as alternative courses, magnet schools, and distance learning represent valuable means of encouraging students to pursue their interests.

The public school system historically has been one of the most extensively regulated and controlled activities of government; consequently, it has been one in which innovation often has been stifled. The current interest in emphasizing mastery rather than course titles provides a welcome opportunity to reverse this inhibition of educational innovations.

GOVERNANCE ISSUES

Appropriately enough, education reform involves an examination of how instruction is delivered in the public schools. Yet no such review would be complete without a look at how the system is operated. The traditional roles of the different levels of government are likely to be profoundly affected by the effort to meet the increased demands and growing expectations for our schools.

Education always has been primarily a function of state governments. Even though the U.S. Constitution fails to mention education, there has been a limited federal role in funding school programs for decades. Generally, this financial support has been restricted to services for certain targeted populations--such as special education, vocational education, and remedial education for economically disadvantaged children.

FEDERAL AND STATE ROLES

In recent years, the percentage of school costs paid with federal funds has declined dramatically. At its highest level, federal funds did not exceed 7 percent of the costs and today constitute, on average, less than 3 percent of a typical school district's total revenues. Although federal aid has been decreased, federal mandates have increased. In many areas, such as asbestos and lead in drinking water, federal mandates require the local school districts to expend more dollars than are provided to the district by Washington.

Many of the regulations imposed by Harrisburg and Washington are highly prescriptive and genuinely burdensome. They represent a vast intrusion into local school operations. The promulgation of these burdensome mandates should be reassessed in order to allow the schools adequate energy, resources, and time to be devoted to the primary mission of the public schools: the effective instruction of children. Unfortunately, that mission is curtailed when already limited federal and state funding must be diverted to mandated programs which often do little to actually enhance the educational program.

In Pennsylvania, for example, Act 372 of 1972 requires each school board that provides transportation for its own pupils to also transport students to nonprofit, private schools within a ten-mile radius of the district's boundaries. This transportation expense can be staggering to school districts with many nonpublic students or to those districts that encompass wide geographic areas. It can cost as much as $20,000 a year to transport one student to a private school.

The statewide cost of this mandate is substantial. In 1990-91 school boards spent $466 million to transport 1,158,000 students, 15.7 percent of whom attended private schools. That means that a minimum of $73.2 million was spent on nonpublic school student transportation during this one year. Although the state appropriated $48.2 million to the school districts to defray this cost, the balance of $25 million remained to be paid by the school districts. This extra expense for public schools inflates local school budgets and necessitates diverting badly needed funds from instructional programs for the districts' own students.

Another example of a financially burdensome mandate is Pennsylvania's Prevailing Wage Act of 1961. This Act requires school boards to pay prevailing wage rates to their workers and to seek separate bids from contractors who perform various aspects of construction for all construction projects that exceed $25,000. The provisions of the Prevailing Wage Act have inflated construction costs to school districts, since these "prevailing wages" typically are identical to union-scale rates in large metropolitan areas. Further, as a result of the mandate, many small contractors are effectively excluded from bidding. In addition, the current threshold figure of $25,000 was established over 30 years ago. If it had been allowed to rise consistently with the national construction cost index, today it would exceed $120,000.

Estimates vary, but many believe that costs for school construction projects could be reduced by 10-30 percent if the Prevailing Wage Law were revised. For example, a 1991 survey by the Associated Builders and Contractors revealed that the school districts polled could have realized a 14.3 percent savings on school construction if the act had not been in effect. Based on total estimated expenditures of $600 million for such projects each year, a repeal of the Prevailing Wage Law could save Pennsylvania school districts at least $86 million annually.

While both the administration and General Assembly have expressed interest in the issue of mandates within the past few years, actual relief from such costly regulation has not been forthcoming. Until the burden of such mandates on school boards is eased, many efforts to improve and expand actual instructional programs will be stifled.

Of necessity, much of the leadership for lessening this burden must come at the state level. School boards must be given the flexibility and resources necessary to institute meaningful educational reform. In their respective roles, the governor and General Assembly have a clear duty to ensure that state regulation is minimized, and that, in current efforts to institute curriculum reform, expected educational outcomes are well defined, sufficient funding is being provided, and state oversight is designed to encourage local decision-making and innovation in successfully achieving the goals established for public schools.

Easing burdensome mandates on school boards, fully funding those still in force, and evaluating the financial and instructional impact of any existing or proposed mandates will ensure that the school boards' focus will be on the continuing enhancement of the educational program in

Pennsylvania's public schools. In addition, approaching state regulation in this manner recognizes that local school officials are best able to design and manage programs to meet the educational needs of their communities.

ROLE OF THE SCHOOL BOARD

The critical element in making school reform and educational innovations succeed is the local school board itself. The 4,500 volunteers who serve on those governing bodies across the Commonwealth must be capable of providing leadership and direction for school systems in a time of extraordinary change.

The National School Boards Association has adopted a mission statement which focuses on the overall policymaking role of the local school board as an integral part of the American institution of democratic, representative, and accountable governance.

In its statement, NSBA notes that "The mission of the public schools is to educate each and every child to the fullest of his or her potential. This mission only can be achieved in the context of the new realities of our society and the world at large....The local school board--an integral part of the American institution of representative governance--acts on behalf of the people of each community across our nation to translate this education mission into reality." Further, NSBA outlines a four-fold thrust for leadership by local boards to ensure excellence and equity in the public schools:

- Vision--Setting the course and establishing the commitment to education excellence and equity for all children.
- Structure--Creating an environment designed to ensure all students the opportunity to attain their maximum potential through a sound organizational framework.
- Accountability--Establishing the continuous assessment of all conditions affecting education.
- Advocacy--Serving as education's key advocate on behalf of students and their schools in the community to advance the community's vision for its schools, pursue its goals, encourage progress, energize systemic change and deal with children as whole people in a diversified society.

The NSBA statement concludes that "It is the local school board that can best bring together in our democracy all of the community--parents, community groups and all others concerned about schooling--in an effective and responsible way to initiate and sustain lasting reform of the schools."

In addition, the Pennsylvania School Boards Association seeks to empower local school boards throughout the Commonwealth as they fulfill this role. Approaching its 100th anniversary as the oldest school board association in the nation, PSBA has clearly stated its mission: "...through local and state leaders, to provide the best information, resources and services for boards of school directors so they can make informed decisions on matters affecting the public education system for the students and citizens they serve."

BOARD TRAINING AND TERM OF OFFICE

Some observers have suggested that school directors should be required to participate in training programs. Their contention that such state-mandated instruction is needed may sound appealing, but it actually raises a number of questions and creates some potentially serious problems.

School directors are representatives of the public, providing local lay control of the education system. Mandated training, as a condition for holding office, likely would pose a significant barrier to attracting people to hold the unpaid position of school director. Pennsylvania does not impose training requirements for elected policymakers at any level of government, including members of the General Assembly or the governor who are salaried officials. Where such in-service is mandated, it is related to a specific administrative need and not directed to those who serve in policymaking roles. For instance, training is required for district magistrates, who are members of the minor judiciary, yet typically not persons otherwise educated in the law.

The opposition of school directors to such a mandate does not suggest an aversion to training, however. In fact, the irony of the proposal for mandatory programs is that it virtually ignores the achievement of school board members in the Commonwealth. Pennsylvania provides, on a voluntary basis, far more in-service programs for school directors than any other state in the nation. Since 1984, PSBA alone has recorded more than 70,000 registrations for its extensive array of programs designed to help local school officials better manage their districts.

The secret of this successful voluntary experience is that the programs are designed to meet the needs school directors and their own association identify as being important. These officials, who routinely spend dozens of hours each month on school board business, willingly devote additional time to participate in training because they believe it is helpful--not because a law requires them to do so.

One change affecting school boards is needed, however. Ever since 1978 when the General Assembly reduced the term of office for school directors from six years to four, the average length of service has declined markedly. The result has been enormous turnover at the local level, in turn producing frequent changes in school administration and extensive, sudden shifts in the policy direction of public schools. PSBA believes school reform would be aided considerably by a return to six-year terms for school directors.

Local school boards are the cornerstone of school reform. The record demonstrates they are ready and able to meet the challenge.

PERSONNEL AND STAFFING ISSUES

Public education is a labor-intensive operation, with most of its expense directly attributable to the salaries and benefits of staff. Not surprisingly, numerous laws have been enacted to define, secure, or expand the rights of those employees. Like barnacles on a ship, each alone may appear innocuous enough; taken collectively, they can affect the course being traveled. In the case of the public schools, this labyrinth of regulations and legal protections stifles not only effective administration but most attempts at essential reform as well.

TEACHER CERTIFICATION

One such example is professional certification, a highly prescriptive area of state regulation which restricts personnel to teaching only specified subjects at certain grade levels. It also unduly limits the ability of school boards to assign teachers in a cost-effective and educationally sound manner.

State certification itself is not inappropriate. To the contrary, parents, students, and the general public need to be assured that those who staff school classrooms are qualified to do so. However, as the Commonwealth moves to provide school districts with greater flexibility in developing curriculum, it must do the same for certification as well. Because traditional course titles may no longer describe instructional offerings in the future, areas now cited on teaching certificates are likely to become archaic and literally could preclude school districts from implementing curriculum changes they have designed in order to improve student mastery of academic subject matter. A thorough review of current certification regulations is therefore a necessity in order to promote meaningful educational reform and grant local school boards the flexibility to enhance instructional programs.

Particularly in need of a thorough review are state requirements governing school nurses. Under current law, school nurses are considered "professional employees," and paid on the same salary scale as teachers, even though they often do not have formal teaching responsibilities. In addition, the shortage of available nurses is aggravated by the prescriptive certification requirements, making it extremely difficult for some districts, particularly in rural areas, to comply with the mandated nurse-student ratio of 1:1,500. Rather than mandate educational certification requirements for school nurses, and therefore impose additional costs to school districts, the Commonwealth should ensure that local school boards are granted the flexibility and funding necessary to provide required health services without diminishing the quality of those services.

State government should also be more active in encouraging and facilitating the entry into the teaching profession of those engaged in other careers. Such persons, properly trained and certified, not only broaden the base of experience of teachers in the public schools, they can also fill critical math and science positions, for example, that perennially are among the most difficult positions to keep staffed.

In addition, the Commonwealth should require all public school teachers and administrators to participate in professional development on a regular basis throughout their careers to maintain their certificates or commissions. "Lifetime certification" is an anachronism in a profession which demands that its practitioners be familiar with advances in instructional methods and new technologies.

State policymakers need to deal with other, more controversial topics as well, if the public school system in the Commonwealth is to be truly reformed. Chief among these are the persistent school labor relations problems that have plagued Pennsylvania for more than two decades.

SCHOOL STRIKES

Without question, since its enactment in 1970, the Public Employee Relations Act (Act 195) has had a more dramatic effect on the public schools than any other education statute. Pennsylvania has consistently led the nation in school strikes since that time. With more than 800 strikes during this time, the Commonwealth has experienced one in every four such walkouts. Consequently, the General Assembly and governor joined to enact Act 88 of 1992. This act represents a significant achievement in reforming the Commonwealth's strike laws.

Act 88, which imposes the first limitations on the right-to-strike by teachers and other school employees since public sector bargaining was authorized in the state by Act 195, contains several key provisions that PSBA actively sought:

- A strict, mandatory timeframe for bargaining.
- A prescribed, minimum number of state mediators to be available to assist when negotiations reach impasse.
- Authority for either bargaining party to initiate fact-finding without approval of the state Labor Relations Board.
- Legal standing for the Secretary of Education to intervene whenever a strike threatens completion of the minimum school year required by law.
- A ban on all selective strikes.
- Required 48-hour advance notice of all legally called strikes.

The passage of Act 88 represents a critical, long-overdue milestone on the road to leveling the bargaining process and restoring labor peace in Pennsylvania's public schools. In fact, the annual number of strikes following passage of Act 88 decreased significantly--from 36 in the 1991-92 school year to 15 more than halfway through the 1992-93 school year. The decreased incidence of strikes and increased use of fact-finding in collective bargaining negotiations are directly attributable to the passage of Act 88.

While Act 88 represents a promising start in improving labor relations, it is only a start. Ultimately, the General Assembly also must remove the existing financial incentive to strike by ensuring that teachers lose a day's pay for each day a strike disrupts the regularly scheduled school year. This can be done by assessing teachers 1/180 of their annual salary for each day a strike disrupts the adopted school calendar. To satisfy those who would claim that such legislation unfairly penalizes teachers, PSBA believes school districts should have their own state subsidy payments reduced in the same manner--effectively assessing both sides in the dispute and encouraging a settlement.

Although Act 88 provides a compulsory, nonbinding "arbitration" process, PSBA opposes binding arbitration as the remedy for ending all school strikes. Such arbitration tends to supplant real negotiations and enables an appointed arbitrator, not necessarily accountable to the community, to impose a settlement. This process also restricts the authority of elected officials; school boards are left with little real responsibility in this vital area, other than to raise the taxes necessary to pay for the salaries and benefits awarded by the arbitrator.

FURLOUGHS AND TENURE

In addition to the school strike issue, the General Assembly should consider correcting other restrictions in law which limit the ability of school officials to act. For instance, although the public properly demands efficient administration of the schools, it generally is unaware that state law prohibits the layoff of teachers for economic reasons. (Furloughs are authorized under the School Code only in cases of declining pupil enrollments and changes in the instructional program.) Public schools constitute perhaps the only level of government that is unable to reduce the size of its workforce to accommodate available revenues, an effective, cost-containment tool that is available to all other levels of government and the private sector.

The consequence of this restriction is to force school districts to maintain all programs and staff, especially in the area of non-mandated programs. Thus, local decisionmaking and flexibility is restricted, and an especially heavy burden is placed on local taxpayers who ultimately are required to pay higher taxes. Prohibiting school boards from furloughing professional employees due to economic reasons artificially inflates school costs at a time when money is scarce and unduly hampers a school board's ability to provide a sound educational program within the constraints of state and local economic circumstances.

Further, the requirement that school boards furlough solely on the basis of seniority rather than ability or performance may adversely affect the overall quality of the education program. In addition, following such a staff furlough, teachers with seniority and multiple certifications may be "bumped" into disciplines where they may be certified but have little or no recent experience--or real interest--in teaching. The ultimate losers in these cases are the students.

Another frequently cited limitation placed on school boards and embedded in law for more than 50 years is tenure. Here, however, legislative relief should be pursued deliberately and carefully.

Originally, tenure protection was granted at a time when teachers were strictly at-will employees, able to be fired without cause, prior notice, or any due process rights. Since then, of course, these public employees have accumulated numerous other job protections, including those afforded by the School Code, the Local Agency Law, and collective bargaining agreements.

One course of action would be simply to remove the tenure section of the School Code and allow other existing procedures which govern the discipline of school employees to stand on their own. Such a wholesale change would prove politically difficult even though it likely would be widely applauded by the public as a much-needed reform.

PSBA is concerned that, in responding to pressure to correct the perceived shortcomings of tenure, the General Assembly actually could exacerbate the problems school officials face in attempting to remove unsuitable teachers.

Tenure is wrongly viewed as a sort of impenetrable barrier. In fact, the legal system has clearly defined the basis for removing professional school employees. A half century of court decisions has clarified not only employee rights but also the grounds for school officials to act. In recent years, school boards have been increasingly effective in dealing with this issue. PSBA estimates that up to 90 percent of all cases initiated under the tenure laws have resulted in the removal of the teacher from the classroom.

If these well-established procedures were replaced by new provisions for hearings before arbitrators, for example, the 50 years of experience and court direction would be lost, and legal precedent would have to be re-established on a case-by-case basis. Such a "cure" could prove far worse than the "disease." PSBA believes that the General Assembly should remove tenure from the School Code entirely, but not attempt to supplant it with new due process provisions that could prove unwieldy and counter-productive.

If tenure is not eliminated, then one helpful change would be to delay its award by at least one year. Today, career-long job protection in the form of tenure is granted after two years of successful teaching; on the other hand, permanent certification is not awarded until after three years, at a minimum. At the very least, these two actions ought to be made concurrent.

RELATED ISSUES

Certification regulations, collective bargaining requirements under Act 195, and furlough and tenure restrictions have combined to reduce school boards' flexibility to establish the best possible instructional programs in our public schools. Moreover, additional restrictions governing personnel and staffing within local districts also have hampered this obligation.

For instance, Act 23 of 1991 has a provision on school retirement that created a program to provide up to $55 per month to be paid toward the health care premiums of those public school retirees who are disabled or who have served at least 24.5 years. To fund this new benefit, 0.5 percent was added to the employer contribution rate, thus imposing a higher cost on taxpayers. After the first year of this program, the total cost was estimated to be $32 million, with school districts and the Commonwealth each providing $16 million.

As teacher salaries increase annually, however, school districts will be required to continue the employer contribution rate on those higher salaries. Hence, total district expenditures will continue to escalate. In addition, continuing increases in health insurance premiums and rising costs of health care nationally open the door for future increases in the amount paid to annuitants toward the cost of health care coverage; these trends add further to the school districts' contributions for the benefit.

Another employee benefit which is both expensive and disruptive to the education program is the sabbatical, which is granted by the School Code to those professional employees with at least ten years of experience in Pennsylvania's public schools, five years within a given district. School boards have little discretion in approving sabbaticals for reasons of travel, health, or education, and they typically must employ a long-term substitute for each teacher on sabbatical as well as provide benefits for those substitutes. Further, teachers on a one-year sabbatical retain full benefits, receive at least half of their regular salary, are awarded regular salary increments as though they were in full-time attendance, continue employer-paid membership in the Public School Employees Retirement System, and are guaranteed their position upon returning from leave. Finally, teachers may choose to take "split sabbaticals," which are taken for one-half of a school year or for half of two successive years.

Clearly, sabbaticals impose financial costs and instructional disruptions upon Pennsylvania's public schools. For example, if just four percent of the state's professional school employees were on sabbatical during a school year, the salary cost would total $90.7 million while the benefit cost would amount to approximately $18.1 million. These estimates are based on the current level of employee benefits and wages; currently, the average yearly professional salary is $37,250. In addition, school boards would need to spend valuable resources for long-term substitutes, with the resulting total annual cost of sabbaticals exceeding $225 million. This nearly quarter of a billion dollars, however, does not account for the disruption sabbaticals cause in classroom instruction. That cost is impossible to calculate.

Finally, the state-mandated minimum $18,500 salary for public school teachers required by Act 10 of 1988 imposed an additional financial burden on many school districts least able to afford it, particularly in the form of a "ripple effect" on the salaries of other teachers and school personnel. Although this salary figure may no longer impose additional costs, this minimum salary could be increased at any time in response to political pressure by teachers' unions. That, in turn, could create a new round of ripple effects on future local salary schedules and effectively neutralize the ability of school boards to control personnel costs. State intervention on salary issues, coupled with collective bargaining mandates at the local level, compound any attempts to deal effectively with increasing salary and benefit costs.

Many of the legal provisions affecting school employees are time-honored even if they no longer are timely. They represent the way schools have been regulated for years, and efforts to modify them will prove difficult at best. If the Commonwealth sincerely intends to effect meaningful education reform, state policymakers cannot ignore these issues since they severely restrict the ability of local school officials to manage their own operations.

CONCLUSION

Education reform is at once sweeping in scope, yet narrow in purpose. Educational innovations and reform are an attempt to address numerous elements of the school system to improve student performance.

The present dialogue on educational reform raises many issues, including those which are potentially divisive and politically volatile. Nonetheless, no honest reappraisal of the schools can take place if difficult topics are not brought up for discussion. Consensus cannot be reached unless all opinions are considered.

Surely, the most important question being addressed in this on-going discussion of educational reform is the following: What are the present and future missions of the public schools? The current debate is a challenge to society to clearly identify its expectations for schools. It also is a call for a renewed commitment to education. Certainly, society's expectations for schools will not be met unless we marshall the energy, resources, and time necessary to achieve these goals.

School boards welcome the challenges now being posed. They have been working to take advantage of the flexibility afforded by state government in order to modify the curriculum and restructure their programs to enhance student learning. In many ways, the Commonwealth appears poised to provide some relief from many of the mandates to which local school officials have objected for years. That is a welcomed development indeed.

Flexibility, however, must not become an excuse for state government to further retreat from an appropriate role in funding public schools. It demands just the opposite. Education remains the only public service mandated by the state constitution, and the primary duty to support education rests squarely upon the General Assembly. This requires not only that funding levels be increased but also that the distribution of state aid be more equitable.

A partnership is needed among the General Assembly, the governor, professional educators, the public, and school boards to ensure that the growing expectations of schools are fulfilled. Indeed, school directors are local agents of the General Assembly, charged with responsibility for management of the public schools. School boards are ready to take the actions needed to enhance public education in the Commonwealth. To do so, they need to be given the necessary authority--and to be freed of excessive regulation.

It will not be easy to accomplish this nor will it happen quickly. Educational innovations and reform will occur if all who are concerned with the public schools are willing, over the long term, to see the job through. That commitment would be the most important of all.

ENDNOTE

1. Hudson Institute, *Workforce 2000: Work and Workers for the 21st Century* (Indianapolis, IN: Hudson Institute, June 1987), 97-101.

Epilogue

In 1920, H.G. Wells wrote, "Human history becomes more and more a race between education and catastrophe." Almost three-quarters of a century later, Wells' declaration has assumed meaning and urgency. Although the importance of education is frequently overlooked in society, historian and philosopher Will Durant recognized the fundamental role education plays in any society. He argued that civilization is transmitted from generation to generation by the educational process. What could be more important than the preservation of civilization for future generations?

Therefore, the fact that the nation's school system is at a crossroads is of critical significance to the American people. During the last decade, report after report has depicted the failures and weaknesses of our schools. Even though some of these reports have focused on only some areas, the need for systemic change and educational innovations is assumed by all of them:

The Paideia Proposal--(1982) - Calls for a thorough, general/liberal arts-approach to education for all students.

A Nation At Risk--(1983) - Calls for raising standards, and also addresses the issues of time, teaching, leadership, and fiscal support.

Action for Excellence--(1983) - Stresses the need for improvements in math, science, and technology; effective school-business cooperation; major changes in typical school operations.

High Schools--(1983) - Calls for clearly defined goals, essential student outcomes, and opportunities for professional enhancement for teachers.

Making the Grade--(1983) - Calls for enlightened federal support and emphasizes the need for English language skills.

Academic Preparation for College--(1983-1986) - Identifies essential competencies and knowledge required of college entrants and decries high school diplomas as indicators of knowledge.

A Place Called School--(1984) - Reflects concern with the negative consequences of age-graded, time-structured instructional systems.

Educating Americans for the 21st Century--(1984) - Makes recommendations regarding curriculum and teaching strategies in math, science, and technology.

A Study of High Schools--(1986) - Draws attention to the limiting character of schools' time-bound structure and procedures along with their adverse effect on students.

America 2000: An Educational Strategy--(1991) - Sets forth six national education goals and calls for local and state initiatives to lead the way to reform.

School reformers have argued that high quality education will require a tougher academic curriculum for all students, better teachers, a redesigning of teaching and testing methods, more challenging textbooks, increased parental involvement, and improved public accountability. If these are the required elements to improve American schools, why is effective educational reform so difficult to conduct and achieve? Perhaps the answer can be found in the interdependence of these elements and the education innovations necessary to realize them. Essentially, all of them must be attained if any of them are to make a significant difference in American schooling.

While this anthology may not have revealed the way to collectively achieve the above-listed elements, it has attempted to depict the environment, innovations, and trends in the schools of America, most specifically in Pennsylvania. American education will not, and cannot, reform itself. No enterprise disrupts itself in fundamental ways. No institution can. The majority of leaders of our educational establishments will provide lip service to educational problems, look gravely concerned, deliver speeches on the topic, attend conferences, and receive additional tax revenues graciously, but their institutions will not fundamentally change. Consequently, when the health and well-being of society depends upon changes in major institutions, these changes have to be conducted by individuals and groups that possess an understanding that the need for change far exceeds the importance of maintaining the status quo.

Although some future date may produce a national government that intends to actively pursue educational reform, the primary responsibility for education remains with the states. The responsibility for implementing and conducting educational reform through various innovations rests with our state governments. Vast quantities of political courage and vision will be necessary to secure our society's future well-being by reforming education in what will likely be a stormy political environment.

In the end, however, whether our schools improve rests with individual citizens. The American public needs to take responsibility for the performance of its local school systems. We have been part of the problem; we need to be part of the solution. We need to volunteer, impose ourselves if necessary, as additional assistants for the schools, e.g., career counselors, librarian assistants, lunch monitors, teaching assistants, and tutors. Most importantly, we need to make certain that our children understand the importance of excellent education and have the support necessary to achieve excellence in school. Implementing educational innovations and achieving educational reform is incumbent upon us; it is a task too important to rely on someone else. The future of our children, our community, our state, and our nation will be improved by our collective actions.

ABOUT THE EDITOR

CHARLES E. GREENAWALT, II is an assistant professor of political science and Assistant Director of the Center for Politics and Public Affairs at Millersville University, Millersville, Pennsylvania. He also serves as the senior policy associate for the Commonwealth Foundation. Greenawalt is the former Director of Policy Development and Research for the Pennsylvania State Senate. He received his Ph.D. and M.A. from the University of Virginia and his B.A. from Millersville University.

ABOUT THE CONTRIBUTORS

SUSAN ARISMAN is the Dean of Education at Cheyney University of Pennsylvania in Cheyney, Pennsylvania. She is the former Executive Director of the Pennsylvania Academy for the Profession of Teaching. She is also the former Associate Director of the National Foundation for the Improvement of Teaching and a former teacher at the high school and college level. Dr. Arisman received her Ph.D. from the University of Chicago, M.A. from the University of Minnesota, and B.S. from Marquette University in Milwaukee, Wisconsin.

J. ROBERT COLDIRON served as the Director of the Student Assessment Program of the Pennsylvania Department of Education for 12 years. He was responsible for the implementation of the minimum competency program and directed this program for four years. Dr. Coldiron received his Ph.D. and masters degree from Pennsylvania State University and his B.S. from Emporia State University in Emporia, Kansas.

BRUCE S. COOPER is a professor of educational administration and public policy at Fordham University Graduate School of Education in Bronx, New York. He has written widely on school finance, educational choice, and educational innovations. Dr. Cooper received his Ph.D. and a masters degree from the University of Chicago, and a masters degree and his B.A. from the University of North Carolina at Chapel Hill.

DENNIS DENENBERG is a graduate level professor and Director of the Student Teacher Program at Millersville University, Millersville, Pennsylvania. He is a writer, lecturer, and teacher in the area of curriculum innovation. Dr. Denenberg received his doctorate and masters from Pennsylvania State University, and his B.A. from William and Mary College.

DENIS P. DOYLE is a Senior Fellow at the Hudson Institute. He is a former director of Education Policy Studies and Human Capital Studies at the American Enterprise Institute and a former Fellow at the Brookings Institution. He is also the former Director of the National Institute for Education. Dr. Doyle works as a consultant, policy analyst, and a writer on education. He received his M.A. and B.A. degrees from the University of California at Berkeley.

D. MICHAEL FISHER is serving his fourth term in the Pennsylvania Senate and is Chairman of the Senate Republican Caucus. He has also served as Chairman for the Senate Republican Policy Committee and for the Environmental Resources and Energy Committee. Senator Fisher received his J.D. and A.B. from Georgetown University.

THOMAS J. GENTZEL is the Assistant Executive Director for Governmental Relations for the Pennsylvania School Boards Association. He is the former Executive Director of the Pennsylvania Association of County Commissioners. Mr. Gentzel holds a B.S. from Pennsylvania State University.

DOROTHY L. HAJDU is the Director of the Pennsylvania Teleteaching Project. She has participated in distance education projects from Maine to California. Mrs. Hajdu received her Bachelors Degree from Immaculata College in Immaculata, Pennsylvania, and her post graduate studies at Pennsylvania State University have been in the area of instructional systems and distance education.

ARNOLD HILLMAN has been an advocate for rural schools and communities for the past 20 years. He has been at the forefront of a school finance equity suit filed by the Pennsylvania Association of Rural and Small Schools against the Commonwealth of Pennsylvania. Dr. Hillman received his doctorate from Lehigh University in Bethlehem, Pennsylvania, and masters degrees from Temple University and the New School for Social Research in New York.

E.D. HIRSCH is the Linden Kent Memorial Professor of English at the

University of Virginia. He is a member of the American Academy of Arts and Sciences, and serves on the advisory boards of several academic and literary organizations. He is the founder and president of the non-profit Core Knowledge Foundation, dedicated to excellence and fairness in early education. Dr. Hirsch received his Ph.D. and masters from Yale University and his B.A. from Cornell University.

DAVID W. KIRKPATRICK is the Executive Director of The REACH Alliance (Road to Educational Achievement Through Choice), an advocate of school choice. He is a former teacher, founder of the Pennsylvania Rural Coalition, and former President of the Pennsylvania State Education Association. He received his M.A. from Lehigh University in Bethlehem, Pennsylvania, and his B.S. from North Adams State College in North Adams, Massachusetts.

LEONARD S. KOSHINSKI is a consultant and a project specialist for school/business partnerships and regional strategic planning for the Mon Valley Educational Consortium, in McKeesport, Pennsylvania. Mr. Koshinski received his M.A. from the John Heinz School of Public Policy and Management at Carnegie Mellon University in Pittsburgh, Pennsylvania and his B.A. from Youngstown State University in Youngstown, Ohio.

JOHN A. LEUENBERGER is the Executive Director of the Northwest Tri-County Intermediate Unit of the Pennsylvania Department of Education. He is a national consultant for quality in education and has prepared national publications for many education groups. He is also a former district superintendent, principal, and teacher. Dr. Leuenberger received his Ph.D. from Case Western Reserve University in Cleveland, Ohio, his masters from the University of Pittsburgh, and his B.S. from Thiel College in Greenville, Pennsylvania.

G. TERRY MADONNA is the Director of the Center for Politics and Public Affairs at Millersville University in Millersville, Pennsylvania. He is a professor of political science. Dr. Madonna is an active political analyst and commentator. He received his Ph.D. and M.A. from the University of Delaware and his B.A. from Millersville University.

WILLIAM J. MOLONEY is the Superintendent of the Easton Area School District in Pennsylvania. He is also an active consultant, speaker, and writer. Dr. Moloney serves on the board of the State Superintendents Association, the League of Urban Schools, and the Center for Workforce Preparation and Quality Education in Washington D.C. He has also served as an adjunct education professor at Lehigh University in Bethlehem, Pennsylvania. Dr. Moloney received his Ph.D. from Harvard University, his M.A. and B.A. from Boston College.

ANNE K. MONTEITH is the founder of BEST for PA (Better Education/Sensible Taxation for Pennsylvania); she serves on the boards of Pennsylvania's REACH Alliance (an organizational advocate for school choice) and the Pennsylvania Leadership Council. Mrs. Monteith earned her A.B. from Bucknell University in Lewisburg, Pennsylvania, and her masters from the Professional Photographers of America.

THOMAS V. O'BRIEN is an assistant professor in the Department of Educational Foundations at Millersville University in Millersville, Pennsylvania. Dr. O'Brien received his Ph.D. from Emory University in Atlanta, Georgia, and his bachelors degree from Brown University.

ANNETTE PALUTIS is the President of the Pennsylvania State Education Association. She taught school for 30 years and served as President of PSEA's Northeastern Region for 12 years. Mrs. Palutis received her B.S. from Marywood College in Scranton, Pennsylvania.

HOWARD B. RICHMAN is a research scientist at Carnegie Mellon University in Pittsburgh. He is also the editor of a state-wide homeschooling newsletter. He is the author or co-author of numerous articles, books, and guides about homeschooling and education. Dr. Richman received his doctorate from the University of Pittsburgh, and his bachelors from Carnegie Mellon University.

FREDERICK P. SAMPLE is the former Superintendent of the Bellefonte Area School District in Bellefonte, Pennsylvania, and the former President of Lebanon Valley College in Annville, Pennsylvania. He is also a former high school principal and teacher. Dr. Sample received his Doctorate from Pennsylvania State University, his masters from Western Maryland College in Westminster, Maryland, and his B.A. from Lebanon Valley College.

DEBORAH L. SCHRECKENGOST is the District Administrator for Pennsylvania State Senator John E. Peterson. She has been actively involved in the field of education and distance learning since 1980. Mrs. Schreckengost holds a bachelors degree from Clarion University in Clarion, Pennsylvania.

RUSSEL M. SUTTON served 23 years in the Pennsylvania Department of Education in the area of teacher certification, including nine years as the Chief of the Division of School Staffing, Bureau of Teacher Preparation and Certification. He is a former teacher and lecturer. Mr. Sutton received his masters from Shippensburg State College in Shippensburg, Pennsylvania, and his B.S. from Dickinson College in Carlisle, Pennsylvania.

PHYLLIS V. WALSH is the Community Service Coordinator for Bethlehem Area School District in Bethlehem, Pennsylvania, which has implemented a community service requirement for graduation. In addition, she is a PennSERVE Fellow in Pennsylvania. She received her B.A. from Mansfield University in Mansfield, Pennsylvania, and served as a secondary education instructor for 22 years.

SELDON V. WHITAKER, JR. is the Superintendent of Schools in the State College Area School District in State College, Pennsylvania. He is the co-founder of the Center for Total Quality Schools in the College of Education at Pennsylvania State University. Dr. Whitaker received his doctorate from Northwestern University, his M.S. from the University of Pennsylvania, and his A.B. from Williams College in Williamstown, Massachusetts.

JAMES W. WHITE is a Professor of Educational Foundations at Millersville University in Millersville, Pennsylvania. He is currently serving as President of the Association of Pennsylvania State College and University Faculties. Dr. White received his Ph.D. and masters from the University of Pittsburgh and his B.A. from Susquehanna University in Selinsgrove, Pennsylvania.

JUDITH T. WITMER is a professional writer and educational consultant. She specializes in educational administration and the process of school change, and also serves as an adjunct professor for Temple University. Dr. Witmer received her doctorate and masters from Temple University and her B.A. from Pennsylvania State University.